also by america's test kitchen

Desserts Illustrated

Vegan Cooking for Two

Modern Bistro

Fresh Pasta at Home

More Mediterranean

The Complete Plant-Based Cookbook

Cooking with Plant-Based Meat

Boards

The Savory Baker

The New Cooking School Cookbook:
Advanced Fundamentals

The New Cooking School Cookbook:
Fundamentals

The Complete Autumn and
Winter Cookbook

One-Hour Comfort

The Everyday Athlete Cookbook

Cook for Your Gut Health

Foolproof Fish

Five-Ingredient Dinners

The Ultimate Meal-Prep Cookbook

The Complete Salad Cookbook

The Chicken Bible

The Side Dish Bible

Meat Illustrated

Vegetables Illustrated

Bread Illustrated

Cooking for One

The Complete One Pot

How Can It Be Gluten-Free
Cookbook Collection

The Complete Summer Cookbook

Bowls

100 Techniques

Easy Everyday Keto

Everything Chocolate

The Perfect Cookie

The Perfect Pie

The Perfect Cake

How to Cocktail

Spiced

The Ultimate Burger

The New Essentials Cookbook

Dinner Illustrated

America's Test Kitchen Menu Cookbook

Cook's Illustrated Revolutionary Recipes

Tasting Italy: A Culinary Journey

Cooking at Home with Bridget and Julia

The Complete Mediterranean Cookbook

The Complete Vegetarian Cookbook

The Complete Cooking for Two Cookbook

The Complete Diabetes Cookbook

The Complete Slow Cooker

The Complete Make-Ahead Cookbook

Just Add Sauce

How to Braise Everything

How to Roast Everything

Nutritious Delicious

What Good Cooks Know

Cook's Science

The Science of Good Cooking

Master of the Grill

Kitchen Smarts

Kitchen Hacks

100 Recipes

The New Family Cookbook

The Cook's Illustrated Baking Book

The Cook's Illustrated Cookbook

The America's Test Kitchen Family
Baking Book

America's Test Kitchen Twentieth
Anniversary TV Show Cookbook

The Best of America's Test Kitchen
(2007–2023 Editions)

The Complete America's Test Kitchen
TV Show Cookbook 2001–2023

Healthy Air Fryer

Healthy and Delicious Instant Pot

Mediterranean Instant Pot

Cook It in Your Dutch Oven

Vegan for Everybody

Sous Vide for Everybody

Air Fryer Perfection

Toaster Oven Perfection

Multicooker Perfection

Food Processor Perfection

Pressure Cooker Perfection

Instant Pot Ace Blender Cookbook

Naturally Sweet

Foolproof Preserving

Paleo Perfected

The Best Mexican Recipes

Slow Cooker Revolution Volume 2:
The Easy-Prep Edition

Slow Cooker Revolution

The America's Test Kitchen
D.I.Y. Cookbook

**THE COOK'S ILLUSTRATED
ALL-TIME BEST SERIES**

All-Time Best Brunch

All-Time Best Dinners for Two

All-Time Best Sunday Suppers

All-Time Best Holiday Entertaining

All-Time Best Soups

COOK'S COUNTRY TITLES

Big Flavors from Italian America

One-Pan Wonders

Cook It in Cast Iron

Cook's Country Eats Local

The Complete Cook's Country
TV Show Cookbook

FOR A FULL LISTING OF ALL OUR BOOKS:

CooksIllustrated.com

AmericasTestKitchen.com

praise for **america's test kitchen titles**

Selected as the Cookbook Award Winner of 2021 in the Health and Nutrition category

INTERNATIONAL ASSOCIATION OF CULINARY PROFESSIONALS (IACP) ON *THE COMPLETE PLANT-BASED COOKBOOK*

"An exhaustive but approachable primer for those looking for a 'flexible' diet. Chock-full of tips, you can dive into the science of plant-based cooking or just sit back and enjoy the 500 recipes."

MINNEAPOLIS STAR TRIBUNE **ON** *THE COMPLETE PLANT-BASED COOKBOOK*

"In this latest offering from the fertile minds at America's Test Kitchen the recipes focus on savory baked goods. Pizzas, flatbreads, crackers, and stuffed breads all shine here . . . Introductory essays for each recipe give background information and tips for making things come out perfectly."

BOOKLIST **(STARRED REVIEW) ON** *THE SAVORY BAKER*

"A mood board for one's food board is served up in this excellent guide . . . This has instant classic written all over it."

PUBLISHERS WEEKLY **(STARRED REVIEW) ON** *BOARDS: STYLISH SPREADS FOR CASUAL GATHERINGS*

"Reassuringly hefty and comprehensive, *The Complete Autumn and Winter Cookbook* by America's Test Kitchen has you covered with a seemingly endless array of seasonal fare . . . This overstuffed compendium is guaranteed to warm you from the inside out."

NPR ON *THE COMPLETE AUTUMN AND WINTER COOKBOOK*

"Here are the words just about any vegan would be happy to read: 'Why This Recipe Works.' Fans of America's Test Kitchen are used to seeing the phrase, and now it applies to the growing collection of plant-based creations in *Vegan for Everybody*."

THE WASHINGTON POST **ON** *VEGAN FOR EVERYBODY*

Selected as the Cookbook Award Winner of 2021 in the General category

INTERNATIONAL ASSOCIATION OF CULINARY PROFESSIONALS (IACP) ON *MEAT ILLUSTRATED*

"Another flawless entry in the America's Test Kitchen canon, *Bowls* guides readers of all culinary skill levels in composing one-bowl meals from a variety of cuisines."

BUZZFEED BOOKS ON *BOWLS*

Selected as the Cookbook Award Winner of 2021 in the Single Subject Category

INTERNATIONAL ASSOCIATION OF CULINARY PROFESSIONALS (IACP) ON *FOOLPROOF FISH*

"The book's depth, breadth, and practicality makes it a must-have for seafood lovers."

PUBLISHERS WEEKLY **(STARRED REVIEW) ON** *FOOLPROOF FISH*

"*The Perfect Cookie* . . . is, in a word, perfect. This is an important and substantial cookbook . . . If you love cookies, but have been a tad shy to bake on your own, all your fears will be dissipated. This is one book you can use for years with magnificently happy results."

HUFFPOST **ON** *THE PERFECT COOKIE*

"The book offers an impressive education for curious cake makers, new and experienced alike. A summation of 25 years of cake making at ATK, there are cakes for every taste."

THE WALL STREET JOURNAL **ON** *THE PERFECT CAKE*

"The go-to gift book for newlyweds, small families, or empty nesters."

ORLANDO SENTINEL **ON** *THE COMPLETE COOKING FOR TWO COOKBOOK*

"If you're one of the 30 million Americans with diabetes, *The Complete Diabetes Cookbook* by America's Test Kitchen belongs on your kitchen shelf."

PARADE.COM **ON** *THE COMPLETE DIABETES COOKBOOK*

"True to its name, this smart and endlessly enlightening cookbook is about as definitive as it's possible to get in the modern vegetarian realm."

MEN'S JOURNAL **ON** *THE COMPLETE VEGETARIAN COOKBOOK*

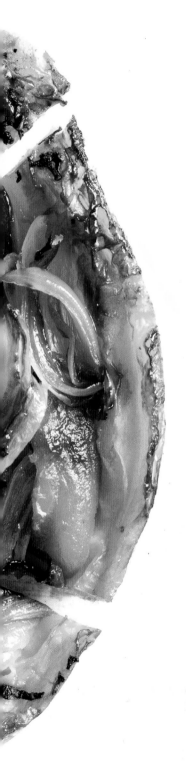

THE COMPLETE
MODERN
PANTRY

350+ WAYS TO COOK WELL WITH WHAT'S ON HAND

AMERICA'S TEST KITCHEN

Library of Congress Cataloging-in-Publication Data has been applied for.

ISBN 978-1-954210-16-5

America's Test Kitchen
21 Drydock Avenue, Boston, MA 02210

Printed in Canada
10 9 8 7 6 5 4 3 2 1

Distributed by
Penguin Random House Publisher Services
Tel: 800.733.3000

pictured on front cover (clockwise from top left)
Pan-Seared Shrimp with Pistachio, Cumin, and Parsley (page 299), Chili Crisp (page 392), Shichimi Togarashi (page 383), Pantry Pesto (page 137), Rustic Butternut Squash and Spinach Tart (page 258), Skillet-Charred Green Beans with Crispy Sesame Topping (page 234), Spaghetti al Tonno (page 122), Skillet-Roasted Pears with Caramel Sauce (page 357), and Lentil Salad with Oranges, Celery, and Pecans (page 196)

pictured on back cover Chana Masala (page 204)

editorial director, books Adam Kowit

executive food editor Dan Zuccarello

deputy food editors Leah Colins and Stephanie Pixley

executive managing editor Debra Hudak

senior editor Sara Mayer

contributing editors Brenna Donovan and Cheryl Redmond

associate editor Sara Zatopek

test cooks Sāsha Coleman, Olivia Counter, Carmen Dongo, Jacqueline Gochenouer, Eric Haessler, Hisham Hassan, José Maldonado, and Patricia Suarez

additional recipe development Garth Clingingsmith and Eva Katz

additional contributions Samantha Block, Camila Chaparro, Hannah Fenton, Joseph Gitter, Laila Ibrahim

kitchen intern Olivia Goldstein

design director Lindsey Timko Chandler

deputy art director Katie Barranger

photography director Julie Bozzo Cote

senior photography producer Meredith Mulcahy

senior staff photographers Steve Klise and Daniel J. van Ackere

staff photographer Kevin White

additional photography Joseph Keller and Carl Tremblay

food styling Joy Howard, Sheila Jarnes, Catrine Kelty, Chantal Lambeth, Gina McCreadie, Kendra McNight, Ashley Moore, Christie Morrison, Marie Piraino, Elle Simone Scott, Kendra Smith, Sally Staub

project manager, publishing operations Katie Kimmerer

senior print production specialist Lauren Robbins

production and imaging coordinator Amanda Yong

production and imaging specialists Tricia Neumyer and Dennis Noble

copy editor Elizabeth Wray Emery

proofreader Kelly Gauthier

indexer Elizabeth Parson

chief creative officer Jack Bishop

executive editorial directors Julia Collin Davison and Bridget Lancaster

contents

welcome to **america's test kitchen**

This book has been tested, written, and edited by the folks at America's Test Kitchen, where curious cooks become confident cooks. Located in Boston's Seaport District in the historic Innovation and Design Building, it features 15,000 square feet of kitchen space including multiple photography and video studios. It is the home of *Cook's Illustrated* magazine and *Cook's Country* magazine and is the workday destination for more than 60 test cooks, editors, and cookware specialists. Our mission is to empower and inspire confidence, community, and creativity in the kitchen.

We start the process of testing a recipe with a complete lack of preconceptions, which means that we accept no claim, no technique, and no recipe at face value. We simply assemble as many variations as possible, test a half-dozen of the most promising, and taste the results blind. We then construct our own recipe and continue to test it, varying ingredients, techniques, and cooking times until we reach a consensus. As we like to say in the test kitchen, "We make the mistakes so you don't have to." The result, we hope, is the best version of a particular recipe, but we realize that only you can be the final judge of our success (or failure). We use the same rigorous approach when we test equipment and taste ingredients.

All of this would not be possible without a belief that good cooking, much like good music, is based on a foundation of objective technique. Some people like spicy foods and others don't, but there is a right way to sauté, there is a best way to cook a pot roast, and there are measurable scientific principles involved in producing perfectly beaten, stable egg whites. Our ultimate goal is to investigate the fundamental principles of cooking to give you the techniques, tools, and ingredients you need to become a better cook. It is as simple as that.

To see what goes on behind the scenes at America's Test Kitchen, check out our social media channels for kitchen snapshots, exclusive content, video tips, and much more. You can watch us work (in our actual test kitchen) by tuning in to *America's Test Kitchen* or *Cook's Country* on public television or on our websites. Listen to *Proof*, *Mystery Recipe*, and *The Walk-In* (AmericasTestKitchen.com/podcasts), to hear engaging, complex stories about people and food. Want to hone your cooking skills or finally learn how to bake—with an America's Test Kitchen test cook? Enroll in one of our online cooking classes. And you can engage the next generation of home cooks with kid-tested recipes from America's Test Kitchen Kids.

Our community of home recipe testers provides valuable feedback on recipes under development by ensuring that they are foolproof. You can help us investigate the how and why behind successful recipes from your home kitchen. (Sign up at AmericasTestKitchen.com/recipe_testing.)

However you choose to visit us, we welcome you into our kitchen, where you can stand by our side as we test our way to the best recipes in America.

facebook.com/AmericasTestKitchen
instagram.com/TestKitchen
youtube.com/AmericasTestKitchen
tiktok.com/@TestKitchen
twitter.com/TestKitchen
pinterest.com/TestKitchen

AmericasTestKitchen.com
CooksIllustrated.com
CooksCountry.com
OnlineCookingSchool.com
AmericasTestKitchen.com/kids

getting started

What's your go-to pantry meal? Maybe it's pasta with butter and cheese, or beans seasoned with garlic and spices. Or perhaps it's a bowl of rice topped with a fried egg and a dash of hot sauce. On occasions when we don't want to cook something involved or haven't recently made it to the supermarket—or simply need to use up what's on hand—a no-fuss pantry meal can be a welcoming, comforting solution.

Pulling together a meal from the odds and ends of the cupboard (and sometimes the fridge or freezer) represents cooking at its most creative: You must work from a limited and somewhat arbitrary set of ingredients to create a satisfying, flavorful dish. It calls on you to pull out the bag of grains from the back corner of the shelf, the spice you haven't used since that one time, or the frozen vegetables buried deep in the freezer. Creating a pantry meal can lead to swaps of necessity, such as when you realize you don't have mozzarella (will cheddar work?), that produce a new invention.

If poking around the pantry leaves you feeling aimless, tired of returning to the same familiar meals, or like there is nothing to make, we encourage you to take another look. Your pantry, every part of it, can lead to something exciting. And using the ingredients you already have will make your cooking more unique, more flavorful, and less wasteful.

Doing this means assuming some degree of flexibility with ingredients. In fact, preparing pantry meals makes you a more flexible cook. Chop carrots instead of sweet potatoes, prepare a dish with a different grain or spice blend, or squeeze a lime when you would have squeezed a lemon. Pay attention to and enjoy how the taste changes. The results can be freeing and, moreover, delicious. A little guidance helps, too, and that's where this book comes in. Every recipe comes with a Pantry Improv box offering tips for riffing on a dish with alternate ingredients to make it easier to utilize what you already have. We bet that using this book will have you reaching for more of the jars, bottles, and tins in your pantry and give your cooking a boost.

As test cooks, we're always asking whether a dish needs a little something else—more crunch, or acid, or a cooling element—and trying various ways to get there. The pages that follow illustrate some of our common strategies for layering and balancing pantry ingredients based on their roles in cooking, an approach that itself encourages improvisation. It doesn't take much, and the process can produce a complex-tasting dish spun from a few humble potatoes or a can of beans.

When you lean in to the ingredients you have, and let them guide how you prepare a particular recipe, you've not only made practical use of your pantry, you've also made a dish your own.

pantry power

Your pantry is an extraordinary resource for creativity and flavor. It's also an ever-evolving collection. Assembling a well-rounded pantry doesn't mean having everything (that's literally impossible). It does mean stocking a mix of ingredients that play a variety of roles in cooking, from starchy bases to spices and seasonings. Toward that end, we've organized our pantry ingredients into categories based on what they contribute to a dish. Within each category, you've got flexibility. Out of lemons? Opt for vinegar. No walnuts? Toast up panko bread crumbs and sprinkle them over food for similar crunch. Stocking items in each category means you can always prepare something tasty to eat. And thinking about your pantry in terms of these categories can make it easier to improvise your next dinner based on what you have on hand.

bulk & bases
Grains, beans, and other starchy foods are the foundation of pantry cooking.

long-storage vegetables & aromatics
Unlock the potential in garlic, onions, potatoes, frozen veggies, and more.

frozen, cured & tinned proteins
Eggs, cheese, tofu, tinned fish, cured meat, and a few freezer standbys are true pantry staples.

crispy, crunchy & chewy toppings
These foods bring texture and richness to make a dish feel complete.

savory umami condiments, seasonings & sprinkles
Flavor-enhancing seasonings add savory, meaty depth to food.

spicy, hot & smoky elements
Spices, chiles, and hot sauces bring pantry meals to life.

acidic & pickled foods
When a dish tastes dull or flat, these bright ingredients can wake it up.

creamy & rich toppings
A dollop or crumble rounds out flavors and turns a dish into its best self.

sweet & sweet-tart flavorings
Not just for baking, these balance salty, bitter, sour, or hot flavors.

cooking liquids & fats & baking items
You get can by with just a few, but more opens doors to delicious places.

bonus: something fresh
These are mostly fresh herbs and chiles. Find out how to extend their shelf life on page 29.

fresh

vegetable

creamy

acidic

crunchy

base

// bulk & bases

Starches are the heart of pantry cooking. Many of our pantry meals start with a can of beans or a scoopful of rice (or both), a package of dried pasta or noodles, or some tortillas or other bread. With pantry cooking, these are often not just the base for layering on other ingredients but the focal point. Simple fried rice is a rice–lover's fried rice, full of deliciously chewy grains and minimal additions that act as seasoning. A can of chickpeas is the focus of chana masala, the beans glimmering in orangey–red sauce. Pasta needs little more than garlic and oil to enrich and flavor an al dente bowl to satisfy cravings day or night.

PASTA

Don't get too hung up on specific pasta shapes when whipping up a pantry meal; they are largely interchangeable and trying a different shape is a fun way to change up a dish. With that said, it is nice to have one long-strand pasta, which is especially good for thinner sauces, a tube shape for trapping thick, meaty sauces, and a short-cut pasta with nooks and crannies such as fusilli or campanelle for holding vegetables, as in pasta salad or Pasta with Caramelized Onions, Pecorino Romano, and Black Pepper (page 112).

small pastas Tiny shapes like orzo, ditalini, tubetti, and conchigliette are nice to add to soups and salads, or to use as the base for stewy pastas like Pasta e Ceci (page 120).

tortellini, gnocchi, and ravioli These pantry mainstays are great for a last-minute meal, and we offer several tricks to doctor them up. When shopping, we like to buy dried cheese tortellini (these steam-pasteurized and dried tortellini tend to have the cheesiest fillings). For gnocchi, we prefer the flavor and texture of vacuum-packed, while packaged ravioli are good both fresh and frozen.

NOODLES

wheat noodles Chinese lo mein noodles made from wheat and eggs are available both fresh and dried, and are incredibly versatile. Dried noodles are convenient, but fresh noodles are delightfully springy when cooked and can be stored in your freezer for up to a month. You can substitute 12 ounces fresh noodles for 8 ounces dried. Japanese yakisoba noodles can also be used in many recipes calling for wheat noodles.

soba noodles Made from buckwheat or a mixture of buckwheat and wheat, soba boast an earthy taste and slightly chewy texture. They're great in broth, and also cold as in Chilled Soba Noodles with Miso Dressing (page 154).

rice noodles The two styles you're most likely to see are flat noodles about ¼ inch wide and thin noodles sometimes labeled "vermicelli." Both must be soaked in hot water before using. Flat rice noodles are often stir-fried after soaking to make them tender, as in Pad Thai (page 164). Vermicelli can be soaked until tender or parsoaked and finished in the pan as with Singapore Noodles (page 162).

ramen noodles The 3-ounce packages of instant ramen that epitomize pantry cooking have many uses. We ditch the flavor packet and use our own seasonings to make Almost-Instant Miso Ramen (page 78) and Gochujang-Tahini Noodles (page 161).

GRAINS AND LEGUMES

rice The types of rice to keep on hand really depends on what you like to make, but having both a long-grain rice and a short- or medium-grain rice allows you to prepare almost any rice dish, and you can add specific rices such as arborio, bomba, or basmati based on your cooking preferences.

other grains Grains can be the foundation of a main dish or salad or added to soups for heft. Most grains can be cooked the same way by boiling them pasta-style using the cooking times on page 173. This gives you the flexibility to incorporate any grain you have into a Grain Bowl (page 172), grain salad (page 174), or other dish.

grits, polenta, and steel–cut oats Not just for breakfast, these form the basis for savory porridges ready to top with the contents of your pantry. (You can make porridge from white rice, too; see page 185.)

beans Inexpensive, healthful beans are a cornerstone of pantry cooking. Don't overlook a dish because you don't have a specific bean; many of the recipes in this book accommodate several types. We also show how to adapt the flavor profile of a dish to spotlight different kinds of beans (as with our easy canned bean soups on page 90). We generally prefer the ease of canned beans but find dried especially useful for developing a flavorful cooking liquid for a stew or soup, such as Lablabi (page 98).

lentils It's nice to have at least one kind of lentil that holds its shape during cooking (such as brown, green, or du Puy) to use in salads and stews and to add to pasta, as well as a lentil that breaks down (we often use red) for pureed soups and dals. And don't pass over convenient canned lentils; they have great texture and flavor.

BREADS

"Bread for dinner" can take many forms. It can be the base for cheesy quesadillas (page 58), sandwiches, and hearty tartines (page 241), and it can be used to make stratas (page 273), croutons (page 389), pita chips (page 388), and bread crumbs. Bread freezes extremely well, so it's worth keeping several kinds in your freezer.

TWO DOUGHS WORTH BUYING

We've found that store-bought pizza dough is just as good as what you'd make at home, and the same goes for more-work-than-its-worth puff pastry. Treat both as part of your "freezer pantry" and you've got a jump-start on dinner. And pizza night is just the start; use dough to make Stromboli (page 340) or Red Pepper Flatbreads (page 338), or use puff pastry to transform humble onions into a caramelized Savory Onion-Apple Tart Tatin (page 256).

// long-storage vegetables & aromatics

This category includes what once would have been stored in a root cellar: vegetables that last for weeks in a cool dark place or the crisper. Many are staples the world over and the building blocks of countless pantry meals. Frozen, canned, and jarred vegetables factor in, too, and have plentiful applications in the kitchen. Rely on them to increase the variety of vibrant vegetables to have at the ready.

garlic Integral to pantry cooking, garlic can be all you need to flavor a dish, and we take full advantage, softening it in oil to become a pasta sauce (page 110) and toasting cloves to bring nuance to chickpea soup (page 76). When garlic isn't the predominant flavor, ¾ teaspoon granulated garlic can replace 1 teaspoon minced garlic. You can also use garlic powder but it must be reconstituted (see page 24).

onion, shallots, scallions, and leeks While flavors vary (yellow onions are bolder, white milder, and red jammier), we use onions interchangeably here, and even trade among alliums. (Want just a bit of onion? Try a shallot.) With alliums always in the pantry, we feature them in big ways. Roasted onions star in Savory Onion-Apple Tarte Tatin (page 256). Scallions create the flavor base of Simple Fried Rice (page 178). Got extra shallots? Make Nasi Goreng (page 182).

ginger If you get into the habit of freezing some of your ginger (see page 31) you'll always have it on hand.

potatoes and other root vegetables (sweet potatoes, carrots, parsnips, celery root, turnips, rutabaga) Unlock the potential of potatoes by stirring them with pasta and pesto (page 124), stuffing them into tacos (page 206), or braising them with vindaloo spices (page 246). While some potato dishes benefit from using either a starchy russet or waxier red potato or Yukon Gold, often any kind will do fine. In fact, many of these recipes accommodate any root vegetable you have; include several to bring variety to a dish.

winter squash (butternut, buttercup, hubbard, kabocha) While a whole squash requires more prep work than precut, it lasts significantly longer and you'll be glad you have it. Winter squash can be used interchangeably here.

cabbage and cauliflower A cabbage in the crisper ensures you always have a leafy vegetable on hand that can be cooked any way you please. Take it beyond soups and slaws and roast the wedges for a salad (page 230), toss sautéed cabbage with noodles or pasta, or sear it hash-style in Bubble and Squeak (page 237). Another durable crucifer, cauliflower is good frozen as well as fresh.

celery and fennel Both can serve as a crunchy addition to salads, an aromatic base, or a braising vegetable. In fact, they work well in many of the same dishes.

canned tomatoes Canned tomatoes come whole, diced, crushed, and pureed. Each is worth keeping on hand but canned whole tomatoes are the most versatile, as you can readily substitute them for others simply by dicing or pureeing them. Their flavor is excellent, lively, and fresh.

frozen and jarred vegetables Stock frozen vegetables! You get lots for your money (preserved at peak freshness) and you can measure out what you need from the freezer. Low-moisture vegetables such as peas, corn, and limas are ideal as they retain their shape. If shape doesn't matter, go for spinach, broccoli, or green beans. We use them in Palak Dal (page 200), Broccoli-Cheese Cornbread (page 330), and Skillet-Charred Green Beans with Crispy Sesame Topping (page 234). We turn to jarred artichoke hearts and roasted red peppers to flavor everything from hummus to shakshuka.

3 WAYS TO USE PAST–THEIR–PRIME VEGETABLES

- Empty-Your-Pantry Vegetable Soup (page 64)
- Quick pickles (page 404)
- Vegetable Broth Base (page 406)

// frozen, cured & tinned proteins

A well-stocked pantry is a storehouse of tasty proteins that can add flavor and substance to meals, either in small amounts or as the focal point. Here, we highlight some of our favorite proteins to keep around for assembling pantry meals, from eggs—that quintessential spur-of-the-moment standby—to cheese, tinned fish, cured meat, packaged tofu and tempeh, and a handful of go-to fresh meats and seafood to store in your freezer.

eggs Take "eggs for dinner" beyond basic by combining them with other pantry items. That could mean a buttery potato roesti topped with a circle of fried eggs (page 266), Mexican chilaquiles (page 264), or several riffs on shakshuka (page 268). Also, don't limit deviled eggs (page 54) to parties: They're a great opportunity to embellish with the contents of your pantry, from pickles to spices.

semifirm cheese (cheddar, Monterey Jack, mozzarella, Gruyère) We get a lot of mileage out of many cheeses, but a semifirm melting cheese can serve as the main protein in recipes, such as Cheese Enchiladas (page 278). Keep a couple on hand and don't be afraid to break with tradition. Yes, that means you can put cheddar on pizza (page 336)!

tinned/smoked seafood (canned tuna; tinned sardines and anchovies; smoked mackerel, trout, and salmon) At once utilitarian and fancy, tinned and smoked fish can be eaten straight from the can, stuffed into a sandwich, flaked over a salad, or even set out in a pantry tapas spread. Tuna (ideally oil-packed) stars in Spaghetti al Tonno (page 122) and we offer 19 updates on classic tuna salad (page 282) to keep lunch interesting. Smoked salmon adds a luxurious touch to pantry meals, from savory pancakes to eggs.

cured meats (bacon, pancetta, salami, smoked chorizo, ham, Spam) The sky's the limit with these options, all useful for adding a small amount of meaty flavor to a dish. In most cases (apart from bacon), avoid thinly sliced cured meats for cooking. Ask for a ¼-inch piece of pancetta or salami, which can be cut into pieces that cook evenly. And remember: The rendered fat from these meats is a valuable flavoring. Use it to sauté aromatics or toast grains.

tofu and tempeh Whether or not you eat meat, these proteins are a pantry cook's best friend. They keep for several weeks and are ready to use for stir-fries, soups, braises, or a crispy sandwich. Firm and extra-firm tofu hold their shape well in high-heat applications and are great marinated. Custardy soft tofu is good pan-fried or braised, but in a pinch, we'll use any tofu we have. Seared slabs of tempeh (page 312) are ready to be dressed in a variety of sauces.

precooked sausage Vacuum-sealed precooked sausage can be the basis of many a pantry meal (like our one-pan dinner of sausage, braised cabbage, and potatoes on page 292), so pick your favorite to keep on hand.

FROZEN EVERYTHING ELSE

Keep a few common cuts of meat and fish in the freezer for greater mealtime flexibility.

- **ground meat (beef, pork, turkey, chicken, plant-based meat)** Stock what you like: Ground meats can often be used interchangeably, as with our Simple (Any) Meat Sauce (page 139).

- **boneless chicken breasts**

- **pork tenderloin** Cook it whole, cut it up for stir-fries, or even slice your own cutlets (see page 284) .

- **frozen fish fillets (salmon, tilapia, or other white fish)**

- **shell-on shrimp**

// crispy, crunchy & chewy toppings

Everyone loves crispy, crunchy, and chewy foods. These ingredients are all about building textural contrasts that can take pasta, noodles, grains, or vegetables to the next level. Since the goal is texture, it generally matters less which particular ingredient you choose than that you use one that has the texture you want. So go nuts—and beyond. Potato chips, popcorn, and dried fruit all have their place. The more variety you include in this category, the more fun your pantry meals will be.

bread crumbs and croutons A handful of boldly seasoned toasted bread crumbs amps up the crunch factor of any dish; sprinkle them on pasta or over vegetables, or use them in a salad in place of croutons for crunch in every mouthful. Start with panko, which has large and fluffy crumbs that provide great crunch; toast them; and season well with salt and pepper. Bring in other flavors: We add maple bread crumbs to roasted carrots, while sesame bread crumbs transform roasted green beans. And croutons (page 389) require only marginally more effort.

nuts and seeds We suggest nuts and seeds so frequently that the pages of this book are sprinkled with them; in addition to crunch they add richness and protein. They can top Butternut Squash Soup (page 84), balance a grain salad (page 174), add texture to pasta or noodles, and level up vegetables. In most cases, any nut or seed will work so use what you have—just make sure to toast them first. Better yet, make Spiced Nuts (page 52).

dried fruit Dried fruit improves more than granola. Its sweetness and chew balance saltier elements in dishes such as Pasta with Capers and Raisins (page 111). And it enhances warm spices in dishes such as Vegetable Tagine with Chickpeas and Olives (page 245). Dried fruit can replace fresh fruit in salads, too. The brightness won't be the same but you'll still have sweetness and tartness.

tortilla strips and chips They add a textured, corny crunch to salads and soups, where they also soak up liquid to become a bit tender. They're often fried, but we bake ours—see page 389. In a pinch, we will use store-bought tortilla chips.

crackers, pretzels, and chips Your snack drawer is a trove of crispy, crunchy goodness that can level up everything from chili to ice cream. Top your next sundae with hot fudge (page 352) and salty potato chips; you'll wonder why you never did before. Popcorn tastes great atop a bowl of tomato soup. Plantain or banana chips add contrast to a cabbage salad (page 230). Pita chips make excellent salad croutons. Kale chips add dimension to creamy soups.

seaweed Toasted nori makes a delicate topping for rice, eggs, fish, noodles, salads, or soups. Use as is or in the seaweed-studded spice blend furikake. Toasted strips of gim (dried seaweed paper) add a flavor, texture, and color to Kimchi Bokkeumbap (page 180). Pretoasted seaweed snacks work great too.

flake sea salt We typically add salt to foods before or during cooking. But sprinkling a finished dish with flake sea salt, such as Maldon or another coarse salt, adds a delicate crunch and discrete pops of brininess that contrast with other flavors. Try seasoning a salad after tossing with flake salt. Sprinkle it on juicy cooked meat or just-baked chocolate chip cookies.

FRY YOUR GARLIC, SHALLOTS, AND CAPERS

Just a few minutes of frying in the microwave turns these potent ingredients into crispy flavor bombs. Once you try them you'll always want to have them at the ready (see page 388 for more information).

// savory umami condiments, seasonings & sprinkles

Umami, a quality of meaty savoriness that brings depth to many dishes, is widely considered the fifth taste. These long-lasting, umami-enhancing ingredients boost the flavor of whatever we're cooking. In some places, the use is subtle: Just a spoonful of fish sauce or tomato paste can add a savory backbone to a soup or stew. But these potent ingredients can also occupy the foreground, serving as the base for a sauce or a one-ingredient sprinkle to add a pop of savoriness to a mild dish.

hard aged cheeses (Parmesan, Pecorino Romano) Umami-producing glutamates in cheese concentrate over time as cheese ages. Parmesan may be king of this category but you can swap in Pecorino Romano or hard aged Manchego, Asiago, or Gouda.

soy sauce The base for a multitude of sauces, marinades, and glazes, soy sauce also deepens the flavor of everything from soups to salad dressings. Mix it with browned butter to make all-purpose Infinite Sauce (page 399).

fish sauce Made from salted, fermented anchovies, this Southeast Asian staple adds complexity and funky depth to everything from a simple cabbage stir-fry (page 232) to rich coconut soup (page 102). We'll substitute it for anchovies when we want an umami boost but don't need anchovy flavor, as in Italian Pasta and Bean Soup (page 95).

Worcestershire sauce Another anchovy derivative that includes malt vinegar, molasses, and tamarind, this pungent sauce is classic in Caesar salad, but try brushing it on steak or tofu or mixing a steakhouse mayonnaise (page 401).

anchovies and anchovy paste Preserved anchovies are packed with glutamates. Traditionally, anchovies add dimension to Caesar dressing, but we use them to intensify savoriness in a variety of dishes, from pasta sauce to beef stew. Anchovy paste can also be used.

hoisin sauce A Cantonese staple, hoisin adds spicy, salty, and sweet elements to stir-fries such as Vegetable Lo Mein (page 166) as well as meats, glazes, and dipping sauces. (Mix it with honey for a sweet-savory glaze; page 401.)

oyster sauce A common stir-fry ingredient made from oysters (vegetarian mushroom versions are also available) this sauce is savory and slightly fishy, with a hint of sweetness.

miso This fermented mixture of soybeans and rice, barley, or rye is incredibly versatile; use it in soups, braises, dressings, and sauces. In addition to flavoring its namesake soup (page 74) and ramen noodles (page 78), we use it to make several simple sauces (page 401).

tomato paste and sun-dried tomatoes All tomatoes add savory qualities to foods, but these ultraconcentrated forms build umami in soups and sauces like Tomato, Bulgur, and Red Pepper Soup (page 101). Briefly sauté tomato paste until it darkens and smells fragrant to develop its flavor.

dried mushrooms All mushrooms are high in umami, but dried ones deliver intense amounts of it. We use dried porcinis and shiitakes to build flavor in long-cooked dishes.

kombu A mainstay in Japanese cooking, this type of kelp is used in dashi (page 74), the first food in which umami was clearly recognized. Try steeping a 4-inch piece in your next batch of lentil soup or in tomato sauce.

bonito flakes These dried fish flakes have a meaty, smoky flavor. In addition to using them to make dashi, add them as a savory garnish to marinated tofu, soups, and noodles.

nutritional yeast This deactivated form of yeast adds a funky, nutty, almost salty flavor (though there's no salt in it) that matches cheese in complexity. Try it in soups, pasta, and salad dressings, or as a "cheesy" popcorn sprinkle.

// spicy, hot & smoky elements

Spices and chiles of all kinds bring food to life, providing warmth, complexity, and aroma. They can add dimension to a salad and introduce flavor profiles of the cuisines of the world. Adding a spice or hot sauce is the simplest way to take a dish beyond basic. And if you don't have a specific spice, hot sauce, or dried chile, don't fret. Look into your pantry and try a different one; see (and taste) how it transforms the dish into something new.

spices Your spice rack is a world of flavor potential in your pantry. So use it! Keep spices well organized so that each one is visible. A great way to use more spices is to make a blend (see pages 381–383) and apply it as a rub for meat and chicken or bloom some in fat as a base for a stew. Or make a spice-infused oil (see page 390).

dried herbs Dried rosemary, sage, oregano, marjoram, and thyme all fare reasonably well in longer-cooked dishes. To replace fresh herbs with dried, use one-third the amount and add early in the cooking process. Those herbs that we consider delicate (such as basil, cilantro, and parsley) lose too much flavor when dried and are best avoided.

ground chiles Red pepper flakes and cayenne are pantry standbys for turning up the heat in everything from soups and sauces to granola (page 49) and ice cream. But there is a world of ground chiles to try. Calabrian chile flakes are fiery; Sichuan chili powder (used in skillet-charred green beans on page 234) offers milder, more aromatic heat. Aleppo pepper conveys a gentle heat and raisin-like sweetness. Don't be afraid to experiment with different kinds.

smoky chiles (chipotles in adobo, chipotle chile powder, smoked paprika) Canned chipotles in adobo are a go-to for adding smokiness and chile heat. Chipotle powder can also be used—it packs a punch. Smoked paprika is milder and can infuse a dish with smoky complexity.

hot sauce When we don't have fresh chiles on hand, we'll often reach for a bottle of hot sauce, which carries more of the fresh chile flavor than dried chiles do. Buy hot sauces with specific chile profiles such as habanero or poblano and use them in place of the fresh ingredient.

chili–garlic sauce and sambal oelek Two Southeast Asian staples, chile-garlic sauce is made with garlic and chiles, while sambal oelek contains chiles only. Both keep for months and are useful for adding chile heat and flavor to marinades and sauces. Make a simple dipping sauce by combining chili-garlic sauce with fish sauce, sugar, and lime juice. We use sambal oelek in Nasi Goreng (page 182).

gochujang This thick, sweet, savory, and spicy paste made from gochugaru (Korean chile flakes) flavors soups, stews, marinades, and sauces. We use it to make a bold sauce for noodles (page 161) and to flavor fried rice (page 180).

chili crisp The pleasure of this flavorful sauce is tactile: Pieces of chiles, garlic, and nuts are deep-fried and jarred in a luxuriously spiced oil. Chili crisp (to make your own, see page 392) has a tingly crispiness that's superb over noodles, rice, greens, or eggs.

harissa A popular smoky North African chili paste, Harissa (page 392) will wake up vegetables, meat, hummus, lentil soup (page 93), and much more. Pair dollops of harissa and yogurt for a spicy-cooling combo.

thai curry paste (red, green, yellow) Beyond their use as a base for Thai curries, these pastes combine chili heat with potent aromatics such as lemongrass, galangal, and makrut limes in pantry form; they're great starting points for soups like Wild Rice Soup with Coconut and Lime (page 102), braises, and even salad dressings (page 230).

// acidic & pickled foods

When we develop recipes we often call for a splash of fresh citrus juice or a touch of vinegar at the end of cooking to awaken the flavors of a dish. When a dish feels flat, adding acid or salt can frequently be the solution. Brined and pickled ingredients hit both of those elements, and they keep for a long time. And vinegar is a great backup for fresh citrus if you don't have any (or vice versa). Whatever you use, get in the habit of seasoning to taste, not just with salt and pepper but also with acid before serving.

VINEGARS

As little as ⅛ teaspoon of vinegar goes a long way in brightening up a dish. We add a finishing touch of vinegar to soups such as Winter Squash and White Bean Soup (page 68), pastas like creamy cheese ravioli (page 134), and vegetables. Vinegar works as an alternative to citrus when you don't have fresh lemons or limes (it can be more acidic, so you may want to season to taste). While most recipes in this book would work with more than one type of vinegar, given their longevity it's worth stocking several kinds; even distilled white vinegar is useful in a pinch.

red and white wine vinegars They're sharp, crisp, subtly fruity, and mostly interchangeable; however, if you don't want to affect a dish's color, use white wine vinegar.

sherry vinegar Warm and toasty flavors add complexity. It's good with earthy grains such as Mushroom Farrotto (page 192) and Spanish-Style Garlic Shrimp (page 300).

rice wine vinegar Less acidic than other vinegars, it's great in milder salad dressings, quick pickles, and stir-fries. We sometimes call for seasoned rice vinegar; to make your own, see page 404.

cider vinegar This one is mellow and slightly sweet; it's great in glazes and slaws or in a pan sauce for pork chops.

balsamic vinegar Balsamic brings sweetness and punch.

Chinese black vinegar Earthy and complex, this vinegar makes a great drizzle for dumplings, noodles, and Congee (page 185).

CITRUS AND PICKLES

lemons and limes A squeeze of lemon or lime provides contrast; it cuts through rich or salty food and brightens mild or mellow flavors. While each citrus fruit has a unique flavor, don't omit that splash of acid just because you don't have the right one. Swapping fresh lemon for lime can be a delightful way to change the character of a dish. If that feels like a step too far, use vinegar. Fresh orange and grapefruit segments are another way to add acidic citrus.

pickled vegetables (cucumbers, jalapeños, pepperoncini, giardiniera, olives, capers) One of the best ingredients in the pantry cook's toolkit, pickles add tang, crunch, salt, and color to liven up any meal. They perk up grain and bean dishes and provide contrast to fresh vegetables. Layer them into a sandwich or add them to a Dutch baby (page 318), fried rice (page 178), or polenta (page 187). Expand your pickle horizons by making quick pickles (page 404) from carrots, celery, or what-have-you.

kimchi This Korean staple conveys many things at once— tang, umami, heat, and crunch. In addition to eating it as an accompaniment to all kinds of meals, try adding it to noodles, soups, hash (page 239), or tuna salad (page 282). More than a condiment, it can be the main ingredient in Kimchi Bokkeumbap (page 180) or Kimchi Jeon (page 60).

sauerkraut Bracing and fresh, sauerkraut is excellent with potatoes (page 266). Stir some into cooked cabbage to create multidimensional flavor (page 292).

USE THAT PICKLE BRINE

Instead of tossing out a jar of pickle juice after finishing the last spear, save that brine for anything that needs a little perking up. But the fun doesn't stop with pickles: Whisk giardiniera liquid into a≈vinaigrette, add pickled jalapeño brine to coleslaw, or slip some pepperoncini juice into a Bloody Mary. Just remember, the vinegar in pickle brine is slightly diluted by water so don't substitute it one-for-one for vinegar or lemon juice.

// creamy & rich toppings

A cooling dollop or crumble of one of these ingredients can balance spice, tame heat, and add richness to lean dishes. Add something creamy and rich to finish soups, beans, grains, and cooked or raw vegetables. Use one of these items as a spread for sandwiches or burgers or as a topping for tacos, or serve as a sauce alongside simply cooked meats.

yogurt If we had to pick one staple in the category of "creamy things to dollop on food," yogurt (Greek or regular) would win. Equally at home with sweet and savory flavors, yogurt is excellent on everything from granola to roasted vegetables and grains to red lentil soup (page 93). While it can act as a sauce on its own, it becomes something more savory with the mere additions of garlic, lemon, and salt, and welcomes fresh herbs and spices, too (see page 396).

sour cream In many recipes, from soups to enchiladas to baked potatoes, sour cream offers more richness than Greek yogurt, but the two are interchangeable.

mayonnaise Like yogurt, mayonnaise can stand on its own as a sauce or spread or provide a blank slate for flavors from chipotle to horseradish (page 401). A dollop of mayonnaise makes a luxurious accompaniment to Fried Eggs with Parmesan and Potato Roesti (page 266) or fideos (page 128). But its most interesting pantry use is adding creamy richness to a bowl of instant ramen noodles (page 78).

nut butters and tahini Peanut butter (or another nut butter), with just a little help from, say, lime juice and soy sauce (page 117) or red curry paste and rice vinegar (page 401) becomes a savory sauce to toss with noodles or spread on tofu, vegetables, chicken, or shrimp. The same holds for tahini—mixed with gochujang it forms a stellar sauce for noodles (page 161).

creamy cheeses (feta, goat, blue, cotija) While the flavors obviously differ among these cheeses, they all serve to add a creamy richness, so if you're just adding a finishing crumble, don't fear making swaps if you don't have a particular cheese on hand. That farro salad or butternut squash soup will be delicious regardless of which you use.

butter, oil, and cream There's nothing like a pat of butter to round out the flavors of a soup or sauce, add gloss to pasta and risotto, and provide a finishing touch to a steak or fish fillet. A drizzle of olive oil or sesame oil contributes aroma and flavor, as well as a luxurious sheen. And a swirl of heavy cream enriches soups, pasta sauces, and spiced braises. If you have extra cream, make Crème Fraîche (page 398).

BONUS: SOMETHING FRESH

Once we've added that final drizzle of oil or dollop of yogurt, we often finish a dish with a scattering of herbs for color and freshness. But the ideal fresh herb isn't always on hand. Here are a few suggestions for finding fresh flavor:

- **swap herbs** A recipe calls for cilantro but all you have is parsley? Use it anyway!

- **add scallion greens** Sliced scallion greens add color and potent fresh favor just like any herb.

- **turn to celery leaves** Those pretty leaves concealed in the heart of your celery make a fantastic garnish and provide delicate herbal flavor.

- **mince fresh chiles** A scattering of minced or sliced fresh chile adds color and freshness in addition to heat.

// sweet & sweet-tart flavorings

Good for more than baking, these sweet and sweet-tart ingredients play a multitude of roles in pantry cooking. Just a spoonful of one can balance a dish that has salty, bitter, sour, or spicy elements. Some offer a neutral sweetness while others bring in caramelized notes or sweet-sour flavors that can perk up a dish by contributing a gentle tang.

sugar Treat sugar as a spice to create a balanced sweet-salty or sweet-sour flavor profile. We typically use white sugar for pure sweetness and turn to brown sugar when we want a more caramelized, rounder flavor. Out of brown sugar? See our substitutions on page 27 or use white sugar in a pinch if a very small amount is needed.

honey and maple syrup These are best used when you want their flavors featured; we often use them interchangeably in pantry cooking, whether it's for sweetening granola or mixing into a dressing. Both play well with spicy flavors: Combine maple syrup or honey with cayenne and add to panko bread crumbs for a punched-up topping for carrots (page 243), or combine either with mustard for a simple glaze for meat. Opt for 100 percent maple syrup rather than one blended with corn syrup.

mirin This Japanese rice wine has a subtle salty-sweet flavor prized in marinades and glazes. We use it to sweeten and brighten the flavor of sauces such as the one used in Chilled Soba Noodles with Miso Dressing (page 154).

ketchup The classic sweet-tangy condiment has plenty of pantry utility beyond squirting onto a hot dog or fries. It combines with Worcestershire and soy sauce to make a tonkatsu-style sauce for crispy breaded cutlets (page 311), and serves as an ingredient in glazes.

kecap manis Pronounced just like "ketchup," kecap is a catchall term for sauce in Indonesia. Kecap manis is the sweetest. Made from soybeans, palm sugar, and seasonings, it has a salty-sweet taste that brings deep flavor to Nasi Goreng (page 182) and makes a great addition to glazes for meat, stews, and dipping sauces.

barbecue sauce A good all-purpose barbecue sauce makes just about anything taste better. Use it as a glaze for chicken wings, stir into baked beans or boiled potatoes for an easy side dish, or brush onto grilled corn.

pomegranate molasses A pantry staple throughout the eastern portion of the Mediterranean region, pomegranate molasses is made by reducing pomegranate juice to a sticky syrup that layers astringent, floral, and faintly bitter notes over a sweet-tart, fruity flavor profile. It can be whisked into vinaigrettes (as in Pomegranate-Honey Vinaigrette on page 225), drizzled over vegetables, brushed onto roast meats, or pureed into dips.

// cooking liquids & fats & baking items

At a minimum, you need some form of fat and/or some kind of liquid (which could be water) to cook pretty much anything, and usually some type of flour to bake. But by expanding your pantry to include just a handful of additional items in these broad categories, you can dramatically increase your options for foods and flavors.

COOKING LIQUIDS

broth Broth can be the cooking liquid for grains, pasta, and noodles; a flavorful medium for cooking vegetables; and the base for a savory sauce. While we love the scrappy homemade broth options on page 406, we often reach for concentrated bouillon. This shelf-stable product is cost-effective and lasts for up to two years once opened. Simply mix it with water to make only as much broth as you need. We particularly like Better than Bouillon Chicken Base.

red and white wine A splash of wine can give nuance to soups (see page 33). If you're simmering food in broth, adding some wine first boosts acidity and adds complexity, as it does in our Fideos with Chickpeas, Fennel, and Kale (page 128). Red wine adds brawny, fruit-forward flavor and a twist of acidity, while white wine (or dry vermouth) brings brightness and acidity to recipes.

Shaoxing wine and dry sherry Many Chinese recipes call for Shaoxing rice wine, an amber wine that contributes savory, nutty flavors. Dry sherry is often a substitute and the reverse is true: Shaoxing wine can be substituted for sherry.

canned coconut milk Coconut milk adds rich flavor and body to soups, curries, stir-fries, and rice dishes such as Chicken and Rice with Turmeric, Coriander, and Cumin (page 291). Coconut milk comes in both regular and light versions; regular coconut milk is creamier but also contains more fat. Do not confuse it with coconut cream or cream of coconut, which contains added sugar and is much sweeter.

FATS

oils Cooking oils such as canola oil and vegetable oil have high smoke points so they're great for sautéing, shallow frying, and stir-frying; they're also good additions to dressings where a neutral flavor is desired. Peanut oil is especially good for frying. Finishing oils such as toasted sesame oil or chili oil are best used raw to add a final drizzle of flavor to a dish. Extra-virgin olive oil is both a cooking oil and a finishing oil; use it to sauté or as an ultraflavorful finishing drizzle.

butter We like unsalted butter for cooking and baking, but salted butter is great for spreading on toast. To get the most out of this pantry staple, make a compound butter (page 403) to dollop over steaks or toss with sautéed vegetables. Better yet, make Ghee (page 403), a form of clarified butter with a rich, nutty aroma that performs well in high-heat applications and keeps for months.

BAKING ITEMS

flour (all-purpose flour, whole-wheat flour, bread flour, chickpea flour) If you bake at all, you probably have all-purpose flour on hand. Whole-wheat flour has many applications for pantry baking: We use it in pizza dough, dinner crepes, and hearty Irish soda bread. And even if you never bake a loaf of bread, bread flour is useful for making pizza dough; we also rely on its high gluten content to make Chinese hand-pulled noodles (page 168). We use chickpea flour to make one of our favorite simple pantry flatbreads, Socca (page 322).

cornmeal The typical supermarket offers a bewildering assortment of cornmeal products, and their labels can be confusing. The same exact dried ground corn can be called yellow grits, polenta, or corn semolina. Labels also advertise fine, medium, and coarse grinds, but no standard definitions exist. Then there's whole-grain versus degerminated cornmeal. For most polenta recipes we call for coarse-ground cornmeal or yellow grits; for most grits recipes we use old-fashioned grits. For cornbread, look for finely ground, whole-grain cornmeal. White and yellow cornmeal can be used interchangeably.

unsweetened cocoa powder Both natural and Dutched cocoa (which has been processed to neutralize its acidity and mellow its astringent notes) work in most recipes, though Dutch-processed cocoa will produce baked goods with a darker color and moister texture.

chocolate Chocolate chips are the most convenient form but we also like bars. We stock a dark chocolate with 60 percent cacao in addition to unsweetened chocolate.

leaveners (baking soda, baking powder) For such indispensable ingredients, leaveners are an afterthought to many, yet the freshness can determine a recipe's outcome. Despite manufacturer claims of one year, we suggest you replace your baking powder every six months.

vanilla extract We all run out of vanilla. On those occasions, you can substitute bourbon or a liqueur such as Grand Marnier.

old-fashioned rolled oats A pantry staple for making granola, folding into cookies, topping fruit crisps (page 365) and, of course, making oatmeal.

no one–hit wonders here

A great pantry ingredient can be used in a variety of ways. We asked our test cooks and editors to share some of their favorite condiments and spice blends along with how they put them to use.

tahini

Stir it into oatmeal with bananas and maple syrup. Stir it into soups and purees to thicken and enrich (carrot, cauliflower, and parsnip all work really well). Or use it to make a super-quick tahini-yogurt sauce (see page 209).

—*Joe Gitter*

harissa

I add it to meatballs and serve with roasted vegetables, feta, herbs, and couscous. It pairs well with salmon. Drizzle it on fried eggs with pita or hard boiled eggs with yogurt, or stir some into shakshuka (see page 268).

— *Hannah Fenton*

adobo

I love adobo seasoning. I use it to marinate proteins, start my sofrito, spice up canned beans, and even add it to popcorn! If I don't have a store-bought blend at home, I make my own (my version is on page 381).

— *Patty Suarez*

thai red curry paste

There is so much flavor in such a little amount of paste. I'll stir it into a "clean-out-your-fridge" stir-fry or into a soup with lots of coconut milk (see page 102). I'll cook it with ground pork for quick weeknight lettuce cups. Sometimes I'll even just turn it into a sauce and toss in some noodles.

— *Samantha Block*

tajín

I sprinkle this "chile-lime-salt" on pineapple and cucumber, grilled chicken or steak (before or after cooking), avocados on tortillas (avocado toast also works), and buttered corn on the cob. It adds a nice hit of salt, acid, and heat when I don't have fresh citrus or chiles on hand.

— *Camila Chaparro*

baharat

Baharat is my favorite spice blend. (You can buy it or make your own; see page 382.) I use it as a seasoning for takeout french fries. I also use it for "taco night" seasoning. And I'll whisk it into some mayo to spread on a sandwich or burger.

— *Hisham Hassan*

five-spice powder

This is my go-to spice blend for everything. I usually pair it with starchy vegetables. Sweet potatoes are a favorite.

— *Olivia Counter*

hoisin

I marinate chicken, pork, and steak with hoisin or rub it on chicken before roasting. I almost always add this to salad dressings. I drizzle it on grain bowls or in soup before eating as a final element of salty-sweet flavor.

— *Sara Mayer*

cholula hot sauce

I'll put it on top of a sliced avocado with sea salt, on scrambled eggs, and on tuna melts.

— *Laila Ibrahim*

chili crisp

I use chili crisp on everything. It has a mellow heat and is pretty flavorful. I have been folding it into rice, noodles, and vegetables. I'll make udon noodles and fold in chili crisp pretty generously and then add a stir-fry of broccoli, snap peas, onions, etc. A spicy bowl of noodles is great chilled or hot.

— *José Maldonado*

greek yogurt

In addition to dolloping on soups, salads, and tacos, it's a blank canvas for flavor mix-ins. I'll make a dressing by thinning it with water and adding herbs, tahini, or chipotle. Or make a ranch dressing with garlic powder, dried dill, oil, a little bit of water.

— *Dan Zuccarello*

hummus

Aside from dipping crudités and pita, I often spread my sandwiches with hummus. I also thin it out with lemon juice and drizzle it over grain bowls or salads (see page 289). A snack I've been loving is rice cakes spread with hummus, sprinkled with dukkah, and drizzled with honey.

— *Brenna Donovan*

wake up **flavor**

Successful pantry cooking isn't about just stocking a wide range of ingredients; it's also about getting the maximum mileage from what you've got. Often, a simple cooking technique can transform a basic pantry staple into a catalyst that revs up flavor. Every one of these tips will help you wake up your meals.

BROWN YOUR BUTTER

Browning butter adds a nutty depth to both sweet and savory dishes. Two key points: Use a light-colored pan so you can easily see the butter change color, and don't walk away—it can darken quickly. Heat the butter over medium heat. Once the water from the butter boils off, it will foam; that's the cue that it's almost ready. As soon as the butter turns chestnut brown and smells toasty, remove the pan from the heat. If you're not using the butter right away, transfer it to another container so it doesn't continue to cook. Browned butter tastes fantastic in cakes, on noodles (page 153), or as a sauce for fish. Or stir in soy sauce and lemon juice to make irresistible Infinite Sauce (page 399).

BROWN TOMATO PASTE, TOO

Tomato paste is a versatile, inexpensive flavor powerhouse that's great for adding concentrated tomato flavor and umami to sauces, soups, and pastas. Tomato paste is full of glutamates that bring out savory flavor. Cook tomato paste with aromatics to release its full flavor. We do this in our Winter Squash and White Bean Soup (page 68).

TOAST PANKO IN THE MICROWAVE

Crisp, airy toasted panko bread crumbs elevate dishes with their light crunch. Toss them with oil in a shallow dish and season them with salt and pepper. Microwave the crumbs, stirring often, until they're deep golden brown, 3 to 5 minutes. Sprinkle them on mac and cheese, roasted vegetables, or just about anything else you can think of.

HYDRATE GARLIC POWDER

The trick to using garlic powder is to hydrate it before cooking, which can be done by mixing it with a little water before adding it to a dish or it will happen naturally when it's applied to wet foods such as raw meat. Hydrating the powder before heating awakens the flavor-producing enzyme, alliinase, which goes dormant when producers dry the garlic (drying happens below 140 degrees to avoid deactivating the alliinase). Heating the powder before hydrating it would kill the enzyme—and any potential for garlic flavor.

BLOOM YOUR SPICES IN FAT

Heating ground spices in oil or butter is called blooming. Blooming changes fat-soluble flavor molecules in spices from a solid state to a liquid one where they mix and interact, thereby producing more complexity. In less than a minute, this process magnifies a spice's flavor, making dishes taste bolder and more well rounded.

CHAR FROZEN VEGGIES

Frozen vegetables are convenient, sure, but exciting? They can be—with a little oil and a lot of heat. Pan searing over high heat adds dramatic color, toasty notes, and a delightful soft-chewy exterior to everyday frozen vegetables like corn Esquites (page 229) and Sichuan-style charred green beans (page 234).

GRIND DRIED MUSHROOMS

Dried shiitake and other mushrooms are glutamate-rich umami powerhouses. We often rehydrate them to use in recipes, but you can also grind them to a powder that gives a quick earthy, meaty flavor boost to all kinds of dishes. Grind dried mushrooms to a fine powder in a spice grinder, and store it in a clean spice jar out of direct sunlight. Add to dishes before or during cooking—not as a final seasoning at the table—so that the powder can hydrate; otherwise, it will taste dry and dusty. Use in stews, chilis, ground beef, risotto, or spice rubs, or on steaks or fish before sautéing. Start with a teaspoon and add more to taste.

USE ANCHOVIES EVERYWHERE

OK, maybe not for dessert, but in just about any savory dish these little fish can be a secret weapon. If you use a large quantity of them, anchovies lend a potent seafood flavor to whatever you're cooking; if you use a judicious amount and mince them (or use anchovy paste), they dissolve and provide depth and savoriness without tasting like fish. But the anchovies themselves aren't the only valuable thing in the can/jar: The oil also carries a wonderful flavor that can be great in vinaigrettes, sauces, and soups or stews. If you cook with anchovies, cook with their oil too!

SALT FOOD EARLY, THEN LATE

We season with salt at different times during the cooking process so it blends in properly: Applying kosher salt to meat in advance of cooking improves flavor and texture; seasoning a salad dressing with table salt ensures the salt dissolves; sprinkling carrots with salt before roasting gives it time to penetrate the vegetables' rigid cell walls; salting stews before braising ensures well-rounded seasoning, as salt's rate of diffusion increases with heat; and seasoning fattier foods such as marbled meat more aggressively than lean foods is smart because fat has a dulling effect on taste. A final sprinkle of coarse finishing salt, on the contrary, isn't meant to provide even seasoning. These colorful, coarse salts heighten the flavor of just about anything—from garden vegetables to a just-seared steak to brownies—and bring out dimension, stimulating the appetite. And their crunch provides surprising textural contrast that makes food pop.

SEASON YOUR SALT

Speaking of finishing salts, kosher salt infused with herbs, spices, or other flavorings delivers distinct, punchy flavor—and it's easy to make in the microwave. For spicy sriracha salt, stir together ½ cup kosher salt and ⅓ cup sriracha. Spread on a large plate and microwave, stirring every 60 seconds, until only slightly damp, 6 to 8 minutes (the mixture will continue to dry as it cools). For smoky salt, replace the sriracha with 1 teaspoon liquid smoke; reduce the microwave time to 1 to 2 minutes.

kitchen substitutions

produce	substitute it with
1 medium onion	= 4 large shallots OR 5 to 6 medium shallots
1 medium leek	= 1 large onion
1 clove fresh garlic	= ¼ teaspoon granulated garlic
1 tablespoon chopped ginger	= ¼ to ⅓ teaspoon ground ginger (to taste)
1 fennel bulb	= 3 celery ribs
3 teaspoons fresh herb	= 1 teaspoon dried
1 lemon	= 1½ to 2 limes
Red-skinned potatoes	= Yukon Gold potatoes
1 ounce fresh spinach	= 1 ounce frozen spinach (in cooked applications) OR 2 ounces frozen spinach (in pasta salads or other uncooked applications)
1 medium vine-ripened tomato	= 6 ounces cherry or grape tomatoes
2 red bell peppers, roasted	= 1 cup jarred roasted red peppers
Frozen fava beans	= frozen shelled edamame, lima beans, or peas
Canned crushed tomatoes	= canned whole or diced tomatoes with their juice (pulse in a food processor)
10 ounces fresh tomatoes	= one 14.5-ounce can whole peeled tomatoes, drained (in cooked applications)

chiles	substitute it with
1 habanero	= 2 Thai chiles
1 Thai chile	= 2 serranos OR 2 jalapeños
1 tablespoon minced fresh jalapeños	= 2 tablespoons jarred jalapeños
2 tablespoons gochugaru	= 2 tablespoons ancho chile powder + ⅛ teaspoon cayenne pepper OR 2 tablespoons Aleppo pepper
1 tablespoon Sichuan chili powder	= 1 tablespoon gochugaru OR 1 tablespoon Aleppo pepper OR 2½ teaspoons ancho chile powder + ½ teaspoon cayenne pepper

chiles (cont.)	substitute it with
1 chipotle in adobe	= ½ teaspoon chipotle powder OR ½ teaspoon smoked paprika + ⅛ teaspoon cayenne
1 teaspoon adobo sauce	= ⅛ teaspoon chipotle powder + ½ teaspoon vinegar + ½ teaspoon tomato paste
Ancho chile powder	= chili powder
2 dried arbol chiles	= 1 tablespoon chili powder
¼ teaspoon red pepper flakes	= ⅛ teaspoon cayenne pepper

liquids	substitute it with
1 tablespoon lemon or lime juice	= 2 teaspoons white wine vinegar
2 tablespoons tamarind juice concentrate	= 1 tablespoon lime juice + 1 tablespoon water
2 tablespoons mirin	= 2 tablespoons sake or white wine + 1 teaspoon sugar OR 2 tablespoons sweet sherry
White wine	= dry vermouth
½ cup wine or vermouth	= ½ cup broth +1 teaspoon wine vinegar or lemon juice (use red or white wine vinegar depending on the wine; add the vinegar or lemon juice just before serving)
Chinese black vinegar	= balsamic vinegar or sherry vinegar
Soy sauce	= tamari
Fish sauce	= Braggs Liquid Aminos
Shaoxing wine	= dry sherry
Honey	= agave or maple syrup
Pomegranate molasses	= balsamic vinegar (but there really is no sub for flavor) OR an equivalent amount of half lemon juice, half molasses
1 tablespoon vanilla	= 2 tablespoons bourbon or Grand Marnier, microwaved until reduced to 1 tablespoon
Sriracha	= sambal oelek or chili-garlic sauce

dairy

dairy		substitute it with
1 cup whole milk	=	⅝ cup skim milk + ⅜ cup half-and-half **OR** ⅔ cup 1 percent low-fat milk + ⅓ cup half-and-half **OR** ¾ cup 2 percent low-fat milk + ¼ cup half-and-half **OR** ⅞ cup skim milk + ⅛ cup heavy cream
1 cup half-and-half	=	¾ cup whole milk + ¼ cup heavy cream **OR** ⅔ cup skim or low-fat milk + ⅓ cup heavy cream
1 cup buttermilk (for baking)	=	¾ cup plain yogurt + ¼ cup whole milk **OR** 1 cup whole milk + 1 tablespoon lemon juice or distilled white vinegar
Cow's milk	=	almond milk or soy milk (better in savory cooking) or oat milk (sweeter, good for baking)
Sour cream	=	full-fat Greek yogurt
Feta	=	goat cheese, queso blanco, or mozzarella
Parmesan	=	Pecorino Romano, Asiago, Grana Padano, cotija, or Manchego

nuts and seeds

nuts and seeds		substitute it with
Peanut butter	=	any nut butter or sunflower seed butter
1 cup tahini	=	6 tablespoons peanut butter blended with 2 tablespoons toasted sesame oil (you want half the amount of tahini) **OR** ⅔ cup sesame seeds, ground in a blender with just enough toasted sesame oil to make a smooth mixture

fats, meat, and fish

fats, meat, and fish		substitute it with
Oil for browning and sautéing	=	canola, olive, refined coconut, grapeseed
Oil for frying	=	vegetable, corn, peanut
1 slice bacon	=	1 ounce pancetta **OR** 1 ounce salt pork
1 anchovy fillet	=	½ teaspoon fish sauce (in recipes where the anchovy is a background flavor) **OR** 1½ teaspoons finely minced water-packed tuna (in pasta sauce and salad dressing)

dry ingredients

dry ingredients		substitute it with
1 cup bread flour	=	1 cup all-purpose flour (bread and pizza crusts may bake up with slightly less chew)
1 cup cake flour	=	⅞ cup all-purpose flour + 2 tablespoons cornstarch
1 teaspoon baking powder	=	¼ teaspoon baking soda + ½ teaspoon cream of tartar (use right away)
1 cup light brown sugar	=	1 cup granulated sugar + 1 tablespoon molasses (pulse in a food processor to combine)
1 cup dark brown sugar	=	1 cup granulated sugar + 2 tablespoons molasses (pulse in a food processor to combine)
Superfine sugar	=	granulated sugar, processed in a food processor for 1 minute
1 cup confectioners' sugar	=	1 cup granulated sugar + 1 teaspoon cornstarch, ground in blender (works well for dusting over cakes, less so in frostings and glazes)
Pasta, specific shape	=	an equal weight of any other shape pasta (do not substitute by volume)
1 teaspoon table salt	=	½ teaspoon Morton Kosher Salt **OR** 2 teaspoons Diamond Crystal Kosher Salt

chocolate

chocolate		substitute it with
1 ounce bittersweet or semisweet chocolate	=	⅔ ounce unsweetened chocolate + 2 teaspoons sugar (better for sturdy recipes such as brownies than delicate cakes or custards)
1 ounce unsweetened chocolate	=	3 tablespoons cocoa powder + 1 tablespoon vegetable oil **OR** 1½ ounces bittersweet or semisweet chocolate (remove 1 tablespoon sugar from recipe)
Dutch processed cocoa	=	natural cocoa (baked goods may be lighter in color and slightly drier)

storage smarts

You can break down your kitchen into three distinct categories: dry (pantry goods), cold (refrigerated goods), and frozen (freezer goods). If you store everything properly, you'll waste less, save more, and ultimately be a more efficient and successful cook. With these simple guidelines, your kitchen and cooking will run as smoothly as our test kitchen does.

MARRY AND DOWNSIZE

Having a pantry full of open or almost-empty boxes isn't an efficient use of space. Marry like items to free up space; if you have multiple boxes of open penne pasta, for example, it's a good idea to combine them in a less bulky container. By transferring dry goods to a tight-fitting plastic or glass container, you're not only creating space in your pantry, you're also prolonging the life of the ingredient. Storing like items together also helps you make a swap when you don't have a specific ingredient; if you don't have, say, farro, you can easily find a different grain that's suitable.

PRACTICE FIFO (FIRST IN FIRST OUT)

A general rule of thumb is that if an ingredient got to your kitchen first, it should be the first to leave! This means check those expiration dates. When you are marrying like ingredients, make sure the ones that expire first get a spot at the top of the container.

KEEP IN THE REFRIGERATOR

eggs Don't store eggs in or near the refrigerator door, where they'll be exposed to warm air whenever you open the refrigerator. Instead, store eggs in the back of the refrigerator, where they will last up to three months (though both the yolks and whites will become looser and their flavor will fade over time).

cheese The crisper drawer is the best location for cheese. Cheese should be wrapped, but not airtight; the ideal material is cheese paper but parchment or wax paper also work. Placing the paper-wrapped cheese in an open plastic bag will help prevent hard varieties like Parmesan from becoming rocks. To store feta cheese that isn't in a brine, place it in a zipper-lock bag, add just enough olive oil to coat the cheese, and seal the bag; it should keep for about a month.

KEEP AT COOL ROOM TEMPERATURE (AND AWAY FROM LIGHT)

canned foods Canned foods can be stored virtually indefinitely, but both taste and nutrition may suffer as the years tick by. Store canned foods in a cool, dry place; dependable recommendations typically indicate that good storage will maintain quality for two to five years. If a can is dented, throw it away.

oils To prevent rancidity, store cooking oils in a cool, dark pantry. Unopened olive oil lasts for one year; once opened, it will last for about three months. Toasted sesame oil and nut oils should be stored in the refrigerator.

spices Keep spices in a cool, dark pantry to prolong their freshness. To keep track of your spices' freshness, it's helpful to label each jar with the date opened; whole spices are good for about two years; ground spices for one year.

sweeteners Store brown sugar in an airtight container; a terra-cotta Brown Sugar Bear will help keep it soft. Keep molasses and honey in the pantry (they will crystallize in the refrigerator). Maple syrup should be refrigerated, as it is susceptible to mold. Syrup also can be kept in the freezer (it won't freeze solid because of its high sugar concentration).

A FEW OF OUR FAVORITE STORAGE ITEMS

- **Home-Complete Over the Door Storage Rack** maximizes pantry space.
- For spices, the U-shaped **Spicy Shelf Deluxe** is a customizable shelf option.
- Formaticum cheese paper wrap and bags keep cheese fresh for weeks.
- A lazy Susan in your fridge lets you see and access foods easily.
- Gusseted vinyl bags from BlueAvocado protect food from freezer burn and are reusable.

pantry produce

apples Apples aren't sensitive to chilling injury and can be stored in the coldest part of the refrigerator (at the back of the bottom shelf) or in the crisper drawer for about a month.

cabbage, carrots, cauliflower, turnips These hardy vegetables do best in the relatively humid environment of the refrigerator crisper drawer. If you buy carrots with leafy greens attached, trim the greens; otherwise, the carrots will lose moisture as they continue to feed their leafy tops. Store loose carrots in an open zipper-lock bag and they should stay firm for a few weeks.

celery Store celery wrapped in aluminum foil for several weeks (foil is not gas tight and allows ethylene produced by the celery to escape, slowing spoilage). To revive limp celery, cut 1 inch off both ends and submerge stalks in a bowl of ice water for 30 minutes.

citrus Keep citrus fruits in the front of the fridge (where the temperature tends to be higher), as they are sensitive to chilling injury.

garlic, onions, shallots Keep at cool room temperature and away from light to prolong their shelf life and delay sprouting. Onions can be stored in the refrigerator, but it's not a good idea, as their odor will affect the other foods around them.

ginger It's best to simply toss ginger into the refrigerator unwrapped. When wrapped in plastic or foil, ginger will grow mold where the condensation is trapped.

leeks, scallions These alliums keep best in the crisper drawer, in plastic bags to contain their odor.

pears Keep unripe pears at cool room temperature and let them ripen slowly. In a pinch, you can speed ripening a bit by storing them in a paper bag. They're ready to eat when the flesh near the neck yields slightly when pressed. If the pears are ready before you are, you can keep them in the crisper drawer for up to five days. Whether they're stored on the counter or in the fridge, keep them away from strong-smelling foods, as pears readily absorb odors.

potatoes, sweet potatoes Keep at room temperature in a cool, dark, well-ventilated spot with space between them to slow down the sprouting process. A paper bag makes a good container. Although potatoes and onions benefit from the same storage conditions, they shouldn't be stored together; onions emit a gas that causes potatoes to sprout quickly.

winter squash Store whole squashes at cool room temperature in a dry spot.

HELP FRESH HERBS AND CHILES LAST LONGER

Basil with its roots attached will last longer. Store it at room temperature, upright in a glass with the root ends submerged in an inch or two of water (change the water every day). Cilantro, dill, mint, parsley, and tarragon can be stored the same way, but in the refrigerator. Wrap marjoram, oregano, or rosemary in damp paper towels and store in a zipper-lock bag in the refrigerator crisper drawer.

Fresh chiles have a relatively brief shelf life in the fridge. To prolong their crisp texture and fresh flavor, slice them in half and submerge them in a brine solution (1 tablespoon table salt per 1 cup of water). Chiles stored like this will retain their crispness, color, and bright heat for several weeks, and after a quick rinse are indistinguishable from fresh chiles. After a month they will begin to soften, but they are still perfectly usable in cooked applications for several more weeks.

building your **freezer pantry**

As an extension of your pantry, the freezer has almost unlimited potential. Freezer storage is a great way to ensure that you have pre-prepped ingredients at the ready for easy meals. It can prolong the shelf life of some dry goods and it can be a better storage choice than the fridge.

soaked beans Dried beans benefit from an overnight soak, and even a quick-soak can take several hours. To save time, soak beans and then drain and freeze. Soaked beans freeze beautifully and are ready to cook without thawing.

cooked rice and grains Cooked rice and grains can also be frozen: Spread the cooked grain in an even layer on a rimmed baking sheet and let it cool completely, then transfer to a zipper-lock freezer bag, seal it, and lay it flat in the freezer.

homemade stocks and sauces Pour small amounts into ice cube trays. After the cubes have frozen, remove them and store them in a zipper-lock freezer bag. Use broth cubes for pan sauces, stir-fry sauces, and vegetable braises. Nonstick muffin tins create slightly larger portions. After the broth has frozen, store the "cups" in a large zipper-lock freezer bag. For larger amounts, line a 4-cup measuring cup with a zipper-lock freezer bag (it holds the bag open so you can use both hands to pour) and pour in the cooled broth or sauce. Seal the bag (double up if you wish) and lay it flat to freeze. This is a good option for gravy, soup, or stew. No matter the size, you can store broth or sauce for up to three months.

scraps for making future stocks Collect vegetable scraps in the freezer in a zipper-lock freezer bag until you have enough to make stock or soup. Don't forget about herb stems and corn cobs. Peels are fine too, as long as they're washed. You can use the same method for chicken and beef trimmings and bones (place them in a separate bag).

whole-wheat flour Left in its original bag, whole-wheat flour goes rancid in as little as three months at room temperature due to oxidation of fat in the germ. Stored in a sealed container in the freezer, it can last up to 12 months.

bread The freezer is a far better place for bread than the refrigerator, where bread undergoes a chemical process called retrogradation, essentially becoming stale. We keep crusty bread, sandwich bread, burger buns, pita, and tortillas on hand at all times, and the freezer keeps them fresh for us. For maximum freshness and ease of use, wrap portions tightly in plastic wrap and then tightly seal (with as little air as possible) in a zipper-lock freezer bag.

meat and poultry We keep a couple simple proteins—such as boneless chicken and pork tenderloin—in the freezer. To freeze in small batches for long-term storage place two chicken breasts, small steaks, or portions of ground meat at≈different locations inside a large zipper-lock freezer bag. Flatten out the bag, forcing the air out, so that the meat portions do not touch. Then fold the bag over in the center and freeze.

buttermilk Frozen buttermilk is great for baking. To freeze it, place some small paper cups on a tray and fill each with ½ cup buttermilk; place tray in freezer until frozen. Then wrap each cup in plastic wrap and store in large zipper-lock freezer bag. Defrost in refrigerator before use.

butter Butter quickly picks up odors and flavors and can turn rancid as its fatty acids oxidize; it lasts about 2½ weeks in the coldest part of the fridge. In the freezer, well-wrapped butter will keep for up to four months.

chipotle chiles in adobo or tomato paste Spoon out each chile, along with a couple teaspoons of adobo sauce, onto different areas of a baking sheet lined with parchment paper and freeze. Or do the same with tablespoons of tomato paste. Transfer the frozen mounds to a zipper-lock freezer bag for storage.

cheese Wrap hard and semifirm cheeses such as Parmesan and cheddar tightly in plastic wrap, seal in a zipper-lock freezer bag, and freeze. Thaw in the refrigerator before using in a recipe. And freeze Parmesan rinds as well; you can add them to simmering soups to enrich and deepen flavor.

citrus zest Remove the zest from the entire fruit. Deposit the grated zest in ½- or 1-teaspoon piles on a plate and freeze. Once the piles are frozen, store them in a zipper-lock freezer bag.

shrimp We prefer frozen to "fresh" (read: "thawed") shrimp. Individually quick frozen (IQF) shrimp are frozen at sea, locking in quality and freshness. They're easy to use in whatever amount you need, and they thaw relatively quickly. Always thaw shrimp in cold water or in the refrigerator.

fish In general, if you want to store fish in the freezer you should buy it frozen. But if fresh fish hasn't been previously frozen (ask at the counter), you can prolong its shelf life just a bit by "short-term freezing": Wrap the fish tightly and store it in the freezer for a couple of days. Defrost in the refrigerator before using.

fresh herbs Place 2 tablespoons chopped fresh mint, oregano, rosemary, sage, parsley, or thyme in each well of an ice cube tray and add water to cover (about 1 tablespoon), then freeze. Once frozen, transfer the cubes to a zipper-lock freezer bag or other freezer container. Add the cubes directly to soups, stews, or sauces.

garlic Peel the cloves, mince or press them through a garlic press, and place the minced garlic in a bowl. Add enough neutral-flavored oil to coat (about ½ teaspoon per clove) and then spoon heaping teaspoons of the mixture onto a baking sheet and freeze. Transfer the frozen portions to a zipper-lock freezer bag. Thaw in the refrigerator (not at room temperature) or use directly from the freezer.

ginger Simply cut fresh ginger into 1-inch pieces and freeze in a zipper-lock freezer bag. Chop or grate directly from the freezer (no need to peel).

nuts Due to their high fat content, nuts go rancid quickly unless frozen. Freeze nuts in a zipper-lock freezer bag. Frozen nuts stay fresh for months. No need to defrost before using; frozen nuts can be chopped as easily as fresh.

wine Measure 1 tablespoon wine into each well of an ice cube tray and freeze. Once frozen, store the wine cubes in a zipper-lock freezer bag or other freezer container. Add to stews and pan sauces.

get scrappy: items not to throw away

Before you relegate food scraps and leftovers to the compost bin or trash can, take a minute to consider their untapped potential. Some of the byproducts of prepping and cooking are kitchen pantry gems in their own right. Here are a few of our favorites.

BACON GREASE

Bacon grease is liquid gold, great for frying eggs, whisking into aioli or a vinaigrette, or using as the fat in cornbread. While the grease is still just warm enough to be liquid, pour it through a strainer into a heatproof container with an airtight lid. Label it with the date and refrigerate for up to one month or pour into ice cube trays and freeze, then transfer the cubes to a zipper-lock freezer bag and freeze for up to a year.

DAY-OLD BREAD

You buy a beautiful baguette and enjoy half of it. The next day, it's hard as a brick. Don't throw it away! Remove the crust, tear the bread into rough 1-inch pieces, and blitz it in the food processor. Toast the crumbs (either dry or with butter or oil) and sprinkle them over mac and cheese, pasta dishes, or broiled fish.

PARMESAN RINDS

Good bacteria and mold grow on the rinds of aged Parmesan cheese, creating strong aromas and myriad flavor compounds. That's one reason why many Italian recipes for Sunday gravy and minestrone call for adding a Parmesan rind, which is a good source of glutamates (and umami flavor). Here in the test kitchen, we save our Parmesan rinds—as well as rinds from other aged cheeses such as Pecorino Romano and Gruyère— for this purpose.

LEFTOVER PICKLE JUICE

Instead of tossing out a jar of pickle juice after finishing the last pickle, use the tangy liquid to make a new condiment. Add thinly sliced onions to the juice and let them marinate in the refrigerator for a few days. The drained onions can be used as a topping for hot dogs or hamburgers or in salads. This method also works well with the spicy packing juice from vinegar peppers.

LEFTOVER STURDY HERBS

You can use your microwave to dry sturdy herbs such as bay leaves, marjoram, mint, oregano, rosemary, sage, and thyme. Place herbs between two layers of paper towels on a plate and microwave for 1 to 3 minutes, checking occasionally, until the herbs are slightly dehydrated. Uncover and let cool completely. Store whole or crumbled in an airtight container for up to one year.

MASHED POTATOES

Freezing mashed potatoes is a practical way to save leftovers. Place 1-cup portions on a parchment paper–lined baking sheet and place the sheet in the freezer. Transfer the frozen potatoes to a large zipper-lock freezer bag and return them to the freezer. To reheat, place a portion in a bowl, cover, and microwave at 50 percent power for about 5 minutes, stirring occasionally, until they're heated through. Use them in Bubble and Squeak (page 237) and you can skip the first couple of steps.

liquid flavor

Boosting the flavor of broths and stocks is a surefire way to both enhance your cooking and get the most mileage from pantry ingredients (as well as scraps and leftovers)— and it's practically effortless.

vegetable scraps For an extra-flavorful broth, toss those vegetable scraps you've been saving in the freezer with a little oil and spread them out on a baking sheet. Roast until golden brown, then combine with water and simmer.

chicken scraps In addition to the trimmings and bones saved from prepping chicken, you can also save the carcass and skin of cooked chicken, including store-bought rotisserie chicken. Hours of simmering releases flavorful marrow from the bones and causes collagen to break down into gelatin for luxurious homemade stock that you can use in soups and stews, pan sauces, and gravies.

shrimp shells When you peel shrimp, don't throw the shells away. Crustacean shells contain loads of proteins, sugars, and flavor-boosting compounds called glutamates and nucleotides. Simmer 4 ounces shrimp shells (harvested from 1½ pounds shrimp) in 1½ cups of water for 5 minutes. (Shrimp flavor compounds are volatile, so a short simmer delivers the best results.) Use for seafood soups, stews, fideos, and risottos.

canned bean liquid Bean canning liquid—essentially a starchy bean broth—can be a useful, tasty ingredient in a number of recipes. Add it to a broth, soup, stew, chili, or any dish that should have a brothy or saucy consistency. The starchy liquid adds flavor and body to the finished dish, a creaminess that's something like what you get when you toss pasta with its own cooking water. Just remember that it's often salty, so adjust seasoning as needed.

wine Once opened, bottles of wine are rarely usable for more than a week. But boxed wine has an airtight inner bag that prevents exposure to oxygen even after the box is opened, so the wine lasts up to one month. Or, for easy substitutions for wine, see page 26.

nutritional yeast Nutritional yeast is grown on a mixture of beet molasses and sugarcane, and then heated to deactivate its leavening power. It packs big savory flavor, thanks to a high level of glutamic acid. Dissolve a tablespoon of nutritional yeast in a cup of boiling water to make a quick vegan broth for cooking. Or use it to enhance vegetable broth with additional savory flavor.

anytime snacks

one-minute **tomato salsa**

MAKES ABOUT 3 CUPS | **SERVES 10 TO 12** | **TOTAL TIME: 10 MINUTES**

why this recipe works For bright, fresh salsa that requires little more effort than opening a jar, we turn to canned tomatoes and jarred jalapeños to give us delicious flavor in record time.

- ½ small red or yellow onion, cut into 1-inch pieces
- ½ cup fresh cilantro leaves (optional)
- ¼ cup jarred sliced jalapeño chiles
- 2 tablespoons lime juice
- 2 garlic cloves, chopped
- ½ teaspoon table salt
- 1 (28-ounce) can diced tomatoes, drained

Pulse onion; cilantro, if using; jalapeños; lime juice; garlic; and salt in food processor until coarsely chopped, about 5 pulses, scraping down sides of bowl as needed. Add tomatoes and pulse until combined, about 3 pulses. Drain salsa briefly in fine-mesh strainer, then transfer to bowl and season with salt and pepper to taste. Serve. (Salsa can be refrigerated for up to 2 days.)

VARIATIONS

one-minute smoky tomato and green pepper salsa

Add 1 green bell pepper, stemmed, seeded, and cut into 1-inch pieces, and 1 tablespoon minced canned chipotle chile in adobo sauce to food processor with onion.

one-minute tomato, pinto bean, and red pepper salsa

Add 1 chopped celery rib and 1 red bell pepper, stemmed, seeded, and cut into 1-inch pieces, to food processor with onion. Stir 1 cup rinsed canned pinto beans into salsa before serving.

one-minute tomato and avocado salsa

Add 1 teaspoon ground cumin to food processor with onion. Stir 1 chopped avocado into salsa before serving.

PANTRY IMPROV

use what you have You can substitute canned whole peeled tomatoes for diced; crush by hand first. You can substitute 2 tablespoons minced fresh jalapeños or serranos for jarred jalapeños.

level up Stir canned black beans or thawed frozen corn into the salsa before serving.

spicy **carrot dip**

MAKES ABOUT 2½ CUPS | SERVES 10
TOTAL TIME: 45 MINUTES, PLUS 30 MINUTES CHILLING

why this recipe works If you have carrots in the crisper drawer and a well-stocked spice cabinet, you've got the makings for this vibrant dip. Adjust the amount of hot sauce to your taste. Serve with pita chips, crusty bread, or crudités.

- 3 tablespoons extra-virgin olive oil, divided, plus extra for serving
- 2 pounds carrots or parsnips, peeled and sliced ¼ inch thick
- ½ teaspoon table salt
- 2 garlic cloves, minced
- ¾ teaspoon ground coriander
- ¾ teaspoon ground cumin
- ¾ teaspoon ground ginger
- ⅛ teaspoon chili powder
- ⅛ teaspoon ground cinnamon
- ⅓ cup water
- 1–2 teaspoons hot sauce
- 1 tablespoon white wine vinegar
- 1 tablespoon roasted, salted pepitas

1 Heat 1 tablespoon oil in large saucepan over medium-high heat until shimmering. Add carrots and salt and cook until carrots begin to soften, 5 to 6 minutes. Stir in garlic, coriander, cumin, ginger, chili powder, and cinnamon and cook until fragrant, about 30 seconds. Add water and hot sauce and bring to simmer. Cover, reduce heat to low, and cook, stirring occasionally, until carrots are tender, 15 to 20 minutes.

2 Transfer carrots to bowl of food processor, add vinegar, and process until smooth, scraping down sides of bowl as needed, 1 to 2 minutes. With processor running, slowly add remaining 2 tablespoons oil until incorporated. Transfer to serving bowl, cover, and refrigerate until chilled, 30 minutes to 1 hour. Season with salt and pepper to taste. Sprinkle with pepitas and drizzle with extra oil. Serve. (Dip can be refrigerated for up to 4 days.)

PANTRY IMPROV

use what you have We like habanero hot sauce here, but any hot sauce will work. Or replace the hot sauce with one or two seeded and minced habanero chiles (cook them in the skillet with the garlic). Substitute toasted pine nuts, almonds, or sunflower seeds for the pepitas. Use red wine vinegar or sherry vinegar instead of white wine vinegar.

level up Sprinkle with chopped fresh cilantro. Top with Crispy Capers (page 388) or Crispy Shallots (page 388). Stir in a dollop of Harissa (page 392) in addition to or instead of the spices.

garlic and rosemary **white bean dip**

MAKES ABOUT 2½ CUPS | SERVES 8 TO 10
TOTAL TIME: 10 MINUTES, PLUS 30 MINUTES RESTING

why this recipe works Fresh lemon juice, garlic, and herbs elevate handy canned white beans to a smooth, elegant dip for parties or everyday snacking. Serve with pita chips, crusty bread, or crudités.

- 2 (15-ounce) cans cannellini beans, rinsed, divided
- ½ cup extra-virgin olive oil, divided
- ¼ cup water
- 2 tablespoons lemon juice
- 2 garlic cloves, minced
- ½ teaspoon chopped fresh rosemary or ⅛ teaspoon dried

1 Process two-thirds of beans, 6 tablespoons oil, water, lemon juice, garlic, and rosemary in food processor until smooth, about 10 seconds, scraping down sides of bowl as needed. Add remaining beans and pulse just to incorporate. Transfer to serving bowl and let sit at room temperature until flavors meld, at least 30 minutes. (Dip can be refrigerated for up to 4 days; bring to room temperature.)

2 Season dip with salt and pepper to taste. To serve, make small well in center and pour remaining 2 tablespoons oil into well.

PANTRY IMPROV

use what you have Other white beans such as small white beans can be used instead of cannellini beans; you can even use pinto beans or chickpeas. Feel free to use other herbs such as thyme or sage instead of rosemary.

level up Use 2 or more cloves of roasted garlic instead of raw. Sprinkle with smoked paprika.

provençal-style **anchovy dip**

MAKES ABOUT ¾ CUP | SERVES 4 | TOTAL TIME: 45 MINUTES

why this recipe works Tinned anchovies merit a prime spot in your pantry for their almost magical ability to add deep savor to sauces, stews, and dressings without making their presence known. But the potent Provençal dip called anchoïade puts their flavor front and center, supported by two other cupboard staples: garlic and olive oil. Our version also adds the less obvious choices of almonds and raisins. When boiled and pureed, the almonds take on a smooth consistency that helps keep the dip cohesive and provides richness, while the raisins provide subtle sweetness. Because extra-virgin olive oil can become bitter if overprocessed, wait until the dip is mostly smooth before slowly drizzling it in. If you've got fresh chives, add them for texture and a pop of color. Serve with slices of toasted baguette or crudités.

⅓ cup almonds
10 anchovy fillets (¾ ounce), rinsed, patted dry, and minced
1 tablespoon raisins
1 tablespoon lemon juice, plus extra for seasoning
1 garlic clove, minced
½ teaspoon Dijon mustard
⅛ teaspoon pepper
Pinch table salt
2 tablespoons extra–virgin olive oil, plus extra for serving
1½ teaspoons minced fresh chives, divided (optional)

1 Bring 4 cups water to boil in medium saucepan over medium-high heat. Add almonds and cook until softened, about 20 minutes. Drain and rinse well.

2 Process drained almonds, anchovies, 2 tablespoons water, raisins, lemon juice, garlic, mustard, pepper, and salt in food processor to mostly smooth paste, about 2 minutes, scraping down sides of bowl as needed. With processor running, slowly add oil and process to smooth puree, about 2 minutes.

3 Transfer mixture to bowl; stir in 1 teaspoon chives, if using; and season with salt and extra lemon juice to taste. (Dip can be refrigerated for up to 2 days; bring to room temperature before serving.) Sprinkle with remaining ½ teaspoon chives, if using, and drizzle with extra oil before serving.

PANTRY IMPROV

use what you have Replace chives with fresh basil or 1 teaspoon minced fresh rosemary. Use white wine or sherry vinegar in place of the lemon juice.

hummus

MAKES ABOUT 2 CUPS | SERVES 8
TOTAL TIME: 15 MINUTES, PLUS 30 MINUTES RESTING

why this recipe works Paired with crunchy vegetables or crispy chips, rolled up in a wrap, tucked into a pita pocket—any way you enjoy it, hummus is the quintessential pantry dip. Composed of simple ingredients in its most basic form—chickpeas, tahini, olive oil, garlic, and lemon juice—it's a versatile backdrop for flavorful toppings from crispy toasted garlic (shown here) to juicy pomegranate seeds and all manner of herbs, nuts, spices, and condiments. Our streamlined recipe uses a food processor to quickly turn convenient canned chickpeas into a smooth dip. Creating an emulsion is the key to avoiding grainy hummus: First we grind the chickpeas and slowly add a mixture of water and lemon juice. We next whisk the olive oil and tahini together and drizzle the mixture into the chickpeas while processing to create a lush, light puree. Earthy cumin, garlic, and a pinch of cayenne keep the flavors balanced.

- ¼ cup water, plus extra as needed
- 3 tablespoons lemon juice
- 6 tablespoons tahini
- 2 tablespoons extra–virgin olive oil
- 1 (15–ounce) can chickpeas, rinsed
- 1 small garlic clove, minced
- ½ teaspoon table salt
- ¼ teaspoon ground cumin
  Pinch cayenne pepper

1 Combine water and lemon juice in small bowl. In separate bowl, whisk tahini and oil together.

2 Process chickpeas, garlic, salt, cumin, and cayenne in food processor until almost fully ground, about 15 seconds. Scrape down sides of bowl with rubber spatula. With machine running, add lemon juice mixture in steady stream. Scrape down sides of bowl and continue to process for 1 minute. With machine running, add tahini mixture in steady stream and process until hummus is smooth and creamy, about 15 seconds, scraping down sides of bowl as needed.

3 Transfer hummus to serving bowl, cover with plastic wrap, and let sit at room temperature until flavors meld, about 30 minutes. (Hummus can be refrigerated for up to 5 days; adjust consistency with up to 1 tablespoon warm water as needed.) Serve.

PANTRY IMPROV

use what you have White beans such as cannellini can be used instead of chickpeas.

level up Add up to ¼ cup roasted red peppers or olives, or up to 1 tablespoon lemon zest or roasted garlic, to the food processor with the lemon juice. Sprinkle with chopped fresh parsley. Top with Crispy Garlic (page 388). For extra flavor and color, garnish the hummus before serving; see pages 42–43 for ideas.

dressing up **hummus**

Whether you made your own hummus or are digging into a container of store–bought, toppings are not only pretty but also add complementary flavors and textures that make hummus a treat. They can be as simple as a swirl of olive oil and a sprinkle of spice, or something a bit more substantial. Take inspiration from the topping combinations offered here or personalize your hummus with whatever flavors speak to you. Serve with Pita Chips (page 388).

- A sprinkle of fresh herbs (parsley, cilantro, or dill) and/or spices (smoked paprika, cumin, curry powder, sumac, or Za'atar—page 383)

- Chopped preserved lemons and Roasted Garlic (page 384)

- Spiced Roasted Chickpeas (page 51) and smoked paprika or sumac

- Everything Bagel Seasoning (page 383) and Quick Sweet and Spicy Pickled Red Onions (page 404)

- Minced fresh or jarred jalapeño and lime zest

- Pomegranate seeds and chopped toasted walnuts or pecans

- Spiced Seeds (page 386) and Chipotle Coriander Oil (page 390)

- Sun-dried tomatoes (plus the oil!) and olives

- Harissa (page 392), toasted pine nuts, and sumac

- Minced chipotle chile in adobo, cilantro leaves, and lime juice and/or zest

- Roasted red peppers, toasted walnuts, and pomegranate molasses

- Jarred or thawed frozen artichoke hearts and lemon zest

- Capers, olives, and parsley leaves

- Crispy Capers (page 388), chopped fresh rosemary, and flake sea salt

- Caramelized Onions (page 384) or Crispy Garlic (page 388) and Baharat (page 382)

spicy **whipped feta**

MAKES 2 CUPS | SERVES 8 | TOTAL TIME: 5 MINUTES

why this recipe works In mere minutes, you can turn a hunk of tangy feta cheese into a light, creamy dip that is soft enough to be scooped up with a piece of bread. Cayenne gives the dip a spicy kick but you can omit it if you want or use the smaller amount. Serve with pita chips, pita bread, or cucumber spears.

1	pound feta cheese, rinsed and patted dry, cut into ½-inch pieces (4 cups)
⅓	cup extra-virgin olive oil, plus extra for drizzling
1	tablespoon lemon juice
¼–½	teaspoon cayenne pepper
½	teaspoon pepper

Process all ingredients in food processor until smooth, about 20 seconds, scraping down sides of bowl as needed; transfer to serving bowl. (Dip can be refrigerated for up to 2 days; bring to room temperature.) Drizzle with extra oil before serving.

PANTRY IMPROV

level up Stir in chopped fresh herbs, sun-dried tomatoes, or chopped olives. Replace 8 ounces of feta with 1 cup jarred roasted red peppers, rinsed, patted dry, and chopped to make a red pepper rendition known in Greece as htipiti.

---

spinach and artichoke dip

MAKES ABOUT 5 CUPS | SERVES 10 TO 12 | TOTAL TIME: 1¼ HOURS

why this recipe works We use bright, tender marinated artichokes and plenty of garlic along with frozen spinach and a combination of three cheeses for a creamy, flavorful dip. One 12-ounce jar of marinated artichoke hearts yields the 1⅓ cups called for here. Use the large holes of a box grater to shred the Gouda and a rasp-style grater to grate the Parmesan. Serve with tortilla chips, crusty bread, pita chips, or crudités.

- 1 tablespoon extra-virgin olive oil
- 3 garlic cloves, minced
- 11 ounces frozen spinach, thawed and squeezed dry
- 8 ounces cream cheese, softened
- 6 ounces Gouda cheese, shredded (1½ cups)
- 3 ounces Parmesan or Pecorino Romano cheese, grated (1½ cups)
- 1⅓ cups marinated artichoke hearts, chopped
- 1 cup mayonnaise
- ¼ teaspoon pepper
- ⅛ teaspoon cayenne pepper

1 Adjust oven rack to middle position and heat oven to 400 degrees. Heat oil in 12-inch skillet over medium-high heat until shimmering. Add garlic and cook until fragrant, about 30 seconds. Add spinach and cook until liquid has evaporated, about 4 minutes.

2 Off heat, add cream cheese and stir until melted and combined, about 1 minute. Stir in Gouda, Parmesan, artichokes, mayonnaise, pepper, and cayenne. Transfer to 2-quart baking dish and smooth top with rubber spatula. (Dip can be cooled completely, wrapped in plastic wrap, and refrigerated for up to 2 days. When ready to serve, continue with step 3, increasing baking time by 10 minutes.)

3 Bake until spotty golden brown and bubbling around edges, about 22 minutes. Let cool for 10 minutes. Serve.

PANTRY IMPROV

use what you have Substitute goat cheese for the cream cheese. Try cheddar or mozzarella instead of Gouda. Jarred artichoke hearts (rinsed and patted dry) or frozen thawed artichoke hearts will work if you can't find marinated. You can replace the mayonnaise with plain yogurt. Use fresh baby spinach instead of frozen.

vegan **nacho dip**

MAKES ABOUT 2 CUPS | SERVES 8 | TOTAL TIME: 45 MINUTES

why this recipe works This creamy, gooey, tangy, downright-cheesy-tasting dip is sure to score a home run with vegans and nonvegans alike. What's more, it's incredibly easy to make with ingredients from the pantry and, surprisingly, the vegetable bin: We build the base using neutral-tasting potatoes. Whirring the boiled potatoes in the blender at high speed releases lots of their gummy, gluey starch, giving them a stretchy, cheese-like texture. We blend in a few other key ingredients—carrot for a hint of sweetness and color, nutritional yeast for funky depth, and a bit of vegetable oil for richness and fluidity—for a dip with a pleasing orange color, mildly earthy flavor, and ultracreamy texture. A combination of sautéed onion, garlic, chipotle chile, cumin, mustard powder, and a splash of hot sauce adds Tex-Mex appeal. Serve with tortilla chips or crudités.

12 ounces russet potatoes, peeled and
    cut into 1–inch pieces
 1 small carrot, peeled and cut into
    ½-inch pieces (⅓ cup)
 3 tablespoons vegetable oil, divided
1½ tablespoons nutritional yeast
 1 teaspoon hot sauce or ¼ cup jarred
    sliced jalapeños
1½ teaspoons distilled white vinegar
 1 teaspoon table salt
⅓ cup finely chopped onion
 1 garlic clove, minced
½ teaspoon minced canned chipotle chile in
    adobo sauce
⅛ teaspoon ground cumin
⅛ teaspoon mustard powder

1 Bring 2 quarts water to boil in medium saucepan over high heat. Add potatoes and carrot and cook until tender, about 12 minutes; drain in colander.

2 Combine cooked vegetables, ⅓ cup water, 2 tablespoons oil, nutritional yeast, hot sauce, vinegar, and salt in blender. Pulse until chopped and combined, about 10 pulses, scraping down sides of blender jar as needed. (You will need to stop processing to scrape down sides of blender jar several times for mixture to come together.) Process mixture on high speed until very smooth, about 2 minutes.

3 Meanwhile, heat remaining 1 tablespoon oil in now-empty saucepan over medium-high heat until shimmering. Add onion and cook until softened and lightly browned, 3 to 5 minutes. Stir in garlic, chipotle, cumin, and mustard and cook until fragrant, about 30 seconds; remove from heat.

4 Stir processed potato mixture into onion mixture in saucepan and bring to brief simmer over medium heat to heat through. Transfer to bowl and serve immediately. (To rewarm cooled nacho dip, microwave, covered, in 30-second bursts, whisking at each interval and thinning with water as needed, or rewarm on the stovetop, whisking occasionally and thinning with water as needed.)

> **PANTRY IMPROV**
>
> **use what you have** We especially like the vegetal taste of a poblano hot sauce but any hot sauce will work. Or sauté ⅓ cup minced fresh poblano chile with the onion and omit the hot sauce.

parmesan–pepper **popcorn**

MAKES 14 CUPS | **SERVES 14** | **TOTAL TIME: 20 MINUTES**

why this recipe works This stovetop popcorn is just as easy as the microwave kind, and you can customize it with your favorite flavor combinations. No need to shake the pan as the corn pops.

- 3 tablespoons vegetable oil
- ½ cup popcorn kernels
- 2 tablespoons unsalted butter, melted
- 1 ounce Parmesan or Pecorino Romano cheese, grated (½ cup)
- 2 teaspoons pepper
- ¼ teaspoon table salt

1 Heat oil and 3 kernels in large saucepan over medium-high heat until kernels pop. Remove pan from heat, add remaining kernels, cover, and let sit for 30 seconds.

2 Return pan to medium-high heat. Continue to cook with lid slightly ajar until popping slows to about 2 seconds between pops. Transfer popcorn to large bowl. Add melted butter and toss to coat popcorn. Add Parmesan, pepper, and salt and toss to combine. Serve.

VARIATIONS
buttermilk ranch popcorn
Omit Parmesan and pepper. Add 1 tablespoon buttermilk powder, 1 tablespoon chopped fresh cilantro, 2 teaspoons dried dill, ¼ teaspoon garlic powder, and ¼ teaspoon onion powder with salt.

chocolate popcorn
Omit Parmesan and pepper. Add 1 tablespoon unsweetened cocoa powder, 1 tablespoon confectioners' sugar, and 1 teaspoon ground cinnamon with salt.

sriracha–lime popcorn
Omit Parmesan and pepper. Add 1½ teaspoons sriracha to melted butter. Add 1 teaspoon grated lime zest with salt.

PANTRY IMPROV

level up Toss with nutritional yeast, garlic powder, Barbecue Spice Blend (page 382), or Adobo (page 381). Omit the cheese and pepper and mix in chocolate chips, peanuts, coconut, and/or M&M'S.

maple-pecan **skillet granola**

MAKES ABOUT 3 CUPS | **SERVES 4** | **TOTAL TIME: 45 MINUTES**

why this recipe works It's so easy to treat yourself to fresh homemade granola, you may never go back to store-bought. Our small-batch recipe doesn't even require turning on the oven. We start by toasting pecans in a skillet to enhance their flavor. Stirring frequently after adding the oats ensures even cooking. Maple syrup holds the nuts and oats together while imparting a balanced sweetness. Salt, cinnamon, and vanilla round out the flavors. And cooling the granola in a single layer on a parchment-lined baking sheet allows us to break it into crunchy clumps. You can sub in any number of nuts and spices to make your own custom granola blend; just don't use quick or instant oats in this recipe—old-fashioned oats provide the perfect amount of chew. It's important to stir the granola frequently in step 2 to ensure that the mixture cooks evenly.

- ¼ cup maple syrup
- 1 teaspoon vanilla extract
- ½ teaspoon ground cinnamon
- ¼ teaspoon table salt
- 2 tablespoons vegetable oil
- ½ cup pecans, chopped coarse
- 1½ cups (4½ ounces) old-fashioned rolled oats

1 Combine maple syrup, vanilla, cinnamon, and salt in bowl; set aside. Line baking sheet with parchment paper.

2 Heat oil in 12-inch nonstick skillet over medium heat until shimmering. Add pecans and cook, stirring frequently, until fragrant and just starting to darken in color, about 4 minutes. Add oats and cook, stirring frequently, until oats are golden and pecans are toasted, about 6 minutes.

3 Add maple syrup mixture to skillet and cook, stirring frequently, until absorbed and mixture turns shade darker, about 3 minutes. Transfer granola to prepared sheet, spread into even layer, and let cool for 20 minutes. Break granola into bite-size pieces and serve.

PANTRY IMPROV

use what you have Substitute honey or agave for the maple syrup. Any warm spice such as nutmeg, garam masala or cardamom works in place of the cinnamon. Feel free to use any nut you like here.

level up Stir in cayenne pepper with the cinnamon. Serve over yogurt and fruit to make a parfait, serve over oatmeal, or sprinkle on top of Any Fruit Milkshakes (page 360). Stir in flaked shredded coconut, chocolate chips, or dried fruit off heat at the end.

bbq **party mix**

MAKES ABOUT 5 CUPS | SERVES 6 | TOTAL TIME: 1 HOUR

why this recipe works This party mix is a genius way to turn a few cups of cereal, chips, pretzels, and/or nuts—whatever's on hand—into a crunchy, salty, and irresistible snack. Bold seasonings such as chili powder, cayenne, and dried oregano hold their flavor through baking (unlike subtler spices like paprika and onion powder). A blend of tangy, spicy bottled barbecue sauce and sweet, nutty melted butter ties it all together.

- 5 cups combination of Corn or Rice Chex cereal, corn chips, Melba toast rounds, pretzels, and/or smoked almonds
- 3 tablespoons unsalted butter, melted
- 2 tablespoons barbecue sauce
- ½ teaspoon chili powder
- ¼ teaspoon dried oregano
- ⅛ teaspoon cayenne pepper

1 Adjust oven rack to middle position and heat oven to 250 degrees. Toss cereal, corn chips, Melba toast, pretzels, and/or almonds together in large bowl. Whisk melted butter and barbecue sauce together in separate bowl, then drizzle over cereal mixture. Sprinkle with chili powder, oregano, and cayenne and toss until well combined.

2 Spread mixture over rimmed baking sheet and bake, stirring every 15 minutes, until golden and crisp, about 45 minutes. Let cool to room temperature. Serve. (Mix can be stored at room temperature for up to 1 week.)

PANTRY IMPROV

use what you have Any mix of chips and/or unsweetened cereal and nuts works in this recipe. You can substitute any dried spice blend you like for the chili powder, oregano, and cayenne.

spiced **roasted chickpeas**

SERVES 6 | TOTAL TIME: 1½ HOURS, PLUS 30 MINUTES COOLING

why this recipe works Roasting canned chickpeas gives them a crisp, airy texture that makes them a most poppable snack—as well as a great topper for hummus, salads, or roasted vegetables. We achieve crispiness by first microwaving the chickpeas for about 10 minutes to burst them open at the seams so they release interior moisture before baking them. We finish with a dusting of spices: paprika, coriander, turmeric, allspice, cumin, and cayenne. You'll need a 13 by 9-inch metal baking pan for this recipe; a glass or ceramic baking dish will result in uneven cooking.

2   (15-ounce) cans chickpeas
3   tablespoons extra-virgin olive oil
2   teaspoons paprika
1   teaspoon ground coriander
½   teaspoon ground turmeric
½   teaspoon ground allspice
½   teaspoon ground cumin
½   teaspoon sugar
⅛   teaspoon table salt
⅛   teaspoon cayenne pepper

1   Adjust oven rack to middle position and heat oven to 350 degrees. Place chickpeas in colander and drain for 10 minutes. Line large plate with double layer of paper towels. Spread chickpeas over plate in even layer. Microwave until exteriors of chickpeas are dry and many have ruptured, 8 to 12 minutes.

2   Transfer chickpeas to 13 by 9-inch metal baking pan. Add oil and stir until evenly coated. Using spatula, spread chickpeas into single layer. Transfer to oven and roast for 30 minutes. Stir chickpeas and crowd toward center of pan. Continue to roast until chickpeas appear dry, slightly shriveled, and deep golden brown, 20 to 40 minutes. (To test for doneness, remove a few paler chickpeas and let cool briefly before tasting; if interiors are soft, return to oven and test again in 5 minutes.)

3   Combine paprika, coriander, turmeric, allspice, cumin, sugar, salt, and cayenne in small bowl. Transfer chickpeas to large bowl and toss with spice mixture to coat. Season with salt to taste. Let cool fully before serving, about 30 minutes. (Chickpeas can stored in airtight container for up to 7 days.)

PANTRY IMPROV

use what you have   You can use any combination of spices or a single spice in place of the spices we use. We particularly love these combos: chili powder, sugar, and garlic powder; coriander, cumin, and smoked paprika; or—used on their own—garam masala, sumac, or herbes de provence.

---

spiced nuts

SERVES 16 | TOTAL TIME: 1¼ HOURS, PLUS 30 MINUTES COOLING

why this recipe works There's no shame in snacking on nuts straight from the cupboard, but these spiced nuts are an easy upgrade with a double punch of protein and flavor. We toss the nuts in a mixture of egg white, water, and salt, which gives them a nice crunch when baked and helps the spices (whatever blend appeals to you) adhere.

- 1 large egg white
- 1 tablespoon water
- 1 teaspoon table salt
- 1 pound pecans, raw cashews, walnuts, or whole unblanched almonds, or a combination
- ⅔ cup superfine sugar
- 2 teaspoons cumin
- 1 teaspoon cayenne pepper
- 1 teaspoon paprika

1 Adjust oven racks to upper-middle and lower-middle positions and heat oven to 275 degrees. Line 2 rimmed baking sheets with parchment paper. Whisk egg white, water, and salt together in medium bowl. Add nuts and toss to coat. Let nuts drain in colander for 5 minutes.

2 Mix sugar, cumin, cayenne, and paprika together in clean medium bowl. Add nuts and toss to coat. Spread nuts evenly over prepared baking sheets. Bake until nuts are dry and crisp, about 50 minutes, stirring occasionally. Let nuts cool completely on baking sheets, about 30 minutes. Break nuts apart and serve. (Spiced nuts can be stored in airtight container for up to 1 week.)

PANTRY IMPROV

use what you have If you can't find superfine sugar, process granulated sugar in a food processor for 1 minute. Any combination of spices works instead of the cumin, cayenne, and paprika, or use a single spice blend such as barbecue spice blend, garam masala, chili powder, curry powder, ras el hanout, or everything bagel seasoning. For a sweet version, try cinnamon and cardamom.

devils on horseback

MAKES 16 PIECES | SERVES 8 | TOTAL TIME: 1¼ HOURS

why this recipe works This retro appetizer makes a huge flavor impact with a short list of long-lasting ingredients: smoky, crispy bacon; sweet dates; and tangy blue cheese. We freeze the blue cheese to make it easier to crumble and then split the dates open with a paring knife and stuff the crumbles inside. The dates' natural stickiness seals them back up nicely. We wrap just half a slice of bacon around each date to avoid a lot of overlap (and gumminess) and place the devils seam side down on a wire rack set in a rimmed baking sheet to cook. The bacon slices seal around the dates (no need for skewers) and the dates shed grease and crisp all around. Use tender dates—we like Deglet Noors—that measure at least 1¼ inches in length; smaller, drier dates are difficult to stuff. Do not use thick-cut bacon in this recipe.

- 2 ounces blue cheese
- 16 pitted dates, about 1¼ inches long
- 8 slices bacon

1 Adjust oven rack to middle position and heat oven to 400 degrees. Set wire rack in aluminum foil–lined rimmed baking sheet. Freeze blue cheese until firm, about 20 minutes.

2 Cut through 1 long side of each date and open like book. Crumble blue cheese and divide evenly among dates. Close dates around blue cheese and squeeze lightly to seal (dates should be full but not overflowing).

3 Lay bacon slices on cutting board and halve each slice crosswise. Working with 1 date at a time, place blue cheese–filled date on end of 1 halved bacon slice and roll to enclose date. Place wrapped dates seam side down on prepared rack.

4 Bake until bacon is browned, 27 to 30 minutes, rotating sheet halfway through baking. Let cool for 10 minutes. Serve with toothpicks.

PANTRY IMPROV

use what you have Use goat cheese instead of blue cheese. You can use prunes or dried figs instead of dates.

level up Add diced roasted red peppers or chopped toasted walnuts to the blue cheese filling.

deviled eggs

MAKES 12 PIECES | SERVES 12 | TOTAL TIME: 20 MINUTES

why this recipe works The best deviled eggs start with the best hard-cooked eggs. Conventional wisdom insists that older eggs peel more easily than fresh ones, but who wants to worry about how old their eggs are? Our recipe for Easy-Peel Hard-Cooked Eggs calls for placing cold eggs directly into hot steam, making it easy to peel the eggs after cooking no matter when you bought them. Pantry basics such as mustard and vinegar flavor our main deviled egg filling, while our variations reach deeper into the cupboard as well as the fridge for olives, pickles, cheeses, and fresh herbs. This recipe can be doubled. If you don't have a pastry bag, you can use a zipper-lock bag with the corner snipped off to fill the egg halves.

1 full recipe (6 eggs) Easy-Peel Hard-Cooked Eggs (page 274)
2 tablespoons mayonnaise or low-fat mayonnaise
1 tablespoon sour cream
½ teaspoon distilled white vinegar
½ teaspoon spicy brown mustard
¼ teaspoon sugar
⅛ teaspoon table salt
⅛ teaspoon pepper

1 Peel eggs and halve lengthwise. Transfer yolks to fine-mesh strainer set over medium bowl. Using spatula, press yolks through strainer into bowl. Stir in mayonnaise, sour cream, vinegar, mustard, sugar, salt, and pepper. (Egg whites and filling can be refrigerated separately for up to 2 days. Wrap egg whites in double layer of plastic wrap. Transfer filling to zipper-lock bag, squeeze out air, and seal.)

2 Arrange egg whites on serving platter. Using spoon or pastry bag fitted with large plain or open-star tip, divide yolk mixture among whites. Serve.

VARIATIONS

blue cheese deviled eggs
Use a mild blue cheese such as Stella Blue here.

Substitute cider vinegar for distilled white vinegar and Dijon mustard for brown mustard. Increase amount of pepper to ¼ teaspoon and stir ¼ cup crumbled blue cheese into yolk mixture in step 1.

dill pickle deviled eggs
Avoid dried dill here. Used in this quantity, it will taste dusty and stale.

Substitute dill pickle juice for distilled white vinegar and yellow mustard for brown mustard. Stir 1 tablespoon finely chopped dill pickles and 1 tablespoon finely chopped fresh dill into yolk mixture in step 1.

herbed deviled eggs
You can substitute finely chopped watercress for the chervil.

Substitute white wine vinegar for distilled white vinegar and Dijon mustard for brown mustard. Stir 2 teaspoons each finely chopped fresh tarragon, fresh parsley, fresh chives, and fresh chervil into yolk mixture in step 1.

spanish-style deviled eggs
For a smoky, spicy kick, use smoked rather than sweet paprika.

Substitute sherry vinegar for distilled white vinegar. Stir ¼ cup finely chopped pimento-stuffed green olives, ¼ cup shredded cheddar cheese, and 1 teaspoon paprika into yolk mixture in step 1.

PANTRY IMPROV

use what you have You can use all mayonnaise or all sour cream here or you can substitute plain yogurt for both. Any vinegar will work here. Dijon or whole-grain mustard can be substituted for the spicy brown mustard.

level up Stir chopped smoked trout or salmon, or crispy crumbled bacon, into yolk mixture. Stir chopped cornichons or capers into yolk mixture. Stir a spice or spice blend into yolk mixture: try up to ¼ teaspoon curry powder, chili powder, cumin, coriander, or turmeric. Top with chopped capers or minced anchovy fillets. Stir up to 2 tablespoons chopped fresh herbs such as chives or parsley into yolk mixture or sprinkle fresh herbs on top.

anything **in a blanket**

MAKES 32 PIECES | SERVES 8 TO 10 | TOTAL TIME: 1 HOUR

why this recipe works Puff pastry replaces refrigerated crescent roll dough in this modern upgrade of the childhood classic, for the same ease of use with flakier, crispier results. We wrap it around the traditional cocktail franks, but bite-size pieces of any savory sausage will work just as well. After spacing them on a baking sheet to allow for the inevitable and desired puffing, we brush each little piggy with egg wash and sprinkle generously with Parmesan cheese and everything bagel seasoning for a pop of savory flavor. The salty-sweet-spicy dipping sauce is easy to pull together from the pantry while the bundles bake. To thaw frozen puff pastry, let it sit either in the refrigerator for 24 hours or on the counter for 30 minutes to 1 hour. One 10- to 13-ounce package of cocktail franks usually contains 32 franks.

pigs

1	(9½ by 9–inch) sheet puff pastry, thawed
1	large egg, lightly beaten with 1 tablespoon water
32	cocktail franks, patted dry
¼	cup grated Parmesan or Pecorino Romano cheese
2	tablespoons Everything Bagel Seasoning (page 383)
½	teaspoon pepper

mustard sauce

⅓	cup yellow mustard
2	tablespoons cider vinegar
2	tablespoons packed brown sugar
1	tablespoon ketchup
½	teaspoon Worcestershire sauce
½	teaspoon hot sauce
¼	teaspoon pepper

1 **for the pigs** Adjust oven rack to middle position and heat oven to 400 degrees. Line rimmed baking sheet with parchment paper. Unfold puff pastry on lightly floured counter and roll into 12 by 9-inch rectangle with short side parallel to edge of counter, flouring top of dough as needed.

2 Using chef's knife or pizza wheel, trim dough to 12 by 8-inch rectangle. Cut dough lengthwise into eight 1-inch strips. Cut dough crosswise at three 3-inch intervals. (You should have thirty-two 3 by 1-inch dough strips.)

3 Lightly brush 1 row of dough strips with egg wash. Roll 1 frank in each dough strip and transfer bundle, seam side down, to prepared sheet. Repeat with remaining dough strips and franks, spacing bundles ½ inch apart.

4 Combine Parmesan, bagel seasoning, and pepper in bowl. Working with a few bundles at a time, brush tops with egg wash and sprinkle with Parmesan mixture. Bake until pastry is golden brown, about 23 minutes.

5 **for the sauce** Meanwhile, whisk all ingredients together in bowl.

6 Let pigs cool on sheet for 10 minutes. Serve with mustard sauce.

PANTRY IMPROV

use what you have Substitute any flavor of cooked chicken sausage, tofu sausage, kielbasa, or breakfast sausage for the cocktail franks: Slice the sausage into 4 by 1-inch pieces. Use sesame seeds or poppy seeds (or a combo) in place of the everything bagel seasoning. If you don't have the ingredients for the mustard sauce, serve these with any mustard you have on hand. You can also substitute pizza dough for the puff pastry.

quesadillas

MAKES 2 FOLDED 8-INCH QUESADILLAS | SERVES 2 | TOTAL TIME: 30 MINUTES

why this recipe works A traditional quesadilla doesn't require a long list of complicated ingredients; rather, it's a satisfying snack you can assemble quickly from a few staples. Here, we fill lightly toasted tortillas simply with cheese and jarred jalapeños. We brush the quesadillas with oil and return them to the heat until the tortillas are well browned and the cheese is fully melted. Using small 8-inch tortillas and folding them in half around the filling allows you to cook two at once in the same skillet. Make sure you wait a few minutes before cutting and eating these quesadillas; straight from the skillet, the melted cheese will ooze out. Serve with salsa or sour cream.

- 2 (8-inch) flour tortillas
- 2 ounces Monterey Jack cheese, shredded (½ cup)
- 1 tablespoon minced jarred jalapeños (optional)
  Vegetable oil for brushing tortillas

1 Heat 10-inch nonstick skillet over medium heat until hot, about 2 minutes. Place 1 tortilla in skillet and toast until soft and puffed slightly at edges, about 2 minutes. Flip tortilla and toast until puffed and slightly browned, 1 to 2 minutes. Slip tortilla onto cutting board. Repeat to toast second tortilla while assembling first quesadilla. Sprinkle ¼ cup cheese and half of jalapeños, if using, over half of toasted tortilla, leaving ½-inch border around edge. Fold tortilla in half and press to flatten. Brush top generously with oil, sprinkle lightly with kosher salt, and set aside. Repeat to form second quesadilla.

2 Place both quesadillas in skillet, oiled sides down; cook over medium heat until crisp and well browned, 1 to 2 minutes. Brush tops with oil and sprinkle lightly with kosher salt to taste. Flip quesadillas and cook until second sides are crisp, 1 to 2 minutes. Transfer quesadillas to cutting board and let cool for 3 minutes. Halve each quesadilla and serve.

PANTRY IMPROV

use what you have Pepper Jack or cheddar cheese can be substituted for the Monterey Jack.

level up Add canned beans, cooked shredded chicken, cooked ground beef or pork, or roasted vegetables to the quesadillas with the cheese.

gochujang and cheddar **pinwheels**

MAKES 18 PINWHEELS | **SERVES 6 TO 8**
TOTAL TIME: 40 MINUTES, PLUS 1 HOUR CHILLING

why this recipe works This easy, savory finger food pairs pantry-friendly gochujang with sharp cheddar cheese and sesame seeds to create a wildly delicious filling for pinwheels made with convenient store-bought puff pastry. Sliced into thin rounds and baked, these two-bite swirls are crispy and cheesy and burst with umami, heat, nuttiness, and a touch of sweetness. Be sure to use gochujang paste, which comes in a tub, instead of gochujang sauce, which comes in a bottle and has a different consistency. To thaw frozen puff pastry, let it sit either in the refrigerator for 24 hours or on the counter for 30 minutes to 1 hour.

- 1 (9½ by 9–inch) sheet puff pastry, thawed
- 2 tablespoons gochujang paste
- 2 ounces sharp cheddar cheese, shredded (½ cup)
- 3 tablespoons minced fresh chives, divided (optional)
- 1 tablespoon sesame seeds
- 1 large egg beaten with 1 teaspoon water

1 Unfold puff pastry on lightly floured counter and roll into 10-inch square. Spread gochujang evenly over entire surface of pastry, leaving ½-inch border along top edge. Sprinkle evenly with cheddar; 2 tablespoons chives, if using; and sesame seeds. Gently roll rolling pin over toppings to press into pastry.

2 Starting at edge of pastry closest to you, roll into tight log and pinch seam to seal. Wrap in plastic wrap and refrigerate until firm, about 1 hour. (Rolled pastry log can be refrigerated for up to 2 days before slicing and baking.)

3 Adjust oven rack to middle position and heat oven to 400 degrees. Line rimmed baking sheet with parchment paper and set inside second rimmed baking sheet. Using sharp serrated or slicing knife, trim ends of log, then slice log into ½-inch-thick rounds (you should have 18 rounds) and space them about 1 inch apart on prepared sheet.

4 Brush pastries with egg wash and bake until golden brown and crispy, 14 to 16 minutes, rotating sheet halfway through baking. Transfer pinwheels to wire rack; sprinkle with remaining 1 tablespoon chives, if using; and let cool for 5 minutes. Serve warm or at room temperature.

PANTRY IMPROV

use what you have Any melty cheese such as Monterey Jack or mozzarella can be substituted for the cheddar. Cilantro or parsley can be substituted for the chives.

kimchi jeon

MAKES ONE 10-INCH PANCAKE | SERVES 2 | TOTAL TIME: 40 MINUTES

why this recipe works Like other fermented foods, kimchi has a long shelf life, which means it's a natural choice to keep on hand when you want to add spice and tang to soups, rice, and noodles. Using it in a savory pancake promotes kimchi from condiment to main player. The key to success here is to prevent the kimchi, with its relatively high moisture content, from making the pancake soggy. We drain the pickled cabbage but reserve 2 tablespoons of liquid for the batter. Binding the kimchi with just this liquid, one egg white, and a little flour really encourages the kimchi to shine. Scallions add color and freshness. Flipping the delicate pancake to cook on the second side without it breaking and the kimchi falling out can be challenging, so we gently slide the pancake onto a plate and invert it onto another plate. This allows us to easily slide the pancake, browned side up, back into the skillet to brown the second side. The pantry-friendly dipping sauce provides a salty-sweet counterpoint to the kimchi's spiciness. This recipe can be easily doubled; make the pancake batter in two separate bowls and cook the pancakes in two batches.

dipping sauce
- 5 tablespoons plus 1 teaspoon sugar
- 5 tablespoons plus 1 teaspoon soy sauce
- 5 tablespoons plus 1 teaspoon water
- 1½ teaspoons unseasoned rice vinegar
- 1 garlic clove, minced

pancake
- ¼ cup (1¼ ounces) all-purpose flour
- 1 large egg white
- 1 cup cabbage kimchi, drained with 2 tablespoons juice reserved, chopped coarse
- 4 scallions, white parts sliced thin, green parts cut into 1-inch lengths
- 3 tablespoons vegetable oil, divided

1 for the dipping sauce Simmer all ingredients in small saucepan over medium heat, stirring occasionally, until thickened and reduced to about ¾ cup, about 5 minutes. Let cool completely before serving.

2 for the pancake Whisk flour, egg white, and reserved kimchi juice together in large bowl. Stir in scallions and kimchi until well combined.

3 Heat 2 tablespoons oil in 10-inch nonstick skillet over medium-high heat until shimmering. Add pancake batter and spread into even layer with rubber spatula. Cook until well browned around edges, about 4 minutes. Run spatula around edge of pancake and shake skillet to loosen. Slide pancake onto large plate.

4 Heat remaining 1 tablespoon oil in now-empty skillet over medium heat until shimmering. Invert pancake onto second large plate, then slide it, browned side up, back into skillet. Cook until pancake is well browned on second side, about 4 minutes. Slide pancake onto cutting board, cut into wedges, and serve with dipping sauce.

PANTRY IMPROV

level up Drizzle with Chili Crisp (page 392) or Sichuan Chili Oil (page 390). Stir drained canned tuna or thinly sliced or ground cooked pork into pancake batter.

soups, stews & chilis

empty-your-pantry **vegetable soup**

SERVES 4 | TOTAL TIME: 1¼ HOURS

2 tablespoons extra-virgin olive oil, plus extra for serving

2 onions, chopped

1 teaspoon table salt

¼ cup dry white wine or dry vermouth

4 cups vegetable broth or chicken broth

4 cups water

½ cup pearl barley

1 garlic clove, peeled and smashed

4 sprigs fresh thyme or ½ teaspoon dried

1 Parmesan or Pecorino Romano cheese rind

1 bay leaf

1 pound Yukon Gold potatoes, peeled and cut into ½-inch pieces

8 ounces turnips, peeled and cut into ¾-inch pieces

2 carrots, peeled and cut into ½-inch pieces

1 teaspoon lemon juice or white wine vinegar

why this recipe works This utterly flexible recipe takes advantage of the root vegetables kicking around your fridge (just about any will work) and turns them into a comforting soup. Sautéed onions provide a flavor base, which you can enhance in any number of ways; we use white wine, garlic, herbs, and a Parmesan rind, but see Pantry Improv for more options. Barley (or another grain) brings heft. A splash of citrus brightens everything up.

1 Heat oil in Dutch oven over medium-high heat until shimmering. Add onions and salt and cook until softened, 8 to 10 minutes. Stir in wine and cook until nearly evaporated, about 2 minutes.

2 Stir in broth, water, barley, garlic, thyme sprigs, Parmesan rind, and bay leaf and bring to simmer. Reduce heat to medium-low, partially cover, and simmer gently for 25 minutes.

3 Stir in potatoes, turnips, and carrots and simmer until barley and vegetables are tender, 18 to 23 minutes. Off heat, discard thyme sprigs, bay leaf, and Parmesan rind. Stir in lemon juice and season with salt and pepper to taste. Drizzle individual portions with extra oil before serving.

PANTRY IMPROV

use what you have Replace onions with 2 cups thinly sliced leeks or use a combo. Use red potatoes, parsnips, rutabaga, and/or celery root in place of some or all of the root vegetables; you will need a total of 1½ to 2 pounds. Use long-grain brown rice, oat berries, or farro in place of the barley (the cooking time may change; see page 173). If you don't have a cheese rind, omit it or add ¼ cup shredded Parmesan.

level up Add a few dried porcini mushrooms (grind them in a spice grinder) and/or 2 teaspoons soy sauce with the herbs. Add drained canned beans along with the root vegetables. Stir in up to 2 cups frozen vegetables or diced cooked protein at the end and let sit off heat to warm through. Top with grated Parmesan, croutons (page 389), herbs, Pantry Pesto (page 137), sour cream, or Greek yogurt.

VARIATIONS

spring vegetable soup with pesto

Pop open a jar of store-bought pesto or use our Pantry Pesto (page 137).

Omit turnips and reduce potatoes to 8 ounces. Substitute 1 fennel bulb, cut into ½-inch pieces, for carrots. Stir 2 zucchini, cut into ½-inch pieces, into soup after root vegetables are tender and simmer until zucchini is tender, about 5 minutes. Stir ¼ cup pesto into soup before serving, passing extra pesto separately.

vegetable soup with eggplant and harissa

Omit Parmesan rind. Stir 2 tablespoons harissa paste into softened onions and cook until fragrant, about 1 minute, before adding wine. Add 1 (15-ounce) can diced tomatoes with broth. Substitute 1 pound eggplant, peeled and cut into ¾-inch pieces, for potatoes.

vegetable soup with mushrooms, paprika, and dill

Omit wine. Use just 1 onion and sauté with 8 ounces sliced mushrooms. Stir 2 tablespoons paprika into softened onions and mushrooms; cook until fragrant, about 1 minute. Reduce water to 3½ cups and add ½ cup dry sherry or dry marsala with broth. Stir ⅓ cup chopped fresh dill into soup and dollop servings with sour cream and extra chopped dill.

hearty **cabbage soup**

SERVES 4 TO 6 | TOTAL TIME: 1¼ HOURS

why this recipe works Like the comforting Irish favorite colcannon, this cabbage and potato soup fills and warms you up. Many cabbage soups rely on smoky bacon or sausage for backbone; for a pantry-friendly vegetable soup, we use smoked hot paprika to contribute a hint of smokiness. Caraway seeds bring out the sweetness of the cabbage and evoke sausage flavors. This is a great place to use our Vegetable Broth Base or Chicken Stock (page 406), but store-bought broth works fine.

1 Melt butter in Dutch oven over medium heat. Add onion and salt and cook until softened, 5 to 7 minutes. Stir in garlic, caraway seeds, thyme, and paprika and cook until fragrant, about 30 seconds.

2 Stir in wine, scraping up any browned bits, and simmer until nearly evaporated, about 1 minute. Stir in broth, cabbage, potatoes, carrots, and bay leaf and bring to simmer. Reduce heat to medium-low, cover, and simmer gently until vegetables are tender, about 30 minutes. Discard bay leaf and season with salt and pepper to taste. Serve.

PANTRY IMPROV

use what you have Substitute fennel seeds for the caraway seeds and a combination of smoked paprika and a pinch of cayenne for the smoked hot paprika. Use shredded coleslaw mix in place of the cabbage. Use parsnips, rutabaga, and/or celery root in place of some or all of the root vegetables; you will need 1½ pounds total.

level up Top with fresh herbs (try minced chives, dill, or parsley), a dollop of sour cream, Greek yogurt, or Smoked Paprika Sauce (page 396), and/or croutons (see page 389).

---

2 tablespoons unsalted butter

1 onion, chopped fine

½ teaspoon table salt

2 garlic cloves, minced

1 teaspoon caraway seeds

½ teaspoon minced fresh thyme or ¼ teaspoon dried

½ teaspoon smoked hot paprika

¼ cup dry white wine or dry vermouth

4 cups vegetable or chicken broth

½ small head green cabbage, halved, cored, and cut into ¾-inch pieces (2 cups)

8 ounces red or Yukon Gold potatoes, unpeeled, cut into ¾-inch pieces

2 carrots, peeled and cut into ½-inch pieces

1 bay leaf

winter **squash and white bean soup**

SERVES 4 TO 6 | TOTAL TIME: 1 HOUR

2 pounds butternut squash, peeled and seeded

4 cups vegetable or chicken broth, plus extra as needed

3 tablespoons unsalted butter, divided

2 teaspoons soy sauce

8 ounces leeks, white and light-green parts only, halved lengthwise, sliced thin, and washed thoroughly

2 teaspoons tomato paste

2 garlic cloves, minced

½ teaspoon table salt

¼ teaspoon pepper

1 (15-ounce) can cannellini beans

½ teaspoon white wine vinegar

why this recipe works Silky-smooth squash soup has its merits (see page 84), but for something less labor-intensive try this on for size. Chunks of sweet squash pair beautifully with creamy white beans for a rustic soup with heft and varying textures. In an efficient move, we simmer half the squash in broth to make a "squash stock," which we then mash to create a soup base with body and flavor. The remaining squash gets cut into cubes, which cook in our soup until tender. This method was designed for butternut squash as it makes good use of the unwieldy bell-shaped base (that part goes into the stock) as well as the neck (which is more easily cut into cubes), but other winter squash work, too. To balance the squash's sweetness, we add two savory pantry staples, soy sauce and tomato paste. And we make sure to include the canned bean liquid, which gives the soup both savoriness and body. Since squash soups can be lean, we use butter, not oil, to enrich it. A swirl of pesto (see Pantry Improv) makes a good soup even better.

1   Cut round bulb section of butternut squash (about half of total squash) into rough 2-inch wedges or pieces. Bring squash pieces, broth, 2 tablespoons butter, and soy sauce to boil in large saucepan over high heat. Reduce heat to medium, partially cover, and simmer vigorously until squash is very tender and starting to fall apart, about 20 minutes. Remove pot from heat and use potato masher to mash squash, still in broth, until completely broken down. Cover to keep warm; set aside.

2   While broth cooks, cut remaining squash into ½-inch pieces. Melt remaining 1 tablespoon butter in Dutch oven over medium heat. Add leeks and tomato paste and cook, stirring occasionally, until leeks are softened and tomato paste is darkened, about 5 minutes. Stir in garlic and cook until fragrant, about 30 seconds. Add squash pieces, salt, and pepper and cook, stirring occasionally, for 5 minutes. Add squash broth and bring to simmer. Partially cover and cook for 10 minutes.

3   Add beans and their liquid, partially cover, and cook, stirring occasionally, until squash is just tender, 15 to 20 minutes. Adjust consistency with extra hot broth as needed. Stir in vinegar and season with salt and pepper to taste. Serve.

PANTRY IMPROV

use what you have Substitute other varieties of winter squash such as buttercup, hubbard, kabocha, or sugar pumpkin for the butternut. Substitute 1 thinly sliced onion for the leeks. Other canned white beans will work here.

level up Top with fresh herbs, a dollop of pesto (page 137), sour cream or Greek yogurt, and/or croutons (see page 389).

tortilla soup

SERVES 4 | TOTAL TIME: 45 MINUTES

4 (6–inch) corn tortillas, cut into ½-inch–wide strips

2 tablespoons vegetable oil, divided

1 (14.5–ounce) can whole peeled tomatoes, drained

½ onion, chopped coarse

2 garlic cloves, peeled

8–10 sprigs fresh cilantro, plus leaves for serving (optional)

2 teaspoons fresh oregano leaves or ½ teaspoon dried

1–3 teaspoons minced canned chipotle chile in adobo sauce

¼ teaspoon table salt

4 cups chicken or vegetable broth

12 ounces bone-in chicken pieces, trimmed (optional)

Lime wedges

why this recipe works This soup has it all: silky broth, amped-up spice, and a satisfying crunchy garnish. The home-run ingredient here is chipotle chile in adobo sauce, which brings a hit of smoky heat in just one can (add as much or as little as you want, depending on your spiciness threshold). Pureeing the chipotle with pantry standbys such as canned tomatoes, garlic, and onion ensures a smooth base to the soup, and cooking the puree before adding broth gives the soup a deeper, complex flavor. Poaching bone-in chicken pieces in the broth brings extra chickeny intensity, but if you don't have chicken on hand feel free to skip it and maybe add rice or beans instead if you want. If you have homemade broth (our scrappy versions are on page 406) this is a good time to use it, but store-bought works well.

1 Adjust oven rack to middle position and heat oven to 425 degrees. Toss tortilla strips with 1 tablespoon oil and bake on rimmed baking sheet until crisp and deep golden, about 14 minutes, stirring occasionally. Season with salt to taste, and let cool on paper towel–lined plate.

2 Meanwhile, process tomatoes; onion; garlic; cilantro sprigs, if using; oregano; and chipotle in food processor until smooth, scraping down sides of bowl as needed. Heat remaining 1 tablespoon oil in Dutch oven over high heat until shimmering. Add tomato-onion mixture and salt and cook, stirring frequently, until mixture has darkened in color, about 10 minutes.

3 Stir in broth, scraping up any browned bits. Add chicken, if using, and bring to simmer. Cover, reduce heat to medium-low, and cook until breasts register 160 degrees and drumsticks/thighs register 175 degrees, about 20 minutes. Transfer chicken to cutting board, let cool slightly, then shred into bite-size pieces using two forks, discarding skin and bones.

4 Stir shredded chicken into soup and let sit until heated through, about 2 minutes. Place portions of tortilla strips in serving bowls and ladle soup over top. Serve with cilantro leaves, if using, and lime wedges.

PANTRY IMPROV

use what you have Substitute 1 cup store-bought tortilla strips or crumbled tortilla chips for the fresh strips. Use smoked paprika and a pinch of cayenne or chili powder in place of the chipotle. Substitute shredded cooked chicken, cooked rice, or canned beans for chicken.

level up Serve with diced avocado, crumbled cheese (such as cotija), and/or crema.

quick **beef and vegetable soup**

SERVES 4 | TOTAL TIME: 30 MINUTES

why this recipe works With little more effort than opening a can of beef soup, you can skip the tinny flavor and enjoy a deeply satisfying bowl thanks to a simple hack: Simmer ground beef in broth. Ground beef (a freezer standby) releases flavor quickly into the hot broth, imbuing this soup with true beefiness. Root vegetables make it hearty; whichever kind you use, be sure to cut them into small pieces to speed up the cooking time. Frozen green beans are a natural fit and canned tomatoes add brightness. The seasonings are nice and simple: just oregano, salt, and pepper. As with other brothy soups, the pot appreciates whatever else you have to give it, whether fresh herbs or a handful of grains.

1   Cook beef, onion, oregano, salt, and pepper in Dutch oven over medium-high heat, breaking up beef with spoon until no longer pink, about 6 minutes. Add broth, tomatoes and their juice, potatoes, and carrots. Bring to boil, reduce heat to low, and simmer, covered, until potatoes are almost tender, 10 to 15 minutes.

2   Add green beans and cook, uncovered, until vegetables are tender and soup has thickened slightly, 10 to 12 minutes. Season with salt and pepper to taste. Serve.

1   pound ground beef

1   onion, chopped

1   tablespoon minced fresh oregano or 1 teaspoon dried

1   teaspoon table salt

½   teaspoon pepper

4   cups beef or chicken broth

1   (14.5–ounce) can diced tomatoes

8   ounces Yukon Gold or red potatoes, unpeeled, cut into ½–inch pieces

2   carrots, peeled and cut into ½–inch pieces

6   ounces frozen cut green beans

PANTRY IMPROV

use what you have Use thyme instead of oregano. Use parsnips, rutabaga, radish, or celery root in place of some or all of the root vegetables; you will need a total of 1 pound. You can substitute fresh green beans for the frozen: trim and cut into 1-inch lengths. Use frozen corn instead of (or in addition to) the green beans.

level up Add rinsed and minced dried mushrooms with the broth for a savory boost. Stir up to ½ cup precooked grains into the soup with the green beans. Sprinkle with fresh parsley before serving.

miso soup with wakame and tofu

SERVES 4 | TOTAL TIME: 40 MINUTES

dashi

8 cups water

½ ounce kombu

2 cups bonito flakes

soup

1 tablespoon wakame

¼ cup white or red miso

7 ounces silken tofu, cut into ½–inch pieces

3 scallions, sliced thin (optional)

why this recipe works Miso soup is a classic Japanese warmer made with its namesake fermented soybean paste that's mixed into dashi, a traditional stock made from two pantry-friendly ingredients: kombu (dried kelp) and flakes of shaved, dried, and smoked bonito (a fish in the tuna family). Unlike many stocks that require long simmering, dashi comes together in a matter of minutes and creates an umami-rich backbone for the sweet and savory miso. Miso soup can include a variety of additions, most traditionally tofu and wakame (a type of seaweed) but also seafood and vegetables. Do not wash or wipe off the chalky, white powder on the exterior of the kombu; it is a source of flavor. To create a vegan dashi, omit the bonito flakes.

1 for the dashi Bring water and kombu to boil in large saucepan over medium heat. When water reaches boil, immediately remove from heat and discard kombu or save for another use. Stir in bonito flakes and let sit for 5 minutes. Strain dashi through fine-mesh strainer into large container; discard solids. (Dashi can be refrigerated for up to 5 days.)

2 for the soup Soak wakame in cold water until softened, about 15 minutes; drain and set aside. Whisk miso and 1 cup dashi in small bowl until combined. Bring remaining dashi to simmer in now-empty saucepan over medium-high heat. Off heat, stir in miso mixture.

3 Divide tofu and wakame among individual serving bowls. Ladle soup into bowls, sprinkle with scallions, if using, and serve immediately.

PANTRY IMPROV

level up Simmer thin slices or small pieces of root vegetables such as carrots, radishes, and squash with dashi until tender before adding miso. Stir delicate vegetables such as spinach, napa cabbage, or mushrooms into the hot dashi and let sit until tender before stirring in the miso; return to a brief simmer if necessary. Add cooked noodles to the serving bowls before ladling in the soup. Drizzle with sesame oil or chili oil, or sprinkle with sesame seeds, crumbled nori, or furikake.

VARIATIONS

miso soup with white fish and carrots

Red snapper, halibut, mahi-mahi, striped bass, and swordfish all work well here.

Omit tofu and wakame. Add 1 cup thinly sliced carrots to dashi before bringing to simmer in step 2. Once dashi is simmering, stir in 8 ounces firm white fish fillets, cut into 1-inch pieces. Reduce heat to medium-low, cover, and gently simmer until fish flakes apart when gently prodded with paring knife, about 6 minutes. Using slotted spoon, transfer fish to individual serving bowls before stirring miso mixture into dashi.

miso soup with squash and spinach

Butternut, buttercup, hubbard, kabocha, or sugar pumpkin all work well here.

Omit tofu and wakame. Add 8 ounces peeled winter squash, cut into ½-inch pieces, to dashi before bringing to simmer in step 2; cook until tender, about 15 minutes. Off heat, stir 2 ounces baby spinach into soup and let sit until slightly wilted, 1 minute. Stir miso mixture into soup and proceed with recipe.

miso soup with udon and mushrooms

Somen or ramen will also work here.

Omit tofu and wakame. Bring 4 quarts water to boil in large pot. Add 6 ounces dry udon noodles and cook, stirring often, until tender. Drain noodles and divide among individual serving bowls. Add 4 ounces thinly sliced mushrooms to dashi before bringing to simmer in step 2.

chickpea noodle soup

SERVES 4　|　TOTAL TIME: 1 HOUR

2 tablespoons vegetable oil

1 onion, chopped fine

2 carrots, peeled and
  sliced ¼ inch thick

2 celery ribs, sliced ¼ inch thick

¼ teaspoon pepper

3 tablespoons nutritional yeast

2 teaspoons minced fresh thyme
  or ¾ teaspoon dried

2 bay leaves

4 cups vegetable broth

1 (15–ounce) can chickpeas

¼ cup ditalini

why this recipe works You don't have to be vegan to enjoy this plant-based take on chicken noodle soup, which tastes surprisingly savory and comes together easily with pantry items. The "meatiness" is achieved courtesy of umami-packed nutritional yeast, a shelf-stable sprinkle with a nutty, almost tangy taste that enhances the soup with a flavor reminiscent of Grandma's. The savory dust is so potent, we've been known to stir a tablespoon into a cup of boiling water for a quick, serviceable cooking broth, but here it transforms vegetable broth. Chickpeas add heartiness and a creamy texture.

1　Heat oil in Dutch oven over medium heat until shimmering. Add onion, carrots, celery, and pepper and cook, stirring occasionally, until softened, 5 to 7 minutes. Stir in nutritional yeast, thyme, and bay leaves and cook until fragrant, about 30 seconds.

2　Stir in broth and chickpeas and their liquid and bring to boil. Reduce heat to medium-low and simmer, partially covered, until flavors meld, about 10 minutes.

3　Stir in pasta; increase heat to medium-high; and boil until just tender, about 10 minutes. Off heat, discard bay leaves and season with salt and pepper to taste. Serve.

> **PANTRY IMPROV**
>
> **use what you have** You can use other small pasta such as tubetti, ditali, elbow macaroni, or small shells instead of the ditalini. You can substitute any canned white beans for the chickpeas.
>
> **level up** Sprinkle with fresh herbs such as parsley. Stir in up to 1 cup shredded cooked protein such as chicken or diced ham.

almost-instant **miso ramen**

SERVES 4 | **TOTAL TIME: 25 MINUTES**

- 2 tablespoons white or red miso
- 8 cups chicken or vegetable broth, divided
- 3 tablespoons toasted sesame oil
- 6 scallions, white parts minced, green parts sliced thin on bias
- 1 (2-inch) piece ginger, peeled and cut into matchsticks
- 3 (3-ounce) packages ramen noodles, seasoning packets discarded

why this recipe works Instant ramen, the quintessential last-minute meal, provides the perfect opportunity to flex your pantry creativity. The tangly noodle brick offers a blank canvas for add-ins, but first we ditch the seasoning packet and instead build an umami-rich base by blending miso with broth. Scallions pull double-duty, providing an allium backbone as well as a fresh garnish, and fresh ginger adds lively aromatic flavor (keep some in your freezer so it's always on hand). It might not be instant, but it's close. This soup is endlessly riffable and the variations give you some ideas: Try adding a jammy, soft-cooked egg or kimchi, or see what results when you stir mayo into the broth. (It really takes things up a notch!)

Whisk miso and ½ cup broth together in bowl. Cook oil, scallion whites, and ginger in Dutch oven over medium-high heat until fragrant, about 30 seconds. Stir in remaining 7½ cups broth and bring to boil. Add noodles and cook, stirring often, until tender. Off heat, stir in miso mixture and season with salt and pepper to taste. Divide soup among serving bowls and sprinkle with scallion greens. Serve.

PANTRY IMPROV

use what you have Homemade dashi (page 74) works well in place of the chicken broth. Use ½ cup grated onion instead of scallions. Substitute 12 ounces fresh ramen for the dried.

level up Add cooked protein (chicken, pork, beef, or tofu); blanched or sautéed vegetables (bok choy, broccoli, or mushrooms); tender, raw vegetables (bean sprouts or sliced radish); and/or canned or frozen vegetables (edamame, bamboo shoots, or corn). Top with Crispy Shallots (page 388). Serve with Shichimi Togarashi (page 383), chili oil, or sriracha. For a richer broth: Whisk 2 eggs and 2 tablespoons mayonnaise into the miso-broth mixture. Whisk 1 cup of heated broth into the egg-miso mixture. Off the heat, slowly stir the miso mixture into the soup.

VARIATIONS

almost–instant miso ramen with soft–cooked egg

Bring saucepan of water to a boil. Gently lower 2–4 eggs into boiling water and simmer for 7 minutes. When eggs are almost finished cooking, combine 2 cups ice cubes and 2 cups cold water in bowl. Transfer eggs to ice bath and let sit until just cool enough to handle, about 30 seconds. (Eggs can be refrigerated, unpeeled, for up to 3 days.) Peel and cut eggs in half, then nestle into soup before serving.

almost–instant miso ramen with pork and kimchi

Cook 1 pound ground pork with 1 tablespoon vegetable oil in Dutch oven over medium heat until no longer pink, about 5 minutes; transfer to bowl. Proceed with recipe in now-empty pot, substituting 1 tablespoon gochujang paste for 1 tablespoon miso and adding ½ cup chopped cabbage kimchi with scallion whites. Top individual portions evenly with pork, 1 cup thawed frozen corn, and ½ cup chopped kimchi.

rich and creamy miso ramen with shiitake mushrooms and bok choy

If using large bok choy, slice it 1 inch thick.

Add 8 ounces thinly sliced shiitake mushroom caps and 1 to 2 heads baby bok choy, quartered length-wise, to Dutch oven with scallion whites; cook for 2 minutes. Whisk 2 eggs and 2 tablespoons mayonnaise into miso-broth mixture. Whisk 1 cup heated broth into egg-miso mixture. Off heat, slowly stir miso mixture into soup.

creamy leek (or onion) and potato soup

SERVES 4 | TOTAL TIME: 1½ HOURS

why this recipe works Even when you're getting to the end of your pantry, you probably have a potato hanging around. The beauty of this soup (beyond its deliciousness) is that it uses just one single potato to create a meal for four. And while leeks are the traditional allium for this soup, there's no reason not to use onions instead, or a combination. Speaking of leeks, while it's common to trim away the tough dark green portions, those ends contain plenty of flavor, which we extract by simmering them in broth for greater depth. (Save leek trimmings in your freezer for just such an occasion.) If you're using onions, simmer their skins instead, or just use plain broth. With our broth ready, we simmer the remaining vegetables. A whir in the blender releases just enough starch from the potato to give the soup a creamy texture without getting gluey (it's a single potato, after all). We add a slice of bread to thicken the soup a touch more. Use the lowest setting on your toaster to dry out the bread without overbrowning it. You can use an immersion blender to process the soup directly in the pot in step 4.

1   Bring dark green leek pieces and broth to boil in large saucepan over high heat. Reduce heat to low, cover, and simmer 20 minutes. Strain broth through fine-mesh strainer into medium bowl, pressing on solids to extract as much liquid as possible; set aside. Discard solids in strainer and rinse out saucepan.

2   Melt butter in now-empty saucepan over medium-low heat. Stir in sliced white and light green leeks and salt. Reduce heat to low and cook, stirring frequently, until vegetables are softened, about 10 minutes.

3   Increase heat to high, stir in reserved broth, potato, bay leaf, and thyme sprig and bring to boil. Reduce heat to low and simmer until potato is tender, about 10 minutes. Stir in bread and simmer until bread is completely saturated and starts to break down, about 5 minutes.

4   Discard bay leaf and thyme sprig. Working in batches, process soup in blender until smooth, 1 to 2 minutes. Return soup to clean saucepan and bring to brief simmer. Adjust consistency with extra hot broth as needed. Season with salt and pepper to taste. Serve.

1   pound leeks, white and light green parts halved lengthwise, sliced thin, and washed thoroughly; dark green parts halved, cut into 2-inch pieces, and washed thoroughly

3   cups vegetable or chicken broth, plus extra as needed

3   tablespoons unsalted butter

½   teaspoon table salt

4   ounces russet potato, peeled, halved lengthwise, and sliced ¼ inch thick

1   bay leaf

1   sprig fresh thyme or ⅛ teaspoon dried

1   slice bread, lightly toasted and torn into ½-inch pieces (1 cup)

PANTRY IMPROV

use what you have No leeks? Use an equal amount of onions and/or shallots; save the peels and use in place of the leek greens.

level up Top with fresh herbs (try chives, scallions, parsley, or dill), a dollop of sour cream or Greek yogurt, hot sauce, shredded or crumbled cheese, crispy bacon, and/or croutons (see page 389).

creamless creamy **tomato soup**

SERVES 4 TO 6 | TOTAL TIME: 40 MINUTES

2 tablespoons extra-virgin olive oil, divided, plus extra for serving

½ onion, chopped fine

1 garlic clove, minced

1 bay leaf

Pinch red pepper flakes (optional)

1 (28-ounce) can whole peeled tomatoes

1 cup vegetable or chicken broth, plus extra as needed

1 slice bread, crust removed, torn into 1-inch pieces (1 cup)

2 teaspoons packed brown sugar

why this recipe works Leagues better than canned soup, this rainy-day favorite benefits from choosing a different can: whole peeled tomatoes, which offer superior tomato flavor. That flavor stands out even more without any flavor-dulling cream. Instead of cream, we use a trick: Add a slice of bread, along with a little brown sugar. This combo gives us a tomato soup with the creamy sweetness that dairy usually brings. For an even smoother soup, pass it through a fine-mesh strainer after blending. Or, if you don't mind a slightly coarser soup, you can use an immersion blender to process the soup directly in the pot in step 2.

1 Heat 1 tablespoon oil in large saucepan over medium-high heat until shimmering. Add onion; garlic; bay leaf; and pepper flakes, if using, and cook until onion is softened, about 5 minutes. Stir in tomatoes and their juice. Using potato masher, mash tomatoes until coarsely ground. Stir in broth, bread, and sugar. Bring to simmer and cook, stirring occasionally, until bread is completely saturated and starts to break down, about 5 minutes.

2 Discard bay leaf. Working in batches, process soup and remaining 1 tablespoon oil in blender until smooth, 1 to 2 minutes. Return pureed soup to clean pot and bring to brief simmer. Adjust consistency with extra hot broth as needed and season with salt and pepper to taste. Drizzle individual portions with extra oil before serving.

PANTRY IMPROV

use what you have Use fire-roasted tomatoes for extra depth of flavor; diced tomatoes will also work well. Substitute other ground chiles or warm spices such as cumin or cinnamon for the pepper flakes.

level up Stir 1 tablespoon brandy into the soup with the broth. Top with fresh herbs (try minced chives or parsley), a dollop of sour cream or Greek yogurt, crumbled cheese or shaved Parmesan, toasted nuts and seeds, crispy shallots (see page 388), and/or croutons (see page 389).

butternut squash soup

SERVES 4 TO 6 | TOTAL TIME: 55 MINUTES

- 2 tablespoons extra-virgin olive oil
- 3 pounds butternut squash (1 large squash), peeled, seeded, and cut into 1-inch pieces (8 cups)
- 2 shallots, chopped
- 2 garlic cloves, minced
- 2 teaspoons minced fresh sage or ½ teaspoon dried
- 4 cups vegetable or chicken broth, plus extra as needed
- ¼ teaspoon table salt
- ¼ teaspoon pepper
- ¼ cup heavy cream (optional)

why this recipe works If you went through the trouble of lugging a large butternut squash home from the supermarket, make it worth your while and turn it into a creamy, aromatic, and hearty soup. This minimalist recipe builds flavor by browning the squash pieces with shallots. Sage, a classic pairing with squash, brings piney, herbal notes. A little heavy cream adds a touch of richness, but if you're fresh out then skip it—the soup is plenty creamy on its own. While the simplicity of a pureed squash soup is part of its charm, it always welcomes creative add-ins, which can range from spices to something hearty such as lentils or sausage. If necessary, you can use an immersion blender to process the soup directly in the pot in step 3.

1   Heat oil in Dutch oven over medium heat until shimmering. Add squash and shallots; cook until vegetables are softened and lightly browned, about 10 minutes. Stir in garlic and sage and cook until fragrant, about 30 seconds.

2   Stir in broth, salt, and pepper and bring to simmer, scraping up any browned bits. Reduce heat to medium-low, cover, and cook until squash is tender, about 15 minutes.

3   Working in batches, process soup in blender until smooth, 1 to 2 minutes. Return pureed soup to clean pot and bring to brief simmer. Off heat, stir in cream, if using. Adjust consistency with extra broth as needed. Season with salt and pepper to taste. Serve.

PANTRY IMPROV

use what you have Substitute other varieties of winter squash such as buttercup, hubbard, kabocha, or sugar pumpkin for the butternut. You can substitute rosemary or thyme for the sage.

level up Top with fresh herbs; a dollop of pesto, sour cream, or Greek yogurt; crumbled blue cheese or goat cheese; toasted nuts and seeds; and/or croutons (see page 389).

VARIATIONS

butternut squash soup with fennel, blue cheese, and pine nuts

Reduce amount of squash to 2 pounds and add 1 large fennel bulb, cut into 1-inch-thick strips, with squash. Substitute 1 teaspoon fennel seeds for sage. Sprinkle portions with crumbled blue cheese and toasted pine nuts before serving.

butternut squash soup with sausage and apple

Any flavor or style of ground meat or plant-based sausage will work here.

Add 8 ounces ground sausage to hot oil and cook, breaking up meat with wooden spoon, until lightly browned. Using slotted spoon, transfer meat to bowl and set aside. Add squash and shallot to fat left in pot and proceed with recipe. Top with crumbled sausage and apple cut into matchsticks.

southwestern butternut squash and lentil soup

Do not substitute brown or green lentils for the red lentils.

Reduce amount of squash to 2 pounds. Substitute ½ teaspoon ground cumin for sage. Add 1 cup dried red lentils, picked over and rinsed, with broth. Stir 2 tablespoons minced fresh cilantro and 2 teaspoons minced canned chipotle chile in adobo sauce into soup before serving.

soup **garnishes**

Most soups (and pureed soups especially) benefit from a garnish, which could be anything from a simple drizzle of olive oil or a dollop of sour cream to chopped vegetables to flavor enhancers such as hot sauce or a spoonful of pesto. Think of the final topping as the last chance to add complementary flavor, texture, and color. Want something more ambitious? Try toasted nuts, crispy croutons, a drizzle of spiced butter, or one of our ideas below. You can add garnishes to each bowl of soup before serving, or offer them separately so that people can customize their bowls.

TOPPING IDEAS

- Sour cream, chopped fresh herbs, and a squeeze of lemon or lime

- Greek yogurt, Harissa (page 392), and Spiced Roasted Chickpeas (page 51)

- Chili Crisp (page 392) or Sichuan Chili Oil (page 390) and a Soft-Cooked Egg (page 274)

- Crispy Shallots (page 388) and crumbled nori or Shichimi Togarashi (page 383)

- Chopped nuts, blue cheese, and Crispy Capers (page 388)

- Yogurt and kale chips or sliced radishes

- Bean sprouts, a Soft-Cooked Egg (page 274), and sriracha

- Parmesan Crisps (page 389), crispy crumbled bacon or pancetta, and olive oil or Rosemary Oil (page 390)

- Crumbled Easy-Peel Hard-Cooked Eggs (page 274), yogurt, and chopped fresh herbs

- Tortilla Strips (page 389), diced avocado and/or tomato, and sour cream

- Diced avocado, pickled radishes or Quick Sweet and Spicy Pickled Red Onions (page 404), chopped tomato or cucumber, and sliced chiles

- Brown Sugar–Balsamic Glaze (page 399), fresh herbs, and Classic Croutons (page 389)

shrimp bisque

SERVES 4 | TOTAL TIME: 40 MINUTES

2   tablespoons unsalted butter

1   pound shrimp, peeled and shells reserved, shrimp deveined and chopped

1   onion, chopped

1   carrot, peeled and chopped

1   celery rib, chopped

¼   cup all–purpose flour

3   tablespoons tomato paste

1   garlic clove, minced

1   cup dry white wine or dry vermouth

4   cups water

2   sprigs fresh thyme or ¼ teaspoon dried

1   cup heavy cream

why this recipe works While there's no denying that tender, juicy bites of shrimp are a welcome addition to any shrimp bisque, it's the shells that really imbue this velvety soup with flavor. Build up a stash of shells in your freezer, and you'll be ready to make bisque any time the mood strikes. Use shrimp as the protein if you've got it, or add cut-up pieces of any white fish you might have on hand.

1   Melt butter in Dutch oven over medium heat. Cook shrimp shells until spotty brown, about 5 minutes. Stir in onion, carrot, and celery and cook until softened and lightly browned, 6 to 8 minutes. Add flour and cook, stirring constantly, until golden, about 2 minutes. Stir in tomato paste and garlic and cook until fragrant and paste begins to darken, about 2 minutes.

2   Stir in wine, scraping up any browned bits, and cook until thickened, 2 to 3 minutes. Stir in water and thyme sprigs, bring to simmer, and cook until slightly thickened, about 30 minutes.

3   Strain broth through fine-mesh strainer into large saucepan, pressing on solids to extract as much liquid as possible; discard solids. (Broth can be refrigerated for up to 24 hours.) Stir in cream and bring to brief simmer. Off heat, add chopped shrimp, cover pot, and let sit until shrimp are cooked through, about 5 minutes. Season with salt and pepper to taste. Serve.

PANTRY IMPROV

use what you have You can use 4 ounces reserved shrimp shells (from your freezer) in step 1 and 12 ounces white fish fillets, cut into ½-inch pieces, in step 3, in place of shrimp.

level up Use bottled clam juice in place of all or a portion of the water for an extra briny soup. Stir 1 tablespoon dry sherry or Madeira into the soup with the cream. Sprinkle portions with fresh herbs (try minced chives or dill). Serve with croutons (see page 389) or oyster crackers.

easy canned **black bean soup**

SERVES 4 | TOTAL TIME: 25 MINUTES

2 (15–ounce) cans black beans

2½ cups vegetable or chicken broth, plus extra as needed

1–3 teaspoons minced canned chipotle chile in adobo sauce

¼ cup plain Greek yogurt or sour cream

Lime wedges (optional)

why this recipe works When we set out to develop a group of pantry-friendly soup recipes, we challenged ourselves to see how short we could make the ingredient lists but still create flavorful, comforting soups. Lucky for us (and our taste buds), a can of beans is so much more than just the beans. The bean liquid here does some heavy lifting, providing body, silky texture, and deep flavor—enough so that we didn't need a lot of herbs or aromatics to make these soups sing. A base of smoky, fruity chipotle chiles in adobo sauce gives the main soup character and depth of flavor. We blend half of the beans after cooking, which thickens the soup. Greek yogurt brings extra creaminess and tanginess. Change up the beans (even canned lentils work great here!) and you've got a whole new soup. For a spicier soup, use the larger amount of chipotle.

1 Bring beans and their liquid, broth, and chipotle to simmer in large saucepan over medium-low heat, and cook, stirring occasionally, until beans begin to break down, 5 to 7 minutes.

2 Process half of soup in blender until smooth, about 1 minute. Return processed soup to saucepan and bring to brief simmer. Off heat, stir in yogurt and adjust consistency with extra hot broth as needed. Season with salt and pepper to taste. Serve with lime wedges, if using.

PANTRY IMPROV

use what you have Substitute other canned beans for the black beans (see variations for some ideas). Use smoked paprika and a pinch of cayenne or chili powder in place of the chipotle.

level up Stir up to 1 cup frozen vegetables, shredded or diced cooked chicken, or smoked fish into the soup after pureeing. Serve with fresh herbs (cilantro is perfect), diced avocado, crumbled cheese (try cotija), hot sauce, crema, and/or crumbled tortilla chips or croutons (see page 389).

easy canned chickpea and garlic soup

Toast 6 garlic cloves in large saucepan over medium heat until skins are just beginning to brown, about 5 minutes. Let cool slightly, then discard skins. Substitute canned chickpeas for black beans, garlic for chipotle, and lemon wedges for lime wedges. Add 1 teaspoon grated lemon zest to blender with soup. Top with Crispy Garlic (page 388) if desired.

easy canned white bean and sun–dried tomato soup

Substitute canned white beans for black beans, ⅓ cup chopped oil-packed sun-dried tomatoes for chipotle, and lemon wedges for lime wedges. Add ¼ cup grated Parmesan cheese to blender with soup.

easy canned lentil and chorizo soup

Omit yogurt and chipotle. Cook 8 ounces chopped Spanish-style chorizo sausage in large saucepan over medium heat until rendered, 5 to 7 minutes. Transfer sausage to bowl; do not clean saucepan. Substitute canned brown lentils for black beans. Add 1 teaspoon red wine vinegar to blender with soup. Sprinkle with sausage before serving.

red lentil soup with warm spices

SERVES 4 TO 6 | TOTAL TIME: 45 MINUTES

why this recipe works Small red lentils break down quickly into a creamy, thick puree—perfect for a smooth and satisfying soup. Their mild flavor does require a bit of embellishment, though. Here we sauté onion in olive oil and use the mixture to bloom fragrant ras el hanout, a spice blend commonly used in North African cuisines. Tomato paste and garlic complete the base before the lentils are added, and a mix of broth and water gives the soup a full, rounded character. After only 15 minutes of cooking, the lentils are soft enough to be pureed with a whisk (no extra equipment necessary!).

1 Heat oil in large saucepan over medium heat until shimmering. Add onion and salt and cook until softened, about 5 minutes. Stir in tomato paste, ras el hanout, and garlic and cook until fragrant, about 2 minutes.

2 Stir in broth, water, and lentils and bring to vigorous simmer. Cook, stirring occasionally, until lentils are soft and about half are broken down, about 15 minutes.

3 Whisk soup vigorously until broken down to coarse puree, about 30 seconds. Adjust consistency with extra hot broth as needed. Stir in lemon juice and season with salt and extra lemon juice to taste. Drizzle individual portions with extra oil before serving.

2 tablespoons extra-virgin olive oil, plus extra for drizzling

1 large onion, chopped fine

1 teaspoon table salt

1 tablespoon tomato paste

2 teaspoons ras el hanout

1 garlic clove, minced

4 cups vegetable or chicken broth, plus extra as needed

2 cups water

10½ ounces (1½ cups) dried red lentils, picked over and rinsed

1 tablespoon lemon juice or white wine vinegar, plus extra for seasoning

---

PANTRY IMPROV

use what you have If you don't have ras el hanout, use a combination of ¾ teaspoon ground coriander, ½ teaspoon ground cumin, ¼ teaspoon ground ginger, ¼ teaspoon pepper, ⅛ teaspoon ground cinnamon, and pinch cayenne. Yellow lentils can be used in place of red; do not substitute brown or green lentils.

level up Serve with fresh herbs (try cilantro), a dollop of Greek yogurt or sour cream, and/or a drizzle of Harissa (page 392).

italian **pasta and bean soup**

SERVES 4 TO 6 | TOTAL TIME: 50 MINUTES

why this recipe works The Italian classic pasta e fagioli started out as peasant food—cucina povera—but now is universally embraced. This homage delivers outstanding flavor and perfect al dente pasta—and thanks to smart use of canned beans and canned tomatoes, it doesn't take all afternoon to make. First, cook pancetta in a Dutch oven and then cook the vegetables in the rendered fat before adding a couple minced anchovies for umami depth. Adding the tomatoes and beans together lets them absorb flavor from each other as they simmer, and chicken broth adds richness without turning this into a chicken soup. A Parmesan rind infuses the soup with a subtle savory complexity.

1 Heat oil in Dutch oven over medium heat until shimmering. Add pancetta and cook until rendered, 3 to 5 minutes. Stir in onion and celery and cook until softened, about 5 minutes. Stir in garlic, anchovies, oregano, and pepper flakes and cook until fragrant, about 30 seconds.

2 Stir in broth, scraping up any browned bits. Stir in tomatoes and their juice, beans, Parmesan rind, and salt. Bring to simmer and cook until flavors meld, about 10 minutes.

3 Bring soup to boil over medium-high heat. Stir in orzo and cook until al dente, about 8 minutes. Discard Parmesan rind and season with salt and pepper to taste. Drizzle individual portions with extra oil and sprinkle with grated Parmesan before serving.

1 tablespoon extra-virgin olive oil, plus extra for drizzling

2 ounces pancetta or bacon, chopped fine

1 onion, chopped fine

1 celery rib, chopped fine

3 garlic cloves, minced

2 anchovy fillets, rinsed and minced

1 teaspoon dried oregano

⅛ teaspoon red pepper flakes

3 cups chicken or vegetable broth

1 (15-ounce) can diced tomatoes

1 (15-ounce) can cannellini beans, rinsed

1 Parmesan cheese rind, plus grated Parmesan for serving

½ teaspoon table salt

½ cup orzo

PANTRY IMPROV

use what you have Substitute 1 teaspoon fish sauce for the anchovies; add with the broth. Use other canned white beans in place of cannellini. Substitute ¼ cup shredded Parmesan for the rind. Use other small pasta shapes such as ditalini, small shells, tubettini, or elbows.

level up Serve with chopped fresh herbs (try parsley or basil) and/or dollop with pesto (see page 137).

spicy pinto bean soup

SERVES 4 TO 6 | **TOTAL TIME: 1½ HOURS, PLUS 8 HOURS SOAKING**

1½ tablespoons table salt for brining

8 ounces (1¼ cups) dried pinto beans, picked over and rinsed

1½ ounces (3 or 4) dried ancho or pasilla chiles, stemmed, seeded, and torn into 1–inch pieces (¾ cup)

1 (14.5–ounce) can whole peeled tomatoes, drained

1 onion, quartered

3 garlic cloves, peeled

1 tablespoon minced canned chipotle chile in adobo sauce

1 tablespoon dried oregano

3 tablespoons vegetable oil

1 teaspoon table salt

7 cups vegetable or chicken broth, plus extra as needed

2 bay leaves

why this recipe works This silky, spicy bean soup is inspired by sopa tarasca, a dish from Michoacán, Mexico, that is generally a puree of pinto beans seasoned with ancho or pasilla chiles. Our version features deep chile flavor from two different varieties: Anchos or pasillas provide subtle sweetness, and chipotles in adobo contribute smoky flavor with a bit of acidity. We process the chiles with tomatoes, onion, garlic, and oregano in a blender to create a vibrant puree, which we cook in hot oil to concentrate its flavor. If you're pressed for time, you can quick-soak your beans. Combine salt, water, and beans in large Dutch oven and bring to boil. Remove from heat, cover, and let sit for 1 hour. Drain and rinse well. If you want, you can use an immersion blender to process the soup directly in the pot in step 4.

1 Dissolve 1½ tablespoons salt in 2 quarts cold water in large container. Add beans and soak at room temperature for at least 8 hours or up to 24 hours. Drain and rinse well.

2 Toast anchos in Dutch oven over medium-high heat, stirring frequently, until fragrant, 2 to 6 minutes. Transfer to blender and let cool slightly, about 5 minutes. Add tomatoes, onion, garlic, chipotle, and oregano and process until smooth, about 30 seconds.

3 Heat oil in now-empty pot over medium-high heat until shimmering. Add ancho-tomato mixture and salt and cook, stirring frequently, until mixture has darkened in color and liquid has evaporated, about 10 minutes. Stir in broth, bay leaves, and beans, scraping up any browned bits, and bring to simmer. Cover, reduce heat to low, and simmer gently until beans are tender, 1 to 1½ hours.

4 Discard bay leaves. Working in batches, process soup in clean, dry blender until smooth, 1 to 2 minutes. Return soup to now-empty pot and bring to brief simmer. Adjust consistency with extra hot broth as needed and season with salt and pepper to taste. Serve.

PANTRY IMPROV

use what you have If you don't have whole dried chiles, substitute 2 tablespoons jarred chili powder and add it to the blender with the tomatoes. Navy, small red, and cannellini beans work well in place of pinto. Use 2 fresh tomatoes, halved, for the canned.

level up Top with fresh herbs, crumbled cheese (cotija, feta, or goat), a drizzle of sour cream or crema, toasted nuts and/or seeds, diced avocado, and/or crumbled tortilla chips.

lablabi

1 pound (2¾ cups) dried chickpeas, picked over and rinsed

1 onion, chopped fine

½ cup harissa, divided

4 garlic cloves, minced

2 teaspoons ground cumin

1 teaspoon table salt

2 tablespoons lemon juice, plus lemon wedges for serving

¼ cup chopped fresh cilantro (optional)

why this recipe works Dinner—or lunch, or breakfast—is served with this simple but superlatively satisfying Tunisian chickpea soup. And it's really all about the dried chickpeas: They're simmered in only water until they're just tender and their flavor becomes omnipresent, giving the soup meatiness (rather than broth doing that job). Traditional aromatics of garlic, cumin, and harissa are added in the final minutes of simmering for an invigorating brew. This soup is traditionally enhanced with extras for a meal; crusty bread, one of the most common, is highly recommended to help soak up all the delectable broth. A squeeze of lemon and a dollop of additional harissa are also traditional and add freshness. From there, myriad other toppings can make the dish as filling as you wish, from hard-cooked eggs to canned tuna. Don't be afraid to try several different combinations. To make your own harissa, see page 392.

1 Combine chickpeas and 2 quarts water in large container. Let soak at room temperature for at least 8 hours or up to 24 hours. Drain and rinse well.

2 Bring chickpeas and 10 cups water to boil in Dutch oven. Reduce heat and simmer, stirring occasionally until chickpeas are just tender, 30 to 45 minutes. (Skim any loose bean skins or foam from surface of liquid as beans cook.)

3 Stir in onion, ¼ cup harissa, garlic, cumin, and salt and cook until vegetables are softened and chickpeas are tender, 10 to 15 minutes. Off heat, stir in lemon juice and season with salt to taste. Divide soup among individual bowls and top with cilantro, if using, and remaining ¼ cup harissa. Serve.

PANTRY IMPROV

use what you have Though they're not traditional, any dried white beans would work instead of the chickpeas.

level up Serve with crusty bread, drizzle with extra-virgin olive oil, and/or top with flaked canned tuna, capers, pitted green olives, lemon wedges, hard-cooked eggs, or Greek yogurt.

tomato, bulgur, and red pepper soup

SERVES 4 | TOTAL TIME: 1 HOUR

why this recipe works Bulgur is classic in salads and pilafs, but it's a great addition to soups as well: Not only does bulgur absorb the soup's flavors, it also does the soup a good turn by releasing starch to create a silky texture. Here bulgur enriches a Turkish-inspired tomato and red pepper soup, which takes on a smoky depth of flavor thanks to smoked paprika and canned fire-roasted tomatoes. Jarred roasted red peppers increase the soup's pantry appeal and add another subtly smoky touch. (Yes, fresh red bell peppers work, too, so use what you have.) Since bulgur cooks quickly, stir it in toward the end so it has just enough time to become tender. And don't confuse bulgur with cracked wheat, which has a much longer cooking time and will not work in this recipe.

1   Heat oil in Dutch oven over medium heat until shimmering. Add onion, salt, and pepper and cook until onion is softened and lightly browned, 6 to 8 minutes. Stir in garlic, dried mint, paprika, and pepper flakes and cook until fragrant, about 30 seconds. Stir in tomato paste and cook for 1 minute.

2   Stir in wine, scraping up any browned bits, and simmer until reduced by half, about 1 minute. Add tomatoes and their juice and cook, stirring occasionally, until tomatoes soften and begin to break apart, about 10 minutes.

3   Stir in broth, water, and bulgur and bring to simmer. Reduce heat to low, cover, and simmer gently until bulgur is tender, about 20 minutes. Stir in red peppers and season with salt and pepper to taste. Serve, sprinkling individual bowls with mint, if using.

2   tablespoons extra-virgin olive oil

½   onion, chopped

¼   teaspoon table salt

¼   teaspoon pepper

2   garlic cloves, minced

½   teaspoon dried mint, crumbled

½   teaspoon smoked paprika

   Pinch red pepper flakes

2   teaspoons tomato paste

¼   cup dry white wine or dry vermouth

1   (28-ounce) can diced fire-roasted tomatoes

2   cups vegetable or chicken broth

1   cup water

¼   cup medium-grind bulgur, rinsed

1   cup jarred roasted red peppers, rinsed, patted dry, and chopped

¼   cup chopped fresh mint (optional)

PANTRY IMPROV

use what you have Use traditional diced tomatoes in place of fire-roasted tomatoes. Substitute dried oregano or marjoram for the dried mint. Two fresh red bell peppers can be used in place of the jarred; chop the peppers and add with the onion. Other size grinds of bulgur can be used; adjust cooking time as needed.

level up Stir in 1 cup of canned beans for a heartier soup.

wild rice soup with coconut and lime

SERVES 4 TO 6 | TOTAL TIME: 1¾ HOURS

2 tablespoons vegetable oil

2 onions, chopped fine

6 garlic cloves, minced

2 tablespoons grated fresh ginger

4 cups chicken or vegetable broth

2 (14–ounce) cans coconut milk, divided

1 cup wild rice, picked over and rinsed

2 lemongrass stalks, trimmed to bottom 6 inches and smashed with back of knife (optional)

4 sprigs fresh cilantro, plus leaves for serving (optional)

3 tablespoons fish sauce, divided, plus extra for seasoning

3 tablespoons lime juice (2 limes), plus lime wedges for serving

1 tablespoon sugar

1 tablespoon Thai red or green curry paste

why this recipe works The secret to this hearty, flavor-packed soup is cooking the wild rice in a gorgeously aromatic base, essentially steeping it in a mixture of garlic, ginger, fish sauce, coconut milk, and broth. Lemongrass and cilantro sprigs (save the leaves for a garnish) are optional but delicious additions. But not to worry if you don't have them on hand: There's plenty of flavor happening in the final moments of this soup when another can of coconut milk, more fish sauce, lime juice, and curry paste (plus a little sugar to balance everything out) get whisked together and then stirred into the finished product. This technique prevents their flavors from dulling during the cooking process so they remain bright and at the forefront.

1   Heat oil in Dutch oven over medium heat until shimmering. Add onions and cook until softened, about 5 minutes. Stir in garlic and ginger and cook until fragrant, about 30 seconds. Stir in broth; 1 can coconut milk; rice; lemongrass, if using; cilantro sprigs, if using; and 1 tablespoon fish sauce. Bring to simmer and cook until rice is tender, about 1 hour.

2   Discard lemongrass. Whisk remaining 1 can coconut milk, remaining 2 tablespoons fish sauce, lime juice, sugar, and curry paste together in bowl. Stir coconut-milk mixture into soup and return to brief simmer. Season with extra fish sauce and salt and pepper to taste. Serve with cilantro leaves, if using, and lime wedges.

PANTRY IMPROV

use what you have Use other grains such as brown rice, farro, oat berries, or wheat berries in place of the wild rice; adjust the cooking time as needed (see page 173).

level up Add sliced tender vegetables (such as mushrooms, zucchini, napa cabbage, or bok choy) with the coconut-milk mixture in step 2. Add 1-inch pieces of chicken, white fish, or shrimp during the final 10 minutes of simmering. Serve with chopped peanuts and/or chili oil.

quick **bean chili**

SERVES 4 TO 6 | TOTAL TIME: 45 MINUTES

1 tablespoon vegetable oil

1 onion, chopped fine

3 tablespoons chili powder

1–3 teaspoons minced canned chipotle chile in adobo sauce

2 teaspoons ground cumin

4 (10–ounce) cans Ro-tel Original Diced Tomatoes & Green Chilies

4 (15–ounce) cans beans, preferably two different kinds, rinsed

why this recipe works This recipe is as close as you can get to opening up a can of chili, but it's so much more delicious. Instead of opening a single can, open many—9 to be exact. Take, ideally, two different varieties of beans (any you have in your pantry will do just fine), the killer combo of Ro-tel canned tomatoes and green chilies (never fails), and chipotle chile in adobo (an old standby!), and you're well on your way to a crowd-pleasing chili. Pureeing some of the bean and tomato mixture gives the chili body, and helps make the whole dish more cohesive. No one will ever guess it came mostly from a can. Gussy up this base with tequila and lime, add some heft with sweet potatoes and/or meat (dealer's choice!), or eat it as-is. It's sure to satisfy. For a spicier chili, use the larger amount of chipotle.

1   Heat oil in Dutch oven over medium-high heat until shimmering. Add onion and cook until softened, about 5 minutes. Stir in chili powder, chipotle, and cumin and cook until fragrant, about 30 seconds. Stir in tomatoes and their juice and beans and bring to simmer.

2   Reduce heat to medium-low, cover, and simmer gently, stirring occasionally, for 15 minutes. Process 2 cups chili in blender until smooth, about 1 minute. Stir puree into pot and bring to brief simmer. Season with salt and pepper to taste. Serve.

> **PANTRY IMPROV**
>
> **use what you have** Pinto, kidney, black, cannellini, or navy beans can be used in this recipe, either a single variety or a combination of beans. Canned diced tomatoes (traditional or fire roasted) can be used in place of the Ro-tel tomatoes.
>
> **level up** Serve with diced avocado, chopped onion, cilantro, lime wedges, sour cream, and/or shredded Monterey Jack or cheddar cheese.

VARIATIONS

quick bean chili with tequila and lime

Add 2 tablespoons tequila and 1 tablespoon honey to chili with tomatoes. Stir additional 1 tablespoon tequila, 1 teaspoon grated lime zest, and 1 tablespoon lime juice into chili before serving.

smoky bean chili with sweet potatoes

Butternut squash will also work well in place of the sweet potato.

Add ½ teaspoon liquid smoke and 12 ounces sweet potatoes, peeled and cut into ½-inch pieces, with tomatoes.

quick bean chili with ground meat

Brown 1½ pounds ground beef, turkey, pork, or plant-based ground meat in hot oil before adding onion; cook, breaking up meat with wooden spoon until firm crumbles form.

butternut squash and peanut chili with quinoa

SERVES 4 | TOTAL TIME: 1½ HOURS

1½ pounds butternut squash, peeled, seeded, and cut into ½-inch pieces (4 cups)

1 onion, chopped

¼ cup vegetable oil, divided

1 teaspoon table salt, divided

¼ teaspoons pepper

4 cups vegetable or chicken broth, divided, plus extra as needed

½ cup dry-roasted salted peanuts, chopped, divided

1 tablespoon grated fresh ginger

2 garlic cloves, minced

½ teaspoon ground coriander

¼ teaspoon ground cinnamon

¼ teaspoon cayenne pepper

1 (14.5-ounce) can diced tomatoes

1 (14-ounce) can coconut milk

½ cup prewashed quinoa

why this recipe works This stick-to-your-ribs vegetable chili is aromatic and boldly flavored with garlic, ginger, and warm spices. It gets its silky body from a combination of blended dry-roasted salted peanuts and squash; we roast the squash with chopped onion until the vegetables start to char around the edges, giving the chili incredible flavor. A combination of canned tomatoes and coconut milk make a creamy but bright broth, and nutty quinoa adds heartiness and subtle pops of texture. Serve with hot sauce.

1 Adjust oven rack to middle position and heat oven to 450 degrees. Toss squash and onion with 2 tablespoons oil, ½ teaspoon salt, and pepper. Arrange vegetables in even layer over rimmed baking sheet and roast, stirring occasionally, until tender, 45 to 50 minutes, rotating sheet halfway through roasting.

2 Process ½ cup roasted vegetables, 1 cup broth, and 2 tablespoons peanuts in food processor until smooth, about 1 minute.

3 Heat remaining 2 tablespoons oil in Dutch oven over medium-high heat until shimmering. Add ginger, garlic, coriander, cinnamon, cayenne, and remaining ½ teaspoon salt and cook until fragrant, about 30 seconds. Stir in remaining 3 cups broth, tomatoes and their juice, coconut milk, and quinoa and bring to boil. Reduce heat to low and simmer, stirring occasionally, until quinoa is tender, about 15 minutes.

4 Stir in pureed vegetable mixture and remaining roasted vegetables and cook until heated through, about 3 minutes. Season with salt and pepper to taste. Adjust consistency with extra hot broth as needed. Serve, sprinkling individual portions with remaining peanuts.

PANTRY IMPROV

use what you have Substitute other varieties of winter squash such as buttercup, hubbard, kabocha, or sugar pumpkin for the butternut.

level up Serve with diced avocado, chopped onion, cilantro, lime wedges, sour cream, crumbled tortilla chips, and/or shredded Monterey Jack or cheddar cheese.

pasta &
noodles

PANTRY SAUCES TO HAVE ON HAND

pasta with **garlic and oil**

SERVES 4 | **TOTAL TIME: 40 MINUTES**

¼ cup extra–virgin olive oil

2 tablespoons plus ½ teaspoon minced garlic, divided

¼ teaspoon red pepper flakes

12 ounces pasta

Table salt for cooking pasta

Grated Parmesan or Pecorino Romano cheese

why this recipe works The late-night pasta monster will be tamed with this dead-simple, quick, and highly adaptable dish made from pantry items. The secret to making a great pasta sauce from little more than garlic and oil lies in how you treat the garlic. We toast a full 2 tablespoons of garlic in ¼ cup of olive oil over low heat just until it turns a sweet and buttery pale golden brown. (Don't let it go any darker or it will taste harsh.) Cooking the pasta in just 2 quarts of salted water gives us extra-starchy cooking water, some of which we stir into the finished pasta (the starch helps the oil cling to the pasta). Adding a little minced raw garlic to the sauce at the end creates a garlicky duality between the sweetness of the toasted garlic and the fire of the raw garlic. From here, you can feel free to embellish with other additions, as the variations show. Any type of pasta (or even a mix of pastas) will work here; if using multiple types of pasta, stagger their additions to the boiling water based on their recommended cooking times.

1 Combine oil and 2 tablespoons garlic in 8-inch nonstick skillet. Cook over low heat, stirring occasionally, until garlic is pale golden brown, 9 to 12 minutes. Off heat, stir in pepper flakes; set aside.

2 Bring 2 quarts water to boil in large pot. Add pasta and 2 teaspoons salt and cook, stirring frequently, until al dente. Reserve 1 cup cooking water, then drain pasta and return it to pot. Add remaining ½ teaspoon garlic, reserved garlic-oil mixture, and reserved cooking water to pasta in pot. Stir until pasta is well coated with oil and no water remains in bottom of pot. Season with salt and pepper to taste. Serve, passing Parmesan separately.

PANTRY IMPROV

use what you have Replace the cheese with toasted panko bread crumbs, or use both. If you are using fresh pasta, increase the amount of pasta to 1¼ pounds.

level up Add chopped fresh parsley, basil, oregano, or tarragon to the pasta with reserved garlic-oil mixture. Serve with a fried egg.

VARIATIONS

pasta with shrimp, lemon, and parsley

Add 1 pound shrimp to cooked garlic-oil mixture and continue to cook, covered, over medium heat until shrimp are opaque throughout, about 5 minutes. Add 2 teaspoons grated lemon zest plus 2 tablespoons juice to skillet with pepper flakes. Add 2 tablespoons chopped fresh parsley to pasta with reserved garlic-oil mixture.

pasta with capers and raisins

Add 3 tablespoons minced capers, 3 tablespoons minced raisins or currants, 1 tablespoon lemon juice, and 2 minced anchovy fillets to pasta with reserved garlic-oil mixture.

pasta with olives and almonds

Add 1 cup chopped olives, ½ cup toasted sliced almonds, and 1 tablespoon lemon juice to pasta with reserved garlic-oil mixture.

pasta with **caramelized onions, pecorino romano, and black pepper**

SERVES 4 | TOTAL TIME: 40 MINUTES

12 ounces pasta

½ teaspoon table salt, plus salt for cooking pasta

1 tablespoon unsalted butter

1 tablespoon coarsely ground pepper

2 cups Caramelized Onions (page 384)

1½ ounces Pecorino Romano or Parmesan cheese, shredded (¾ cup), plus extra for serving

¼ cup chopped fresh parsley (optional)

1 tablespoon white wine vinegar

why this recipe works Caramelized onions (made quickly using our pre-steaming method) improve everything from sandwiches to soups. Often a spoonful is all you need for flavor, but in this pantry pasta dish the onions become the main event. We cook down a few pounds of onions until caramelized and then balance their complex sweetness with a hefty tablespoon of coarsely ground black pepper, salty Pecorino Romano, and a splash of vinegar. We recommend a pasta shape with nooks and crannies that will hold on to the onions, such as campanelle or cavatappi.

1   Bring 4 quarts water to boil in large pot. Add pasta and 1 tablespoon salt and cook, stirring occasionally, until al dente. Reserve 1½ cups cooking water, then drain pasta and return it to pot.

2   While pasta cooks, melt butter in 10-inch skillet over medium heat. Add pepper and cook until fragrant, about 1 minute. Add onions and salt and cook, stirring occasionally, until onions are warmed through, about 4 minutes.

3   Add Pecorino; parsley, if using; vinegar; onions; and 1 cup reserved cooking water to pasta and stir to combine. Season with salt and pepper to taste. Serve, adjusting consistency with remaining reserved cooking water as needed and passing extra Pecorino separately.

PANTRY IMPROV

use what you have Don't worry if you don't have enough onions to make a full 2 cups of caramelized onions. The pasta will still be delicious with less. Other wine vinegars such as sherry vinegar can be used. Swap in other fresh herbs such as basil or chives.

level up Top with dollops of ricotta or mascarpone or torn bits of mozzarella or burrata. Drizzle with chile or herb oil.

bottom-of-the-box pasta
with butter and cheese

SERVES 4 | TOTAL TIME: 35 MINUTES

12 ounces pasta

½ teaspoon table salt, plus salt for cooking pasta

4 ounces Parmesan cheese, grated (2 cups), plus extra for serving

5 tablespoons unsalted butter, cut into 5 pieces

PANTRY IMPROV

use what you have Any mix of pasta will work here. If you are using fresh pasta, increase the amount to 1¼ pounds.

level up Thaw frozen peas or spinach under hot water; drain well and sprinkle over pasta after tossing vigorously in step 3. Add minced parsley, basil, oregano, or tarragon to the pasta before tossing in step 3. Serve with sliced cooked chicken or poached shrimp.

---

why this recipe works We all have those pasta odds and ends buried at the back of the pantry; a few ounces of farfalle, a handful of elbows. Here's your permission to cook any combo for a creamy, comforting bowl of pasta bound together—simple as can be—with butter and cheese. The basic sauce, which hearkens to the original fettuccine Alfredo, proves that you don't need any cream, or eggs for that matter, to create a clingy sauce that thoroughly coats your pasta. What you do need is a cupful of starchy pasta cooking water, plenty of vigorous stirring, and just a bit of patience. Combine the hot pasta and other ingredients in the pot, stir for a minute, let rest, and then stir again. The rest allows errant drips of water to be absorbed, and the second stir fully incorporates the cheese. Real Parmigiano-Reggiano cheese (a worthwhile pantry staple) grated on a rasp-style grater will give you the creamiest results. Do not adjust the amount of water for cooking the pasta. Stir the pasta frequently as it cooks to avoid sticking; if using multiple types of pasta, stagger their additions to the boiling water based on their recommended cooking times. Move quickly after draining the pasta; you're relying on the residual heat from both the pasta and the cooking water to help the cheese and butter melt. For the best results, warm ovensafe dinner bowls in a 200-degree oven for 10 minutes prior to serving and serve the pasta hot.

1 Bring 3 quarts water to boil in large pot. Add pasta and 1 tablespoon salt and cook, stirring frequently, until al dente. Reserve 1 cup cooking water, then drain pasta and return it to pot.

2 Add Parmesan, butter, salt, and reserved cooking water to pot. Set pot over low heat and, using tongs, toss and stir vigorously to thoroughly combine, about 1 minute. Remove pot from heat, cover, and let pasta sit for 1 minute.

3 Toss pasta vigorously once more so sauce thoroughly coats pasta and any cheese clumps are emulsified into sauce, about 30 seconds. (Mixture may look wet at this point, but pasta will absorb excess moisture as it cools slightly.) Season with salt to taste.

4 Divide pasta among individual bowls. (Use rubber spatula as needed to remove any clumps of cheese stuck to tongs and bottom of pot.) Serve immediately, passing extra Parmesan separately.

3–ingredient combinations
for pasta and noodles

When you've got a box of pasta or noodles, you've always got a meal on hand. A few high–flavor ingredients from the pantry are all it takes to spruce them up for a quick, tasty dinner. Save some of the pasta or noodle cooking water to thin out the sauces or to help melt the cheese or miso; the cooking water is a key ingredient that is a gimme, though often treated as an afterthought. A drizzle of olive, toasted sesame, or other oil is often necessary, too.

pasta

- Garlic, olive oil, jarred or thawed frozen artichokes

- Capers, diced tomatoes or tomato sauce, olives

- Sun-dried tomatoes (and their oil), fresh herbs, olives

- Crispy Capers (and their oil, page 388), bread crumbs, lemon zest

- Thawed frozen corn, ricotta or Spicy Whipped Feta (page 44), Rosemary Oil (page 390)

- Crispy bacon (and its rendered fat), Perfect Poached Eggs (page 275), grated Parmesan

- Boursin, thawed frozen spinach or fresh baby spinach, sun-dried tomatoes

- Pantry Pesto (page 137), thawed frozen peas, fresh mozzarella cheese

- Flaked smoked trout, crème fraîche or ricotta cheese, lemon zest

noodles

- Chili Crisp (page 392), scallions, grated fresh ginger

- Sliced scallions, toasted sesame oil, Shichimi Togarashi (page 383)

- Miso, minced raw or sautéed shallot, furikake

- Sweet soy sauce, ramen seasoning packet, Sichuan Chili Oil (page 390)

- Toasted sesame oil, scallions, thawed frozen green beans

- Peanut butter, lime juice, soy sauce

- Minced garlic, fish sauce, melted butter

- Perfect Poached Eggs (page 275), Sichuan Chili Oil (page 390), frozen thawed edamame or thinly sliced snow peas

pasta alla gricia

SERVES 4 | TOTAL TIME: 30 MINUTES

why this recipe works The Romans are masters of devising decadent pasta dishes from pantry staples. Some focus on cheese or tomatoes, but pasta alla gricia is decidedly about the cured pork. Guanciale (cured hog jowl) is the traditional porky choice, but you can also use pancetta (from the belly). Cook the pasta to al dente in half the usual amount of water (omitting salt since the pork and cheese add plenty). Add this extra-starchy water to the rendered pork fat and reduce the mixture to concentrate the starch and break up the fat into smaller droplets for a creamy consistency. We recommend buying a thick piece of pancetta from the deli and avoiding presliced products. What if you have only bacon? Neither pancetta nor guanciale is traditionally smoked, so bacon will alter the character of the recipe. It may not be pasta alla gricia, but it will still taste pretty good.

8 ounces pancetta, sliced ¼ inch thick

1 tablespoon extra-virgin olive oil

12 ounces rigatoni

1 teaspoon coarsely ground pepper, plus extra for serving

2 ounces Pecorino Romano or Parmesan cheese, grated fine (1 cup), plus extra for serving

1 Slice each round of pancetta into rectangular pieces that measure about ½ inch by 1 inch.

2 Heat pancetta and oil in Dutch oven over medium-low heat, stirring frequently, until fat is rendered and pancetta is deep golden brown but still has slight pinkish hue, 8 to 10 minutes, adjusting heat as necessary to keep pancetta from browning too quickly. Using slotted spoon, transfer pancetta to bowl; set aside. Pour fat from pot into liquid measuring cup (you should have ¼ to ⅓ cup fat; discard any extra). Return fat to Dutch oven.

3 While pancetta cooks, set colander in large bowl. Bring 2 quarts water to boil in large pot. Add pasta and cook, stirring often, until al dente. Drain pasta in prepared colander, reserving cooking water.

4 Add pepper and 2 cups reserved cooking water to Dutch oven with fat and bring to boil over high heat. Boil mixture rapidly, scraping up any browned bits, until emulsified and reduced to 1½ cups, about 5 minutes. (If you've reduced it too far, add more reserved cooking water to equal 1½ cups.)

5 Reduce heat to low, add pasta and pancetta, and stir to evenly coat. Add Pecorino and stir until cheese is melted and sauce is slightly thickened, about 1 minute. Off heat, adjust sauce consistency with remaining reserved cooking water as needed. Transfer pasta to platter and serve immediately, passing extra pepper and extra Pecorino separately.

PANTRY IMPROV

use what you have Use other short cut pasta in place of the rigatoni. If you can find guanciale, we recommend using it and increasing the browning time in step 2 to 10 to 12 minutes. You can also use bacon in place of the pancetta.

level up Serve with a green vegetable or salad to balance the richness of this pasta.

pasta e ceci

SERVES 4 | TOTAL TIME: 1 HOUR

2 ounces pancetta or bacon,
  cut into ½-inch pieces

1 small carrot, peeled and cut into
  ½-inch pieces

1 small celery rib, cut into
  ½-inch pieces

4 garlic cloves, peeled

1 onion, halved and cut into
  1-inch pieces

1 (14-ounce) can whole peeled
  tomatoes, drained

¼ cup extra-virgin olive oil,
  plus extra for serving

2 teaspoons minced fresh rosemary
  or ½ teaspoon dried

1 (15-ounce) can chickpeas,
  undrained

2 cups water

1 teaspoon table salt

8 ounces (1½ cups) ditalini

1 tablespoon lemon juice

1 ounce Parmesan or Pecorino
  Romano cheese, grated (½ cup)

why this recipe works Pasta and chickpeas go way back as a pantry pairing. The Italian dish that combines them is cheap and hearty and packed with satisfying flavor. Just about every Italian house has a version, which can include simple aromatics such as onion, celery, carrot, and garlic and flavorful additions like pancetta and rosemary. Our version uses all of the aforementioned ingredients, but the dish is flexible and forgiving. If you're out of, say, celery, or don't have any pancetta or bacon, this recipe squeezes so much flavor from each ingredient that the result will still be good. (And there are other ways to boost flavor if needed; see Pantry Improv.) We start by blitzing our vegetables and meat in the food processor to make a soffritto; we cook this until a fond starts to form in the pot, which we deglaze with tomatoes. Definitely use the whole can of chickpeas, liquid and all, for more body and savoriness. Giving the chickpeas a 10-minute head start before adding the pasta makes them creamy and allows a portion to break down for a thicker texture. Lemon and fresh herbs (if you have them) will brighten things up.

1 Process pancetta in food processor until ground to paste, about 30 seconds, scraping down sides of bowl as needed. Add carrot, celery, and garlic and pulse until finely chopped, 8 to 10 pulses. Add onion and pulse until onion is cut into ⅛- to ¼-inch pieces, 8 to 10 pulses. Transfer pancetta mixture to large Dutch oven. Pulse tomatoes in now-empty food processor until coarsely chopped, 8 to 10 pulses. Set aside.

2 Add oil to pancetta mixture in Dutch oven and cook over medium heat, stirring frequently, until fond begins to form on bottom of pot, about 5 minutes. Add rosemary and cook until fragrant, about 1 minute. Stir in tomatoes, chickpeas and their liquid, water, and salt and bring to boil, scraping up any browned bits. Reduce heat to medium-low and simmer for 10 minutes. Add pasta and cook, stirring frequently, until tender, 10 to 12 minutes. Stir in lemon juice and season with salt and pepper to taste. Serve, passing Parmesan and extra oil separately.

PANTRY IMPROV

use what you have Use other small pasta such as orzo, tubetti, elbow macaroni, or small shells, but make sure to substitute by weight and not by volume. Diced or whole peeled tomatoes will work instead of canned. Use red wine vinegar instead of lemon juice.

level up Add 1 anchovy fillet and ¼ teaspoon red pepper flakes with the rosemary. Sprinkle with chopped fresh parsley before serving.

spaghetti al tonno

SERVES 4 | TOTAL TIME: 50 MINUTES

2 (5- to 7-ounce) jars/cans olive oil–packed tuna, drained

1 tablespoon lemon juice

1 teaspoon table salt, divided, plus salt for cooking pasta

½ teaspoon pepper, divided

¼ cup extra–virgin olive oil, divided, plus extra for drizzling

1½ tablespoons minced garlic, divided

3 anchovy fillets, rinsed, patted dry, and minced

¼–½ teaspoon red pepper flakes

1 (14.5-ounce) can whole peeled tomatoes, drained with juice reserved, crushed by hand to small pieces

12 ounces spaghetti

6 tablespoons chopped fresh parsley, divided (optional)

why this recipe works Canned tuna stars in this gutsy weeknight savior, a true meal from the cupboard with a flavor that is anything but pedestrian. Plenty of olive oil is a must here to give the dish sufficient richness. Using oil-packed canned tuna also helps in that regard (if you happen to have a fancy glass jar of oil-packed tuna, this is a great opportunity to use it). When it comes to seasonings, the kitchen-sink approach doesn't pay off. We focus our flavorings on garlic, red pepper flakes for heat, and a small amount of canned tomatoes, crushed by hand to produce small, supple pieces. Three anchovies enhance the seafood profile and provide a briny backbone. To ensure that the tuna stays moist and silky, we stir it into slightly underdone spaghetti along with our tomato mixture off the heat and simply let it warm through. This not only gently warms the fish so that it holds onto its moisture but also hedges against mushy spaghetti. For a spicier dish, use the full ½ teaspoon of red pepper flakes.

1 Bring 4 quarts water to boil in large pot. While water comes to boil, gently stir tuna, lemon juice, ¼ teaspoon salt, and ¼ teaspoon pepper together in small bowl.

2 Heat 2 tablespoons oil, 1 tablespoon garlic, anchovies, and pepper flakes in large saucepan over medium heat, stirring occasionally, until oil sizzles gently and anchovies break down, 1½ to 2 minutes. Stir in tomatoes and their juice and ½ teaspoon salt. Bring to gentle simmer and cook, stirring occasionally, until slightly thickened, 6 to 7 minutes. Cover and keep warm over low heat.

3 Add pasta and 1 tablespoon salt to boiling water. Cook, stirring often, until barely al dente. Reserve ½ cup cooking water. Drain pasta and return it to pot. Off heat, add tomato mixture, remaining ¼ teaspoon salt, remaining ¼ teaspoon pepper, and remaining 1½ teaspoons garlic and toss until pasta is well coated. Add tuna mixture and toss gently. Cover and set aside for 3 minutes so flavors can meld and pasta can finish cooking.

4 Adjust consistency of sauce with reserved cooking water as needed. Add ¼ cup parsley, if using, and remaining 2 tablespoons oil and toss to combine. Season with salt and pepper to taste. Drizzle individual portions with extra oil and sprinkle with remaining 2 tablespoons parsley. Serve.

PANTRY IMPROV

use what you have We prefer spaghetti or linguine for this dish, but short or tubular shapes such as penne, fusilli, farfalle, ziti, or rigatoni also work. Likewise, we prefer oil-packed tuna and whole peeled tomatoes, but if you happen to have water-packed tuna or diced tomatoes instead, don't let that stop you.

level up Top with toasted bread crumbs, Crispy Shallots (page 388), or Crispy Capers (page 388).

pasta with **pesto, potatoes, and green beans**

SERVES 4 | **TOTAL TIME: 40 MINUTES**

8 ounces red potatoes, peeled and cut into ½-inch pieces

Table salt for cooking vegetables and pasta

8 ounces frozen cut green beans

12 ounces gemelli, penne, trofie, or any short-cut pasta

2 tablespoons unsalted butter, cut into ½-inch pieces and chilled

1 tablespoon lemon juice

½ teaspoon pepper

¾ cup basil pesto

why this recipe works Combining two humble pantry starches, potatoes and pasta, might seem to promise a hearty—if heavy—dinner. But this classic dish from Liguria, Italy achieves a remarkable lightness and creaminess. This is accomplished by boiling chunks of potatoes in salted water (the same water we later use to cook the pasta) and then vigorously stirring them with pasta, pesto, and green beans. The process of stirring sloughs off the corners of the potatoes, releasing starch that combines with the pesto and some pasta cooking water to produce a luscious, creamy sauce. Better yet, the potatoes and pasta together act as a blank canvass for the vibrant basil pesto for which Liguria is known (soaking up all the flavorful oils). There is absolutely nothing wrong with opening a jar of store-bought pesto here. This one-pot meal is also an excellent reason to defrost a box of frozen green beans.

1 Bring 4 quarts water to boil in large pot. Add potatoes and 1 tablespoon salt and cook for 8 minutes. Stir in green beans and continue to cook until potatoes are tender but still hold their shape, 1 to 3 minutes. Using slotted spoon, transfer vegetables to rimmed baking sheet. (Do not discard water.)

2 Bring potato cooking water back to boil, add pasta, and cook, stirring often, until al dente. Reserve 1 cup cooking water, then drain pasta and return it to pot. Add butter, lemon juice, pepper, potatoes and green beans, pesto, and ¾ cup reserved cooking water and stir vigorously with rubber spatula until sauce takes on creamy appearance. Adjust consistency with remaining ¼ cup reserved cooking water as needed and season with salt and pepper to taste. Serve immediately.

PANTRY IMPROV

use what you have Yukon gold potatoes or white boiling potatoes can be used in place of the red potatoes. Fresh green beans, trimmed and cut into 1-inch pieces, can be used in place of frozen; frozen peas are also a good option.

level up Make your own pesto. See our Pantry Pesto (page 137) for different options.

bucatini with **peas, kale, and pancetta**

SERVES 4 | TOTAL TIME: 45 MINUTES

why this recipe works Pancetta, broth, and white wine form a flavor trio to infuse this one-pot pasta with savory complexity; the pasta drinks up the rich liquid as it cooks. After crisping the pancetta (bacon works, too), we use the rendered fat to warm garlic and lemon zest before adding wine, broth, and water and simmering pasta vigorously to cook it through and reduce the liquid. A couple of frozen vegetables (several good choices here) contribute freshness: Add them during the last few minutes so they don't over-soften. A final handful of grated cheese binds the cooking liquid into a cohesive sauce. We love how thick-stranded, hollow bucatini absorbs the sauce, but regular spaghetti is perfectly good here.

1 Cook pancetta in Dutch oven over medium heat until rendered and crisp, 6 to 8 minutes. Using slotted spoon, transfer pancetta to paper towel–lined plate. Add garlic and lemon zest to fat left in pot and cook until fragrant, about 30 seconds. Stir in wine, scraping up any browned bits, and cook until nearly evaporated, about 3 minutes. Stir in water, broth, and pasta and bring to vigorous simmer. Reduce heat to medium, cover, and cook, stirring gently and often, until pasta is nearly tender, 8 to 10 minutes.

2 Uncover, stir in kale and peas and simmer until heated through, about 4 minutes. Add Parmesan and stir vigorously until pasta is creamy and well coated, about 30 seconds. Season with salt and pepper to taste. Serve, sprinkling individual portions with pancetta.

2 ounces pancetta or bacon, cut into ½-inch pieces

2 garlic cloves, minced

2 teaspoons grated lemon zest

½ cup dry white wine or dry vermouth

2½ cups water

2 cups chicken or vegetable broth

12 ounces bucatini or spaghetti

5 ounces frozen kale, thawed and squeezed dry

1 cup frozen peas

1 ounce Parmesan or Pecorino Romano cheese, grated (½ cup), divided

---

PANTRY IMPROV

use what you have Other frozen leafy greens such as spinach will work in place of kale, and frozen fava beans or edamame can be substituted for the peas. Or stir in 5 ounces (5 cups) fresh baby kale.

level up Top each serving with toasted panko bread crumbs, fresh herbs, and/or extra lemon zest. Dollop with ricotta or mascarpone, or sprinkle with crumbled goat cheese.

fideos with **chickpeas, fennel, and kale**

SERVES 4 | TOTAL TIME: 55 MINUTES

8   ounces fideo noodles

3   tablespoons extra–virgin olive oil, divided

1   onion, chopped fine

1   fennel bulb, 1½ teaspoons fronds minced, stalks discarded, bulb halved, cored, and sliced thin

½   teaspoon table salt, divided

1   (14.5–ounce) can diced tomatoes, drained and chopped fine, juice reserved

3   garlic cloves, minced

1½   teaspoons smoked paprika

2¾   cups chicken or vegetable broth

1   (15–ounce) can chickpeas, rinsed

8   ounces frozen kale or spinach, thawed and squeezed dry

½   cup dry white wine or dry vermouth

½   teaspoon pepper

¼   cup sliced almonds, toasted

Lemon wedges

why this recipe works A cousin of paella, fideos ("noodles" in Spanish) is a one-pan dish of short, thin, toasted noodles (which are also called fideos) simmered in a smoky sauce with additions such as meat or seafood. Fideos are so flavorful they also work great in a vegetarian, pantry-friendly meal. We first toast the noodles, which contributes nuttiness and color. Onion and fresh fennel provide an aromatic base. We then cook diced tomatoes with garlic and smoked paprika, add wine for complexity, and simmer the pasta with chickpeas until tender. A run under the broiler creates a nice crunchy surface. You will need a 12-inch broiler-safe skillet for this recipe. The skillet will be quite full once you add the pasta; we recommend using a straight-sided skillet or sauté pan for easier stirring.

1   Toss noodles and 1 tablespoon oil in broiler-safe 12-inch skillet until pasta is evenly coated. Toast pasta over medium-high heat, stirring frequently, until browned and releases nutty aroma (pasta should be color of peanut butter), 6 to 10 minutes; transfer to bowl.

2   Wipe out now-empty skillet, add remaining 2 tablespoons oil, and heat over medium-high heat until shimmering. Add onion, sliced fennel, and ¼ teaspoon salt and cook until onion is softened, about 5 minutes. Stir in tomatoes and cook until mixture is thick, dry, and slightly darkened in color, 4 to 6 minutes.

3   Reduce heat to medium, stir in garlic and paprika, and cook until fragrant, about 30 seconds. Stir in toasted pasta until thoroughly combined. Stir in broth, chickpeas, kale, wine, pepper, reserved tomato juice, and remaining ¼ teaspoon salt. Increase heat to medium-high and bring to simmer. Cook uncovered, stirring occasionally, until liquid is slightly thickened and pasta is just tender, 8 to 10 minutes. Meanwhile, adjust oven rack 5 to 6 inches from broiler element and heat broiler.

4   Transfer skillet to oven and broil until surface of pasta is dry with crisped, browned spots, 5 to 7 minutes. Let cool for 5 minutes, then sprinkle with almonds and fennel fronds and serve with lemon wedges.

PANTRY IMPROV

use what you have You can use spaghettini or thin spaghetti in place of fideos; loosely wrap the pasta in a dish towel, then press the bundle against the corner of the counter to break into 1- to 2-inch lengths. Substitute small white beans for chickpeas. Use minced fresh herbs in place of (or in addition to) fennel fronds. Substitute toasted seeds or other chopped nuts for almonds.

level up Serve with Easy Garlic Mayonnaise (page 398) or Greek yogurt.

skillet **tortellini supper**

SERVES 4 | TOTAL TIME: 50 MINUTES

8 ounces dried cheese tortellini

Table salt for cooking pasta

4 ounces bacon or pancetta,
cut crosswise into ¼–inch strips

4 garlic cloves, minced

1 cup heavy cream

½ teaspoon pepper

2 cups frozen peas or fava beans,
thawed

1 ounce Parmesan or Pecorino
Romano cheese, grated (½ cup),
plus extra for serving

1 teaspoon grated lemon zest
plus 2 teaspoons juice

why this recipe works Dried tortellini are a pantry mainstay for us. Here we dress them up with a creamy, bacon-y sauce and dig into our freezer for veggies (peas or other legumes) to add pops of color and freshness. We remove the pasta from the boiling water while slightly underdone and let it finish cooking in the sauce, along with some pasta cooking water. This allows the pasta to absorb the sauce's flavor while releasing starch that thickens the sauce to better coat the tortellini for a more cohesive dish.

1 Bring 4 quarts water to boil in large pot. Add pasta and 1 tablespoon salt and cook, stirring frequently, until not quite al dente, about 8 minutes. Reserve 1 cup cooking water, then drain pasta; set aside.

2 Meanwhile, cook bacon in 12-inch skillet over medium heat until crispy, 5 to 7 minutes. Using slotted spoon, transfer bacon to paper towel–lined plate.

3 Pour off all but 1 teaspoon fat from skillet. Add garlic and cook until fragrant, about 30 seconds. Stir in cream, pepper, pasta, and ½ cup reserved cooking water, and bring to simmer over medium heat. Cook, stirring often, until tortellini is al dente and sauce has thickened and coats pasta, 4 to 7 minutes. Stir in peas, Parmesan, and lemon zest and juice and cook until warmed through, about 1 minute, adjusting consistency with remaining reserved cooking water as needed. Season with salt and pepper to taste. Sprinkle with reserved bacon and serve, passing extra Parmesan separately.

> **PANTRY IMPROV**
>
> **use what you have** Use blue cheese instead of Parmesan. You can substitute medium shells, penne, or ziti for the tortellini.
>
> **level up** Stir baby spinach or baby kale into the pasta at the end. Sprinkle with chopped toasted nuts.

gnocchi, cauliflower, and gorgonzola gratin

SERVES 4 | TOTAL TIME: 40 MINUTES

why this recipe works Making gnocchi from scratch isn't hard, but it's not exactly a weeknight activity, so we keep vacuum-sealed gnocchi (available in the pasta aisle) on hand for when the craving strikes. For true comfort, we use them in a cheesy baked gratin studded with cauliflower. While the water boils for the gnocchi, we brown and parcook the cauliflower, and stir in blue cheese, cream, and a splash of sherry (no sherry? try using Shaoxing wine) and let everything get melty and thickened. With a sprinkle of bread crumbs and a few minutes under the broiler, dinner is ready.

1 Bring 4 quarts water to boil in large pot. Adjust oven rack about 5 inches from broiler element and heat broiler. Pulse bread, melted butter, salt, and pepper in food processor until mixture resembles coarse crumbs, about 6 pulses.

2 Add gnocchi and 1 tablespoon salt to boiling water and cook until tender and gnocchi are floating, about 4 minutes. Drain gnocchi and transfer to plate.

3 Meanwhile, melt remaining 2 tablespoons butter in 12-inch skillet over medium-high heat. Add cauliflower and cook until lightly browned, about 5 minutes. Add blue cheese, cream, sherry, and thyme and cook until cheese is melted and sauce is thickened, about 5 minutes. Stir in gnocchi and simmer until gnocchi are heated through, about 1 minute. Season with salt and pepper to taste.

4 Transfer gnocchi and cauliflower to 13 by 9-inch broiler-safe baking dish. Sprinkle bread crumbs evenly over surface and broil until crumbs are lightly browned, 3 to 5 minutes. Serve.

- 2 slices bread, torn into large pieces (2 cups)
- 2 tablespoons unsalted butter, melted, plus 2 tablespoons unsalted butter
- ¼ teaspoon table salt, plus salt for cooking gnocchi
- ⅛ teaspoon pepper
- 1 pound vacuum-packed gnocchi
- 1 large head cauliflower (3 pounds), cored and cut into 1-inch florets
- 4 ounces blue cheese, crumbled (1 cup)
- ¾ cup heavy cream
- 4 teaspoons dry sherry or Shaoxing wine
- 1 tablespoon minced fresh thyme or ¾ teaspoon dried

PANTRY IMPROV

use what you have We particularly like gorgonzola cheese here but any blue cheese will work. You can substitute broccoli or romesco for the cauliflower.

cheese ravioli **with pumpkin cream sauce**

SERVES 4 | TOTAL TIME: 50 MINUTES

1½ pounds fresh cheese ravioli

⅛ teaspoon plus ½ teaspoon table salt, divided, plus salt for cooking pasta

5 tablespoons unsalted butter, divided

¼ cup blanched hazelnuts, chopped

12 fresh sage leaves (optional)

1 teaspoon sherry vinegar

¼ cup finely chopped shallot

¼ teaspoon ground nutmeg

1 cup heavy cream

½ cup canned unsweetened pumpkin puree

1 ounce Parmesan or Pecorino Romano cheese, grated (½ cup)

why this recipe works Packaged ravioli never had it so good. After a weekend of making pies and sage-infused stuffing during the autumn season, we often end up with a pantry filled with half-used ingredients, and it can be challenging to find uses for them. This decadent but fast pasta dinner reimagines that leftover canned pumpkin as a luscious cream-enriched sauce for ravioli (fresh or frozen: your choice). If you have any sage leaves on hand, fry them in butter for the ultimate crispy garnish, and toss in some chopped hazelnuts (or, really, any nuts) for richness and crunch.

1   Bring 4 quarts water to boil in large pot. Add pasta and 1 tablespoon salt and cook, stirring often, until al dente. Reserve ½ cup cooking water, then drain pasta.

2   Meanwhile, melt 4 tablespoons butter in 12-inch nonstick skillet over medium heat. Add hazelnuts and sage, if using, and cook until butter and hazelnuts are both browned and fragrant, about 4 minutes, and removing the sage when the leaves turn crispy (probably 1 minute before the brown). Transfer to heatproof bowl and stir in vinegar and ⅛ teaspoon salt.

3   Melt remaining 1 tablespoon butter in now-empty skillet over medium heat. Add shallot, nutmeg, and remaining ½ teaspoon salt and cook, stirring occasionally, until shallot is softened, about 3 minutes. Stir in cream and pumpkin and bring to simmer. Cook until thickened, about 5 minutes. Off heat, stir in Parmesan. Add pasta and toss to combine. Adjust consistency with reserved cooking water as needed. Serve, topped with sage and hazelnut butter.

PANTRY IMPROV

use what you have Red or white wine vinegar can be used instead of the sherry vinegar. Almonds, walnuts, or pecans make a nice sub for the hazelnuts. Any filled ravioli or tortellini works here.

level up Sprinkle with fresh herbs. Stir baby spinach into the sauce or serve with a green salad.

pantry sauces to have on hand

Many of the best pasta sauces get their character from pantry staples: cans of tomatoes (preferable to fresh most months) and hearty beans, jars of briny olives and capers and umami–rich sun–dried tomatoes, tins of anchovies, and, of course, garlic and olive oil. Toasted nuts add richness, flavor, and substance. These sauces are also a great way to use up whatever fresh herbs you may have hanging out in the fridge, from basil to beyond.

pantry pesto

**makes about 1½ cups | enough for 2 pounds pasta
total time: 30 minutes**

This all-purpose recipe for green pesto is perfect for using up any fresh leafy herbs you have on hand such as basil, parsley, cilantro, or even tarragon; it also takes well to baby greens like arugula. Regardless of the base, there are a few requirements: Use a high-quality extra-virgin olive oil (its flavor will shine through), toast the garlic (to tame its fiery flavor), and add some type of nut or seed (for richness and body). When you're tossing the pesto with cooked pasta, it is important to add some pasta cooking water to achieve the proper sauce consistency. Pounding the greens helps bring out their flavorful oils.

- 6 garlic cloves, unpeeled
- ½ cup nuts such as pine nuts, walnuts, pistachios, or sunflower seeds
- 4 cups fresh leafy herbs such as basil, parsley, cilantro, or tarragon and/or baby greens such as arugula, spinach, and kale
- 1 cup extra–virgin olive oil
- 1 ounce Parmesan or Pecorino Romano cheese, grated fine (½ cup)

1 Toast garlic in 8-inch skillet over medium heat, shaking skillet occasionally, until softened and spotty brown, about 8 minutes. When garlic is cool enough to handle, remove and discard skins and chop coarsely. Toast pine nuts in now-empty skillet over medium heat, stirring often, until golden and fragrant, 4 to 5 minutes.

2 Place basil in 1-gallon zipper-lock bag. Pound bag with flat side of meat pounder or with rolling pin until all leaves are bruised.

3 Process garlic, pine nuts, and basil in food processor until finely chopped, about 1 minute, scraping down sides of bowl as needed. With processor running, slowly add oil until incorporated. Transfer pesto to bowl, stir in Parmesan, and season with salt and pepper to taste. (Pesto can be refrigerated for up to 3 days or frozen for up to 3 months. To prevent browning, press plastic wrap flush to surface or top with thin layer of olive oil. Bring to room temperature before using.)

VARIATIONS

sun–dried tomato pesto
Reduce garlic to 3 cloves and oil to ½ cup. Substitute ¼ cup chopped walnuts for pine nuts and 1 cup oil-packed sun-dried tomatoes for basil; skip step 2.

kale and sunflower seed pesto
Reduce garlic to 2 cloves, basil to 1 cup, and oil to ½ cup. Substitute ½ cup sunflower seeds for pine nuts. Add 4 ounces baby kale to processor with basil.

green olive and orange pesto
Reduce garlic to 2 cloves and oil to ½ cup. Substitute ½ cup slivered almonds for pine nuts and 1½ cups fresh parsley leaves for basil. Add ½ cup pitted brine-cured olives and ½ teaspoon grated orange zest plus 2 tablespoons juice to processor with garlic.

classic marinara sauce

makes about 4 cups | enough for 1 pound pasta
total time: 45 minutes

Starting with canned tomatoes makes for a sauce that can be enjoyed year-round. By definition, a marinara sauce contains tomatoes, onions, garlic, and herbs; from there, the variations are endless—but no matter what goes in, the result should be more than the sum of its parts. A relatively brief simmer—a hallmark of marinara—gives way to a deeply flavorful sauce.

- 2 (28–ounce) cans whole peeled tomatoes
- 3 tablespoons extra–virgin olive oil, divided
- 1 onion, chopped fine
- 2 garlic cloves, minced
- 2 teaspoons minced fresh oregano or ½ teaspoon dried
- ½ teaspoon table salt
- ¼ teaspoon pepper
- Sugar

1 Drain tomatoes in fine-mesh strainer set over bowl. Using hands, open tomatoes and remove and discard seeds and cores. Let tomatoes drain for 5 minutes. (You should have about 2½ cups juice; if not, add water as needed to equal 2½ cups.) Measure out and reserve ¾ cup tomatoes separately.

2 Heat 2 tablespoons oil in large saucepan over medium heat until shimmering. Add onion and cook until softened and lightly browned, 5 to 7 minutes. Stir in garlic and oregano and cook until fragrant, about 30 seconds. Stir in remaining tomatoes and increase heat to medium-high. Cook, stirring often, until liquid has evaporated and tomatoes begin to brown and stick to saucepan, 10 to 12 minutes.

3 Stir in tomato juice, salt, and pepper, scraping up any browned bits. Bring to simmer and cook, stirring occasionally, until sauce is thickened, 8 to 10 minutes.

4 Transfer sauce to food processor, add reserved tomatoes, and pulse until slightly chunky, about 8 pulses. Return sauce to now-empty saucepan and bring to brief simmer. Stir in remaining 1 tablespoon oil. Season with salt, pepper, and sugar to taste. (Sauce can be refrigerated for up to 1 week or frozen for up to 1 month.)

VARIATION
vodka cream marinara sauce

Add ¼ teaspoon red pepper flakes to onions with garlic. Add ½ cup heavy cream and ⅓ cup vodka to skillet with tomato juice in step 3.

simple (any) meat sauce

makes about 6 cups | enough for 2 pounds pasta
total time: 1 hour

We love our meat sauce on pasta or just spooned straight from the pot. To achieve a deep, meaty flavor without overcooking, we don't brown the meat before stewing it with tomatoes. Instead, we make the most of the browned bits (fond) left behind after sautéing onion—scraping them up into the tomatoes distributes deep flavor throughout the sauce. A simple bread-and-milk panade ensures tender meat.

- 1   slice bread, torn into pieces (1 cup)
- ¼   cup whole milk
- ½   teaspoon table salt
- ½   teaspoon pepper
- 1   pound ground beef, pork, lamb, turkey, or 12 ounces plant-based meat
- 1   tablespoon extra-virgin olive oil
- 1   onion, chopped fine
- 6   garlic cloves, minced
- 1   tablespoon tomato paste
- ¼   teaspoon red pepper flakes
- ¼   cup water
- 1   tablespoon minced fresh oregano or 1 teaspoon dried, divided
- 1   (28-ounce) can crushed tomatoes

1   Pulse bread, milk, salt, and pepper in food processor until paste forms, about 8 pulses. Add beef and pulse until mixture is well combined, about 6 pulses.

2   Heat oil in large saucepan over medium heat until shimmering. Add onion and cook until softened and well browned, 6 to 10 minutes. Stir in garlic, tomato paste, and pepper flakes and cook until fragrant and tomato paste begins to brown, about 1 minute. Stir in water and 2 teaspoons fresh oregano (if using dried, add full amount), scraping up any browned bits. Add meat mixture and cook, breaking up meat with wooden spoon, until no longer pink, 2 to 4 minutes.

3   Stir in tomatoes, bring to simmer, and cook until sauce has thickened and flavors have blended, about 30 minutes. Stir in remaining 1 teaspoon fresh oregano and season with salt and pepper to taste. (Sauce can be refrigerated for up to 3 days or frozen for up to 1 month.)

chickpea–mushroom bolognese

makes 6 cups | enough for 2 pounds pasta
total time: 1 hour

Mushrooms and canned chickpeas form the base of a vegetarian version of a savory, unctuous, meaty sauce. Make sure to rinse the chickpeas after pulsing them in the food processor or the sauce will be too thick.

- 10 ounces cremini mushrooms
- 6 tablespoons extra–virgin olive oil, divided
- 1 teaspoon table salt
- 1 onion, chopped
- 5 garlic cloves, minced
- 1¼ teaspoons dried oregano
- ¼ teaspoon red pepper flakes
- ¼ cup tomato paste
- 1 (28–ounce) can crushed tomatoes
- 2 cups vegetable or chicken broth
- 1 (15–ounce) can chickpeas, rinsed
- 2 tablespoons chopped fresh basil (optional)

1 Pulse mushrooms in two batches in food processor until chopped into ⅛- to ¼-inch pieces, 7 to 10 pulses, scraping down sides of bowl as needed. (Do not clean workbowl.)

2 Heat 5 tablespoons oil in Dutch oven over medium-high heat until shimmering. Add mushrooms and salt and cook, stirring occasionally, until mushrooms are browned and fond has formed on bottom of pot, about 5 minutes.

3 While mushrooms cook, pulse onion in food processor until finely chopped, 7 to 10 pulses, scraping down sides of bowl as needed. (Do not clean workbowl.) Transfer onion to pot with mushrooms and cook, stirring occasionally, until onion is soft and translucent, about 5 minutes. Combine remaining 1 tablespoon oil, garlic, oregano, and pepper flakes in bowl.

4 Add tomato paste to pot and cook, stirring constantly, until mixture is rust-colored, 1 to 2 minutes. Reduce heat to medium and push vegetables to sides of pot. Add garlic mixture to center and cook, stirring constantly, until fragrant, about 30 seconds. Stir in tomatoes and broth; bring to simmer over high heat. Reduce heat to low and simmer sauce for 5 minutes, stirring occasionally.

5 While sauce simmers, pulse chickpeas in food processor until chopped into ¼-inch pieces, 7 to 10 pulses. Transfer chickpeas to fine-mesh strainer and rinse under cold running water until water runs clear; drain well. Add chickpeas to pot and simmer until sauce is slightly thickened, about 15 minutes. Stir in basil, if using, and season with salt and pepper to taste. (Sauce can be refrigerated for up to 2 days or frozen for up to 1 month.)

puttanesca sauce

makes about 3 cups | enough for 1 pound pasta
total time: 30 minutes

This sauce is supersavory thanks to a bold combination of anchovies, olives, and capers. It's not only great on pasta—try serving it over fish or chicken.

- 2 tablespoons unsalted butter
- ¼ cup finely chopped onion
- 4 anchovy fillets, rinsed and minced
- ½ teaspoon red pepper flakes
- ½ teaspoon table salt
- 1 teaspoon minced fresh oregano or
  ¼ teaspoon dried
- 2 garlic cloves, minced
- 1 (28-ounce) can crushed tomatoes
- ¼ teaspoon sugar
- ¼ cup pitted olives, chopped
- 3 tablespoons capers, rinsed and minced
- 1 tablespoon extra-virgin olive oil

1 Melt butter in medium saucepan over medium-low heat. Add onion, anchovies, pepper flakes, salt, and oregano and cook, stirring occasionally, until onion is softened and lightly browned, 3 to 5 minutes. Stir in garlic and cook until fragrant, about 30 seconds.

2 Stir in tomatoes and sugar, bring to simmer, and cook until thickened slightly, about 10 minutes. Off heat, stir in olives, capers, and oil. Season with salt and pepper to taste. (Sauce can be refrigerated for up to 1 week or frozen for up to 1 month.)

white clam sauce

makes 2 cups | enough for 1 pound pasta
total time: 35 minutes

- 2 shallots, minced
- 2 tablespoons extra-virgin olive oil
- 4 garlic cloves, minced
- 2 (6.5-ounce) cans chopped clams
- 1 cup chicken or vegetable broth
- 1 (8-ounce) bottle clam juice
- 2 tablespoons unsalted butter

Cook shallots, oil, and garlic in 12-inch skillet over medium heat until shallots are just golden and garlic is fragrant, about 2 minutes. Add clams and their juice, broth, and bottled clam juice; increase heat to medium-high; and bring to boil. Cook until sauce is reduced to 2 cups, about 15 minutes. Off heat, whisk in butter and season with salt and pepper to taste.

garlic cream sauce

makes about 2 cups | enough for 1 pound pasta
total time: 35 minutes

- 1 tablespoon unsalted butter
- 8 garlic cloves, minced
  Pinch red pepper flakes
- ¾ cup dry white wine
- 1 cup whole milk
- 1 cup heavy cream
- 1 ounce Parmesan cheese, grated (½ cup)
- ¼ teaspoon table salt
- ¼ teaspoon pepper
- 2 tablespoons minced fresh parsley (optional)

Melt butter in medium saucepan over medium heat. Add garlic and pepper flakes and cook until fragrant, about 30 seconds. Add wine, bring to simmer, and cook until reduced to ¼ cup, about 5 minutes. Whisk in milk, cream, Parmesan, salt, and pepper. Bring to simmer and cook until Parmesan has melted and sauce is thickened, about 5 minutes. Stir in parsley and season with salt and pepper to taste. Serve immediately.

one-pot penne
with quick tomato sauce

SERVES 4 | TOTAL TIME: 45 MINUTES

3 tablespoons extra-virgin olive oil

2 garlic cloves, minced

1 (28-ounce) can crushed tomatoes

¾ teaspoon table salt

½ teaspoon pepper

½ teaspoon sugar

¼ teaspoon dried oregano

3 cups water, plus extra as needed

1 pound penne

why this recipe works Consider this your blueprint for making a one-pot pasta to simmer right in the sauce, whether you want a simple tomato sauce or hearty ragu. Any way you take it, the key to getting al dente pasta and just-thick-enough sauce starts with the right ratio of liquid to pasta, which we achieve by using 3 cups of water and a large can of tomatoes for a pound of pasta. We cover the pot so the sauce doesn't dry out (though you'll want to give the pasta an occasional stir) and then lift the lid at the end to let the sauce reduce. Starch released from the pasta thickens the sauce, helping it cling nicely. Cooking garlic and other seasonings such as capers or red pepper flakes in oil before adding the tomatoes builds a nice flavor base.

1 Cook oil and garlic in Dutch oven over medium heat until fragrant, 1 to 2 minutes. Stir in tomatoes, salt, pepper, sugar, and oregano. Bring to simmer and cook for 5 minutes.

2 Stir in water and pasta and bring to vigorous simmer. Reduce heat to medium, cover, and cook, stirring occasionally, until pasta is nearly tender, about 12 minutes. (If sauce becomes too thick, add extra water as needed.)

3 Uncover and continue to simmer, stirring often, until pasta is tender and sauce has thickened, 3 to 5 minutes. Season with salt and pepper to taste. Serve.

PANTRY IMPROV

use what you have Other short pasta shapes such as ziti, farfalle, and campanelle can be substituted for the penne.

level up Add anchovy fillets, capers, olives, and/or pepper flakes to the pot with the tomatoes. Cook ground meat (sausage, beef, or chicken) and/or chopped fresh vegetables (such as bell peppers, fennel, and zucchini) in oil until lightly browned and/or softened before adding the garlic. Stir frozen peas, jarred artichokes, or baby spinach into the cooked pasta and let sit until heated through. Top with fresh herbs, shredded cheese, and/or dollops of ricotta.

VARIATIONS

one-pot penne with sausage ragu

Coarsely chop 1 carrot, 1 celery rib, ½ onion, and garlic, then pulse in food processor until finely ground. Heat oil in Dutch oven over medium-high heat until shimmering. Add vegetables and 8 ounces Italian sausage, casings removed. Cook, breaking up meat with wooden spoon, until vegetables are softened and sausage is no longer pink, about 5 minutes. Add 1 cup dry red wine and cook until nearly evaporated, about 5 minutes. Stir in tomatoes and proceed with recipe.

one-pot shrimp fra diavolo

Increase oil to 6 tablespoons and garlic to 4 cloves. Substitute ½ teaspoon red pepper flakes for oregano. After uncovering pasta, stir in 12 ounces peeled and deveined shrimp and continue to simmer as directed. Stir ¼ cup minced fresh parsley and 2 tablespoons minced pepperoncini or hot cherry peppers, plus 1 tablespoon brine, into pasta before serving.

one-pot penne with olives, capers, and eggplant

Microwave 1 pound eggplant, cut into 1-inch pieces, on paper towel–lined plate until slightly wilted, about 5 minutes. Heat oil in Dutch oven over medium-high heat until just smoking. Add eggplant and cook until well browned and fully tender, about 5 minutes. Add garlic and cook until fragrant, about 30 seconds. Proceed with recipe, stirring ½ cup chopped olives and 1 tablespoon capers into pasta before serving.

fresh pasta without a machine

makes 1 pound | serves 4 to 6
total time: 1½ hours, plus 1 hour resting

Homemade pasta speaks to the resourcefulness that is the heart of pantry cooking. Adding six egg yolks creates a soft dough easily rolled out by hand. If using a high-protein flour like King Arthur, use seven egg yolks. The longer the dough rests in step 2, the easier it will be to roll out. Avoid adding too much flour when rolling out pasta, which may result in excessive snapback. Serve with any of the sauces on pages 137–141.

- 2 cups (10 ounces) all-purpose flour, plus extra as needed
- 2 large eggs plus 6 large yolks
- 2 tablespoons extra-virgin olive oil
- Table salt for cooking pasta

1 Process flour, eggs and yolks, and oil in food processor until mixture forms cohesive dough that feels soft and is barely tacky to touch, about 45 seconds. (If dough sticks to your fingers, add up to ¼ cup flour, 1 tablespoon at a time, until barely tacky. If dough doesn't become cohesive, add up to 1 tablespoon water, 1 teaspoon at a time, until it just comes together; process 30 seconds longer.)

2 Turn out dough onto dry counter and knead until smooth, 1 to 2 minutes. Shape dough into 6-inch-long cylinder. Wrap in plastic wrap and let rest at room temperature for at least 1 hour or up to 4 hours.

3 Cut cylinder crosswise into 6 equal pieces. Working with 1 piece of dough at a time (rewrap remaining dough), dust both sides with flour, place cut side down on clean counter, and press into 3-inch square. Using heavy rolling pin, roll into 6-inch square. Dust both sides of dough lightly with flour.

4 Starting at center of square, roll dough away from you in 1 motion. Return rolling pin to center of dough and roll toward you in single motion. Repeat rolling steps until dough sticks to counter and measures roughly 12 inches long. Lightly dust both sides of dough with flour and continue to roll until dough measures roughly 20 inches long and 6 inches wide, frequently lifting dough to release it from counter. (You should be able to easily see outline of your fingers through dough.) If dough firmly sticks to counter and wrinkles when rolled out, dust dough lightly with flour.

5 Transfer pasta sheet to clean dish towel and let stand, uncovered, until firm around edges, about 15 minutes; meanwhile, roll out remaining dough.

6 Starting with 1 short end, gently fold pasta sheet at 2-inch intervals until sheet has been folded into flat, rectangular roll. Using sharp chef's knife, slice crosswise into 3/16-inch-thick noodles. Use your fingers to unfurl noodles and transfer to baking sheet. Repeat folding and cutting remaining sheets of dough. Cook noodles within 1 hour or freeze.

7 to cook pasta Bring 4 quarts water to boil in large pot. Add pasta and 1 tablespoon salt and cook until tender but still al dente, about 3 minutes. Drain pasta and toss with sauce; serve immediately.

VARIATIONS

fresh spinach pasta without a machine
Process 4 ounces frozen chopped spinach, thawed and thoroughly squeezed dry, with eggs and yolks until finely ground, before adding flour and oil.

fresh tomato pasta without a machine
Process 2 tablespoons tomato paste with eggs and yolks until finely ground, before adding flour and oil.

fresh lemon–black pepper pasta without a machine
Add 1 tablespoon grated lemon zest and 1 teaspoon ground pepper to processor with remaining ingredients.

buttered **spaetzle**

SERVES 4 | TOTAL TIME: 45 MINUTES

why this recipe works With little more than flour, eggs, and milk you can make your own chewy, buttery, noodle-y dumplings, aka, spaetzle. Serve them with all manner of stewy dishes, or make them the main: Stir in browned sausages, sautéed onions and cabbage, and shredded cheese and call it dinner. Make sure to let the batter rest to allow the gluten to relax for more tender spaetzle. Shaping the spaetzle is as easy as pressing the batter through small holes of some kind of gadget into boiling water: We rig a makeshift spaetzle-maker by poking holes into a disposable aluminum pan.

1 Whisk flour, salt, pepper, and nutmeg together in large bowl. Whisk milk and eggs together in second bowl. Slowly whisk milk mixture into flour mixture until smooth. Cover and let rest for 15 to 30 minutes.

2 While batter rests, use scissors to poke about forty ¼-inch holes in bottom of disposable pan. Bring 4 quarts water to boil in Dutch oven.

3 Add 1 tablespoon salt to boiling water and set prepared disposable pan on top of Dutch oven. Transfer half of batter to disposable pan. Use spatula to scrape batter across holes, letting batter fall into water. Boil until spaetzle float, about 1 minute. Using spider skimmer or slotted spoon, transfer spaetzle to colander set in large bowl to drain. Repeat with remaining batter.

4 Discard any accumulated water in bowl beneath colander. Pour spaetzle into now-empty bowl. Add melted butter and toss to combine. Serve.

- 2 cups all-purpose flour
- ¾ teaspoon table salt, plus salt for cooking spaetzle
- ½ teaspoon pepper
- ¼ teaspoon ground nutmeg
- ¾ cup whole milk
- 3 large eggs
- 1 (13 by 9-inch) disposable aluminum pan
- 2 tablespoons unsalted butter, melted

PANTRY IMPROV

use what you have Use other warm spices in place of the nutmeg.

level up Make it crispy: Before tossing the spaetzle with butter, heat 2 tablespoons vegetable oil in 12-inch nonstick skillet over medium-high heat until shimmering, add the spaetzle and cook, stirring occasionally, until golden and crispy around edges, 5 to 7 minutes. Stir in browned sausage, sautéed cabbage and onions, and/or shredded swiss cheese.

sautéed buttery egg noodles
with cabbage and fried eggs

SERVES 4 | TOTAL TIME: 40 MINUTES

8 ounces egg noodles

¼ teaspoon plus ⅛ teaspoon table salt, divided, plus salt for cooking noodles

3 tablespoons unsalted butter

3 cups coarsely chopped green or red cabbage

1 small onion, sliced thin

¾ teaspoon caraway seeds

½ teaspoon plus ⅛ teaspoon pepper, divided

1 tablespoon vegetable oil

4 large eggs

why this recipe works Who can say no to buttered noodles? This ultra-comforting take on haluski, the Eastern European cabbage and egg noodle dish, proves that the basics don't have to be boring. We start by sautéing cabbage and onion in butter to develop some nice browning—along with caraway seeds for mild anise notes—and then add cooked noodles right to the skillet with some reserved pasta water so they can soak up all of the good stuff. Finally, we top each serving with a fried egg—the runny yolk adds creaminess and saucy cohesion.

1   Bring 4 quarts water to boil in Dutch oven. Add noodles and 1 tablespoon salt and cook, stirring often, until al dente, 10 to 12 minutes. Reserve 1 cup cooking water, then drain noodles and set aside. Wipe out pot.

2   Melt butter in now-empty pot over medium-high heat. Add cabbage, onion, and ¼ teaspoon salt and cook, stirring occasionally, until vegetables are softened and beginning to brown, 6 to 8 minutes. Stir in caraway seeds and cook until fragrant, about 30 seconds. Stir in ½ teaspoon pepper, reserved cooked noodles, and ½ cup reserved cooking water, scraping up any browned bits, and simmer until reduced slightly, 1 to 2 minutes. Adjust consistency with remaining reserved cooking water as needed and season with salt and pepper to taste.

3   Meanwhile, heat oil in 12-inch nonstick skillet over medium-high heat until shimmering. Add eggs to skillet and sprinkle with remaining ⅛ teaspoon salt and remaining ⅛ teaspoon pepper. Cover and cook for 1 minute. Remove skillet from heat and let sit, covered, for 15 to 45 seconds for runny yolks, 45 to 60 seconds for soft but set yolks, or about 2 minutes for medium-set yolks. Serve noodles topped with egg.

PANTRY IMPROV

use what you have No caraway? Try fennel seeds, or omit.

level up Sprinkle with fresh minced dill. Add chopped smoked kielbasa or ham, or cooked ground pork. Dollop with sour cream or cottage cheese.

pasta salad with salami and sun-dried tomato vinaigrette

SERVES 4 | TOTAL TIME: 35 MINUTES

dressing

- ¾ cup oil-packed sun-dried tomatoes, minced, plus 2 tablespoons packing oil
- ¼ cup red wine vinegar, plus extra for seasoning
- 1 garlic clove, minced
- ¾ teaspoon pepper
- ¾ teaspoon table salt
- ¼ cup extra-virgin olive oil

salad

- 8 ounces fusilli (3 cups)
  Table salt for cooking pasta
- 4 (¼-inch-thick) slices deli salami or pepperoni (8 ounces), cut into 1-inch-long matchsticks
- 4 (¼-inch-thick) slices deli provolone or sharp cheddar cheese (8 ounces), cut into 1-inch-long matchsticks
- ½ cup pitted brine-cured olives, sliced crosswise

why this recipe works Pasta salad is a potluck favorite that checks all the cheesy, meaty, tangy, and carb-y boxes. But it's also perfect for a casual meal at home and a great excuse to clean out your pantry. Taking a cue from Italian antipasto, the main recipe incorporates supersavory flavors by way of deli ingredients such as thick-cut salami, olives, and a bright vinaigrette accented by sun-dried tomatoes and their packing oil. The variations bring fresh vegetables into the mix, from asparagus to eggplant.

1 for the dressing Whisk tomatoes, vinegar, garlic, pepper, and salt together in large bowl. Whisking constantly, drizzle in olive oil and tomato oil; set aside.

2 for the salad Bring 4 quarts water to boil in large pot. Add pasta and 1 tablespoon salt and cook, stirring often, until tender. Drain pasta, rinse with cold water, and drain again, leaving pasta slightly wet.

3 Add salami, provolone, olives, and pasta to dressing and toss to combine. Season with salt, pepper, and extra vinegar to taste. Serve. (To make ahead, toss pasta, salami, cheese, and olives with half of vinaigrette; refrigerate pasta mixture and remaining vinaigrette separately for up to 2 days. To serve, bring to room temperature. Stir ¼ cup boiling water into remaining vinaigrette and add to salad; toss to combine.)

PANTRY IMPROV

use what you have Any wine vinegar will work here. Try other deli meats and cheeses. Other small pastas with nooks and crannies to capture the dressing will work here, or use shelf-stable tortellini.

level up Use Roasted Garlic (page 384) in place of fresh. Add minced fresh herbs to the dressing. Add chopped baby spinach, baby kale, or baby arugula to the salad just before serving. Add other jarred or pickled vegetables such as artichokes, roasted red peppers, pepperoncini, or giardiniera.

VARIATIONS

tortellini salad with grilled eggplant, zucchini, and peppers

Any store-bought basil pesto will work here, or make Pantry Pesto (page 137).

Slice 1 pound eggplant into 1-inch-thick rounds. Halve 2 zucchini lengthwise. Halve, stem, and seed 1 bell pepper. Lightly toss vegetables with extra-virgin olive oil. Grill over hot fire until tender and lightly charred, 8 to 10 minutes; cut into 1-inch pieces. Whisk ½ cup pesto, 2 tablespoons water, and 1 tablespoon white wine vinegar together in large bowl. Substitute basil dressing for tomato dressing, tortellini for fusilli, and grilled vegetables for salami, provolone, and olives. Stir ¼ cup shaved Parmesan into salad just before serving.

orecchiette salad with asparagus and tomatoes

Omit sun-dried tomatoes and increase oil to 6 tablespoons. Substitute white wine vinegar for red wine vinegar and add 1 tablespoon Dijon mustard to dressing. Substitute orecchiette for fusilli. Substitute 1 pound blanched asparagus, cut into 1-inch lengths, and 8 ounces cherry or grape tomatoes, halved, for salami, provolone, and olives. Stir ¼ cup coarsely chopped fresh basil, parsley, and/or mint into salad just before serving.

farfalle salad with broccoli and avocado

Omit sun-dried tomatoes, salami, provolone, and olives. Increase oil to 6 tablespoons, and substitute 3 tablespoons lemon juice for vinegar and farfalle for fusilli. Add 12 ounces blanched fresh broccoli florets (or thawed frozen), coarsely chopped, and 2 diced avocados to dressing with pasta. Stir ¼ cup chopped toasted almonds into salad just before serving.

browned butter–soy noodles
with pan–seared tofu

SERVES 4 | TOTAL TIME: 1 HOUR

why this recipe works The glorious combination of soy sauce and butter has been used for years, especially in Japanese cooking. It's everything you want in a sauce: rich, sweet, salty, and umami. The combo tastes good on almost anything, but it's particularly incredible on noodles. We add a twist by browning the butter, which adds a pleasant nuttiness. (Use a stainless steel pan for a better visual on the browning and to avoid burning.) After taking the skillet off the heat, we add garlic and pepper flakes before stirring in soy sauce. This is when that "wow" moment happens. The butter bubbles up and absorbs the soy, transforming into a rich, nutty, salty, slightly caramel-like sticky sauce that gives off the most wonderful aroma. Lastly, we incorporate just enough lemon juice to balance the richness of the butter and stir in our noodles. These noodles are great on their own but opportunities for toppings are virtually endless.

1 Thoroughly pat tofu dry with paper towels. Sprinkle with salt and pepper, then gently toss with cornstarch. Transfer tofu to strainer and shake gently to remove excess cornstarch. Heat oil in 12-inch skillet over medium-high heat until just smoking. Add tofu and cook, turning as needed, until crisp and browned on all sides, 8 to 10 minutes; transfer to a plate. Wipe skillet clean with paper towels.

2 Bring 4 quarts water to boil in large pot. Add noodles and 1 tablespoon salt and cook, stirring often, until almost tender (center should still be firm, with slightly opaque dot). Reserve 1 cup cooking water, then drain pasta and return it to pot.

3 Meanwhile, melt butter in now-empty skillet over medium-high heat, swirling occasionally, and continue to cook until butter is browned and releases nutty aroma, about 1½ minutes. Off heat, stir in garlic and pepper flakes and cook using residual heat from skillet until fragrant, about 1 minute. Stir in soy sauce and lemon juice.

4 Add sauce and ½ cup reserved cooking water to noodles and cook over low heat, stirring occasionally, until flavors meld and noodles are tender, about 1 minute. Season with salt and pepper to taste and adjust consistency with remaining reserved cooking water as needed. Top individual portions of noodles with tofu and scallions, if using. Serve.

14 ounces firm or extra–firm tofu, cut into 1–inch pieces

¾ teaspoon table salt, plus salt for cooking noodles

¾ teaspoons white pepper

2 tablespoons cornstarch

2 tablespoons vegetable oil

1 pound dried yakisoba noodles

6 tablespoons unsalted butter

5 cloves garlic, minced

½ teaspoon red pepper flakes

2 tablespoons soy sauce

1½ tablespoons lemon juice

4 scallions, sliced (optional)

PANTRY IMPROV

use what you have Use rice vinegar in place of the lemon juice. You can use 12 ounces of fresh yakisoba noodles in place of dried. Lo mein or spaghetti can also be substituted.

level up Bulk up the noodles further with stir-fried or sautéed vegetables, fresh bean sprouts, and/or thinly sliced radishes.

chilled soba noodles
with miso dressing

SERVES 4 | TOTAL TIME: 40 MINUTES

- 8 ounces dried soba noodles
- 1 (8–inch square) sheet nori (optional)
- 3 tablespoons white, yellow, red, or brown miso
- 3 tablespoons mirin
- 2 tablespoons toasted sesame oil
- 1 tablespoon sesame seeds
- 1 teaspoon grated fresh ginger
- ¼–½ teaspoon red pepper flakes
- 3 scallions, sliced thin on bias (optional)

why this recipe works Chewy buckwheat soba noodles can be slurped in hot broth, but we also love them cold or at room temperature in this casual noodle dish. An umami-rich, pantry-friendly miso dressing (any color of miso will work) clings to the noodles without overpowering their distinct taste. From here, the salad is easily customizable. Eat the noodles by themselves or incorporate a mix of fresh vegetables you need to use up; they'll add color and crunch. Whichever vegetables you choose, it's nice to cut them into varying shapes (thin slices, matchsticks, or half moons) so they incorporate better into the noodles. Strips of toasted nori add more texture and a subtle briny taste. This dish isn't meant to be very spicy, but if you like heat, use the full ½ teaspoon of red pepper flakes.

1   Bring 4 quarts water to boil in large pot. Add noodles and cook, stirring occasionally, until noodles are cooked through but still retain some chew. Drain noodles and rinse under cold water until chilled. Drain well and transfer to large bowl.

2   Grip nori sheet, if using, with tongs and hold about 2 inches above low flame on gas burner. Toast nori, flipping every 3 to 5 seconds, until nori is aromatic and shrinks slightly, about 20 seconds. (If you do not have a gas stove, toast nori on rimmed baking sheet in 275-degree oven until it is aromatic and shrinks slightly, 20 to 25 minutes, flipping nori halfway through toasting.) Using scissors, cut nori into four 2-inch strips. Stack strips and cut crosswise into thin strips.

3   Combine miso, mirin, oil, 1 tablespoon water, sesame seeds, ginger, and pepper flakes in small bowl and whisk until combined. Add dressing to noodles and toss to combine. Add scallions and nori, if using, and toss well to evenly distribute. Season with salt to taste and serve.

PANTRY IMPROV

use what you have Plain pretoasted seaweed snacks can be substituted for the toasted nori, if desired.

level up Add vegetables: Crisp raw vegetables such as thinly sliced cucumber, snow or sugar snap peas, radishes, cucumber, and bell pepper are all good options. Bulk up the noodles with pan-seared tofu, shredded cooked chicken, or a roasted fish fillet.

soba noodles **with pork, scallions, and shichimi togarashi**

SERVES 4 | TOTAL TIME: 35 MINUTES

why this recipe works Seared slices of pork, nutty soba noodles, and a sweet-savory sauce combine for a meaty noodle dish that can be enhanced with fresh vegetables like mushrooms and bean sprouts if you have them. Soy sauce, mirin, and rice vinegar plus ginger and garlic make for a flavorful sauce, but to really heighten the soba noodles' flavor, we add a big sprinkle of the Japanese spice blend shichimi togarashi (or seven-spice blend) which adds peppery, aromatic, and citrusy notes. Reserve a portion of the starchy noodle cooking water to adjust the consistency of the sauce before serving.

2 tablespoons vegetable oil, divided

1½ pounds pork tenderloin, trimmed and sliced thin crosswise

6 garlic cloves, minced

1 tablespoon grated fresh ginger

½ cup soy sauce

¼ cup mirin

¼ cup rice vinegar

8 ounces soba noodles

Table salt for cooking noodles

4 scallions, sliced thin (optional)

2 tablespoons shichimi togarashi

1   Heat 1 tablespoon oil in 12-inch skillet over high heat until just smoking. Add pork in single layer and cook, without moving, for 1 minute. Stir and continue to cook until pork is lightly browned around edges and little pink remains, about 3 minutes; transfer to bowl.

2   Add remaining 1 tablespoon oil to now-empty skillet and heat over medium-high heat until shimmering. Add garlic and ginger and cook until fragrant, about 30 seconds. Stir in soy sauce, mirin, rice vinegar, and pork and cook for 1 minute. Remove from heat and cover to keep warm.

3   Meanwhile, bring 4 quarts water to boil in large pot. Add noodles and 1 tablespoon salt and cook, stirring often, until al dente. Reserve ½ cup cooking water, then drain noodles and return to pot. Stir in pork mixture and scallions, if using, and adjust consistency with reserved cooking water as needed. Sprinkle individual portions with shichimi togarashi. Serve.

PANTRY IMPROV

use what you have Use boneless chicken breasts or 1-inch tofu cubes instead of pork. Use 2 tablespoons toasted sesame seeds and 1 teaspoon red pepper flakes in place of shichimi togarashi.

level up In step 2, increase oil to 2 tablespoons; brown 10 ounces shiitake mushroom caps, quartered, for 4 minutes before adding the garlic and ginger. Add 3 cups bean sprouts to the pan along with the sauce ingredients.

spicy **peanut rice noodles**

SERVES 4 | TOTAL TIME: 35 MINUTES

why this recipe works For a quick bowl of noodles that hits every tastebud, we combine rice noodles with edamame (a freezer staple) and crunchy cabbage and drape it all with a rich peanut sauce that's a little spicy, a little sweet, and a little acidic. Once you've soaked the noodles, whisk together the peanut sauce (only six ingredients if you count the water) and cook the edamame until its just speckled with brown but still retains a crisp-tender texture. After removing the edamame from the pan, finish cooking the noodles in the same pan with the sauce and shredded cabbage, and a bit more water if needed, until they are perfectly tender and chewy. Finish with scallions and herbs, if you have them, and a squeeze of sriracha.

1 Bring 2 quarts water to boil in large pot. Remove from heat, add noodles, and stir to separate. Let noodles soak until soft and pliable but not fully tender, 8 to 10 minutes, stirring halfway through soaking. Drain noodles and rinse under cold running water until water runs clear, shaking to remove excess water.

2 Meanwhile, whisk peanut butter, lime juice, soy sauce, sriracha, sugar, and 3 tablespoons water together in bowl; set aside. Heat 4 teaspoons oil in 14-inch flat-bottomed wok or 12-inch nonstick skillet over medium heat until shimmering. Add edamame and cook until spotty brown, about 3 minutes; transfer to clean bowl. Heat remaining 4 teaspoons oil in now-empty skillet over medium heat until shimmering. Add noodles, cabbage, and peanut sauce and cook until noodles are well coated and tender, about 2 minutes, adjusting consistency with water, 1 tablespoon at a time, as needed.

3 Off heat, sprinkle noodles with edamame and basil, if using. Serve with lime wedges and drizzle with extra sriracha.

12 ounces (¼-inch-wide) rice noodles

½ cup creamy or chunky peanut butter

2 tablespoons plus 2 teaspoons lime juice, plus lime wedges for serving

2 tablespoons plus 2 teaspoons soy sauce

4 teaspoons sriracha, plus extra for serving

2 teaspoons packed brown sugar

2 tablespoons plus 2 teaspoons vegetable oil, divided

1 cup frozen edamame

2 cups (6 ounces) shredded red or green cabbage

¼ cup chopped fresh basil, cilantro, and/or scallions (optional)

PANTRY IMPROV

use what you have You can use sambal oelek or chili-garlic sauce in place of sriracha. Use coleslaw mix instead of shredded cabbage.

level up Bulk up the noodles with pan-seared tofu, shredded cooked chicken, or a roasted fish fillet.

gochujang–tahini noodles

SERVES 4 | TOTAL TIME: 35 MINUTES

why this recipe works This noodle bowl is as simple and craveable as it gets. A combination of gochujang, rice vinegar, and hoisin creates a pantry-friendly sauce that's a little zingy and a little sweet. The addition of tahini and sesame oil provides richness without overwhelming the noodles. We always have some packets of ramen hanging around, so we often reach for those to pair with this sauce, but other wheat noodles work equally well. No matter which noodles you choose, be sure to cook them until tender but still resilient and rinse them to remove excess starch. This ensures your noodles have the right amount of chew and don't stick together. Enjoy these noodles served simply or include as many or as few toppings as you like.

1 Whisk gochujang, vinegar, tahini, hoisin, soy sauce, oil, and garlic together in large bowl.

2 Meanwhile, bring 4 quarts water to boil in large pot. Add noodles and cook, stirring occasionally, until noodles are cooked through but still retain some chew. Drain noodles, rinse under warm water, and drain again. Toss noodles in bowl with sauce to thoroughly combine. Portion noodles into individual bowls and top with scallions, if using, and sesame seeds. Serve.

5 tablespoons gochujang paste

3 tablespoons unseasoned rice vinegar

2 tablespoons tahini

2 tablespoons hoisin sauce

2 tablespoons soy sauce

1 tablespoon toasted sesame oil

2 garlic cloves, minced

4 (3–ounce) packages ramen noodles, seasoning packets discarded

4 scallions, sliced thin (optional)

1 tablespoon toasted sesame seeds

PANTRY IMPROV

use what you have Any type of wheat noodle will work here; we have had good success with somen, soba, udon, and thin spaghetti. Crushed peanuts or sunflower seeds are a good swap for toasted sesame seeds.

level up Include a medley of raw or thawed frozen vegetables for crispness. Thinly sliced cucumber, snow or sugar snap peas, radishes, carrots, bell pepper, edamame, corn, and/or peas are all good options. We also enjoy the crunch and sweetness of pickled vegetables and Asian pear. Bulk up the noodles with pan-seared tofu, shredded cooked chicken, or a roasted fish fillet.

singapore noodles

SERVES 4 TO 6 | TOTAL TIME: 1¼ HOURS

- 8 ounces rice vermicelli
- ¼ cup plus 2 teaspoons vegetable oil, divided
- 2 tablespoons curry powder
- 2 large shallots, sliced thin
- 3 garlic cloves, minced
- 1 teaspoon grated fresh ginger
- ⅛ teaspoon cayenne pepper
- 2 tablespoons soy sauce
- 1 teaspoon sugar
- 12 ounces extra–large shrimp (21 to 25 per pound), peeled, deveined, tails removed, and cut into ½–inch pieces
- 4 large eggs, lightly beaten
- ⅔ cup chicken or vegetable broth
- 4 scallions, cut into ½–inch pieces (optional)
- 2 teaspoons lime juice, plus lime wedges for serving

why this recipe works Thin, resilient rice noodles, Chinese seasonings—garlic, ginger, soy sauce—and fragrant curry powder come together in this stir-fry which, despite its name, is native to Hong Kong. The curry powder (likely a British influence) lends a distinctive aroma balanced by a little sugar for sweetness and bright lime juice. Overall, the typical ingredient list is simple—dried noodles, a handful of seasonings, eggs, shrimp, and vegetables. Some versions add roast pork or ham. Some go heavier on veggies such as bean sprouts or cabbage; others focus on the noodles. Regardless of add-ins, this stir-fry isn't saucy; instead it's light, almost fluffy. To distribute the seasonings evenly and avoid grittiness, we bloom the curry powder and aromatics in oil, releasing fat-soluble flavor compounds while also keeping the dish from tasting too lean. We cook our shrimp and eggs in the pan in stages, adding a bit more oil with each to assure browning and avoid sticking. (If you want to add vegetables, see Pantry Improv.) Finally, we simmer our softened noodles with chicken broth until the liquid is absorbed before returning all the components to the pan and tossing to heat through.

1 Bring 4 quarts water to boil in large pot. Remove from heat, add noodles, and let sit, stirring occasionally, until soft and pliable but not fully tender. Drain noodles and rinse under cold running water until chilled. Drain noodles again and transfer to large bowl.

2 Meanwhile, add 3 tablespoons oil, curry powder, shallots, garlic, ginger, and cayenne to 14-inch flat-bottomed wok or 12-inch nonstick skillet and cook over medium-low heat, stirring occasionally, until fragrant, about 4 minutes. Add curry mixture, soy sauce, and sugar to bowl with noodles and toss until well combined; set aside.

3 Wipe pan clean with paper towels. Heat 2 teaspoons oil in now-empty pan over medium-high heat until just smoking. Add shrimp and increase heat to high. Cook, tossing shrimp slowly but constantly, until just opaque, about 2 minutes; transfer to medium bowl.

4   Heat remaining 1 tablespoon oil in now-empty pan over high heat until shimmering. Add eggs and scramble quickly using rubber spatula. Continue to cook, scraping slowly but constantly along bottom and sides of pan, until eggs just form cohesive mass, 15 to 30 seconds (eggs will not be completely dry). Transfer to bowl with shrimp and break up any large curds.

5   Return pan to high heat, add broth, and bring to simmer. Add noodles and cook, tossing slowly but constantly, until liquid is absorbed, about 2 minutes. Add shrimp mixture and scallions, if using, and cook, tossing slowly but constantly, until mixture is thoroughly combined and heated through, about 2 minutes. Off heat, add lime juice and toss to combine. Serve, passing lime wedges separately.

PANTRY IMPROV

use what you have You can use chicken, tofu, pork, or ham instead of some or all of the shrimp.

level up Add vegetables: Add 1 sliced bell pepper when cooking the shrimp. Add 1 cup sliced cabbage before cooking shrimp. Stir 4 ounces (2 cups) bean sprouts into the noodles with the shrimp mixture and scallions.

pad thai

SERVES 4 | TOTAL TIME: 1 HOUR

8 ounces (¼-inch-wide) rice noodles

2 tablespoons plus 2 teaspoons vegetable oil, divided

½ teaspoon table salt

¼ teaspoon plus 3 tablespoons sugar, divided

4 ounces daikon radish, peeled and cut into 1½-inch-long matchsticks

4 scallions, white and light green parts minced, dark green parts cut into 1-inch lengths (optional)

2 tablespoons dried shrimp (optional)

1 garlic clove, minced

¼ cup fish sauce

3 tablespoons tamarind juice concentrate

2 teaspoons distilled white vinegar

1–3 teaspoons sriracha, plus extra for serving

4 large eggs, lightly beaten

¼ cup dry-roasted peanuts, chopped coarse

Lime wedges

why this recipe works Pad thai, the famous noodle dish and street food, is built on Thai pantry staples such as rice noodles, vinegar, fish sauce, and tamarind. With a well-stocked pantry, this stir-fry comes together at a moment's notice and accommodates whatever protein you choose to add, from tofu and shrimp to chicken or beef. To make it, we soak rice noodles in boiling water to soften them until pliable but not fully tender, as they will continue to soften during stir-frying. While they soak, we mix our sauce, a sweet, salty, sour, and hot blend of sugar, fish sauce, tamarind juice concentrate, vinegar, and sriracha. Softly scrambled eggs bulk up the dish. Peanuts add crunch, as do radishes, which we quick-pickle for just 15 minutes. Dried shrimp (they'll last forever in your pantry) bring greater umami depth, but it's fine to leave them out if you don't have them. For a spicier dish, use the larger amount of sriracha. This dish progresses quickly after step 2; it's important that your ingredients are ready to go by then.

1   Bring 4 quarts water to boil in large pot. Remove from heat, add noodles, and let sit, stirring occasionally, until soft and pliable but not fully tender. Drain noodles and rinse under cold running water until chilled. Drain noodles well again and toss with 2 teaspoons oil; set aside.

2   Combine ¼ cup water, salt, and ¼ teaspoon sugar in small bowl. Microwave until steaming, about 30 seconds. Add radishes and let sit for 15 minutes. Drain and set aside.

3   Combine minced scallions and dried shrimp, if using, 1 tablespoon oil, and garlic in second small bowl; set aside. Whisk fish sauce, tamarind juice concentrate, vinegar, sriracha, and remaining 3 tablespoons sugar in third small bowl until sugar has dissolved; set aside.

4   Heat remaining 1 tablespoon oil in 14-inch flat-bottomed wok or 12-inch nonstick skillet over medium-high heat until shimmering. Add eggs and scramble quickly using rubber spatula. Continue to cook, scraping slowly but constantly along bottom and sides of pan, until eggs just form cohesive mass, 15 to 30 seconds (eggs will not be completely dry). Transfer to bowl and break up any large curds.

5 Return now-empty pan to medium heat. Add dried shrimp mixture and cook, mashing mixture into pan, until fragrant, about 30 seconds. Add reserved noodles, reserved fish sauce mixture, and eggs and cook, tossing slowly but constantly, until mixture is thoroughly combined and noodles are well coated and tender, 2 to 4 minutes. Off heat, fold in radishes and scallion greens, if using. Sprinkle with peanuts. Serve with lime wedges, passing extra sriracha separately.

PANTRY IMPROV

use what you have If you don't have tamarind juice concentrate, substitute a combination of 1½ tablespoons of lime juice and 1½ tablespoons of water; omit the lime wedges. Any radishes can be used in place of the daikon. A minced shallot will work in place of scallions. You can use sambal oelek or chili-garlic sauce in place of sriracha.

level up Add a protein: Cook up to 12 ounces of shrimp; thinly sliced chicken breast, flank steak, or pork tenderloin; or 1-inch cubes of firm tofu in 2 teaspoons hot oil before cooking the eggs; transfer to a bowl and add back to the pan with the noodles in step 5. Add bean sprouts to the noodles with the pickled radishes.

vegetable lo mein

SERVES 4 | TOTAL TIME: 45 MINUTES

sauce

- ½ cup vegetable or chicken broth
- 3 tablespoons soy sauce
- 2 tablespoons Shaoxing wine or dry sherry
- 2 tablespoons oyster sauce
- 2 tablespoons hoisin sauce
- 1 teaspoon toasted sesame oil
- 1 teaspoon cornstarch
- ⅛ teaspoon five–spice powder

stir–fry

- 8 ounces dried lo mein noodles
- 2 tablespoons vegetable oil, divided
- 2 garlic cloves, minced
- 2 teaspoons grated fresh ginger
- 1 onion, halved and sliced ½ inch thick
- ½ small head green cabbage, halved, cored, and sliced ½ inch thick (3 cups)
- 3 carrots, peeled and sliced on bias ⅛ inch thick

why this recipe works Chewy Chinese noodles are the star of lo mein, which may get its name from the Cantonese "lou minh," meaning "stirred noodles." After being boiled, the fresh or dried noodles are stir-fried with a sauce and then tossed with vegetables or meat—or both. Part of the fun of lo mein is that it's endlessly customizable with mix-ins. Here we offer not only ideas for improvising with different vegetables and meats you may have on hand, but give four different sauce options. Whether in a flat-bottom wok or a skillet, we cook our vegetables first and then incorporate aromatic garlic and ginger to cook for just 30 seconds. As for the noodles, we boil them until almost tender, drain them, and then rinse them of excess starch before tossing them into the stir-fry—along with the sauce—at the end of cooking. This allows the noodles to soak up the sauce's flavor without becoming mushy. This dish progresses quickly, so it's important that all of your ingredients are ready to go. You will need a 14-inch flat-bottomed wok or 12-inch nonstick skillet for this recipe.

1 for the sauce Whisk all ingredients together in bowl.

2 for the stir-fry Bring 4 quarts water to boil in large pot. Add noodles and cook, stirring often, until almost tender (center should still be firm, with slightly opaque dot). Drain noodles and rinse under cold running water until chilled. Drain noodles again and set aside.

3 Combine 1 tablespoon oil, garlic, and ginger in small bowl. Heat remaining 1 tablespoon vegetable oil in 14-inch flat-bottomed wok or 12-inch nonstick skillet over medium-high heat until just smoking. Add onion and increase heat to high. Cook, tossing slowly but constantly, until onion begins to soften, 1 to 2 minutes. Add cabbage and carrots and cook until vegetables are crisp-tender, 4 to 6 minutes. Push vegetables to 1 side of pan. Add garlic mixture to clearing and cook, mashing mixture into pan, until fragrant, about 30 seconds. Stir garlic mixture into vegetables.

4 Whisk sauce mixture to recombine. Return pan to medium heat. Add sauce and reserved noodles and increase heat to high. Cook, tossing slowly but constantly, until noodles and vegetables are heated through, about 2 minutes. Serve.

VARIATIONS

vegetable lo mein with hot-and-sour sauce
Omit five-spice powder. Whisk 2 tablespoons distilled white vinegar and 1 tablespoon chili-garlic sauce or sriracha into sauce.

vegetable lo mein with garlic-basil sauce
Omit five-spice powder. Whisk ¼ cup chopped fresh basil and 4 minced garlic cloves into sauce.

vegetable lo mein with sesame sauce
Omit five-spice powder. Increase sesame oil to 1 tablespoon. Whisk 1 tablespoon toasted sesame seeds and 1 teaspoon chili-garlic sauce or sriracha into sauce.

biang biang mian

SERVES 4 | TOTAL TIME: 1¼ HOURS, PLUS 12 HOURS RESTING

dough

2⅓   cups (12¾ ounces) bread flour

¾   teaspoon table salt, plus salt for cooking noodles

1   cup water

1   tablespoon vegetable oil

chili oil vinaigrette

10–20   dried Thai bird chiles, ground fine

½   cup vegetable oil

2   garlic cloves, sliced thin

1   (1-inch) piece fresh ginger, peeled and sliced thin

1   tablespoon Sichuan peppercorns

½   cinnamon stick

1   star anise pod

2   tablespoons soy sauce

2   tablespoons Chinese black vinegar

1   tablespoon toasted sesame oil

1   teaspoon sugar

why this recipe works If you have bread flour on hand then you can make some of the most satisfyingly chewy noodles you'll ever eat: Biang biang noodles, or hand-pulled noodles, a popular dish from the Shaanxi province of China, are handmade, flat, belt-like noodles often served with lots of hot peppers and chili oil. The name describes the sound made when the noodles are slapped against a table to stretch them. To achieve the perfect chew and texture, we use high-protein bread flour and an extended resting time, which allows the strong gluten network to relax and makes the stretching process easier. Once you master this technique, the noodles are a breeze to make, and the possibilities for noodle dishes are virtually endless. Here we dress the noodles in a simple Sichuan-inspired chili oil vinaigrette. The chiles used here are pretty spicy; scale back accordingly if desired. It is critical to rest the dough for at least 12 hours (and up to 48 hours). Note that after 24 hours the surface of the dough may develop small black speckles. This oxidation has no impact on flavor or safety.

1 **for the dough** Whisk flour and salt together in bowl of stand mixer. Add water and oil. Fit stand mixer with dough hook and mix on low speed until all flour is moistened, 1 to 2 minutes. Increase speed to medium and knead until dough is smooth and satiny, 10 to 12 minutes. (Alternatively, mix dough in food processor.) Transfer dough to counter, knead for 30 seconds, and shape into 9-inch log. Wrap log in plastic wrap and refrigerate for at least 12 hours or up to 48 hours.

2 **for the chili oil vinaigrette** Place bird chiles in large bowl and set fine-mesh strainer on top; set aside. Add vegetable oil, garlic, ginger, peppercorns, cinnamon stick, and star anise to small saucepan and cook over medium-high heat until sizzling. Reduce heat to low and gently simmer until garlic and ginger are lightly browned, 10 to 12 minutes. Pour oil mixture through strainer into bowl with chiles; discard solids in strainer. Stir chili oil to combine and let cool for 5 minutes. Stir in soy sauce, vinegar, sesame oil, and sugar until combined; set aside. (Vinaigrette can be refrigerated for up to 4 days; bring to room temperature and whisk to recombine before using.)

3 Unwrap dough, transfer to lightly oiled counter, and, using bench scraper or knife, divide into 6 equal pieces (each 1½ inches wide). Cover with plastic wrap and let rest for 20 minutes.

4 Oil both sides of 1 piece of dough and flatten into 7 by 3-inch rectangle, with long side parallel to edge of counter. Gently grasp each short end of dough. Stretch dough and slap against counter until noodle is 32 to 36 inches long (noodle will be between 1/16 and 1/8 inch thick). (If dough is hard to stretch to this length or is snapping back significantly, set aside on counter and let rest for 10 minutes. Meanwhile, continue stretching remaining pieces of dough.)

5 Place noodle on counter. Pinch center of noodle with forefinger and thumb of each hand and pull apart with even pressure in both directions to rip seam in middle of noodle and create 1 continuous loop. Cut loop to create 2 equal-length noodles. Set aside noodles on lightly oiled counter (do not let noodles touch) and cover with plastic. Repeat stretching and cutting with remaining pieces of dough.

6 Meanwhile, bring 4 quarts water to boil in large pot. Add 1 tablespoon salt and half of noodles and cook, stirring occasionally, until noodles float and turn chewy-tender, 45 to 60 seconds. Transfer noodles to bowl with chili vinaigrette and toss to combine. Return water to boil and repeat with remaining noodles. Transfer to serving platter. Serve.

PANTRY IMPROV

use what you have Use balsamic vinegar in place of Chinese black vinegar. Use 1 pound fresh Chinese wheat noodles, lo mein, or ramen in place of the hand-pulled noodles. You can use other small dried chiles in place of the dried Thai bird chiles.

level up Top with coarsely chopped cilantro sprigs and thinly sliced scallions.

grains
& beans

grain bowls

One of our favorite kinds of pantry meal is the freestyle grain bowl. Start by cooking your grain of choice. Top the grain with little bits of protein, some vegetables, pickles, a drizzle of sauce, and a crunchy element for a variety of flavors and textures. The combinations listed here show just how versatile bowls can be, so feel free to use what you have. Season each bowl with salt and pepper to taste.

COOKING GRAINS

(1 cup dry grains = 2½ cups cooked; 1½ cups dry grains = 4 cups cooked)
Bring 4 quarts water to boil in large pot and add 1 teaspoon table salt.
Stir in grains and cook until tender, following timing below. Drain well.
Refrigerate cooled grains for up to 3 days.

pearl barley	20 to 40 minutes	**wild rice**	35 to 40 minutes
farro	15 to 30 minutes	**wheat berries**	60 to 70 minutes
freekeh	30 to 45 minutes	**oat berries**	45 to 50 minutes
long-grain white rice	10 to 15 minutes	**rye berries**	50 to 70 minutes
long-grain brown rice	25 to 30 minutes		

- Brown rice, shredded chicken, celery, fried eggs (page 275), and Chili Crisp (page 392)

- Farro, flaked smoked trout or mackerel, orange segments, Make-Ahead Sherry-Shallot Vinaigrette (page 395), and capers

- Wild rice, thawed frozen corn, black beans, Quick Sweet and Spicy Pickled Red Onions (page 404), Avocado-Lime Yogurt Sauce (page 398), and crumbled cotija

- White rice, sliced steak, carrots, thawed frozen spinach, Perfect Fried Eggs (page 275), and kimchi with juice

- Brown rice, cooked ground pork, thawed frozen green beans, sliced water chestnuts, and Sichuan Chili Oil (page 390)

- Wheat berries, flaked canned salmon, celery, sun-dried tomatoes, and All-Purpose Herb Sauce (page 396)

- Freekeh, roasted sweet potatoes, thawed frozen spinach, Make-Ahead Vinaigrette (page 395), and Spiced Roasted Chickpeas (page 51)

- Farro, roasted butternut squash, crumbled blue cheese, Yogurt Sauce (page 396), and toasted pepitas

- White rice, tofu, thawed frozen edamame, shredded cabbage, Peanut-Sesame Sauce (page 399), and scallions

- Wild rice, sausage, Quick Fennel Pickles (page 404), dried fruit, shaved Manchego, olive oil, and pomegranate molasses

- White rice, thawed frozen asparagus, cherry tomatoes, Quick Carrot Pickles (page 404), and Pantry Pesto (page 137)

- Couscous, cannellini beans, Perfect Poached Eggs (page 275), tomato sauce, and crumbled feta

- Freekeh, cooked shrimp, thawed frozen corn, shredded cheddar, and Chili-Coriander Sauce (page 396)

- Barley, seared tofu, roasted cauliflower, Peanut-Sesame Sauce (page 399), and toasted nuts

- Farro, shredded chicken, apples, thawed frozen spinach, Make-Ahead Vinaigrette (page 395), and Spiced Seeds (page 386)

- Wheat berries, flaked canned salmon, thawed frozen green beans, Yogurt Sauce (page 396), and fresh herbs

grain salad with dried fruit, cheese, and nuts

SERVES 4 | TOTAL TIME: 15 MINUTES

3 tablespoons extra-virgin olive oil

2 tablespoons red wine vinegar

1 small shallot, minced

½ teaspoon table salt

½ teaspoon pepper

2½ cups cooked grains such as wheat berries or farro

1 cup chopped radicchio

1 cup loosely packed fresh parsley leaves (optional)

½ cup pecans or walnuts, toasted and chopped coarse, divided

¼ cup dried cherries or cranberries

1 ounce blue cheese, crumbled (¼ cup)

why this recipe works A pot of tender-chewy grains is the foundation for an abundance of dishes; we like to keep a stash on hand for adding to soups and sides and whipping up salads. A grain salad can be made with any grain, of course, but it's a nice way to use the heartiest grains (such as wheat berries, farro, and oat berries) that may receive less regular kitchen attention. Their chewy texture contrasts well with other salad elements. Those elements might include something creamy, something nutty, something fruity, and something crisp and/or leafy—a formula that pretty much ensures a salad with plenty of flavor and textural interest. Here we use blue cheese, toasted pecans, dried cherries, parsley, and radicchio, which, like cabbage, keeps for a while in your crisper. Let precooked grains come to room temperature before using. To cook grains, see page 173 for our cooking chart.

Whisk oil, vinegar, shallot, salt, and pepper together in large bowl. Add wheat berries; radicchio; parsley, if using; half of pecans; and cherries and toss to combine. Season with salt and pepper to taste. Transfer to serving bowl and sprinkle with blue cheese and remaining pecans. Serve.

PANTRY IMPROV

use what you have Any cooked grain works: Try rye berries, oat berries, freekeh, or wild rice. Substitute goat cheese or any soft, crumbled cheese for the blue cheese. Any nut or combination of nuts or seeds works here. Vary the parsley with fresh baby spinach, cilantro, or baby arugula. Use other bitter greens such as endive in place of the radicchio, or use celery. White wine or sherry vinegar works instead of the red wine vinegar.

level up Add fresh fruit such as orange segments or apple slices in addition to or instead of the cherries.

barley salad with celery and miso dressing

SERVES 4 | TOTAL TIME: 20 MINUTES

why this recipe works This grain salad is sure to perk up your senses, as it's full of crunchy vegetables; nutty, chewy barley; and a savory-sweet miso dressing. Most of the barley we buy has been pearled, meaning that part of its hull has been removed. This helps it cook faster but also means it releases a lot of starch during cooking that can cause clumping. Boiling it in a large volume of water removes the sticky starch for pleasing, distinct grains. Let the barley come to room temperature before tossing it with the dressing. Adjust the amount of pepper flakes to suit your taste.

Whisk vinegar, miso, soy sauce, sesame oil, vegetable oil, ginger, garlic, sugar, and pepper flakes together in large bowl. Add barley to bowl with dressing and toss to coat. Add celery; carrot; and cilantro, if using, and stir to combine. Season with salt and pepper to taste. Serve.

PANTRY IMPROV

use what you have Any grain can be substituted for the barley (see the grain cooking chart page 173). If you don't have seasoned rice vinegar, you can make your own (see page 404).

level up Sprinkle with chopped nuts or Crispy Shallots (page 388). To make the salad heartier, add up to 1 cup white beans, seared tofu, or chopped, cooked chicken or shrimp.

1½ tablespoons seasoned rice vinegar

1½ teaspoons white or red miso

1½ teaspoons soy sauce

1½ teaspoons toasted sesame oil

1½ teaspoons vegetable oil

1 teaspoon grated fresh ginger

1 garlic clove, minced

½ teaspoon packed brown sugar

¼ teaspoon red pepper flakes

2 cups cooked pearl barley (page 173)

1 celery rib, sliced thin on bias

1 carrot, peeled and grated

¼ cup minced fresh cilantro (optional)

simple **fried rice**

SERVES 4 | TOTAL TIME: 30 MINUTES

3 large eggs

1½ teaspoons kosher salt, divided

2 tablespoons vegetable oil, divided

1 carrot, peeled and cut into
¼–inch pieces

4 ounces Spam or ham steak,
cut into ½–inch pieces (¾ cup)

4 scallions, white and green parts
separated and sliced

4 cups cooked jasmine rice or
long–grain white rice,
room temperature

¼ teaspoon pepper

½ cup frozen peas

PANTRY IMPROV

use what you have You can use
any proteins and vegetables in this
recipe as long as you keep to the
ratio of roughly 1 part chopped
proteins and vegetables to 2½ parts
rice so that the finished product is
appropriately grain-heavy.

level up Top with Chili Crisp
(page 392) or quick pickled
vegetables (page 404).

---

why this recipe works The perfect leftovers dish of stir-fried rice made with yesterday's rice, simple seasonings, and modest mix-ins makes for an incredibly satisfying meal. Day-old rice works best; the stiff, dry clumps relax during cooking into tender-firm, distinct grains and can be pushed around without turning mushy. This fried rice needs no ginger or garlic, spices, or sauce. It's really all about the rice, so don't overdo it with mix-ins. Cooking sliced scallion whites in oil infuses the rice with subtle oniony savoriness. To make fluffy, tender pockets of scrambled eggs, we pour beaten eggs into smoking-hot oil; the eggs puff as their water rapidly turns to steam. If you don't have day-old rice, cook your rice 2 hours ahead, spread it on a rimmed baking sheet, and let it cool completely before chilling it for 30 minutes. All rice should be roughly room temperature when you stir-fry. You will need a 14-inch flat-bottomed wok or a 12-inch nonstick skillet for this recipe. If using a wok, make sure that it is well seasoned so that the rice does not stick.

1   Beat eggs and ¼ teaspoon salt in bowl until well combined. Heat 2 teaspoons oil in 14-inch flat-bottomed wok or 12-inch carbon-steel or cast-iron skillet over medium-high heat until just smoking. Add eggs and cook, stirring frequently, until very little liquid egg remains, 30 to 60 seconds. Transfer to large plate.

2   Add 1 teaspoon oil to now-empty pan and reduce heat to medium. Add carrot and ¼ teaspoon salt and cook, stirring frequently, until just beginning to brown, 2 to 4 minutes. Add Spam and cook, stirring frequently, until Spam is warmed through, 1 to 2 minutes. Transfer to plate with eggs.

3   Add scallion whites and remaining 1 tablespoon oil to now-empty pan. Cook, stirring constantly, until fragrant, about 1 minute. Add rice and stir until combined. (It's OK if some clumps of rice remain.) Spread into even layer. Sprinkle pepper and remaining 1 teaspoon salt evenly over rice. Continue to cook, stirring frequently and pressing on rice with spatula to break up clumps, until grains are separate and heated through, 2 to 5 minutes. Add peas, egg mixture, and scallion greens and cook, stirring frequently and using edge of spatula to break eggs into small pieces, until peas are warmed through, about 2 minutes. Serve.

VARIATIONS

broccoli, bean sprout, and ham fried rice

Substitute chopped broccoli for carrot, ¾ cup cubed ham steak or char siu for Spam, and bean sprouts for peas.

mushroom, chicken, and napa cabbage fried rice

Substitute chopped mushrooms for carrots, ¾ cup shredded, cooked chicken for Spam, and thinly sliced napa cabbage for peas.

three pea fried rice

Omit Spam. Substitute sliced sugar snap peas for carrots and decrease cooking time to 1 to 2 minutes. Add 1 cup pea sprouts or microgreens in with peas.

kimchi bokkeumbap

SERVES 4 | TOTAL TIME: 1 HOUR, PLUS 30 MINUTES COOLING

- 1 (8–inch square) sheet gim
- 2 tablespoons vegetable oil, divided
- 4 ounces Spam or ham steak, cut into ¼–inch pieces (¾ cup)
- 1 large onion, chopped
- 6 scallions, white and green parts separated and sliced thin on bias
- 1¼ cups cabbage kimchi, drained with ¼ cup juice reserved, cut into ¼–inch strips
- ¼ cup water
- 4 teaspoons soy sauce
- 4 teaspoons gochujang paste
- ½ teaspoon pepper
- 3 cups cooked short–grain white rice, room temperature
- 4 teaspoons toasted sesame oil
- 1 tablespoon sesame seeds, toasted

why this recipe works Kimchi fried rice is pantry cooking on the fly that unites two Korean staples: At its core is leftover cooked rice stir-fried with cabbage kimchi. But from there it becomes unscripted and personal, since the umami-charged base is just the thing to capture refrigerator odds and ends. You might find it bulked up with ham, Spam, sausage, or seafood; seasoned with gochujang, plum extract, or oyster sauce; dolloped with mayonnaise; topped with crumbled gim; or bundled in an omelet. Day-old rice works best; in a pinch, cook your rice 2 hours ahead, spread it on a rimmed baking sheet, and let it cool completely before chilling it for 30 minutes. Rice should be roughly room temperature when you stir-fry. You'll need at least a 16-ounce jar of kimchi; if it doesn't yield ¼ cup of juice, make up the difference with water. If using soft, well-aged kimchi, omit the water and reduce the cooking time at the end of step 2 to 2 minutes. You will need a 14-inch flat-bottomed wok or a 12-inch nonstick skillet. If using a wok, make sure that it is well seasoned so that the rice does not stick.

1   Grip gim with tongs and hold 2 inches above low flame on gas burner. Toast gim, turning every 3 to 5 seconds, until gim is aromatic and shrinks slightly, about 20 seconds. (If you do not have a gas stove, toast gim on rimmed baking sheet in 275-degree oven until gim is aromatic and shrinks slightly, 20 to 25 minutes, flipping gim halfway through toasting.) Using kitchen shears, cut gim into four 2-inch-wide strips. Stack strips and cut crosswise into thin strips.

2   Heat 1 tablespoon vegetable oil in 14-inch flat-bottomed wok or 12-inch nonstick skillet over medium-high heat until shimmering. Add Spam, onion, and scallion whites and cook, stirring frequently, until onion is softened and Spam is beginning to brown at edges, 6 to 8 minutes. Stir in kimchi and reserved juice, water, soy sauce, gochujang, and pepper. Cook, stirring occasionally, until kimchi turns soft and translucent, 4 to 6 minutes.

3   Add rice; reduce heat to medium-low; and cook, stirring and folding constantly until mixture is evenly coated, about 3 minutes. Stir in sesame oil and remaining 1 tablespoon vegetable oil. Increase heat to medium-high and cook, stirring occasionally, until mixture begins to stick to skillet, about 4 minutes. Transfer to serving bowl. Sprinkle with sesame seeds, scallion greens, and gim and serve.

PANTRY IMPROV

use what you have Plain pretoasted seaweed snacks can be substituted for the gim; omit toasting. Substitute plum extract or oyster sauce for the gochujang paste. Use cooked Chinese sausage instead of Spam. Try ¼ cup minced shallot in place of the scallion whites.

level up Top each portion with a fried or poached egg. Add cooked fresh, tinned, or smoked seafood. Top the rice with shredded cheese and cover the skillet until melted.

nasi goreng

SERVES 4 | TOTAL TIME: 1¼ HOURS

7 large shallots, peeled (4 whole, 3 sliced thin)

4 large garlic cloves, peeled

3 tablespoons kecap manis

2 tablespoons fish sauce

2–4 teaspoons sambal oelek or sriracha

¼ teaspoon table salt

4 large eggs

½ cup vegetable oil

4 cups cooked long–grain white rice, room temperature

4 large scallions, sliced thin (optional)

Lime wedges

why this recipe works Indonesia's nasi goreng (literally "fried rice") packs an umami punch. It stir-fries leftover rice with sambal, a sweet soy sauce called kecap manis, and shrimp paste. It's all topped with tender eggs and crispy shallots. The resulting dish boasts great complexity, and while you can add meat, seafood, or vegetables, as some do, it's substantial as is. While sambals are often made from scratch with fresh chiles and aromatics, we rely on a pantry-friendly staple, sambal oelek, and we substitute fish sauce for shrimp paste. If you don't have day-old rice, you can cook rice 2 hours ahead, spread it on a rimmed baking sheet, and let it cool completely before chilling it for 30 minutes. Rice should be roughly room temperature when you stir-fry. You will need a 14-inch flat-bottomed wok or a 12-inch nonstick skillet with a tight-fitting lid. If using a wok, make sure that it is well seasoned so that the rice does not stick. If you like, serve with traditional accompaniments of sliced cucumber and tomato wedges.

1 Pulse whole shallots and garlic in food processor until coarse paste forms, about 15 pulses, scraping down sides of bowl as needed; transfer to small bowl and set aside. Whisk kecap manis, fish sauce, and sambal oelek together in second small bowl; set aside. Whisk eggs and salt together in separate bowl; set aside.

2 Add oil and sliced shallots to 14-inch flat-bottomed wok or 12-inch nonstick skillet and cook over medium heat, stirring constantly, until shallots are golden and crispy, 5 to 8 minutes. Using slotted spoon, transfer shallots to paper towel–lined plate and season with salt to taste. Pour off and reserve oil. Wipe pan clean with paper towels.

3 Heat 1 teaspoon reserved oil in now-empty pan over medium heat until shimmering. Using paper towel, wipe out pan, leaving thin film of oil on bottom and sides. Add half of egg mixture and gently tilt and shake pan until mixture forms even 10-inch round omelet (if using wok, egg will go up sides of pan). Cover and cook until bottom of omelet is spotty brown and top is just set, about 30 seconds. Loosen edges of omelet with rubber spatula and slide onto cutting board. Gently roll omelet into tight log. Cut log crosswise into 1-inch segments (leaving segments rolled). Repeat with 1 teaspoon reserved oil and remaining egg mixture.

4   Break up large clumps of rice with your fingers. Heat 3 tablespoons reserved oil in now-empty pan over medium heat until shimmering. Add shallot-garlic mixture and cook, mashing mixture into pan, until golden, 3 to 5 minutes. Add rice and kecap manis mixture and cook, tossing constantly, until mixture is evenly coated, about 3 minutes. Increase heat to medium-high and cook, tossing occasionally, until mixture is heated through, about 4 minutes. Off heat, stir in scallions, if using. Garnish with egg segments and crispy shallots. Serve with lime wedges.

congee

SERVES 4 | TOTAL TIME: 1 HOUR

why this recipe works Savory, warming rice porridge is a welcome breakfast throughout China and neighboring countries. But it's also lunchtime fare and a popular late-night snack. In the style of congee given here, the pantry-friendly toppings are more than just accents; they're the focal point. They can be as simple as peanuts, soy sauce, and chili oil, or as substantial as stir-fried meat, eggs, or fried shallots. The key is to mix textures and flavors, and to be creative. To create a silky, viscous porridge that can suspend our toppings, we employ a 13:1 ratio of liquid to rice, and a vigorous simmer that breaks down the grains more rapidly than the typical 90-minute gentle simmer. To prevent the congee from boiling over, we rinse excess starch from the rice and wedge a wooden spoon between the lid and the side of the pot, which gives the water bubbles a chance to escape.

¾ cup long-grain white rice or jasmine rice

1 cup vegetable or chicken broth

¾ teaspoon table salt

Dry-roasted peanuts, chopped coarse

Chili oil

Soy sauce

Chinese black vinegar

1 Place rice in fine-mesh strainer and rinse under cold running water until water runs clear. Drain well and transfer to Dutch oven. Add broth, salt, and 9 cups water and bring to boil over high heat. Reduce heat to maintain vigorous simmer. Cover pot, tucking wooden spoon horizontally between pot and lid to hold lid ajar. Cook, stirring occasionally, until mixture is thickened, glossy, and reduced by half, 45 to 50 minutes.

2 Serve congee in bowls, passing peanuts, chili oil, soy sauce, and vinegar separately.

TOPPING
stir-fried ground pork

Toss 8 ounces ground pork, 1 tablespoon water, ¼ teaspoon table salt, and ⅛ teaspoon baking soda in bowl until thoroughly combined. Add 1 minced garlic clove, 1 teaspoon minced fresh ginger, 1 teaspoon soy sauce, 1 teaspoon Shaoxing wine, 1 teaspoon cornstarch, ½ teaspoon sugar, and ¼ teaspoon white pepper and toss until thoroughly combined. Heat 1 teaspoon vegetable oil in 12-inch nonstick skillet over medium-high heat until just smoking. Add pork mixture and cook, breaking meat into ¼-inch pieces with wooden spoon, until pork is no longer pink and just beginning to brown.

> **PANTRY IMPROV**
>
> **use what you have** You can substitute a 2:1 ratio of rice vinegar and balsamic vinegar for the Chinese black vinegar here.
>
> **level up** For freshness, top with sliced scallions and cilantro leaves. Top with Crispy Shallots (page 388). For a more substantial congee, top with Stir-Fried Ground Pork or Soft-Cooked Eggs (page 274).

no-fuss **parmesan polenta**

SERVES 4 | TOTAL TIME: 1¼ HOURS

why this recipe works A bowl of creamy polenta will transform anything you add to it into comfort food: roasted squash or cabbage, broiled broccoli rabe or radicchio, sautéed mushrooms or eggplant; the list goes on. This recipe makes it easier to enjoy polenta any way you please by eliminating the time-consuming step of stirring for upwards of an hour for creamy results. Adding a pinch of baking soda is the key: It softens the cornmeal's endosperm, which cuts down on the cooking time and encourages the granules to release their starch for a silky consistency. Coarse-ground degerminated cornmeal such as yellow grits (with grains the size of couscous) works best in this recipe. Avoid instant and quick-cooking products, as well as whole grain, stone-ground, and regular cornmeal. If the polenta bubbles or sputters even slightly after the first 10 minutes, the heat is too high and you may need to move the saucepan to a smaller burner.

1 Bring water to boil in heavy-bottomed large saucepan over medium-high heat. Stir in salt and baking soda. Slowly pour cornmeal into water in steady stream while stirring back and forth with wooden spoon or rubber spatula. Bring mixture to boil, stirring constantly, about 1 minute. Reduce heat to lowest possible setting and cover.

2 After 5 minutes, whisk polenta to smooth out any lumps, about 15 seconds. (Make sure to scrape sides and bottom of saucepan.) Cover and continue to cook, without stirring, until grains of polenta are tender but slightly al dente, about 25 minutes. (Polenta should be loose and barely hold its shape; it will continue to thicken as it cools.)

3 Remove from heat, stir in Parmesan and butter, and season with pepper to taste. Let stand, covered, for 5 minutes. Serve, drizzling each portion with oil and passing extra Parmesan separately. (Polenta can be refrigerated for up to 2 days.)

7½ cups water

1½ teaspoons table salt

     Pinch baking soda

1½ cups coarse-ground cornmeal

4 ounces Parmesan cheese, grated (2 cups), plus extra for serving

2 tablespoons unsalted butter

   Extra-virgin olive oil for drizzling

PANTRY IMPROV

use what you have You can use just about any hard cheese, such as Pecorino Romano, aged Manchego, or aged Gouda, in place of the Parmesan.

level up Sprinkle with fresh herbs, toasted sliced almonds or pine nuts, and/or chopped sun-dried tomatoes. Drizzle with balsamic vinegar. For a heartier meal, serve with a wedge of rich cheese or top with roasted, sautéed, or grilled vegetables; a fried egg; cooked meat; or Simple (Any) Meat Sauce (page 139).

savory oatmeal with corn, jalapeños, and cotija

SERVES 4 | TOTAL COOK TIME: 35 MINUTES, PLUS 12 HOURS SOAKING

why this recipe works Leave the cinnamon on the shelf: This cheesy take on steel-cut oats (a pantry hero) taps into the savory side of the porridge. If you've never served savory oatmeal, doing so effectively doubles your options for enjoying the wholesome grain. To keep breakfast (or dinner, for that matter) fast, we turn to our 10-minute overnight method for preparing the oats. We stir them into boiling water the night before so the grains can hydrate and soften; the oats then need only 4 to 6 minutes of simmering the next day to become thick and creamy. Chili powder infuses the oats with smoky, spicy flavor. Meanwhile, we quickly prepare our mix-ins, browning frozen corn and adding in cotija cheese and pickled jalapeños (with a splash of brine). We stir everything together and let it sit for 5 minutes so the oats can reach the ideal consistency before topping with a dollop of jarred salsa. The oatmeal will continue to thicken as it cools. If you prefer a looser consistency, thin the oatmeal with boiling water. There's no need to thaw the corn before cooking.

1 Bring water to boil in large saucepan over high heat. Remove pan from heat; stir in oats and salt. Cover pan and let stand overnight.

2 Stir broth and chili powder into oats and bring to boil over medium-high heat. Reduce heat to medium and cook, stirring occasionally, until oats are softened but still retain some chew and mixture thickens and resembles warm pudding, 4 to 6 minutes.

3 While oats cook, heat oil in 10-inch skillet over medium-high heat until shimmering. Add corn and cook, stirring frequently, until starting to brown and pop, about 4 minutes. Reduce heat to low, add shallot, and cook, stirring constantly, until shallot is slightly softened, about 1 minute. Stir corn mixture, two-thirds of cotija, and jalapeños and brine into oats. Let stand for 5 minutes. Season with salt and pepper to taste. Serve, topping each portion with salsa and remaining cotija.

3 cups water

1 cup steel-cut oats

¼ teaspoon table salt

1 cup chicken or vegetable broth

2 teaspoons chili powder

2 teaspoons vegetable oil

1 cup frozen corn

1 shallot, chopped fine

3 ounces cotija cheese, crumbled (¾ cup), divided

1 tablespoon chopped jarred jalapeño chiles plus 1 teaspoon brine

¼ cup jarred salsa

PANTRY IMPROV

use what you have Any jarred salsa works here.

level up For a heartier breakfast, top each serving with ½ thinly sliced avocado or a fried or soft-cooked egg. Sprinkle with fresh cilantro. Substitute other frozen vegetables for the corn; we like sliced peppers or chopped onions.

almost hands–free risotto
with parmesan

SERVES 4 | TOTAL TIME: 50 MINUTES

- 5 cups chicken or vegetable broth
- 1½ cups water
- 4 tablespoons unsalted butter, divided
- 1 large onion, chopped fine
- ¾ teaspoon table salt
- 1 garlic clove, minced
- 2 cups Arborio or short–grain white rice
- 1 cup dry white wine or dry vermouth
- 2 ounces Parmesan or Pecorino Romano cheese, grated (1 cup)
- 1 cup frozen peas, thawed
- 1 teaspoon lemon juice
- ¼ cup chopped fresh parsley (optional)

PANTRY IMPROV

use what you have Substitute tarragon, chives, or basil for the parsley. Substitute any sautéed or roasted vegetable, frozen corn, or frozen fava beans for the peas.

level up Stir in up to 1 cup shredded or diced cooked chicken or ham or poached or sautéed shrimp. Stir in baby kale or spinach with the Parmesan.

---

why this recipe works Risotto is a fantastic platform for utilizing the contents of your pantry. From hearty winter vegetables and frozen vegetables to hard cheeses and cooked meats, everything gets bound in mouthfuls of creamy rice. The creaminess, however, typically comes from half an hour of stovetop stirring. Not here. To minimize the need for constant stirring, we cook the risotto in a Dutch oven rather than a saucepan, which ensures more even heat distribution. We also add most of the broth at once, rather than in small increments as is typical. We cover the pot and simmer the rice until almost all the broth has been absorbed, stirring just twice. After pouring in the final addition of broth, we stir the pot for a few minutes and then take it off the heat. The rice turns out thickened, velvety, and just barely chewy, ready to welcome any add-ins. This mostly hands-off method does require precise timing, so we strongly recommend using a timer. The consistency of risotto is largely a matter of taste, so if you prefer a brothy risotto, add extra broth in step 4. This is a great place to use homemade broth if you have it (see page 406).

1 Bring broth and water to boil in large saucepan over high heat. Cover and reduce heat to medium-low to maintain gentle simmer.

2 Melt 2 tablespoons butter in Dutch oven over medium heat. Add onion and salt and cook until onion is softened, about 5 minutes. Stir in garlic and cook until fragrant, about 30 seconds. Stir in rice and cook, stirring often, until grain edges begin to turn translucent, about 3 minutes.

3 Stir in wine and cook, stirring constantly, until fully absorbed, 2 to 3 minutes. Stir in 5 cups hot broth mixture. Reduce heat to medium-low, cover, and simmer until almost all liquid has been absorbed and rice is just al dente, 16 to 19 minutes, stirring twice during cooking.

4 Add ¾ cup hot broth mixture and stir gently and constantly until risotto becomes creamy, about 3 minutes. Stir in Parmesan. Remove pot from heat, cover, and let stand for 5 minutes. Stir in remaining 2 tablespoons butter; peas; lemon juice; and parsley, if using. Season with salt and pepper to taste. Before serving, stir in remaining hot broth mixture as needed to loosen consistency of risotto.

VARIATIONS

almost hands–free risotto with fennel and saffron

Omit peas. Add 1 fennel bulb, cored and chopped fine, to pot with onion and cook until softened, about 12 minutes. Add ¼ teaspoon ground coriander and pinch saffron threads to pot with garlic.

almost hands–free risotto with chicken

Nestle 1 pound boneless skinless chicken breasts into simmering broth in step 1 and cook until chicken registers 160 degrees, about 10 minutes. Transfer chicken to cutting board and shred into bite-size pieces; cover and keep broth warm. Stir shredded chicken into risotto with peas.

almost hands–free red wine risotto with beans

Omit peas. Substitute dry red wine for white wine. Add 2 tablespoons tomato paste with garlic and 6 ounces diced salami with rice. Stir 1 (15-ounce) can pinto beans, rinsed, into risotto with last addition of broth. Stir 2 teaspoons red wine vinegar into risotto with butter.

mushroom **farrotto**

SERVES 4 | TOTAL TIME: 1¼ HOURS

1½ cups whole farro

¾ ounce dried porcini mushrooms, rinsed

6 cups water or broth, divided

4 tablespoons unsalted butter, divided

½ onion, chopped fine

1½ teaspoons table salt, divided

1 garlic clove, minced

2 teaspoons minced fresh thyme or ½ teaspoon dried

¾ teaspoon pepper

1½ ounces Parmesan or Pecorino Romano cheese, grated (¾ cup)

2 tablespoons minced fresh chives (optional)

2 teaspoons sherry vinegar

why this recipe works You can make risotto-style dishes with grains other than rice, as this twist featuring farro illustrates. There's just one pitfall: the bran. Arborio rice has been stripped of its bran, and thus readily gives up its amylopectin, the starch molecule that makes risotto creamy. Farro retains much of its bran, which provides nutrients and earthy flavor but traps starch inside the grain. "Cracking" the farro by whizzing it in a blender solves the problem. We prefer the flavor and texture of whole farro here. Do not use quick-cooking or pearled farro. The consistency of farrotto is largely a matter of personal taste; if you prefer a looser texture, add more of the hot water in step 7.

1   Pulse farro in blender until about half of grains are broken into smaller pieces, about 6 pulses.

2   Microwave mushrooms and 1 cup water in covered bowl until steaming, about 1 minute. Let sit until softened, about 5 minutes. Drain mushrooms in fine-mesh strainer lined with coffee filter. Transfer liquid to medium saucepan and finely chop mushrooms.

3   Add remaining 5 cups water to saucepan and bring to boil over high heat. Reduce heat to medium-low to maintain gentle simmer.

4   Melt 2 tablespoons butter in Dutch oven over medium-low heat. Add onion, mushrooms, and ½ teaspoon salt and cook until onion has softened, 3 to 4 minutes. Add garlic and cook until fragrant, about 30 seconds. Add farro and cook, stirring frequently, until grains are lightly toasted, about 3 minutes.

5   Stir 5 cups hot water into farro, reduce heat to low, cover, and cook until almost all liquid has been absorbed and farro is just al dente, about 25 minutes, stirring twice during cooking.

6   Add thyme, remaining 1 teaspoon salt, and pepper and continue to cook, stirring constantly, until farro becomes creamy, about 5 minutes.

7   Remove pot from heat. Stir in Parmesan; chives, if using; vinegar; and remaining 2 tablespoons butter. Season with salt and pepper to taste. Adjust consistency with remaining hot water as needed. Serve immediately.

PANTRY IMPROV

use what you have Red wine vinegar or white wine vinegar can be used instead of sherry vinegar. You can use any dried mushrooms instead of porcini.

level up Sauté up to 12 ounces fresh mushrooms in Dutch oven before cooking onion. Blanch 4 ounces asparagus in broth and stir in with Parmesan.

black beans and rice

SERVES 4 | TOTAL TIME: 1 HOUR

1 (15–ounce) can black beans, undrained

2¼ cups chicken or vegetable broth, plus extra as needed

2 tablespoons vegetable oil

½ onion, chopped fine

½ teaspoon table salt

½ teaspoon pepper

1½ cups long–grain white rice, rinsed

3 garlic cloves, minced

½ teaspoon dried oregano

¼ teaspoon ground cumin

1 bay leaf

why this recipe works Rice and beans are a comforting combination and a staple preparation the world over. This version uses the simplest of pantry seasonings—garlic, onion, oregano, and cumin—to build great flavor, and offers plenty of leeway to vary the type of beans, the seasonings, and the add-ins if you desire. Toasting the rice in oil until the edges turn translucent helps the grains to hold their shape and not turn mushy. Canned beans offer weeknight ease, and we reserve and use their starchy liquid to add color to the white rice. We cook the rice and beans together with chicken broth, the reserved bean liquid, and the sautéed onion for 20 minutes and let them sit for 10 minutes before fluffing with a fork. Rinse the rice in a fine-mesh strainer under running water until the water runs almost clear, about 2 minutes, stirring the rice a few times with your hand.

1   Place beans in fine-mesh strainer set over 4-cup liquid measuring cup and let drain for 5 minutes; reserve bean liquid. Add enough broth to bean liquid to equal 2½ cups and stir to combine. Set aside beans and broth mixture.

2   Heat oil in 12-inch nonstick skillet over medium-high heat until shimmering. Add onion, salt, and pepper and cook until onion is softened and beginning to brown, about 4 minutes. Add rice and cook, stirring frequently, until the edges begin to turn translucent and rice is fragrant, about 2 minutes. Stir in garlic, oregano, and cumin and cook until fragrant, about 30 seconds. Stir in bay leaf, beans, and broth mixture and bring to boil. Cover, reduce heat to medium-low, and cook, without stirring, for 20 minutes.

3   Off heat, let sit, covered, for 10 minutes. Discard bay leaf. Gently fluff rice with fork and season with salt and pepper to taste. Serve.

PANTRY IMPROV

use what you have Use any kind of canned beans. Utilize spice blends, such as creole or cajun, in place of oregano and cumin.

level up Add finely chopped vegetables such as carrot, fennel, and bell pepper with the onion in step 2. Stir cooked meat or tofu; baby greens; or thawed, frozen vegetables into the rice before letting it sit in step 3. Top with toasted nuts, crispy bacon, pickles, herbs, tomatoes, or avocado.

VARIATIONS

red beans and rice with andouille

Substitute kidney beans or small red beans for black beans, thyme for oregano, and 2 teaspoons paprika for cumin. Add 8 ounces andouille sausage, sliced ¼ inch thick, ¼ cup finely chopped green bell pepper, and ¼ cup finely chopped celery with onion; increase cooking time to 8 minutes. After fluffing rice, stir in 2 teaspoons red wine vinegar and sprinkle with 2 thinly sliced scallions. Serve with hot sauce.

lentils and rice with spiced beef

Substitute canned brown or black lentils for black beans and ¾ teaspoon pumpkin pie spice for oregano. Increase cumin to 2 teaspoons. Add 8 ounces ground beef to skillet with onion and cook, breaking up meat with wooden spoon until no longer pink, about 6 minutes. After fluffing rice, sprinkle with Crispy Shallots (page 388) and ¼ cup chopped fresh parsley or dill. Serve with yogurt.

butter beans and rice with tomato salad

Combine 12 ounces halved cherry tomatoes, 1 teaspoon grated lemon zest, 2 tablespoons lemon juice, 2 tablespoons extra-virgin olive oil, and ½ cup coarsely chopped fresh parsley, basil, and/or dill in bowl. Season with salt and pepper to taste; set aside. Substitute butter beans for black beans and ½ teaspoon ground coriander for cumin. Top individual portions with tomato salad before serving.

lentil salad with oranges, celery, and pecans

SERVES 4 | TOTAL TIME: 1 HOUR, PLUS 1 HOUR BRINING

1 cup dried brown or green lentils or lentilles du Puy (French lentils), picked over and rinsed

¾ teaspoon table salt, divided, plus salt for brining

2 tablespoons cider vinegar

1 shallot, minced

1 tablespoon honey or agave syrup

½ teaspoon dried mint

¼ cup extra-virgin olive oil

1 orange, peel and pith cut away, fruit cut into 8 wedges, then sliced crosswise ¼ inch thick

2 celery ribs, sliced thin on bias, plus ¼ cup celery leaves

¼ cup pecans or walnuts, toasted and chopped coarse, divided

why this recipe works A good lentil salad is a lesson in contrasts: Pair sweet with tart, crunchy with creamy or juicy, and you can create a dish from everyday pantry items that looks and tastes impressive. For lentils with a firm-tender bite and to soften their skins without blowouts, we brine dried lentils in warm salt water for an hour. To further ensure uniformly tender lentils, we cook them in the oven, which provides gentle, even heat. Next we choose our components: Sliced celery ribs add color and crispness while celery leaves provide a lovely herbaceous element. Orange segments add pops of bright juiciness to contrast with toasted nuts. A honey and cider vinaigrette brings more sweetness to contrast with the earthy lentils.

1   Place lentils and 1 teaspoon salt in bowl. Cover with 4 cups warm water (about 110 degrees) and soak for at least 1 hour or up to 24 hours. Drain well. (Brined, drained lentils can be refrigerated for up to 2 days.)

2   Adjust oven rack to middle position and heat oven to 325 degrees. Combine drained lentils, 4 cups water, and ½ teaspoon salt in medium ovensafe saucepan. Cover, transfer to oven, and bake until lentils are tender, 40 minutes to 1 hour. Drain lentils well.

3   Whisk vinegar, shallot, honey, mint, and remaining ¼ teaspoon salt together in large bowl. While whisking constantly, slowly drizzle in oil until combined. Add drained lentils, orange slices, celery and leaves, and 2 tablespoons pecans and toss to combine. Season with salt and pepper to taste.

4   Sprinkle with remaining 2 tablespoons pecans. Serve warm or at room temperature. (Lentil salad can be refrigerated for up to 3 days.)

white bean and tuna salad

SERVES 4 | TOTAL TIME: 10 MINUTES

why this recipe works With the simplicity of this flavorful pantry salad, using good ingredients makes a difference. Reach for the olive oil–packed tuna if you have it. A good olive oil contributes fresh, fruity flavor. Sherry vinegar adds complexity. Parsley isn't strictly needed but provides welcome freshness. A single shallot adds just enough bite without being harsh. If you like to cook dried beans, this is a lovely way to enjoy them.

Remove tuna from container and discard packing oil. Coarsely flake tuna into medium bowl. Add beans; oil; parsley, if using; shallot; vinegar; salt; and pepper flakes and stir to combine. Serve.

- 1 (6-ounce) can olive oil–packed tuna
- 2 (15-ounce) cans cannellini beans, rinsed
- ¼ cup extra-virgin olive oil
- ¼ cup very coarsely chopped fresh parsley (optional)
- 1 shallot, sliced into thin rings
- 4 teaspoons sherry vinegar
- ¼ teaspoon table salt
- ¼ teaspoon red pepper flakes

PANTRY IMPROV

use what you have Use canned butter beans or small white beans instead of cannellini. To substitute cooked dried beans, you'll need 3½ cups cooked beans. Try fresh mint or 2 tablespoons chopped fresh oregano instead of parsley. You can substitute ¼ cup thinly sliced red onion for the shallot. We prefer oil-packed tuna here, but if you happen to have water-packed tuna, don't let that stop you, or feel free to substitute canned salmon for the tuna. Red wine vinegar or white wine vinegar can be used instead of the sherry vinegar.

level up Serve on toast or over salad greens and top with thinly sliced vegetables or grated hard cheese to create a heartier meal. Stir chopped carrots and/or celery, chopped olives, capers, or diced cooked egg into the tuna salad. Stir in some blanched green beans or thawed, frozen cut green beans.

---

palak dal

SERVES 4 | TOTAL TIME: 1¼ HOURS

4½ cups water

10½ ounces (1½ cups) dried red lentils, picked over and rinsed

1 tablespoon grated fresh ginger

¾ teaspoon ground turmeric

6 ounces frozen spinach, thawed and squeezed dry

1½ teaspoons table salt

3 tablespoons ghee

1½ teaspoons brown or yellow mustard seeds

1½ teaspoons cumin seeds

1 large onion, chopped

15 curry leaves, roughly torn (optional)

6 garlic cloves, sliced

4 whole dried arbol chiles

1 serrano chile, halved lengthwise, or 1–2 whole dried Thai bird chiles

1½ teaspoons lemon juice, plus extra for seasoning

⅓ cup chopped fresh cilantro (optional)

why this recipe works Nourishing, satisfying, and packed with flavor, dal is served daily in many Indian households. Dal is the Hindi term for dried peas, beans, and legumes; dal also refers to dishes made from them. Palak dal incorporates spinach (palak in Hindi). It begins by simmering dal with spices before adding a pile of spinach. Using red lentils, which break down quickly, keeps the cooking time short, and a whisk breaks them down even more. Next comes the real genius: tadka, a seasoning technique central to Indian cuisine. Fry whole spices (here: cumin, mustard seeds, chiles, and curry leaves) in a few tablespoons of fat and use the fragrant mixture as a gorgeous garnish that adds extraordinary flavor. Fresh curry leaves add a wonderful aroma (store extra leaves in the freezer), but you can omit them. Monitor the spices carefully during frying, reducing the heat if necessary to prevent scorching. To make your own ghee, see page 403.

1   Bring water, lentils, ginger, and turmeric to boil in large saucepan over medium-high heat. Reduce heat to maintain vigorous simmer. Cook, uncovered, stirring occasionally, until lentils are soft and starting to break down, 18 to 20 minutes.

2   Whisk lentils vigorously until coarsely pureed, about 30 seconds. Continue to cook until lentils have consistency of loose polenta or oatmeal, up to 5 minutes. Stir in spinach and salt and continue to cook until spinach is fully warmed through, 30 to 60 seconds. Cover and set aside off heat.

3   Melt ghee in 10-inch skillet over medium-high heat. Add mustard seeds and cumin seeds and cook, stirring constantly, until seeds sizzle and pop, about 30 seconds. Add onion and cook, stirring frequently, until onion is just starting to brown, about 5 minutes. Add curry leaves, if using; garlic; arbols; and serrano and cook, stirring frequently, until onion and garlic are golden brown, 3 to 4 minutes.

4   Add lemon juice to lentils and stir to incorporate. (Dal should have consistency of loose polenta. If too thick, loosen with hot water, adding 1 tablespoon at a time.) Season with salt and extra lemon juice to taste. Transfer dal to serving bowl and spoon onion mixture on top. Sprinkle with cilantro, if using, and serve.

PANTRY IMPROV

use what you have Dried whole cayenne or pequín chiles are good substitutions for dried arbols, or use ½ teaspoon ground cayenne. You can substitute 1½ teaspoons red pepper flakes for the serrano or Thai bird chiles. Substitute browned butter for the ghee; discard browned butter solids before using.

level up Serve the dal with naan and basmati or another long-grain white rice.

stovetop **white bean casserole**

SERVES 4 | TOTAL TIME: 1 HOUR

- 5 tablespoons extra-virgin olive oil, divided
- 4 slices crusty bread, cut into ½-inch pieces (about 4 cups)
- ¾ teaspoon table salt, divided
- 1 onion, chopped fine
- 3 garlic cloves, minced
- 1 teaspoon minced fresh thyme or ¼ teaspoon dried
- 1 (14-ounce) can diced tomatoes
- 4 carrots, peeled, halved lengthwise, and sliced ½ inch thick
- 2 (15-ounce) cans cannellini beans, undrained

why this recipe works Simmer beans in an aromatic sauce, toss on a crunchy bready layer, and you have satisfying, endlessly riffable dinner that can be composed of the barest pantry essentials, or made heartier with add-ins such as chicken, vegetables, or cheese. For our core recipe, we develop the sauce's flavor by browning aromatic onion in a skillet, adding some garlic and thyme, and using canned tomatoes to deglaze the pan. Saving the starchy liquid from the canned beans and adding it to the sauce gives the sauce a long-simmered texture and flavor. As for the crunchy topping, toasted bread crumbs are a common choice, but we aim for maximum crunch by toasting lightly seasoned and oiled bread cubes in a skillet until golden and crisp, and sprinkle them over our casserole just before serving.

1   Heat ¼ cup oil in 12-inch skillet over medium heat until shimmering. Add bread and ¼ teaspoon salt and toast, stirring frequently, until deep golden brown and crisp, 8 to 10 minutes; transfer to bowl and set aside.

2   Add onion, remaining 1 tablespoon oil, and remaining ½ teaspoon salt to now-empty skillet and cook until onion is softened and lightly browned, 5 to 7 minutes. Stir in garlic and thyme and cook until fragrant, about 30 seconds.

3   Fold in tomatoes, carrots, and beans with their canning liquid. Bring to simmer and cook, stirring occasionally, until sauce has thickened and carrots are tender, 25 to 30 minutes. (If sauce thickens before carrots are tender, stir in up to ¼ cup water.)

4   Off heat, season with salt and pepper to taste. Top with croutons and let rest for 10 minutes before serving.

PANTRY IMPROV

use what you have Rosemary, sage, or Italian seasoning works in place of thyme. Use whole peeled tomatoes instead of diced; crush them by hand and add their juices. Substitute 8 ounces of other root vegetables for the carrots.

level up Add spices to the bread while toasting or toss croutons with grated cheese, nuts, or herbs. Nestle 4 sausages or 4 browned chicken thighs, skin side up, in the skillet (cook meat to 165 degrees).

VARIATIONS

stovetop white bean casserole with bacon, spinach, and rosemary

Cook 4 slices of bacon, cut into 1-inch pieces, in 12-inch skillet over medium heat until rendered and crisp, 5 to 7 minutes; transfer to bowl. Pour off all but ¼ cup fat from skillet (or add extra oil if necessary) and use in place of oil in step 1. Substitute 2 teaspoons minced fresh rosemary for thyme. Stir 4 ounces baby spinach into bean mixture until wilted before removing skillet from heat in step 4. Sprinkle casserole with bacon along with croutons.

stovetop white bean casserole with chicken thighs and butternut squash

Pat 4 (5- to 7-ounce) bone-in chicken thighs dry and sprinkle with ¼ teaspoon table salt and ¼ teaspoon pepper. Heat 2 teaspoons extra-virgin olive oil in 12-inch skillet over medium-high heat until just smoking. Cook chicken, skin side down, until skin is crisped and well browned, 8 to 10 minutes; transfer to plate. Discard fat and proceed with recipe, substituting sage for thyme and 2 cups ½-inch peeled butternut squash pieces for carrots. Nestle chicken, skin side up, into bean mixture before simmering and cook until chicken registers 175 degrees.

stovetop white bean casserole with zucchini, smoked paprika, and parmesan croutons

Toss cooled croutons with ¼ cup grated Parmesan. Add 1 teaspoon smoked paprika with garlic and thyme. Add 1 zucchini or summer squash, quartered lengthwise and sliced 1 inch thick, with tomatoes.

chana masala

SERVES 4 | TOTAL TIME: 50 MINUTES

1 small red or yellow onion, quartered, divided

10 sprigs fresh cilantro, stems and leaves separated (optional)

1 (1½-inch) piece ginger, peeled and chopped coarse

2 garlic cloves, chopped coarse

2 serrano chiles, stemmed, halved, seeded, and sliced thin crosswise, divided

3 tablespoons vegetable oil

1 (14.5-ounce) can whole peeled, diced, or crushed tomatoes

1 teaspoon paprika

1 teaspoon ground cumin

½ teaspoon ground turmeric

½ teaspoon fennel seeds

2 (15-ounce) cans chickpeas, undrained

1½ teaspoons garam masala

½ teaspoon table salt

Lime wedges

why this recipe works One of North India's most popular vegetarian dishes, chana masala is quick and easy to prepare. Its allure runs deep, with golden, creamy chickpeas glimmering in a fragrantly spiced orangey-red tomato sauce. We fry a paste of onion, cilantro, ginger, garlic, and chiles in a full 3 tablespoons of oil for richness before stirring in paprika, cumin, turmeric, and fennel seeds. We then add tomatoes and chickpeas, as well as the bean liquid for body and savory depth. Cooking our foundational spices at the beginning ensures that they permeate the dish, but we reserve sweet, delicate garam masala until the end to preserve its aroma. A generous garnish of more onion, chiles, and cilantro adds vibrancy and texture. You'd never guess that most of the ingredients in this recipe are from the pantry. Because the sodium contents of canned chickpeas and tomatoes vary, we include only a small amount of salt; season to taste with additional salt at the end of cooking. If you prefer a spicier dish, leave the seeds in the serrano chiles. To make your own garam masala, see page 382.

1   Chop three-quarters of onion coarse; reserve remaining quarter for garnish. Cut cilantro stems, if using, into 1-inch lengths. Process chopped onion, cilantro stems, ginger, garlic, and half of serranos in food processor until finely chopped, scraping down sides of bowl as necessary, about 20 seconds. Combine onion mixture and oil in large saucepan. Cook over medium-high heat, stirring frequently, until onion is fully softened and beginning to stick to saucepan, 5 to 7 minutes.

2   While onion mixture cooks, process tomatoes and their juice in now-empty food processor until smooth, about 30 seconds. Add paprika, cumin, turmeric, and fennel seeds to onion mixture and cook, stirring constantly, until fragrant, about 1 minute. Stir in chickpeas and their liquid and processed tomatoes and bring to boil. Adjust heat to maintain simmer, then cover and simmer for 15 minutes. While mixture cooks, chop reserved onion fine.

3   Stir garam masala and salt into chickpea mixture and continue to cook, uncovered and stirring occasionally, until chickpeas are softened and sauce is thickened, 8 to 12 minutes. Season with salt to taste. Transfer to wide, shallow serving bowl. Sprinkle with chopped onion; remaining serranos; and cilantro leaves, if using; and serve, passing lime wedges separately.

PANTRY IMPROV

use what you have Substitute ¾ teaspoon Kashmiri chile powder, 2 teaspoons cayenne, or (for a milder dish) 3 teaspoons paprika for the serranos; add the full amount in step 1.

level up This dish is often paired with bhature, deep-fried breads that puff up as they cook; alternatively, serve it with rice or naan. Sprinkle a little garam masala, cumin powder, mango powder (amchoor), and red chili powder over the dish before serving.

sweet potato and bean tacos

SERVES 4 | TOTAL TIME: 1 HOUR

- 3 tablespoons extra-virgin olive oil
- 3 garlic cloves, minced
- 1½ teaspoons ground cumin
- 1½ teaspoons ground coriander
- 1 teaspoon minced fresh oregano or ¼ teaspoon dried
- 1 teaspoon table salt
- ½ teaspoon pepper
- 12 ounces sweet potatoes, peeled and cut into ½-inch pieces
- 1 onion, halved and sliced ½ inch thick
- 1 (15-ounce) can beans, rinsed
- ¼ cup chopped fresh cilantro (optional)
- 12 (6-inch) corn or flour tortillas, charred

why this recipe works One great thing about the proliferation of taco restaurants is the varied plant-based fillings that are featured, from poblanos to mushrooms and more. It inspired us to create this pantry-friendly combo of sweet potatoes, onion, and beans, which we season with fragrant garlic, cumin, coriander, and oregano. Roasting the vegetables produces caramelized exteriors and tender interiors. Of course, tacos can enclose all kinds of vegetables; the variations offer additional ideas.

1   Adjust oven racks to upper-middle and lower-middle positions and heat oven to 450 degrees. Whisk oil, garlic, cumin, coriander, oregano, salt, and pepper together in large bowl. Add potatoes and onion to oil mixture and toss to coat.

2   Spread vegetable mixture in even layer over 2 aluminum foil–lined rimmed baking sheets. Roast vegetables until tender and golden brown, about 30 minutes, stirring vegetables and switching and rotating sheets halfway through roasting.

3   Return vegetables to now-empty bowl, add beans and cilantro, if using, and gently toss to combine. Divide vegetables evenly among warm tortillas. Serve.

PANTRY IMPROV

use what you have Any beans can be used in this recipe. You can substitute chili powder for the cumin and coriander.

level up Top with your favorite taco toppings such as Quick Sweet and Spicy Pickled Red Onions (page 404) and Avocado-Lime Yogurt Sauce (page 398), crema, or Greek yogurt. Top with sliced radishes.

VARIATIONS

sweet potato, bean, and poblano tacos

Roast 4 poblano chiles, seeded and cut into ½-inch-wide strips, with potatoes and onions. Top with Avocado-Lime Yogurt Sauce (page 398).

sweet potato and bean tacos with mango and cabbage slaw

Combine 3 cups shredded green cabbage or green coleslaw mix, ¾ cup finely chopped mango, 2 tablespoons lime juice, 1 tablespoon chopped fresh cilantro, 1 tablespoon minced jalapeño, and ¼ teaspoon table salt in bowl, cover, and let sit for 30 minutes. Serve on tacos.

smoky sweet potato and mushroom tacos

Roast 8 ounces mushrooms, cut into 1-inch pieces, with potatoes and onions. Add 1 teaspoon smoked paprika to spice mixture. Top with crumbled cotija or queso fresco and Quick Sweet and Spicy Pickled Red Onions (page 404).

spiced chickpea gyros
with tahini yogurt

SERVES 4 | TOTAL TIME: 30 MINUTES

why this recipe works This fast, supersatisfying vegetarian dinner reimagines protein-rich canned chickpeas by making them the star filling in a roll-up sandwich. Mashing the chickpeas lightly breaks up their skins and allows them to soak up the flavors of the seasonings. Red onion, pepperoncini, and cucumber (if you have it) add three different kinds of crunch.

1   Combine yogurt, tahini, and ½ teaspoon salt in small bowl; set aside.

2   Using potato masher, very coarsely mash chickpeas in medium bowl. Stir chili-garlic sauce, cumin, and remaining ½ teaspoon salt into chickpeas; set aside.

3   Spread reserved yogurt sauce evenly over 1 side of each pita (use all of it). Divide reserved chickpea mixture; cucumber, if using; pepperoncini; and onion evenly among pitas. Fold pitas in half, wrap tightly in parchment paper, and serve.

1 cup plain Greek yogurt

¼ cup tahini

1 teaspoon table salt, divided

2 (15-ounce) cans chickpeas or white beans, rinsed

2 tablespoons chili-garlic sauce

2 teaspoons ground cumin

4 (8-inch) pita breads, lightly toasted

½ cucumber, halved lengthwise and sliced thin on 3-inch bias (optional)

½ cup pepperoncini, stemmed and sliced into thin rings

¼ cup thinly sliced red or yellow onion

PANTRY IMPROV

use what you have Jarred sliced jalapeños can be used instead of the pepperoncini.

level up For more heat, serve with extra chili-garlic sauce.

chickpea salad sandwiches

SERVES 4 | TOTAL TIME: 15 MINUTES

why this recipe works Sandwiches made with chicken or tuna salad are old standbys; we wanted to put a modern spin on this category by using protein-packed chickpeas as our salad base while still retaining all the richness and saucy texture of a traditional deli salad. Mayonnaise (plant-based or egg-based) helps the cause, but too much of it masks the savory chickpea flavor, so we use some of the chickpeas to make a hummus-style puree. We buzz a portion of the chickpeas with mayo, water, and lemon juice in the food processor for the perfect creamy binder. After adding the remaining chickpeas we briefly pulse the mixture to give us good textural contrast. To round out the salad we turn to classic flavors: Chopped celery provides crunch, dill pickle brings salty brininess, and red onion and herbs offer a bright, fresh finish. This chickpea salad makes a creamy, luscious sandwich sure to satisfy any lunchtime craving.

1 Process ¾ cup chickpeas, mayonnaise, water, lemon juice, and salt in food processor until smooth, about 30 seconds, scraping down sides of bowl as needed.

2 Add remaining chickpeas to food processor and pulse until coarsely chopped with some larger pieces remaining, about 4 pulses.

3 Combine chickpea mixture; celery; pickles; onion; and parsley, if using, in large bowl and season with salt and pepper to taste. Spread chickpea salad evenly over 4 bread slices. Top with remaining bread slices and serve.

2 (15-ounce) cans chickpeas or white beans, rinsed, divided

½ cup egg or plant-based mayonnaise or dairy or plant-based Greek yogurt

¼ cup water

1 tablespoon lemon juice

½ teaspoon table salt

2 celery ribs, finely chopped

⅓ cup dill pickles, finely chopped

½ small red onion, chopped fine

2 tablespoons minced fresh parsley, dill, or tarragon (optional)

8 slices bread, toasted

PANTRY IMPROV

use what you have You can substitute 2 thinly sliced scallions for the red onion.

level up Add 1 tablespoon of your favorite spice blend such as curry powder, ras el hanout, chili powder, or garam masala to the chickpea mixture in the food processor in step 1. Top sandwiches with sprouts, sliced tomatoes, lettuce, and/or sliced avocado if desired. This salad is also delicious served in lettuce wraps.

black bean burgers

SERVES 6 | TOTAL TIME: 1 HOUR, PLUS 1 HOUR CHILLING

2 (15–ounce) cans black beans, rinsed

2 large eggs

2 tablespoons all–purpose flour

1 shallot, minced

3 tablespoons minced fresh cilantro (optional)

2 garlic cloves, minced

1 teaspoon ground cumin

½ teaspoon ground coriander

¼ teaspoon table salt

¼ teaspoon pepper

1 teaspoon hot sauce (optional)

1 ounce tortilla chips, crushed coarse (½ cup)

8 teaspoons vegetable oil

6 burger buns, toasted if desired

PANTRY IMPROV

use what you have Two minced scallions can be used instead of the shallot.

level up Serve the burgers with your favorite toppings or with Pub Burger Sauce (page 398) or Easy Garlic Mayonnaise (page 398).

why this recipe works These hearty burgers have a Southwestern flair thanks to a few flavor enhancers (cumin, coriander, hot sauce, and cilantro) plus a pantry hack: ground tortilla chips. Turns out, these chips add flavor as well as an appealing texture to the patties that saves them from venturing into mushy territory, a common pitfall for bean burgers. Eggs and just 2 tablespoons of flour provide further binding without dulling flavor. Thoroughly drying the rinsed canned black beans helps prevent pasty, soggy patties. Refrigerating the mixture for at least an hour allows the starches to absorb some of the eggs' moisture. After an hour, you're ready to form patties and brown the burgers in an oiled skillet. Serve with any of your favorite fixings. When forming the patties it is important to pack them firmly together.

1   Line rimmed baking sheet with triple layer of paper towels and spread black beans over towels. Let stand for 15 minutes.

2   Whisk eggs and flour together in large bowl until uniform paste forms. Stir in shallot; cilantro, if using; garlic; cumin; coriander; salt; pepper; and hot sauce, if using, until well combined.

3   Process tortilla chips in food processor until finely ground, about 30 seconds. Add black beans and pulse until beans are roughly broken down, about 5 pulses. Transfer black bean mixture to bowl with egg mixture and mix until well combined. Cover and refrigerate for at least 1 hour or up to 24 hours.

4   Divide bean mixture into 6 equal portions. Firmly pack each portion into tight ball, then flatten to 3½-inch patty. (Patties can be wrapped individually in plastic wrap, placed in zipper-lock bag, and frozen for up to 2 weeks. Thaw patties before cooking.)

5   Heat 2 teaspoons oil in 10-inch nonstick skillet over medium heat until shimmering. Carefully lay 3 patties in skillet and cook until bottoms are well-browned and crisp, about 5 minutes. Flip patties, add 2 teaspoons oil, and cook second sides until well-browned and crisp, 3 to 5 minutes. Transfer patties to buns and repeat with remaining 3 patties and 4 teaspoons oil. Serve.

beans and greens

SERVES 4 | TOTAL TIME: 40 MINUTES

- 2 tablespoons extra-virgin olive oil, plus extra for drizzling
- 1 onion, chopped fine
- ½ teaspoon table salt
- ½ teaspoon pepper
- 3 garlic cloves, minced
- 1 teaspoon chopped fresh rosemary or ¼ teaspoon dried
- ½ teaspoon red pepper flakes
- ½ cup vegetable or chicken broth
- 1 pound escarole, cabbage, or other hearty greens, trimmed and cut into 2-inch pieces
- 1 (15-ounce) can cannellini beans, rinsed
- 1 ounce Parmesan or Pecorino Romano cheese, grated (½ cup), divided

why this recipe works A comforting pile of braised greens and creamy beans is a convenient way to use up various vegetables you may have lying around, from sturdy cabbage to delicate baby spinach (even frozen greens work). This rendition develops flavor via garlic, rosemary, red pepper flakes, and Parmesan. We sauté the aromatics and then add our greens to wilt down before stirring in cannellini beans to cook for a few minutes. Don't forget to add a final drizzle of olive oil and a sprinkle of cheese for good measure. Don't be alarmed by the volume of greens; they'll cook down significantly.

1   Heat oil in Dutch oven over medium-high heat until shimmering. Add onion, salt, and pepper and cook until onion is softened and beginning to brown, 5 to 7 minutes. Add garlic, rosemary, and pepper flakes and cook until fragrant, about 30 seconds.

2   Reduce heat to medium-low. Stir in broth, scraping up any browned bits. Stir in escarole, cover, and cook, stirring occasionally, until wilted, 6 to 8 minutes.

3   Add beans and cook, uncovered and stirring occasionally, until greens are tender, 5 to 10 minutes. Off heat, stir in ¼ cup Parmesan. Season with salt and pepper to taste. Transfer to serving dish. Sprinkle with remaining ¼ cup Parmesan and drizzle with extra oil. Serve.

PANTRY IMPROV

use what you have Any fresh greens you have on hand will work here; we like escarole, cabbage, spinach, kale, or a mix. Or use frozen spinach or baby spinach. Any canned beans can be used. Substitute thyme for the rosemary. Red onion or 3 large shallots can be substituted for the onion.

level up Stir in cubes of stale bread or Classic Croutons (page 398) to make a ribollita-style dish. Add crumbled sausage with the onion for a meaty dish.

white bean gratin with rosemary and parmesan

SERVES 4 | TOTAL TIME: 30 MINUTES

why this recipe works A creamy, bubbly bean gratin is a comforting and supremely satisfying way to enjoy the contents of your pantry. This quick take is inspired by the Tuscan classic where dried beans are gently cooked for hours until they break down and bind together. We rely on canned beans and mash some of the beans before adding them to the dish, which gives the finished casserole a creamy, saucy texture reminiscent of long-simmered beans in just 10 minutes. Broiling the beans in broth allows them to absorb the rich, savory flavor. Onion, garlic, rosemary, and Parmesan serve as supporting ingredients for a straightforward and savory gratin. You will need an 8-inch square broiler-safe baking dish or pan for this recipe. This recipe can also be doubled using a 13 by 9-inch broiler-safe baking pan.

1   Microwave onion, oil, garlic, and rosemary in medium bowl, stirring occasionally, until onion is softened, about 5 minutes.

2   Adjust oven rack to upper middle position and heat broiler. Add ⅔ cup beans to bowl with onion mixture and mash with potato masher until smooth. Stir in broth and remaining whole beans until combined. Transfer mixture to 8-inch square broiler-safe baking dish or pan and sprinkle evenly with Parmesan. Broil until mixture is bubbling around edges and cheese is golden brown, 5 to 7 minutes. Transfer dish to wire rack and let cool slightly before serving.

- 1 onion, chopped fine
- 2 tablespoons extra-virgin olive oil
- 3 garlic cloves, minced
- 1 teaspoon minced fresh rosemary or ¼ teaspoon dried
- 2 (15-ounce) can cannellini beans, rinsed, divided
- ½ cup vegetable or chicken broth
- 2 ounces Parmesan or Pecorino Romano cheese, grated (1 cup)

PANTRY IMPROV

use what you have Any beans work here: Try pinto or small white beans. Any melty cheese works well; for extra cheesiness, use cheddar or Monterey Jack. Thyme or sage can be substituted for the rosemary. Red onion or 3 large shallots can be substituted for the onion.

level up Stir in thawed frozen spinach or chopped broccoli or green beans. Top with crispy bacon or Crispy Shallots (page 388). Put Classic Croutons (page 389) under the cheese before broiling.

vegetables

carrot and white bean salad
with raisins and almonds

SERVES 4 | TOTAL TIME: 45 MINUTES

why this recipe works Think of this as a quintessential pantry salad—no leafy greens required. Crunchy shredded carrots provide a vegetable base that pairs well with a variety of additions: Think briny, sweet, chewy, nutty, and creamy. We start with olives, raisins, and toasted sliced almonds, plus cayenne for heat and fresh herbs if available. Stirring in a couple cans of creamy white beans makes the salad hearty enough to be a meal. To best incorporate the dressing's flavor, we warm the beans before mixing them with the dressing. Why? The beans' skins are rich in pectin, which breaks down when exposed to heat and moisture, creating a more porous surface for the dressing to penetrate. Letting the dressed beans rest for 30 minutes puts the flavor over the top and allows the beans to cool.

1 Microwave white beans in medium bowl until hot, about 2 minutes. Stir in oil, lime juice, salt, pepper, and cayenne and let sit until flavors meld, about 30 minutes. (Bean mixture can be refrigerated for up to 2 days.)

2 Add carrots; raisins; olives; almond; and mint, if using, to bean mixture and toss to combine. Season with salt and pepper to taste. Serve. (Salad can be refrigerated for up to 2 hours.)

2 (15-ounce) cans white beans or chickpeas, rinsed

¼ cup extra-virgin olive oil

2 tablespoons lime or lemon juice

¾ teaspoon table salt

½ teaspoon pepper

   Pinch cayenne pepper

3 carrots, peeled and shredded

½ cup raisins

½ cup olives, halved

¼ cup sliced almonds, toasted

¼ cup chopped fresh mint or parsley (optional)

PANTRY IMPROV

use what you have Any style of white beans will work. You can substitute any nuts for the almonds and any chopped dried fruit for the raisins. Substitute shredded sturdy vegetables such as beets, celery root, or parsnips for the carrots. Swap in other briny ingredients in place of the olives: try caper berries or pickled hot peppers.

level up Add something fresh (baby arugula or kale, a sprinkle of minced carrot greens, orange or grapefruit segments). Sprinkle the salad with crumbled cheese such as feta or goat cheese.

caesar vegetables

SERVES 4 | TOTAL TIME: 25 MINUTES

why this recipe works Let's be honest: Caesar dressing is too good to be limited to romaine or kale. And since the umami-packed dressing utilizes pantry staples, we can make it any time. If there are no greens on hand when the craving strikes, we poke around to see what can be tossed in the dressing's savory goodness. Green beans—fresh or frozen—are a particularly excellent option. Starting there, we mix a quick dressing with the flavors we love in Caesar: garlic, Worcestershire, and anchovies. Instead of eggs, Dijon mustard produces a lightly thickened emulsion to coat the vegetables. Shavings of Parmesan provide substantial bursts of cheesy nuttiness.

1 for the croutons Toss bread, oil, and pepper in large bowl until bread pieces are coated with oil. Transfer to 12-inch nonstick skillet (reserve bowl). Cook over medium-high heat, stirring occasionally, until golden brown and crispy, 5 to 7 minutes. Return croutons to reserved bowl.

2 for the dressing and green beans Whisk lemon juice, Worcestershire, mustard, garlic, anchovies, pepper, and salt in bowl until combined. Slowly whisk in oil until emulsified; set aside. (Dressing can be made up to 24 hours in advance.)

3 Transfer dressing, green beans, and half of Parmesan to bowl with croutons and toss to combine. Season with salt and pepper to taste. Transfer to serving dish and sprinkle with remaining Parmesan. Serve.

croutons

- 3 ounces bread, cut into ½-inch pieces (3 cups)
- 2 tablespoons extra-virgin olive oil
- ¼ teaspoon pepper

dressing and green beans

- 1½ tablespoons lemon juice
- 1 tablespoon Worcestershire sauce
- 1 tablespoon Dijon mustard
- 3 garlic cloves, minced
- 3 anchovy fillets, minced to paste
- ½ teaspoon pepper
- ¼ teaspoon table salt
- 3 tablespoons extra-virgin olive oil
- 1½ pounds frozen green beans, thawed and patted dry
- 2 ounces Parmesan or Pecorino Romano cheese, shaved with vegetable peeler

---

PANTRY IMPROV

use what you have Use blanched fresh green beans instead of frozen. Or substitute shredded raw brussels sprouts, torn softened kale, or chopped, blanched broccoli or asparagus.

level up Add up to 1 cup halved cherry or grape tomatoes to the salad. Top with poached chicken or shrimp, or poached eggs.

shaved celery salad with pomegranate-honey vinaigrette

SERVES 4 | TOTAL TIME: 30 MINUTES

why this recipe works Celery is a vegetable many of us have hanging out at the bottom of the crisper drawer. Good thing, too, as its uses go far beyond cutting into sticks for snacking. In salad, for instance, the supercrispy, mildly peppery stalk shines. We pair it with celery's sturdier sibling, celery root—which tastes great raw—for a salad that's just as good without greens as it is with a handful of bitter leaves thrown in. (No celery root? Other vegetables work as well; see below.) Toasted nuts, salty Pecorino Romano, and a honey-pomegranate dressing punch up the flavor. A sprinkle of pomegranate seeds further accentuates the salad, or try a different bright fruit. Use the large holes of a box grater to shred the celery root and Pecorino Romano.

1   Whisk pomegranate molasses, vinegar, shallot, honey, salt, and pepper together in large bowl. While whisking constantly, slowly drizzle in oil until combined.

2   Add celery root; celery ribs and leaves; Pecorino; and 2 tablespoons pomegranate seeds, if using, to bowl with dressing and toss gently to coat. Season with salt and pepper to taste. Sprinkle with walnuts and remaining 2 tablespoons pomegranate seeds, if using. Serve.

- 2 tablespoons pomegranate molasses
- 1 tablespoon red wine vinegar
- 1 small shallot, minced
- 2 teaspoons honey or agave syrup
- ¼ teaspoon table salt
- Pinch pepper
- 2 tablespoons extra-virgin olive oil
- 14 ounces celery root, trimmed, peeled, and shredded
- 4 celery ribs, sliced thin on bias, plus ½ cup celery leaves
- 1½ ounces Pecorino Romano or Parmesan cheese, shredded (½ cup)
- ¼ cup pomegranate seeds, divided (optional)
- ½ cup walnuts, toasted and chopped coarse

PANTRY IMPROV

use what you have You can substitute carrots, turnips, or rutabaga for the celery root. Any type of nut or vinegar will work well in this recipe. Use any chopped dried fruit or orange or grapefruit segments in place of pomegranate seeds. You can substitute 1 tablespoon of lemon juice plus 1 tablespoon of molasses for the pomegranate molasses.

level up Add trimmed, chopped frisée, endive, escarole, or other bitter greens or shaved mushrooms to the salad. Add flaked smoked or cooked fresh trout, mackerel, or salmon on top.

---

succotash salad

SERVES 4 | **TOTAL TIME: 50 MINUTES**

¼ cup extra-virgin olive oil

¼ cup white wine vinegar

2 teaspoons honey

½ teaspoon table salt, plus salt for cooking vegetables

¾ teaspoon pepper

½ small red onion, chopped fine

12 ounces frozen whole haricots verts or green beans

2 cups frozen or fresh corn

1½ cups frozen lima beans

why this recipe works Salad from the freezer may be an unexpected move, but a well-stocked freezer can house a bounty of summertime flavors fit to add color and freshness any time of year. Here, we pick some frozen vegetable favorites—corn, haricots verts, and lima beans—and season them thoroughly in well-salted water before adding a simple honey vinaigrette in a salad inspired by succotash. The variations mix fresh and frozen. Have zucchini? Make a green-on-green salad with frozen limas. Or introduce bacon and juicy cherry tomatoes to the mix. Do not confuse frozen haricots verts with french-cut green beans, which will not work here.

1 Whisk oil, vinegar, honey, salt, and pepper together in large bowl. Stir in onion and set aside.

2 Bring 4 quarts water to boil in large pot. Add ¼ cup salt, haricots verts, corn, and lima beans and cook until tender, about 5 minutes. Drain vegetables and rinse under cold water until chilled. Drain well, transfer to bowl with vinaigrette, and toss to combine. Let sit for at least 15 minutes or up to 24 hours. Season with salt and pepper to taste. Serve.

PANTRY IMPROV

use what you have Use other wine vinegars. Substitute fresh trimmed green beans for the frozen; add the green beans to the boiling water 1 minute before adding the corn and lima beans. Substitute frozen fava beans or edamame for the lima beans; one (15-ounce) can of beans can also be substituted.

level up Bulk up the salad with precooked grains or serve with your favorite seared protein. Add ground spices (fennel, coriander, and smoked paprika are good choices) and minced fresh herbs to the dressing. Add fresh ingredients such as halved cherry or grape tomatoes, baby salad greens, and/or sliced radishes to the salad just before serving. Sprinkle with crumbled fresh cheese such as feta or goat cheese and toasted nuts or seeds.

VARIATIONS

succotash salad with bell pepper, avocado, and cilantro

Omit haricots verts and lima beans. Whisk ½ cup minced fresh cilantro and ½ teaspoon ground cumin into dressing. Add 1 red bell pepper, stemmed, seeded, and sliced thin, and 1 (15-ounce) can black beans, rinsed, to dressing with corn. Top salad with 1 diced avocado just before serving.

succotash salad with bacon, cherry tomatoes, and arugula

Omit lima beans. Add ½ cup crispy bacon, 6 ounces halved cherry or grape tomatoes, and 2 cups baby arugula to salad just before serving and toss to combine.

succotash salad with zucchini, dill, and feta

Omit haricots verts. Substitute lemon juice for vinegar. Add 2 small zucchini, cut into ½-inch pieces, to dressing with corn and lima beans. Add ¼ cup chopped fresh dill and 1 cup crumbled feta cheese to salad just before serving and toss to combine.

esquites

SERVES 4 | TOTAL TIME: 1 HOUR

why this recipe works We can't get enough of Mexico's popular street snack of charred corn slathered with rich, tangy crema; coated with salty cotija cheese; and dusted with chili powder, whether we're eating it on the cob (as elote) or in salad form (as esquites). While we don't always have fresh corn on hand for elote, you can make good esquites from frozen corn. Yes, you can char frozen corn in a bit of oil over high heat. Covering the pan prevents the kernels from popping out of the hot skillet and traps steam, which helps cook the corn. Once the corn is toasted, we use the hot skillet to bloom chili powder and lightly cook minced garlic. To tie everything together, we make a simple crema with mayonnaise, sour cream, jarred jalapeños, and lime juice, which we toss with the charred corn and spices before adding crumbled cotija. Cilantro and scallion add freshness and bite, but feel free to leave them out if you don't have them. You will need a 12-inch nonstick skillet with a tight-fitting lid for this recipe.

1   Combine lime juice, sour cream, mayonnaise, jalapeños, and ¼ teaspoon salt in large bowl. Set aside.

2   Heat 1 tablespoon oil in 12-inch nonstick skillet over high heat until shimmering. Add corn and spread into even layer. Sprinkle with remaining ¼ teaspoon salt. Cover and cook, without stirring, until corn touching skillet is charred, about 3 minutes. Remove skillet from heat and let stand, covered, for 15 seconds, until any popping subsides. Transfer corn to bowl with sour cream mixture.

3   Return now-empty skillet to medium heat and add remaining ½ teaspoon oil, garlic, and chili powder. Cook, stirring constantly, until fragrant, about 30 seconds. Transfer garlic mixture to bowl with corn mixture and toss to combine. Let cool for at least 15 minutes.

4   Add cotija; cilantro, if using; and scallion, if using, and toss to combine. Season salad with salt and up to 1 tablespoon extra lime juice to taste. Serve.

1½ tablespoons lime juice, plus extra for seasoning

2   tablespoons sour cream

1   tablespoon mayonnaise

2   tablespoons chopped jarred jalapeño chiles

½   teaspoon table salt, divided

1   tablespoon plus ½ teaspoon vegetable oil, divided

3   cups frozen corn, thawed

1   garlic clove, minced

¼   teaspoon chili powder

2   ounces cotija or feta cheese, crumbled (½ cup)

¼   cup coarsely chopped fresh cilantro (optional)

1   scallion, sliced thin (optional)

PANTRY IMPROV

use what you have Substitute crema or plain Greek yogurt for the sour cream. You can substitute 1–2 fresh serranos or jalapeños, cut into thin rings, for the jarred jalapeños.

level up Turn this into a meal by adding seared shrimp, chicken, or steak.

charred cabbage salad
with torn tofu and plantain chips

SERVES 4 | TOTAL TIME: 1 HOUR

14 ounces firm or extra-firm tofu, torn into bite-size pieces

3 tablespoons seasoned rice vinegar, divided

2 tablespoons lime juice

4 teaspoons grated fresh ginger, divided

1 tablespoon honey or agave syrup

1 tablespoon fish sauce

1 head red cabbage (2 pounds)

7 tablespoons vegetable oil, divided

4 teaspoons Thai red or green curry paste, divided

1 tablespoon ground turmeric, divided

½ teaspoon table salt

1 tablespoon water

2 scallions, sliced thin on bias (optional)

¼ cup plantain or banana chips, crushed

why this recipe works Roasting cabbage wedges transforms them; the edges char and crisp, leaving tender, sweet layers beneath. These sweet-smoky wedges have a multitude of uses, including as a base for a salad. To amp up their flavor even further, we coat the wedges with Thai curry paste and turmeric before roasting. For a hearty salad, we pair the cabbage with tofu. Tearing the tofu into pieces by hand creates a craggy surface area ideal for soaking up flavor—in this case, a sweet-sour lime juice, honey, and fish sauce marinade. This salad benefits from crunchy embellishments: We love plantain chips and bean sprouts, but many options would work. Scallions and a fresh herb (such as Thai or Italian basil) are nice if you have them. A warm dressing of curry paste, turmeric, and ginger, bloomed in the microwave and mixed with seasoned rice vinegar, ties everything together.

1 Adjust oven rack to lowest position and heat oven to 500 degrees. Gently press tofu dry with paper towels. Whisk 1 tablespoon vinegar, lime juice, 2 teaspoons ginger, honey, and fish sauce together in medium bowl. Add tofu and toss gently to coat; set aside for 20 minutes. (Tofu can be refrigerated for up to 24 hours.)

2 Halve cabbage through core and cut each half into 4 approximately 2-inch-wide wedges, leaving core intact (you will have 8 wedges). Whisk ¼ cup oil, 1 teaspoon curry paste, 2 teaspoons turmeric, and salt together in bowl. Arrange cabbage wedges in single layer on aluminum foil–lined rimmed baking sheet, then brush cabbage all over with oil mixture. Cover tightly with foil and roast for 10 minutes. Remove foil and drizzle 2 table-spoons oil evenly over wedges. Return sheet to oven and roast, uncovered, until cabbage is tender and sides touching sheet are well browned, 10 to 15 minutes. Let cool slightly, about 15 minutes.

3 Whisk remaining 2 teaspoons ginger, remaining 1 tablespoon oil, remaining 1 tablespoon curry paste, and remaining 1 teaspoon turmeric together in bowl. Microwave until fragrant, about 30 seconds. Whisk water and remaining 2 tablespoons vinegar into ginger mixture.

4 Chop cabbage coarse and divide among individual plates. Top individual portions with scallions, if using, and tofu. Drizzle with vinaigrette and sprinkle with plantain chips. Serve.

PANTRY IMPROV

use what you have If you don't have plantain chips, chopped macadamia nuts, cashews, or peanuts work fine. Use green cabbage or napa cabbage instead of red cabbage.

level up Sprinkle salad with up to 1 cup bean sprouts. Sprinkle with chopped fresh basil, Thai basil, cilantro, or parsley.

stir-fried cabbage
with shallot and fish sauce

SERVES 4 | TOTAL TIME: 25 MINUTES

1 shallot, minced

3–5 dried Thai bird chiles, stemmed, seeded, and cut into ½-inch lengths

4 teaspoons vegetable oil, divided

1 garlic clove, minced

3 tablespoons water, divided

1 tablespoon fish sauce

2 teaspoons packed brown sugar

1 teaspoon cornstarch

1 small head green or red cabbage (1¼ pounds), cored and cut into 1-inch pieces

½ teaspoon lime juice

¼ cup fresh cilantro leaves (optional)

why this recipe works When there's a cabbage in your crisper, a tasty side dish is never far away, and its uses go far beyond shredding for slaw. Across Southeast Asia cabbage is prized in stir-fries for its ability to quickly transform into something sweet, tender, and crisp. A head of cabbage is uneven, with some thick, tougher leaves and other thin, delicate ones. As a result, simply stir-frying cabbage over high heat can overcook the delicate leaves before the thicker portions cook through. Instead, a quick steam—by adding a splash of water with the cabbage and covering the pan—partially softens the toughest parts without destroying the rest. After uncovering the pan we add aromatic shallot and garlic as well as some dried chiles; once the extra moisture is cooked off we swirl in a sweet-savory mix of brown sugar and fish sauce. A little lime juice brightens and balances out the seasonings. Dried Thai bird chiles are quite spicy so scale back as desired. You will need a 14-inch flat-bottomed wok or a 12-inch nonstick skillet, each with a tight-fitting lid, for this recipe.

1 Combine shallot, Thai bird chiles, 1 teaspoon oil, and garlic in small bowl; set aside. Whisk 1 tablespoon water, fish sauce, sugar, and cornstarch in second small bowl until sugar has dissolved; set aside.

2 Heat remaining 1 tablespoon oil in 14-inch flat-bottomed wok or 12-inch nonstick skillet over medium-high heat until shimmering. Add cabbage and remaining 2 tablespoons water (water will sputter); cover; and cook, shaking pan occasionally, for 3 minutes.

3 Uncover and push cabbage to 1 side of pan. Add reserved shallot mixture to clearing and cook, mashing mixture into pan, until fragrant, about 30 seconds. Stir shallot mixture into cabbage and cook, tossing slowly but constantly, until all water has evaporated and cabbage is crisp-tender, 1 to 2 minutes. Whisk reserved fish sauce mixture to recombine, then add to pan and cook, tossing constantly, until sauce has thickened and coats cabbage, about 30 seconds. Off heat, stir in lime juice and sprinkle with cilantro, if using. Serve.

PANTRY IMPROV

use what you have Substitute Thai or Italian basil for the cilantro. Dried arbol, cayenne, or pequín chiles are good substitutes for the Thai bird chiles, or substitute 1–1½ teaspoons red pepper flakes.

level up Before cooking the cabbage, stir-fry thinly sliced chicken breast, flank steak, pork tenderloin, chopped shrimp, or 1-inch cubes of firm tofu in 2 teaspoons hot oil until cooked through and lightly browned. Transfer to a bowl and add back to the pan with the fish sauce in step 3. Or top with a fried egg.

skillet–charred green beans
with crispy sesame topping

SERVES 4 | TOTAL TIME: 35 MINUTES

3 tablespoons sesame seeds

1 tablespoon panko bread crumbs

1 teaspoon Sichuan peppercorns

2 teaspoons plus 2 tablespoons vegetable oil, divided

1 teaspoon Sichuan pepper flakes

1 teaspoon toasted sesame oil

¾ teaspoon kosher salt

½ teaspoon grated orange zest

1 pound frozen whole green beans, thawed and patted dry

2 scallions, green parts only, sliced thin (optional)

why this recipe works Inspired by Sichuan dry-fried green beans, this high-heat method transforms frozen green beans, taking them from limp and slightly soft to charred and delicious. There are benefits to using frozen green beans here beyond pantry convenience. While fresh beans are great when you want that crisp-tender snap, here we seek a bean with satisfying chew to contrast with the blistered surface. Softening a bean's cell walls takes time, though. In the traditional Sichuan dish, green beans are deep-fried, fully submerged in hot oil, which softens them quickly. But when pan-frying, as we do here, using frozen green beans bypasses the softening stage. To guarantee nice color, we don't stir the beans for the first few minutes—but after that we toss them in the pan so that they blister all over. The charred beans are delicious as is, but are extra-tasty with a crispy topping. We mix one from sesame seeds and toasted panko bread crumbs seasoned with Sichuan peppercorns, Sichuan pepper flakes, and sesame oil, though this combo is easily varied. Be sure to thoroughly dry the green beans before cooking them.

1   Process sesame seeds, panko, and peppercorns in spice grinder or mortar and pestle until uniformly ground to medium-fine consistency that resembles couscous. Transfer sesame mixture to 12-inch nonstick skillet, add 2 teaspoons vegetable oil, and stir to combine. Cook over medium-low heat, stirring frequently, until light golden brown, 5 to 7 minutes. Remove skillet from heat; add pepper flakes, sesame oil, salt, and orange zest; and stir to combine. Transfer sesame mixture to bowl and set aside. Wash and dry skillet thoroughly.

2   Heat remaining 2 tablespoons vegetable oil in clean, dry skillet over high heat until just smoking. Add green beans in single layer. Cook, without stirring, until green beans begin to blister and char, 4 to 5 minutes. Toss green beans and continue to cook, stirring occasionally, until green beans are softened and charred, 4 to 5 minutes. Using tongs, transfer green beans to serving bowl, leaving any excess oil in skillet. Sprinkle with scallions, if using, and sesame mixture and serve.

PANTRY IMPROV

use what you have Substitute gochugaru (Korean red pepper flakes) for Sichuan pepper flakes or use ¼ teaspoon red pepper flakes. If you don't have sesame seeds, use all panko. To make this with fresh green beans, rinse the green beans (do not dry) and microwave them, covered, until tender, 6 to 12 minutes, stirring every 3 minutes. Drain them and dry well on a paper towel–lined plate before using.

level up Add a simple protein such as a fried egg or seared tofu and serve with rice.

bubble and squeak

SERVES 4 | TOTAL TIME: 1 HOUR

why this recipe works A deliciously crispy mess of fried mashed potato and cabbage, bubble and squeak gets its entertaining name from the sound the mixture makes when it pops in the hot skillet. Originally an English version of Irish colcannon or Scottish rumbledethumps, bubble and squeak found a foothold in the United States in potato-rich Maine back in the colonial era. It always contains potato and cabbage (often leftovers), but in Great Britain, it's also a catchall for whatever other vegetables and meats are kicking around the refrigerator. Feel free to improvise accordingly on this simple version. Whatever you add, channel your inner diner cook to "hash" the whole thing right in the hot buttered skillet. Spread the green-flecked mash into an even layer and let it cook, undisturbed, until the bottom is nicely browned. Then dig in, one spatula width at a time, and flip it piece by piece, continuing to flip until you create loads of flavorful, crispy browning.

1   Place potatoes and 1 tablespoon salt in medium saucepan and cover with water by 1 inch. Bring to boil over high heat. Reduce heat to medium and simmer until tip of paring knife inserted into potatoes meets no resistance, 8 to 10 minutes.

2   Drain potatoes and return them to saucepan. Add 3 tablespoons butter and pepper. Using potato masher, mash until smooth. Set aside.

3   Melt 1 tablespoon butter in 12-inch nonstick skillet over medium heat. Add onion and cook until softened, about 4 minutes. Stir in cabbage, 2 tablespoons water, and salt. Cover and cook until cabbage is wilted and lightly browned, 8 to 10 minutes, stirring occasionally. Transfer cabbage mixture to saucepan with potato mixture and stir to combine. Wipe skillet clean with paper towels.

4   Melt 2 tablespoons butter in now-empty skillet over medium-high heat. Add potato-cabbage mixture to skillet and, using rubber spatula, press into even layer. Cook, undisturbed, until bottom is well browned, about 7 minutes.

5   Flip spatula-size portions of potato mixture and lightly repack in skillet. Break remaining 2 tablespoons butter into small pieces and distribute around edge of skillet. Repeat flipping process every few minutes until potato-cabbage mixture is evenly browned, 8 to 10 minutes. Serve.

1½   pounds russet potatoes, peeled and sliced ¼ inch thick

½   teaspoon table salt, plus salt for cooking potatoes

8   tablespoons unsalted butter, cut into 8 pieces, divided

¼   teaspoon pepper

1   small onion, chopped

½   small head savoy cabbage, cored and cut into 1–inch pieces (5 cups)

PANTRY IMPROV

use what you have Any green cabbage works instead of the savoy cabbage, or use brussels sprouts. Use red, Yukon Gold, or sweet potatoes in place of all or some of the russets, or incorporate other root vegetables or winter squash.

level up Add cooked crumbled sausage or bacon, shredded corned beef, or shredded chicken to the skillet with the potato-cabbage mixture. Serve with Perfect Fried Eggs (page 275). Drizzle with any herb oil (see page 390).

anytime **hash**

SERVES 4 | TOTAL TIME: 30 MINUTES

1 pound Yukon Gold potatoes, unpeeled, cut into ½-inch pieces

8 ounces carrots, peeled and cut into ½-inch pieces

8 ounces parsnips, peeled and cut into ½-inch pieces

3 tablespoons vegetable oil, divided

¾ teaspoon table salt

½ teaspoon pepper

1 onion, chopped fine

2 garlic cloves, minced

2 teaspoons minced fresh thyme or ½ teaspoon dried

½ cup heavy cream (optional)

why this recipe works A hash is a great way to use up all kinds of vegetables, and meats, too. We start with a mix of root vegetables—potatoes, carrots, parsnips, and onions—for a basic hash that can be varied with nearly any topping or seasoning. To speed up cooking, we parcook the vegetables in the microwave before we brown and crisp them in a skillet.

1 Toss potatoes, carrots, and parsnips with 1 tablespoon oil, salt, and pepper in bowl. Cover and microwave until potatoes are translucent around edges, 5 to 8 minutes, stirring halfway through microwaving.

2 Heat remaining 2 tablespoon oil in 12-inch nonstick skillet over medium heat until shimmering. Add onion and cook until just beginning to soften, about 2 minutes. Stir in garlic and thyme and cook until fragrant, about 30 seconds.

3 Increase heat to medium-high. Stir in vegetables and cream, if using, and, using back of spatula, gently pack vegetable mixture into skillet and cook undisturbed for 2 minutes. Flip hash, 1 portion at a time, and lightly repack into skillet. Repeat flipping process every few minutes until mixture is well browned, 5 to 10 minutes. (If after 5 minutes you notice vegetable mixture isn't getting brown, increase heat slightly.) Serve.

PANTRY IMPROV

use what you have Russet, red, or sweet potatoes can be used in place of all or part of the Yukon Golds. Use other root vegetables, such as celery root, turnips, radishes, and beets, in place of the carrots and parsnips. Use other hearty herbs instead of thyme or add your favorite spice to the cooked onion.

level up Add cooked crumbled sausage, shredded corned beef, or shredded chicken to the skillet with the onion for a more substantial meal. Alternatively, serve with a simple salad, smoked fish, or eggs. Top with pickled vegetables, cheese, and/or fresh herbs. Serve with a dollop of yogurt, seasoned mayonnaise, or hot sauce.

VARIATIONS

potato, kimchi, and radish hash with fried eggs

Omit parsnips, cream, and thyme. Substitute sesame oil for vegetable oil and daikon radish for carrots in step 1. Add 1 cup drained and chopped cabbage kimchi to skillet with onion. Transfer hash to serving platter and sprinkle with 3 thinly sliced scallions. Wipe skillet clean with paper towels. Heat 1 tablespoon vegetable oil in now-empty skillet over medium-high heat until shimmering. Add 4–8 eggs and sprinkle with salt and pepper to taste. Cover and cook for 1 minute. Remove skillet from heat and let sit, covered, for 15 to 45 seconds for runny yolks, 45 to 60 seconds for soft but set yolks, or about 2 minutes for medium-set yolks. Serve hash with eggs.

beet and potato hash with smoked salmon

Canned or vacuum-sealed cooked beets can also be used here. Use the large holes of a box grater to shred the beets.

Omit thyme and garlic and substitute shredded beets for carrots. Top hash with 4 ounces sliced smoked salmon, 2 tablespoons minced fresh chives, and 1 tablespoon Everything Bagel Seasoning (page 383). Serve with sour cream or yogurt.

sweet potato and ham hash with kale salad

Reduce Yukon Gold potatoes to 12 ounces and substitute 12 ounces sweet potatoes for carrots and parsnips. Add 8 ounces cubed ham steak with onion; increase cooking time to 5 minutes. Toss 4 ounces baby kale or spinach, 2 tablespoons extra-virgin olive oil, and 2 teaspoons hot sauce together in bowl and season with salt and pepper to taste. Top hash with salad and shaved Parmesan cheese before serving.

toppings for **toasts**

The contents of your pantry contain a world of flavors and textures to turn a good piece of toasted bread into a meal. It's a great way to use up that bread that's a day or two past fresh; toasting caramelizes the crumb and makes it sturdy enough to support the toppings. When topping toast, it helps to think in categories: A spread to slather on first, your toppings next, and a flavorful drizzle or something crunchy to finish. Slices of hearty bread make the best toast: Broil ¾-inch slices until deep golden, 1 to 2 minutes per side. Lightly rub 1 side with a clove of garlic. Brush with olive oil and top as desired before sprinkling with kosher or flake salt to taste.

- Pantry Pesto (page 137), white beans, cherry tomatoes, shaved Parmesan

- Compound butter (see page 403), sliced radishes, flake sea salt

- Sliced avocado, flaked hot-smoked salmon or trout, Yogurt Sauce (page 396), capers

- Smashed black beans, Quick Sweet and Spicy Pickled Red Onions (page 404), cherry tomatoes

- Roasted fresh or frozen asparagus, Perfect Poached Eggs (page 275), crumbled nori

- Roasted or sautéed cabbage, Perfect Poached Eggs (page 275), Harissa (page 392)

- Goat cheese, roasted or sautéed mushrooms, fresh herbs

- Ricotta or Spicy Whipped Feta (page 44), Caramelized Onions (page 384), canned artichoke hearts, olive oil drizzle

- Smashed thawed frozen fava beans, edamame, or lima beans; manchego cheese; red pepper flakes; lemon zest

- Hummus (page 41), quick pickles (page 404), chopped toasted nuts

- Roasted vegetables, Hummus (page 41), Dukkah (page 386)

- Peanut butter, banana, honey drizzle, chopped toasted nuts

- Peanut butter, roasted grapes, splash of vinegar

- Pantry Pesto (page 137), sautéed summer squash, toasted pine nuts

- Smashed roasted squash, crumbled blue cheese, baby arugula, olive oil drizzle

- Ricotta cheese or Spicy Whipped Feta (page 44), sardines, lemon zest

- Ricotta, thawed frozen or fresh peaches, arugula

- Boursin, deli-sliced roast beef, baby arugula, sun-dried tomatoes

- Fresh mozzarella cheese, thawed frozen corn, sliced pepperoni, olive oil drizzle

- Tapenade, roasted tomatoes, flake sea salt

skillet-roasted carrots
with spicy maple bread crumbs

SERVES 4 | TOTAL TIME: 40 MINUTES

why this recipe works Sweet, slightly caramelized roasted carrots are a regular addition to our pantry dinners, from grain bowls to salads. But these carrots are a stellar dish in their own right. Dressed up (just a bit) with crispy bread crumbs infused with maple and cayenne, they could be a light meal, perhaps with a dollop of yogurt, a handful of toasted nuts, or a simple sauce. To speed thing up, we move the roasting process to a covered skillet, where we steam the carrots before searing them. Steaming softens the carrots and releases their sugars; this encourages browning and makes the carrots more flexible so that they can be pressed flush against the skillet for optimal color. Once the lid is off, the carrots need only 5 to 7 minutes to develop oven-quality, golden browning. Large carrots from the bulk bin are ideal for this recipe. After cutting the carrots crosswise, quarter lengthwise any pieces that are larger than 1½ inches in diameter and halve lengthwise any pieces that are ¾ to 1½ inches in diameter. Leave whole any carrots that are narrower than ¾ inch. You will need a 12-inch nonstick skillet with a tight-fitting lid for this recipe.

- 3 **tablespoons panko bread crumbs**
- 2 **teaspoons maple syrup**
- 2 **teaspoons plus 2 tablespoons vegetable oil, divided**
- ⅛ **teaspoon plus ½ teaspoon table salt, divided**
- ⅛ **teaspoon cayenne pepper**
- ½ **cup water**
- 1½ **pounds large carrots, peeled, cut crosswise into 3- to 4-inch lengths, and cut lengthwise into even pieces**

1   Combine panko, maple syrup, 2 teaspoons oil, ⅛ teaspoon salt, and cayenne in 12-inch nonstick skillet. Cook over medium-high heat, stirring constantly, until panko is crunchy and caramel-colored, 3 to 5 minutes. Transfer to small bowl and let cool completely. Wipe skillet clean with paper towels.

2   Mix water and remaining ½ teaspoon salt in now-empty skillet until salt is dissolved. Place carrots in skillet, arranging as many carrots flat side down as possible (carrots will not fit in single layer). Drizzle remaining 2 tablespoons oil over carrots. Bring to boil over medium-high heat. Cover and cook, without moving carrots, until carrots are crisp-tender and water has almost evaporated, 8 to 10 minutes.

3   Uncover and gently shake skillet until carrots settle into even layer. Continue to cook, not moving carrots but occasionally pressing them gently against skillet with spatula, until undersides of carrots are deeply browned, 3 to 5 minutes. Stir carrots and flip pale side down. Cook until second side is lightly browned, about 2 minutes. Transfer to serving dish. Sprinkle carrots with panko mixture and serve.

PANTRY IMPROV

use what you have You can use honey or agave syrup instead of maple syrup. Use parsnips instead of carrots.

level up Add chopped, toasted pecans or almonds to the panko mixture. Sprinkle with pomegranate seeds or drizzle with any of our infused oils (see page 390). Serve with Cucumber-Herb Yogurt Sauce (page 396), plain yogurt, or All-Purpose Herb Sauce (page 396); schmear the sauce on a plate and top with the carrots.

vegetable tagine with chickpeas and olives

SERVES 4 | TOTAL TIME: 45 MINUTES

why this recipe works Tagines often mix vegetables, beans, dried fruits, and slow-braised meats. Without the meat, a vegetable tagine becomes more of a pantry occasion, and with canned beans it braises more quickly too. Microwaving the vegetables before adding them to the pot streamlines the cooking process even further. For spices, garam masala and paprika bring balanced warm, floral, and earthy notes. Green olives, raisins, and lemon recall Moroccan flavors. Serve with couscous, rice, or naan. You can make your own garam masala; see page 382.

1 Combine potatoes, carrots, 2 tablespoons oil, salt, and pepper in bowl, cover, and microwave until vegetables begin to soften, about 10 minutes.

2 Meanwhile, heat remaining 2 tablespoons oil in Dutch oven over medium-high heat until shimmering. Add onion and lemon zest and cook until onion begins to brown, about 8 minutes. Stir in garlic, paprika, and garam masala and cook until fragrant, about 30 seconds.

3 Add microwaved potatoes and carrots to Dutch oven and stir to coat with spices. Stir in broth, chickpeas, olives, and raisins. Cover and simmer gently until flavors blend, about 10 minutes. Uncover and simmer until vegetables are tender and sauce is slightly thickened, about 7 minutes. Stir in lemon juice and cilantro, if using, and season with salt and pepper to taste. Serve.

- 1 pound red potatoes, unpeeled, cut into 1/2-inch pieces
- 1 pound carrots, peeled and cut into 1/2-inch pieces
- 1/4 cup extra-virgin olive oil, divided
- 1 teaspoon table salt
- 1/2 teaspoon pepper
- 1 onion, halved and sliced thin
- 4 (3-inch) strips lemon zest, sliced into matchsticks, plus 2 tablespoons juice
- 5 garlic cloves, minced
- 4 teaspoons paprika
- 2 teaspoons garam masala
- 3 cups vegetable or chicken broth
- 2 (15-ounce) cans chickpeas, rinsed
- 1/2 cup pitted brine-cured green olives, halved
- 1/2 cup raisins
- 1/4 cup minced fresh cilantro (optional)

PANTRY IMPROV

use what you have Substitute any white beans for chickpeas. Vary the root vegetables: try Yukon Gold potatoes, parsnips, rutabaga, or celery root (2 pounds total). Use other brine-cured olives, or 1/4 cup capers or jarred jalapeños. Use other chopped dried fruit instead of raisins. Use parsley, mint, or chives in place of cilantro.

level up Serve with a dollop of Greek yogurt. Stir in up to 1 cup cooked, diced protein such as chicken or fish. Stir in a spoonful of chopped preserved lemon before serving.

vindaloo-style **sweet potatoes**

SERVES 4 | TOTAL TIME: 1¼ HOURS

- 2 tablespoons vegetable oil
- 2 onions, chopped fine
- 1 pound sweet potatoes, peeled and cut into ½-inch pieces
- 1 pound red potatoes, unpeeled, cut into ½-inch pieces
- 1½ teaspoons table salt, divided
- 10 garlic cloves, minced
- 4 teaspoons paprika
- 1 teaspoon ground cumin
- ¾ teaspoon ground cardamom
- ½ teaspoon cayenne pepper
- ¼ teaspoon ground cloves
- 2½ cups water, vegetable broth, or chicken broth
- 2 bay leaves
- 1 tablespoon mustard seeds
- 1 (28-ounce) can diced tomatoes
- 2½ tablespoons red wine vinegar
- ¼ cup minced fresh cilantro (optional)

why this recipe works The word "vindaloo" has evolved to indicate a hot curry, but the original dish blends Portuguese and Indian influences in a bright but relatively mild pork braise that's tangy with vinegar, flavored and tinted with Kashmiri chiles, and seasoned with warm spices. We take inspiration from those flavors in this comforting vegetarian stew of sweet and red potatoes. A mix of warm spices provides exceptionally deep flavor, with paprika adding color in place of the Kashmiri chiles. But we found that after 45 minutes of simmering, the potatoes still weren't cooked. A second look at our ingredients showed us why: The acidic environment created by the tomatoes and vinegar was preventing the potatoes from becoming tender. To test our theory, we whipped up another batch, this time leaving out the tomatoes and vinegar until the end, cooking them just enough to mellow their flavors. Sure enough, after just 15 minutes, the potatoes were perfectly tender.

1   Heat oil in Dutch oven over medium heat until shimmering. Add onions, sweet potatoes, red potatoes, and ½ teaspoon salt and cook, stirring occasionally, until onions are softened and potatoes begin to soften at edges, 10 to 12 minutes.

2   Stir in garlic, paprika, cumin, cardamom, cayenne, and cloves and cook until fragrant and vegetables are well coated, about 2 minutes. Gradually stir in water, scraping up any browned bits. Stir in bay leaves, mustard seeds, and remaining 1 teaspoon salt and bring to simmer. Cover, reduce heat to medium-low, and cook until potatoes are tender, 15 to 20 minutes.

3   Stir in tomatoes and their juice and vinegar and continue to simmer, uncovered, until flavors meld and sauce has thickened slightly, about 15 minutes. Discard bay leaves; stir in cilantro, if using; and season with salt and pepper to taste. Serve.

PANTRY IMPROV

use what you have Use all sweet potatoes or red potatoes, or up to 2 pounds of parsnips, rutabaga, and/or celery root. A can of whole peeled tomatoes, chopped, can replace the diced tomatoes. You can vary the spice profile by using 2½ teaspoons garam masala in place of the cumin, cardamom, pepper, and cloves. Any wine vinegar will work. Try mint, parsley, or chives in place of the cilantro.

level up Top with a dollop of yogurt.

bagna cauda potatoes

SERVES 4 | TOTAL TIME: 55 MINUTES

why this recipe works There are times when a single anchovy can bring that perfect, *can't-quite-place-it* savory note to a dish. And there are times like this one, where you'll want to use the whole tin. The reference point is bagna cauda, which means "hot bath": a rustic Italian mix of anchovies, garlic, and usually olive oil that's traditionally served as a dip for vegetables and bread. We think it's too good to be limited to appetizer status, and use it here to bathe warm, tender slices of boiled potatoes; their relatively mild flavor allows the bold sauce to shine. For the best results, use a high-quality extra-virgin olive oil. One 2-ounce can of anchovies usually contains about 11 anchovies. This may seem like a lot of anchovies, but their flavor mellows as they cook.

2 **pounds red potatoes, unpeeled, sliced ½ inch thick**

   Table salt for cooking potatoes

½ **cup extra-virgin olive oil**

1 **(2-ounce) can anchovies, drained and minced**

9 **garlic cloves, minced**

1 **tablespoon lemon juice**

1 **teaspoon pepper**

3 **tablespoons minced fresh chives (optional)**

1 Place potatoes and 1 tablespoon salt in large saucepan, add water to cover by 1 inch, and bring to boil over high heat. Reduce heat to medium and cook until potatoes are fork-tender, about 10 minutes. Drain potatoes and transfer to large bowl; set aside.

2 Add oil, anchovies, and garlic to now-empty saucepan and cook over medium heat until garlic is fragrant, about 4 minutes, stirring occasionally.

3 Immediately add oil mixture, lemon juice, and pepper to bowl with potatoes. Toss to combine. Let sit for 5 minutes. Transfer potatoes to serving platter. Spoon any remaining oil mixture in bowl over top. Sprinkle with chives, if using, and serve.

PANTRY IMPROV

use what you have Boiled or steamed cauliflower, broccoli, or asparagus will work instead of potatoes, but the cooking time will change. Fresh parsley or basil would work in place of the chives.

level up Add canned tuna or a couple of hard-cooked eggs to make this a light meal. Or top with seared salmon or cod.

hasselback **potato casserole**

SERVES 4 | TOTAL TIME: 2 HOURS

3 ounces bacon or pancetta, chopped fine

1 onion, chopped fine

¾ cup chicken or vegetable broth, divided

1 garlic clove, minced

1½ teaspoons minced fresh rosemary or thyme or ¾ teaspoon dried, divided

½ teaspoon table salt

½ teaspoon pepper

2 pounds large russet or Yukon Gold potatoes, unpeeled

3 ounces Gruyère cheese, shredded (1 cup), divided

1 ounce Parmesan or Pecorino Romano cheese, grated (½ cup), divided

why this recipe works This extra-crispy take on potato gratin, credited to chef and author J. Kenji López-Alt, an America's Test Kitchen alumnus, melds potato gratin with Hasselback potatoes (purportedly created by Leif Elisson in 1953 at the Hasselbacken Restaurant Academy in Stockholm). Stacking potato slices vertically allows for crispier browning and better distribution of cheese and seasonings. No wonder the internet went nuts for it. Here is a loaf pan–size version of this dish to indulge our cravings on any night. Using a mandoline ensures that the potato slices are uniformly thin for an unfailingly tender interior and well-browned top. We layer in our own complementary flavors: crispy bacon, onion that caramelizes in the rendered bacon fat, garlic for pungent bite, and piney rosemary. Finally, we incorporate two cheeses, a semifirm melty cheese plus Parmesan, to provide nuttiness and creaminess while structurally melding the potato slices together. Depending on the type and size of the potatoes you use, you should be able to accommodate 3 or 4 crosswise rows.

1 Adjust oven rack to middle position and heat oven to 400 degrees. Cook bacon in 10-inch skillet over medium heat until rendered and crisp, 5 to 7 minutes. Stir in onion and ¼ cup broth. Cover and cook, stirring occasionally, until most of liquid has evaporated, 5 to 7 minutes. Uncover and continue to cook until onion is well browned, about 5 minutes. Stir in garlic, 1¼ teaspoons rosemary, salt, and pepper and cook until fragrant, about 1 minute.

2 Grease 8½ by 4½-inch loaf pan. Using mandoline, slice potatoes crosswise ⅛ inch thick. Combine potatoes, ½ cup Gruyère, ¼ cup Parmesan, bacon-onion mixture, and remaining ½ cup broth in large bowl, breaking up any stacked potatoes and making sure potatoes are well coated.

3 Stack 4 inches of potatoes, then lay stack on its side across short side of pan. Continue stacking and laying down potatoes to create 2 or 3 more rows. (Potato slices should fit snugly without having to be squeezed in; you may not need all of them.) Pour remaining broth mixture in bowl over potatoes. Push any pieces of bacon or onion on top of potatoes down into valleys between rows.

4   Cover pan tightly with aluminum foil and bake for
45 minutes. Uncover and continue to bake until tops of
potatoes are golden brown and paring knife inserted into
potatoes meets very little resistance, about 15 minutes.

5   Combine remaining ¼ teaspoon rosemary, remaining
½ cup Gruyère, and remaining ¼ cup Parmesan in bowl.
Sprinkle potatoes with cheese mixture and bake until cheese
is melted and lightly browned, 8 to 10 minutes. Let cool
slightly before serving.

PANTRY IMPROV

use what you have Any semifirm cheese such
as cheddar, mozzarella, Monterey Jack, or
Emmentaler can be used instead of Gruyère.

level up Serve as a side dish or make it the feature
of a meal with a simple salad. Top leftovers with
fried or poached eggs for a delicious diner-style
breakfast.

twice-baked potatoes
with cheddar and scallions

SERVES 4 | TOTAL TIME: 2 HOURS, PLUS 20 MINUTES COOLING

- 4 russet or sweet potatoes (about 8 ounces each), unpeeled, rubbed lightly with vegetable oil
- 4 ounces sharp cheddar cheese, shredded (1 cup)
- ½ cup sour cream or Greek yogurt
- ½ cup vegetable or chicken broth
- 2 tablespoons unsalted butter, softened
- 3 scallions, sliced thin (optional)
- ½ teaspoon table salt

PANTRY IMPROV

use what you have You can use any crumbled soft cheese or shredded semifirm cheese (such as Monterey Jack or Gruyère) instead of cheddar. Use any fresh herbs instead of scallions.

level up Stir 6 ounces thawed frozen chopped broccoli, spinach, or kale into potato mixture in step 3. Stir up to 1 cup shredded or diced cooked chicken or ham, or black or pinto beans, into potato mixture in step 3. Sprinkle with crispy bacon. Top with salsa, jarred jalapeños, fresh herbs, and/or more sour cream.

why this recipe works Twice-baked potatoes embody the ethos of doing more with less: Mash up the center of a baked potato, leave the shell crispy, and you're rewarded with a variety of textures and flavors in every bite. That filling is also a canvas for flavor (cheese is just the start), making this recipe flexible in the pantry department, and we take things a step further by showing how to twice-bake starchy russets as well as sweet potatoes. (The key with sweet potatoes is to jump-start their cooking in the microwave.) After scooping out the baked potatoes' centers, we return the hollowed-out shells to the oven to keep them crisp. For the filling, we like a base of tangy dairy, broth, cheese, and a small amount of butter. Most potatoes have two relatively flat, blunt sides and two curved sides. Halve the baked potatoes lengthwise so the blunt sides are down once the shells are stuffed, making the potatoes much more stable in the pan during final baking.

1   Adjust oven rack to upper-middle position and heat oven to 400 degrees. If using sweet potatoes, place on large plate and microwave until potatoes yield to gentle pressure and centers register 200 degrees, 6 to 9 minutes, flipping potatoes every 3 minutes.

2   Arrange russet potatoes or microwaved sweet potatoes on aluminum foil–lined rimmed baking sheet and bake until skin is crisp and deep brown and skewer easily pierces flesh, about 1 hour. Transfer potatoes to wire rack and let cool slightly, about 10 minutes. (Leave oven on.)

3   Being careful of hot potatoes, cut each potato in half so that long, blunt sides rest on work surface. Using small spoon, scoop flesh from each half into medium bowl, leaving ⅛- to ¼-inch thickness of flesh in each shell. Arrange shells on now-empty foil-lined baking sheet and return to oven until dry and slightly crisp, about 10 minutes. Meanwhile, mash potato flesh with fork until smooth. Stir in cheddar; sour cream; broth; softened butter; scallions, if using; salt; and pepper to taste until well combined.

4   Remove shells from oven and increase oven setting to broil. Holding shells steady on pan with oven mitt or towel-protected hand, spoon mixture into crisped shells, mounding it slightly at center, and return potatoes to oven. Broil until spotty brown and crisp on top, 10 to 15 minutes. Cool for 10 minutes and serve warm.

VARIATIONS

twice-baked stuffed potatoes with ham, peas, and gruyère

Omit scallions. Substitute Gruyère cheese for cheddar. Stir 4 ounces deli ham, cut into ¼-inch pieces, ½ cup thawed frozen peas, and 1 tablespoon whole grain mustard into potato mixture in step 3.

twice-baked potatoes with chorizo and chipotle

Cook 4 ounces Mexican-style chorizo sausage, casings removed, in 12-inch skillet over medium heat, breaking up meat with spoon, until well browned, 5 to 7 minutes. Stir cooked chorizo into potato mixture in step 3. Substitute Monterey Jack cheese for cheddar and 1 tablespoon minced canned chipotle chile in adobo sauce for pepper.

twice-baked potatoes with smoked salmon and chives

Substitute 4 ounces smoked salmon, cut into ½-inch pieces, for cheddar and 3 tablespoons minced fresh chives for scallions. Sprinkle potatoes with additional chopped chives just before serving.

potato and parmesan tart

SERVES 6 TO 8 | TOTAL TIME: 2 HOURS, PLUS 1 HOUR CHILLING

1½ cups (7½ ounces) all-purpose flour

1 teaspoon table salt, divided

10 tablespoons unsalted butter, cut into ½-inch pieces and chilled

6–7 tablespoons ice water

4 ounces cream cheese

2 ounces Parmesan or Pecorino Romano cheese, grated (1 cup), divided

2 tablespoons extra-virgin olive oil

2 teaspoons Dijon mustard

1½ teaspoons minced fresh rosemary or ½ teaspoon dried, divided

¼ teaspoon pepper

1 large egg, separated

1 pound russet or Yukon Gold potatoes, peeled and sliced ⅛ inch thick

1 shallot, sliced thin

why this recipe works With little more than potatoes, Parmesan, and cream cheese, you have the makings of a buttery, crisp, free-form tart that's a major crowd-pleaser. Slicing the potatoes thin prevents any underdone spots. Folding the potatoes into a mixture of cream cheese, mustard, shallot, and Parmesan flavors them and also secures them in place. A bit of rosemary (or another sturdy herb) serves as a savory pairing for the Parmesan. A light brush of egg white on the pastry dough fosters a golden crust while acting as glue for anchoring a bit more sprinkled-on cheese, making the crust just as savory as the filling. A mandoline makes quick work of evenly slicing the potatoes.

1 Process flour and ½ teaspoon salt in food processor until combined, about 3 seconds. Scatter butter over top and pulse until mixture resembles coarse crumbs, about 10 pulses. Add 6 tablespoons ice water and process until almost no dry flour remains, about 10 seconds, scraping down sides of bowl after 5 seconds. Add up to 1 additional tablespoon ice water if dough doesn't come together.

2 Turn out dough onto lightly floured counter, form into 4-inch square, wrap tightly in plastic wrap, and refrigerate for 1 hour. (Wrapped dough can be refrigerated for up to 2 days or frozen for up to 1 month.)

3 Adjust oven rack to lower-middle position and heat oven to 375 degrees. Line rimmed baking sheet with parchment paper. Let chilled dough sit on counter to soften slightly before rolling, about 10 minutes. Roll dough into 14 by 11-inch rectangle on lightly floured counter, then transfer to prepared sheet.

4 Microwave cream cheese in large bowl until softened, 20 to 30 seconds. Whisk in ½ cup Parmesan, oil, mustard, 1 teaspoon rosemary, pepper, and remaining ½ teaspoon salt until combined, about 20 seconds. Whisk in egg yolk. Add potatoes and shallot to cream cheese mixture and stir to thoroughly coat potatoes.

5 Transfer filling to center of dough. Press filling into even layer, leaving 2-inch border on all sides. Sprinkle 6 tablespoons Parmesan and remaining ½ teaspoon rosemary over filling.

6 Grasp 1 long side of dough and fold about 1½ inches over filling. Repeat with opposing long side. Fold in short sides of dough, overlapping corners of dough to secure. Lightly beat egg white and brush over folded crust (you won't need it all). Sprinkle remaining 2 tablespoons Parmesan over crust.

7 Bake until crust and filling are golden brown and potatoes meet little resistance when poked with fork, about 45 minutes. Transfer sheet to wire rack and let tart cool for 10 minutes. Using metal spatula, loosen tart from parchment and carefully slide onto wire rack; let cool until just warm, about 20 minutes. Cut into slices and serve warm.

PANTRY IMPROV

use what you have Use Boursin instead of cream cheese. Substitute ¼ cup finely chopped red onion for the shallot, and thyme for the rosemary.

level up Serve with a green salad. Top with up to 1 cup shredded or diced cooked chicken or ham. Top with crispy bacon or pancetta. Sprinkle the tart with fresh herbs before serving. Top with fried or poached eggs.

VARIATIONS

potato tart with blue cheese and sun-dried tomatoes

Reduce Parmesan to ½ cup. Use ¼ cup in cream cheese mixture in step 4 and 2 tablespoons to sprinkle over filling in step 5. Add ¼ cup crumbled blue cheese and ¼ cup chopped sun-dried tomatoes to cream cheese mixture in step 4. Sprinkle additional ¼ cup crumbled blue cheese over filling in step 5.

potato tart with brie and crispy bacon

Substitute thyme for rosemary. Reduce Parmesan to ½ cup. Use ¼ cup in cream cheese mixture in step 4 and 2 tablespoons to sprinkle over filling in step 5. Add ¼ cup finely chopped brie cheese, rind removed, and ¼ cup crispy bacon to cream cheese mixture in step 4. Sprinkle additional ¼ cup finely chopped brie cheese, rind removed, and ¼ cup crispy bacon over filling in step 5.

potato tart with caramelized onions and goat cheese

Omit shallots. Reduce Parmesan to ½ cup. Use ¼ cup in cream cheese mixture in step 4 and 2 tablespoons to sprinkle over filling in step 5. Add ¼ cup crumbled goat cheese to cream cheese mixture in step 4 along with 1 cup Caramelized Onions (page 384). Sprinkle additional ¼ cup crumbled goat cheese over filling in step 5.

savory **onion–apple tarte tatin**

SERVES 4 | TOTAL TIME: 1¾ HOURS

1 (9½ by 9–inch) sheet puff pastry, thawed

2 tablespoons extra–virgin olive oil

1 tablespoon sugar

½ teaspoon table salt, divided

2 medium onions (1 cut through root end into 6 wedges, 1 halved and sliced ½ inch thick)

2 Granny Smith apples, peeled, cored, halved, and sliced ½ inch thick

4 teaspoons chopped fresh sage or 1 teaspoon dried

PANTRY IMPROV

use what you have Use other firm apples such as Honeycrisp, Pink Lady, or Cortland, or use pears. Try another hearty herb such as thyme or rosemary instead of the sage. If you don't have puff pastry, store-bought pie crust also works.

level up Serve with a green salad (we especially love watercress or arugula). Drizzle with a make-ahead vinaigrette (see page 395). Sprinkle with crumbled goat cheese or blue cheese.

why this recipe works Yes, tarte Tatin is traditionally an upside-down tart featuring apples caramelized in butter and sugar. But you know what else caramelizes well? Onions. In fact, using onions in a savory version (still with a couple of apples for contrasting sweetness) proves to be a revelation. They quickly pick up beautiful caramelization, while their centers turn meltingly dense and silky. We start with olive oil and just a little sugar in a cold skillet. This allows us to carefully arrange onion wedges in an attractive pinwheel; we fill in the gaps with sliced onion and set the pan on high to jump-start browning. Sliced apple and sage go on top, and then we cover the filling with store-bought puff pastry and finish it in the oven. The apples gently steam and turn into a sage-infused jammy melange, a perfect base for the onions once inverted. To thaw frozen puff pastry, let it sit either in the refrigerator for 24 hours or on the counter for 30 minutes to 1 hour.

1 Adjust oven rack to middle position and heat oven to 375 degrees. Unfold pastry onto lightly floured counter and roll into 11-inch square. Using pizza cutter or sharp knife, cut pastry into 11-inch circle. Transfer to parchment paper–lined rimmed baking sheet, cover loosely with plastic wrap, and refrigerate while preparing filling.

2 Swirl oil over bottom of 10-inch ovensafe nonstick skillet, then sprinkle with sugar and ¼ teaspoon salt. Arrange onion wedges in pinwheel shape, fanning out from center of circle. Fill in gaps with sliced onion. Cook, without stirring, over high heat until onions turn deep golden brown, 7 to 9 minutes (if pan is not sizzling after 2 minutes, adjust cooking time accordingly).

3 Off heat, sprinkle with apples, sage, and remaining ¼ teaspoon salt. Carefully transfer chilled dough to skillet, centering over filling. Being careful of hot skillet, gently fold excess dough up against skillet wall (dough should be flush with skillet edge). Using paring knife, pierce dough evenly over surface 10 times. Transfer skillet to oven and bake until crust is deep golden brown, about 45 minutes. Transfer skillet to wire rack and let cool for 10 minutes.

4 Run paring knife around edge of crust to loosen. Using dish towels or potholders, carefully place serving platter on top of skillet, and, holding platter and skillet firmly together, invert tart onto serving platter. Transfer any onion slices that stick to skillet to tart. Serve.

rustic **butternut squash and spinach tart**

SERVES 4 | TOTAL TIME: 1 HOUR

3 tablespoons extra-virgin olive oil, divided

5 ounces cream cheese, room temperature

1 teaspoon minced fresh thyme or ¼ teaspoon dried

¾ teaspoon table salt, divided

1 garlic clove, minced

1 pound butternut squash, peeled and cut into ½-inch pieces (3 cups)

4 shallots, sliced thin

1 teaspoon pepper

6 ounces frozen spinach or kale, thawed and squeezed dry

1 (9½ by 9-inch) sheet puff pastry, thawed

why this recipe works Between the flaky puff pastry and creamy, cheesy base, this tart makes eating your vegetables feel like a treat. A mixture of cream cheese, herbs, and garlic anchors the topping while adding plenty of flavor. Make sure the cream cheese is at room temperature; otherwise you could tear the tart dough when trying to spread it over the base. It may look like a lot of filling before the tart goes in the oven, but like magic the puff will rise around it. To thaw frozen puff pastry, let it sit either in the refrigerator for 24 hours or on the counter for 30 minutes to 1 hour. To dry the spinach after you thaw it, place the leaves in the center of a clean dish towel, gather the ends of the towel, and twist firmly. Letting the filling cool completely before assembling the pie ensures a crisp crust.

1 Adjust oven rack to upper-middle position and heat oven to 425 degrees. Line rimmed baking sheet with parchment paper. Combine 1 tablespoon oil, cream cheese, thyme, ¼ teaspoon salt, and garlic in small bowl; set aside.

2 Microwave squash in covered bowl until just tender, about 8 minutes; drain if needed. Meanwhile, heat remaining 2 tablespoons oil in 12-inch nonstick skillet over medium heat until shimmering. Add shallots, pepper, and remaining ½ teaspoon salt and cook, stirring frequently, until well browned and softened, 8 to 10 minutes. Toss shallots, butternut squash, and spinach together in bowl until well combined; set aside.

3 Unfold pastry onto lightly floured counter and roll into 10-inch square; transfer to prepared sheet. Lightly brush outer ½-inch border along edges of pastry with water, then fold edges of pastry over by ½ inch, pressing gently to seal. Spread reserved cream cheese mixture evenly over dough, avoiding folded border, then spread butternut squash mixture in even layer over top.

4 Bake until pastry is well browned, 20 to 30 minutes, rotating sheet halfway through baking. Transfer sheet to cooling rack and let cool for 10 minutes. Slice and serve warm or at room temperature.

PANTRY IMPROV

use what you have
Use Boursin instead of the cream cheese mixture. Use other winter squash. You can substitute fresh baby spinach; microwave it with ¼ cup water in a covered bowl until the spinach is wilted, 3 to 4 minutes. Set aside for 1 minute and then drain, pressing with a rubber spatula to release liquid.

level up Top with shredded or diced cooked chicken or ham, or crispy bacon or pancetta. Sprinkle with shredded Gruyère, crumbled blue cheese, chopped nuts, or Crispy Capers (page 388). Drizzle with Rosemary Oil (page 390) or Harissa (page 392).

pantry
proteins

scrambled eggs with pinto beans and cotija cheese

SERVES 4 | TOTAL TIME: 20 MINUTES

8 large eggs

3 tablespoons extra-virgin olive oil, divided

¼ teaspoon table salt

¼ teaspoon pepper

¼ cup jarred sliced jalapeños, chopped coarse

2 garlic cloves, minced

1 (15-ounce) can pinto or black beans, rinsed

¼ cup chopped fresh cilantro, divided (optional)

1 ounce cotija or feta cheese, crumbled (¼ cup)

why this recipe works Eggs fit seamlessly into the pantry cooking repertoire: They last about a month in the fridge, they taste great with a wide range of foods, and they can anchor quick, hearty meals such as this egg scramble. We enhance the eggs' tenderness and richness with olive oil and then incorporate flavor, heft, and textural interest with canned beans, cheese, and fresh vegetables and herbs if we have them. You can easily halve this recipe if desired; use a 10-inch skillet.

1 In medium bowl, beat eggs, 2 tablespoons oil, salt, and pepper with fork until no streaks of white remain. Heat 1 teaspoon oil, jalapeños, and garlic in 12-inch nonstick skillet over medium heat until fragrant, about 1 minute. Add beans and 3 tablespoons cilantro, if using, and cook, stirring frequently, until moisture has evaporated, about 1 minute. Transfer bean mixture to small bowl and set aside. Wash and dry skillet.

2 Heat remaining 2 teaspoons oil in clean, dry skillet over medium-high heat until shimmering. Add egg mixture and, using rubber spatula, constantly and firmly scrape along bottom and sides of skillet until eggs begin to clump and spatula just leaves trail on bottom of skillet, 30 to 60 seconds. Reduce heat to low and gently but constantly fold eggs until clumped and just slightly wet, 30 to 60 seconds. Fold in bean mixture. Transfer to serving dish; sprinkle with cotija and remaining 1 tablespoon cilantro, if using; and serve.

PANTRY IMPROV

use what you have If you don't have jarred jalapeños, use another briny pickled element such as peppadew peppers or pepperoncini. Chives or parsley can be used instead of cilantro. Queso fresco also works instead of cotija or feta.

level up Serve with warm corn or flour tortillas and hot sauce or salsa. Top with flaked smoked or tinned fish, cooked ham, or crispy bacon. You can also add Quick Sweet and Spicy Pickled Red Onions (page 404).

VARIATIONS

scrambled eggs with asparagus, smoked salmon, and chives

Omit jalapeños. Add 1 tablespoon minced fresh chives to eggs in step 1. Reduce garlic to 1 clove. Substitute 8 ounces thin asparagus, trimmed and cut into ½-inch pieces, and 2 tablespoons water for beans and cilantro. Cover and cook until crisp-tender, 3 to 4 minutes. Substitute 2 ounces torn smoked salmon for cotija. Sprinkle eggs with 1 tablespoon minced fresh chives before serving.

scrambled eggs with shiitake mushrooms and feta cheese

Omit jalapeños, beans, and cilantro. Substitute 1 minced shallot and 1 teaspoon minced fresh or ¼ teaspoon dried thyme for garlic and cook until beginning to brown, 2 to 3 minutes. Add 8 ounces thinly sliced shiitake mushrooms and ¼ cup water and cook, stirring, until softened, 5 to 8 minutes. Uncover and continue to cook until moisture has evaporated, 2 to 3 minutes. Substitute feta for cotija.

scrambled eggs with arugula, sun-dried tomatoes, and goat cheese

Omit jalapeños, beans, and cilantro. Substitute ½ finely chopped onion and ⅛ teaspoon red pepper flakes for garlic and cook until softened, about 5 minutes. Add 5 ounces baby arugula and cook just until wilted. Stir 3 tablespoons finely chopped oil-packed sun-dried tomatoes into scrambled eggs along with arugula mixture. Substitute goat cheese for cotija.

spicy chilaquiles with fried eggs

SERVES 4 | TOTAL TIME: 1½ HOURS

16 (6-inch) corn tortillas, cut into 8 wedges

6 tablespoons plus 2 teaspoons extra–virgin olive oil, divided

½ teaspoon table salt, divided

1 onion, chopped fine

2 tablespoons chili powder

3 garlic cloves, minced

1 teaspoon minced canned chipotle chile in adobo sauce

2 (8-ounce) cans tomato sauce

1½ cups vegetable or chicken broth

8 large eggs

¼ teaspoon pepper

1 tablespoon unsalted butter, cut into 4 pieces

4 ounces queso fresco, crumbled (1 cup)

2 tablespoons chopped fresh cilantro (optional)

why this recipe works This Mexican breakfast dish of crisp tortillas simmered in spicy sauce and topped with fried eggs began as a way to use up leftovers. These tortillas are baked with a little oil to ensure that they crisp up and then stirred into a quick, pantry-friendly, aromatic chile sauce flavored with chili powder and chipotle in adobo just before serving. Cracking the eggs into two small bowls and adding them to the pan all at once ensures that all eight are done at the same time. Add a final sprinkle of tangy queso fresco and fresh cilantro, if there's some handy, to round out the dish. To keep the sauced tortillas from softening too much, make sure to coat the crisped tortillas in the sauce just as the eggs finish cooking. For the best texture, we prefer to use 100 percent corn tortillas in this recipe. You will need a 12- or 14-inch nonstick skillet with a tight-fitting lid for this recipe.

1 Adjust oven racks to upper-middle and lower-middle positions and heat oven to 425 degrees. Spread tortillas evenly over 2 rimmed baking sheets. Drizzle each sheet with 2 tablespoons oil, sprinkle with ¼ teaspoon salt, and toss until evenly coated. Bake, stirring occasionally, until tortillas are golden brown and crispy, 15 to 20 minutes, switching sheets halfway through baking.

2 Meanwhile, heat 2 tablespoons oil in Dutch oven over medium heat until shimmering. Add onion and cook until softened, about 5 minutes. Stir in chili powder, garlic, and chipotle and cook until fragrant, about 30 seconds. Add tomato sauce and broth, bring to simmer, and cook, stirring occasionally, until flavors meld, about 10 minutes. Remove pot from heat.

3 Heat remaining 2 teaspoons oil in 12- or 14-inch nonstick skillet over low heat for 5 minutes. Crack eggs into 2 small bowls (4 eggs per bowl) and season with remaining ¼ teaspoon salt and pepper.

4 Increase heat to medium-high and heat until oil is shimmering. Add butter and quickly swirl to coat skillet. Working quickly, pour 1 bowl of eggs in 1 side of skillet and second bowl of eggs in other side. Cover and cook for 2 minutes.

5 Remove skillet from heat and let stand, covered, about 2 minutes for runny yolks (white around edge of yolk will be barely opaque), about 3 minutes for soft but set yolks, and about 4 minutes for medium-set yolks.

6   While eggs finish cooking, return sauce to brief simmer over medium-high heat. Off heat, stir in tortillas, cover, and let sit until tortillas have softened slightly, 2 to 5 minutes. Divide tortilla mixture among individual plates and sprinkle with queso fresco. Slide eggs on top; sprinkle with cilantro, if using; and serve immediately.

PANTRY IMPROV

use what you have Cotija or Monterey Jack works instead of the queso fresco. If you only have canned crushed tomatoes or tomato puree, add it along with some dried oregano and garlic.

level up Serve with hot sauce or salsa and sour cream. Add cooked, shredded chicken or canned beans in with tomato sauce.

fried eggs with parmesan and potato roesti

SERVES 4 | **TOTAL TIME: 1¼ HOURS**

2½   pounds Yukon Gold or russet potatoes, peeled and shredded

1½   teaspoons cornstarch

1¼   teaspoons table salt, divided

⅛   teaspoon plus ¼ teaspoon pepper, divided

5   tablespoons unsalted butter, divided, plus 1 tablespoon cut into 4 pieces and chilled

8   large eggs

2   teaspoons vegetable oil

1   ounce Parmesan or Pecorino Romano cheese, grated (½ cup)

PANTRY IMPROV

use what you have Use cheddar, mozzarella, or Monterey Jack instead of Parmesan.

level up Serve with Easy Garlic Mayonnaise (page 391) or All-Purpose Herb Sauce (page 396). Top with quick pickled vegetables (see page 404) or sauerkraut. Top with Caramelized Onions (page 384), kimchi, or smoked or tinned fish.

---

why this recipe works Swiss roesti—a crisp, golden cake of seasoned grated potatoes fried in butter—topped with a layer of fried eggs is a simple pantry meal that's greater than the sum of its parts. Producing a golden-brown crust isn't a problem using a skillet, but to avoid a gluey interior you'll want to rinse the excess starch from the shredded potatoes before wringing them in a dish towel to eliminate moisture. Tossing the dry potatoes with cornstarch helps hold the cake together. After cooking the roesti, you can use the same skillet to quickly fry the eggs; covering the skillet traps in steam, cooking the eggs from above as well as below. Use the large holes of a box grater to shred the potatoes; for the best texture, shred the potatoes lengthwise into long shreds. Squeeze the potatoes as dry as possible. You will need a 12-inch nonstick skillet with a tight-fitting lid for this recipe.

1   Place potatoes in large bowl and fill with cold water. Using hands, swirl to remove excess starch, then drain, leaving potatoes in colander.

2   Wipe bowl dry. Place one-third of potatoes in center of dish towel. Gather towel ends together and twist tightly to squeeze out moisture. Transfer potatoes to now-empty bowl and repeat process with remaining potatoes in 2 batches. Sprinkle cornstarch, ¾ teaspoon salt, and ⅛ teaspoon pepper over potatoes. Using hands or fork, toss ingredients together until well blended.

3   Melt 2½ tablespoons butter in 12-inch nonstick skillet over medium heat. Add potato mixture and spread into even layer. Cover and cook for 6 minutes. Uncover and, using spatula, gently press potatoes down to form round cake. Cook, occasionally pressing on potatoes to shape into uniform round cake, until bottom is deep golden brown, 8 to 10 minutes.

4   Shake skillet to loosen roesti and slide onto large plate. Add 2½ table-spoons butter to skillet and swirl to coat skillet. Invert roesti onto second plate and slide roesti, browned side up, back into skillet. Cook, occasionally pressing down on roesti, until bottom is well browned, 8 to 10 minutes. Transfer roesti to cutting board and let cool slightly while making eggs. Wipe skillet clean with paper towels.

5   Crack eggs into 2 small bowls (4 eggs per bowl) and sprinkle with remaining ½ teaspoon salt and remaining ¼ teaspoon pepper. Heat oil in now-empty skillet over medium heat until shimmering. Add remaining 1 tablespoon chilled butter to skillet and quickly swirl to coat skillet. Working quickly, pour 1 bowl of eggs in 1 side of pan and second bowl of eggs in other side. Cover and cook for 2 minutes.

6   Remove skillet from heat and let sit, covered, about 2 minutes for runny yolks (white around edge of yolk will be barely opaque), about 3 minutes for soft but set yolks, and about 4 minutes for medium-set yolks. Slide eggs onto roesti, sprinkle with Parmesan, and season with salt to taste. Cut into wedges and serve.

shakshuka with chickpeas, red peppers, and tomatoes

SERVES 4 | TOTAL TIME: 45 MINUTES

2 tablespoons extra-virgin olive oil, plus extra for drizzling

1 onion, chopped fine

1 cup jarred roasted red peppers, rinsed, patted dry, and chopped coarse

1¼ teaspoons table salt, divided

½ teaspoon pepper

3 garlic cloves, minced

1½ teaspoons smoked paprika

1½ teaspoons ground cumin

½ teaspoon red pepper flakes

1 (28-ounce) whole peeled tomatoes, drained with juice reserved, crushed by hand to small pieces

1 (15-ounce) can chickpeas, rinsed

8 large eggs

why this recipe works Enjoyed throughout North Africa and the Middle East, this dish features eggs poached in a bright, punchy tomato sauce fragrant with warm spices and spiked with roasted peppers. Canned and jarred ingredients make this a meal that you can eat any time of day or night. Shakshuka is easy to customize with your choice of proteins (such as the chickpeas here), vegetables, and herbs. Let the runny yolks mingle with the sauce and scoop everything up with pita or crusty bread. You will need a 12-inch nonstick skillet with a tight-fitting lid for this recipe.

1 Heat oil in 12-inch nonstick skillet over medium-high heat until shimmering. Add onion, red peppers, 1 teaspoon salt, and pepper and cook until onion is softened, about 4 minutes. Stir in garlic, paprika, cumin, and red pepper flakes and cook until fragrant, about 1 minute. Stir in tomatoes and reserved juice and chickpeas. Bring to simmer and cook until flavors meld and sauce is slightly thickened, about 5 minutes.

2 Off heat, use back of spoon to make 8 shallow 1½-inch indentations in sauce (seven around perimeter and one in center). Crack 1 egg into each indentation. Spoon sauce over edges of egg whites so that whites are partially covered and yolks are exposed. Sprinkle eggs with remaining ¼ teaspoon salt.

3 Return skillet to medium-high heat and bring to simmer. Cover, reduce heat to medium-low, and cook until egg whites are fully set and yolks are still runny, about 8 minutes, rotating skillet occasionally for even cooking. Drizzle with extra oil and serve immediately.

PANTRY IMPROV

use what you have Use two fresh bell peppers instead of jarred. Chop, add with the onion, and increase the cooking time to about 8 minutes. Substitute white beans for the chickpeas. Use traditional paprika in place of smoked and diced tomatoes instead of whole.

level up Sprinkle shakshuka with fresh herbs (parsley, mint, and cilantro are all good choices), crumbled goat cheese, or feta. Serve with plain yogurt or Yogurt Sauce (page 396).

VARIATIONS

tofu shakshuka with white beans and zucchini

We prefer silken tofu here, but other styles will work.

Omit cumin. Substitute cannellini beans for chickpeas and ½ teaspoon dried oregano for paprika. Add 1 small zucchini, cut into ½-inch pieces with onion; increase cooking time to 8 minutes. Cut one 14-ounce block tofu into 8 pieces; substitute tofu pieces for eggs and simmer, uncovered, in step 3. Sprinkle shakshuka with ½ cup grated Parmesan and ½ cup shredded fresh basil before serving.

garam masala—spiced shakshuka with spinach and yogurt

Substitute 12 ounces frozen spinach, thawed and squeezed dry, for red peppers, and 1 tablespoon Garam Masala (page 382) for paprika and red pepper flakes. Sprinkle shakshuka with ½ cup chopped fresh mint and serve with yogurt.

shakshuka with black beans, chiles, and avocado

Substitute frozen corn for red peppers, 1 tablespoon minced canned chipotle chile in adobo for smoked paprika and red pepper flakes, and black beans for chickpeas. Add ½ cup canned chopped green chiles with tomatoes. Top shakshuka with 1 diced avocado and sprinkle with ½ cup chopped fresh cilantro. Serve with warmed tortillas and lime wedges.

smoked salmon and potato **frittata**

SERVES 4 | TOTAL TIME: 45 MINUTES

why this recipe works Eggs and potatoes are a complementary pair that you can use as the starting point for hearty meals such as this bagel-inspired frittata. Frozen hash browns make the prep completely hassle-free. Smoked salmon and softened cream cheese blend in seamlessly with the egg and potato mixture. A sprinkling of everything bagel seasoning finishes the dish with contrasting crunch. (To make your own, see page 383.) You will need a 12-inch ovensafe nonstick skillet for this recipe.

1   Adjust oven rack to upper-middle position and heat oven to 375 degrees. Microwave half of cream cheese in large bowl until softened, about 20 seconds. Whisk in water until smooth. Whisk in eggs and salt. Combine onion and lemon juice in second bowl; set aside.

2   Heat oil in 12-inch ovensafe nonstick skillet over medium-high heat until shimmering. Add potatoes and cook until tender, about 5 minutes. Stir in egg mixture and salmon. Off heat, scatter remaining cream cheese over top and press lightly to partially submerge. Sprinkle evenly with bagel seasoning. Transfer skillet to oven and bake until frittata is just set in center, 10 to 12 minutes.

3   Using rubber spatula, loosen frittata from skillet and transfer to cutting board. Cut frittata into wedges and serve sprinkled with onion.

4   ounces cream cheese, cut into ½-inch pieces, divided

¼   cup water

10   large eggs

⅛   teaspoon table salt

½   red or yellow onion, sliced thin

2   tablespoons lemon juice

2   tablespoons extra-virgin olive oil

2   cups frozen diced hash brown potatoes

4   ounces smoked salmon, chopped

2½   teaspoons everything bagel seasoning

PANTRY IMPROV

use what you have You can use any smoked, flaked fish instead of the salmon: white fish works especially well. Instead of everything bagel seasoning you can use toasted sesame seeds. Or try Aleppo pepper for a spicier finish, or furikake to enhance the flavor of the smoked salmon.

level up Stir some sautéed mushrooms or red peppers in with the potatoes. Serve with a tomato-onion salad. Dollop with cream cheese. Top with sliced tomatoes, capers, olives, baby arugula, or watercress.

empty-your-breadbox **skillet strata**

SERVES 4 | TOTAL TIME: 35 MINUTES

why this recipe works A strata sounds—and tastes—pretty impressive, but this eggy, cheesy preparation couldn't be easier. It requires just a handful of pantry ingredients and gives you the perfect opportunity to use up odds and ends from your breadbox. If the bread is still fresh, just toast it in a skillet so it won't turn to mush by the end of cooking. Add the egg-and-cheese custard off the heat and finish the strata in the oven for an impressively delicate souffléd texture. Use whatever kind of bread appeals to you, or a mixture (even burger buns or English muffins will work); don't trim the crusts or the strata will be too dense and eggy. You will need a 10-inch ovensafe nonstick skillet for this recipe.

1   Adjust oven rack to middle position and heat oven to 425 degrees. Whisk eggs, milk, and pepper together in bowl, then stir in pepper Jack.

2   Cook bacon in 10-inch ovensafe nonstick skillet over medium-high heat until fat begins to render, about 2 minutes. Add onion and salt and cook until onion is softened and lightly browned, about 6 minutes. Stir in bread until evenly coated and cook, stirring occasionally, until bread is lightly toasted, about 3 minutes.

3   Off heat, fold in egg mixture until slightly thickened and well combined with bread. Gently press on top of strata to help bread soak up egg mixture. Transfer skillet to oven and cook until center of strata is puffed and edges have browned and pulled away slightly from sides of pan, about 12 minutes. Sprinkle with scallions, if using, and serve.

 6 large eggs

1½ cups milk

 ¼ teaspoon pepper

 4 ounces pepper Jack cheese, shredded (1 cup)

 4 ounces bacon or pancetta, chopped fine

 1 onion, chopped fine

 ½ teaspoon table salt

1¼ cups bread cut into 1-inch squares (about 5 slices)

 2 scallions, sliced thin (optional)

PANTRY IMPROV

use what you have Use any semisoft cheese instead of pepper Jack: Cheddar or Monterey Jack works particularly well. Substitute any fresh herbs for the scallions; we especially like parsley, chives, or basil.

level up For some freshness and bite, top with watercress or baby arugula. Or make it a meal by serving the strata alongside a green salad. Sprinkle with Everything Bagel Seasoning (page 383).

eggs

Stored in their carton on a refrigerator shelf (not the door), eggs will keep for a few weeks, at the ready whenever you need them. To turn a side dish into a meal, check out the "level up" suggestions throughout the book, which use eggs cooked in one of these four easy ways. Or make your own combinations: Add hard-cooked eggs to a crisp green salad, or soft-cooked or poached eggs to a wilted salad or brothy noodle dish. Perch a fried egg on a serving of rice or beans, or slip it into a sandwich.

easy-peel hard-cooked eggs

makes 1 to 6 eggs | total time: 40 minutes

Be sure to use eggs that have no cracks and are cold from the refrigerator. You can double this recipe as long as you use a pot and steamer basket large enough to hold the eggs in a single layer. There's no need to peel the eggs right away. They can be stored in their shells for up to five days and peeled when needed.

1–6 large eggs

1   Bring 1 inch water to rolling boil in medium saucepan over high heat. Place eggs in steamer basket. Transfer basket to saucepan. Cover, reduce heat to medium-low, and cook eggs for 13 minutes.

2   When eggs are almost finished cooking, combine 2 cups ice cubes and 2 cups cold water in medium bowl. Using tongs or spoon, transfer eggs to ice bath; let sit for 15 minutes. Peel before using.

soft-cooked eggs

makes 1 to 6 eggs | total time: 20 minutes

Be sure to use eggs that have no cracks and are cold from the refrigerator. Because precise timing is vital to the success of this recipe, we strongly recommend using a digital timer. If you have one, a steamer basket makes lowering the eggs into the boiling water easier. You can serve these eggs in eggcups and with buttered toast for dipping, or you can chill and peel them as for hard-cooked eggs.

1–6 large, extra-large, or jumbo eggs

1   Bring ½ inch water to boil in medium saucepan over medium-high heat. Using tongs, gently place eggs in boiling water (eggs will not be submerged). Cover saucepan and cook eggs for 6½ minutes.

2   Uncover, transfer saucepan to sink, and place under cold running water for 30 seconds. Remove eggs from pan and serve, seasoning with salt and pepper to taste.

perfect fried eggs

makes 4 eggs | **total time: 20 minutes**

Once you raise the heat, don't dawdle; each step from here takes less than a minute. When checking the eggs for doneness, lift the lid just a crack to prevent loss of steam should they need further cooking. To fry just two eggs, use an 8- or 9-inch nonstick skillet and halve the amounts of oil and butter. You can use this method with extra-large or jumbo eggs without altering the timing.

- 2 **teaspoons vegetable oil**
- 4 **large eggs, divided**
- 2 **teaspoons unsalted butter, cut into 4 pieces and chilled**

1 Heat oil in 12- or 14-inch nonstick skillet over low heat for 5 minutes. Meanwhile, crack 2 eggs into small bowl and season with salt and pepper. Repeat with remaining 2 eggs in second small bowl.

2 Increase heat to medium-high and heat until oil is shimmering. Add butter to skillet and quickly swirl to coat skillet. Working quickly, pour 1 bowl of eggs in 1 side of skillet and second bowl of eggs in other side. Cover and cook for 1 minute. Let skillet stand off heat, covered, 15 to 45 seconds for runny yolks (white around edge of yolk will be barely opaque), 45 to 60 seconds for soft but set yolks, and about 2 minutes for medium-set yolks. Slide eggs onto plates and serve.

perfect poached eggs

makes 1 to 4 eggs | **total time: 20 minutes**

Once the cover is removed, you can check the eggs individually, removing them once the white nearest to the yolk is just set. For the best results, be sure to use the freshest eggs possible. This recipe can be used to cook from one to four eggs. To make two batches of eggs to serve all at once, transfer four cooked eggs directly to a large pot of 150-degree water and cover them. This will keep them warm for 15 minutes or so while you return the poaching water to a boil and cook the next batch.

- 1–4 **large eggs**
- 1 **tablespoon distilled white vinegar**
  Table salt for poaching eggs

1 Bring 6 cups water to boil in Dutch oven over high heat. Meanwhile, crack eggs, one at a time, into colander. Let stand until loose, watery whites drain away from eggs, 20 to 30 seconds. Gently transfer eggs to 2-cup liquid measuring cup.

2 Add vinegar and 1 teaspoon salt to boiling water. With lip of measuring cup just above surface of water, gently tip eggs into water, one at a time, leaving space between them. Cover pot; remove from heat; and let stand until whites closest to yolks are just set and opaque, about 3 minutes. If after 3 minutes whites are not set, let stand in water, checking every 30 seconds, until eggs reach desired doneness. (For medium-cooked yolks, let eggs sit in pot, covered, for 4 minutes, then begin checking for doneness.)

3 Using slotted spoon, carefully lift and drain each egg over Dutch oven. Season with salt and pepper to taste, and serve.

matzo brei

SERVES 2 | TOTAL TIME: 20 MINUTES

why this recipe works Matzo brei (Yiddish for "fried matzo") is one of those dishes that has transcended its humble "do-without" origins to become a luxuriously comforting meal. The backbone ingredients are eggs and matzo, an unleavened flatbread made simply from flour and water. Soaking the broken matzo pieces in the whisked eggs cuts out the usual separate step of soaking them in water or milk before cooking. Frying the egg-matzo mixture in butter or schmaltz gives the dish a rich flavor that provides an ideal backdrop for a range of toppings and seasonings. You can take this dish in a savory or sweet direction with equally satisfying results; here we choose savory—and simple—by adding just a bit of chopped onion. The remaining embellishments are up to you. When breaking the matzo, don't worry if the pieces are slightly irregular. Different brands of matzo hydrate at slightly different rates; start checking for softness at the beginning of the time range in step 2.

2½ tablespoons unsalted butter or schmaltz

⅔ cup chopped onion

½ teaspoon pepper, divided

¼ teaspoon table salt, divided

3 large eggs

2 sheets plain, unsalted matzo (about 2 ounces), broken into approximate 1½-inch pieces

1 tablespoon chopped fresh dill (optional)

1 Melt butter in 10-inch nonstick skillet over medium heat. Add onion, ¼ teaspoon pepper, and ⅛ teaspoon salt and cook, stirring occasionally, until onion has softened and started to brown, 6 to 8 minutes.

2 While onion cooks, whisk eggs, remaining ¼ teaspoon pepper, and remaining ⅛ teaspoon salt in medium bowl until no streaks of white remain. Add matzo pieces to egg mixture. Stir and fold until matzo is thoroughly coated with egg and pieces have softened (they should maintain their shape, but you should be able to break them easily with spatula), 2 to 4 minutes.

3 Add matzo mixture to skillet and gently but constantly stir and fold mixture onto itself, scraping along bottom and sides of skillet as needed until eggs are soft and just set, about 2 minutes. Transfer to serving dish; sprinkle with dill, if using; and serve.

PANTRY IMPROV

use what you have Parsley or chives can be substituted for the dill. Substitute Caramelized Onions (page 384) or chopped mushrooms for the onion.

level up Top with flaked, smoked fish such as salmon or white fish, or pastrami. Top with sautéed or pickled vegetables (see page 404), or capers. Dollop with crème fraîche, yogurt, or sour cream. Stir thawed frozen vegetables in with the onion.

cheese enchiladas

SERVES 4 | TOTAL TIME: 1¼ HOURS

2 tablespoons vegetable oil

1 onion or red onion, chopped fine, divided

3 tablespoons chili powder

4 teaspoons tomato paste

4 garlic cloves, minced

3 tablespoons all-purpose flour

3 cups chicken or vegetable broth

12 (6-inch) corn or flour tortillas, warmed

1 pound Monterey Jack cheese, shredded (4 cups), divided

Lime wedges for serving (optional)

PANTRY IMPROV

use what you have Substitute chipotle or ancho chile powder or taco seasoning for chili powder. You can use any semisoft cheese instead of Monterey Jack; try cheddar or pepper Jack.

level up Stir cooked, shredded chicken or canned beans into the cheese before rolling. Serve with whatever toppings you have on hand, such as salsa, chopped avocado, sour cream, and/or cilantro.

why this recipe works This easy Tex-Mex dish can be pulled together from the contents of your cupboard and fridge, but it tastes satisfyingly complex. A heavy dose of chili powder packs some serious spice and earthiness into the bold red sauce. Cooking the chili powder in the skillet along with onion, tomato paste, and garlic adds flavor intensity. Enjoy these enchiladas simply filled with cheese or add in beans, vegetables, or shredded meat.

1 Adjust oven rack to middle position and heat oven to 450 degrees. Heat oil in 12-inch skillet over medium heat until shimmering. Add three-quarters of onion and cook until softened, 3 to 5 minutes. Stir in chili powder, tomato paste, and garlic and cook until fragrant, about 30 seconds. Stir in flour and mash into skillet with wooden spoon until well combined, about 30 seconds. Gradually add broth, whisking constantly to smooth out any lumps. Bring to simmer and cook until thickened slightly, about 4 minutes.

2 Spread 1 cup sauce in bottom of 13 by 9-inch baking dish. Spread ¼ cup cheese across center of 1 warm tortilla, tightly roll tortilla around filling, then place seam side down in prepared dish. Repeat with remaining 11 tortillas (2 columns of 6 tortillas will fit neatly across width of dish).

3 Pour remaining sauce over top of enchiladas and sprinkle with remaining 1 cup cheese. Cover dish with lightly greased aluminum foil and bake until cheese is melted, about 10 minutes. Uncover and continue to bake until sauce is bubbling around edges, about 5 minutes. Let cool for 10 minutes, then sprinkle with remaining onion. (Refrigerate enchiladas for up to 2 days or freeze for up to 1 month). Serve with lime wedges, if using.

tartiflette

SERVES 4 | TOTAL TIME: 1¾ HOURS

8 ounces ripe Camembert cheese, rind left on

1¾ pounds Yukon Gold or red potatoes, unpeeled, halved lengthwise and sliced into ¼-inch half-moons

6 ounces bacon or pancetta, cut into ½-inch pieces

1 large onion, chopped fine

1¼ teaspoons table salt, divided

2½ teaspoons minced fresh thyme or ¾ teaspoon dried

2 garlic cloves, minced

½ cup dry white wine or dry vermouth

½ cup heavy cream

¼ teaspoon pepper

Crème fraîche (optional)

why this recipe works Tartiflette was invented to promote French cheese, but the foundation of this luscious dish is a rustic preparation of potatoes, bacon, and onion—basics we often have on hand. We leave the skins on the potatoes to maximize their earthy flavor. Chopped bacon delivers meaty smokiness, and cooking a chopped onion in the bacon fat ensures that the smoky essence permeates the whole dish. Cream contributes silkiness while a splash of white wine brings welcome acidity to temper the gratin's richness. Finally, we top the potatoes with cubes of Camembert (a stateside stand-in for the traditional Reblochon; see "Pantry Improv" for more possibilities). A quick stint in a hot oven melts the cheese, enveloping the dish in a creamy blanket. If your cheese is very runny, chill it before cutting it and hold the pieces in the freezer until you're ready to use them. A 2-quart baking dish of any dimensions can be used in place of the 8-inch square baking dish. To make your own crème fraîche, see page 398.

1 Adjust oven rack to middle position and heat oven to 400 degrees. Line large plate with paper towels. Grease 8-inch square baking dish. Cut Camembert in half horizontally to create 2 pieces of equal thickness. Cut each half into ¾-inch pieces.

2 Place steamer basket in large saucepan. Add water to barely reach bottom of steamer and bring to boil over high heat. Add potatoes, cover, and reduce heat to medium (small wisps of steam should escape from beneath lid). Cook until potatoes are just cooked through and tip of paring knife inserted into potatoes meets little resistance, 15 to 17 minutes. Leaving potatoes in steamer, remove steamer from saucepan; set aside and let cool slightly, at least 10 minutes.

3 While potatoes cool, cook bacon in 12-inch skillet over medium heat, stirring occasionally, until browned and chewy-crisp, 4 to 6 minutes. Using slotted spoon, transfer bacon to prepared plate; pour off all but 2 tablespoons bacon fat. Add onion and ½ teaspoon salt to fat left in skillet and cook over medium heat, stirring occasionally, until onion is softened and beginning to brown, about 7 minutes. Add thyme and garlic and continue to cook, stirring occasionally, until fragrant, about 2 minutes. Add wine and cook until reduced by half, about 2 minutes. Off heat, stir in cream, pepper, and remaining ¾ teaspoon salt.

4   Add potatoes to skillet and stir gently to coat with onion mixture. Transfer half of potato mixture to prepared dish and spread into even layer. Top evenly with half of bacon. Add remaining potatoes and top evenly with remaining bacon. Arrange Camembert, rind side up, in even layer on top. Bake until bubbling and lightly browned, about 20 minutes. Let cool for 10 minutes before serving. Top each serving with spoonful of crème fraîche, if using.

PANTRY IMPROV

use what you have Alternatives for the Camembert include Taleggio, Brie, Humbolt Fog, Harbison, or Reblochon.

level up Serve the tartiflette with bread and a crisp green salad.

tuna salad

While some take a certain pride in eating the same tuna salad for weeks, months, or even years, why not tap into your pantry and shake things up? Whether you want a creamy mayo-based tuna salad or a bright vinaigrette style, the options for customization are endless. For 3 cans of tuna you want about ½ cup dressing and ¾ cup add-ins. Try our Creamy Tuna Salad or our Vinaigrette-Style Tuna Salad as a starting point!

creamy tuna salad

makes 2 cups | enough for 4 sandwiches

Microwaving the onion in olive oil cooks it and releases its flavor into the oil for the salad.

- ¼ cup finely chopped onion
- 2 tablespoons extra-virgin olive oil
- 3 (6-ounce) cans solid white tuna in water, drained
- ½ cup mayonnaise
- 1 small celery rib, minced
- 2 teaspoons lemon juice
  Pinch sugar

1 Combine onion and oil in small bowl and microwave until onion begins to soften, about 2 minutes; set aside to cool for 5 minutes. Transfer tuna to medium bowl and mash with fork until finely flaked.

2 Add mayonnaise, celery, lemon juice, sugar, and onion mixture to tuna and mix until well combined. Season with salt and pepper to taste. Serve. (Salad can be refrigerated for up to 2 days.)

creamy tuna salad add-ins:

- Cornichons or other pickles and whole-grain mustard
- Easy-Peel Hard-Cooked Eggs (page 274), radishes, and capers
- Curry powder and grapes
- Apples, walnuts, and tarragon
- Wasabi and pickled ginger
- White beans and roasted red peppers
- Easy-Peel Hard-Cooked Eggs (page 274) and fresh herbs
- Chopped dried or fresh fruit
- Kimchi and scallions

vinaigrette-style tuna salad

makes 2 cups | enough for 4 sandwiches

⅓ cup extra-virgin olive oil
1½ tablespoons lemon juice
1 tablespoon Dijon mustard
1 garlic clove, minced
¾ teaspoon table salt
¼ teaspoon pepper
3 (6-ounce) jars oil-packed tuna, drained
1 cup fresh herb leaves such as parsley, chives, or cilantro

Whisk oil, lemon juice, mustard, garlic, salt, and pepper together in large bowl. Reserve 2 tablespoons vinaigrette. Add tuna and parsley to remaining vinaigrette in bowl and toss gently to combine. Drizzle reserved vinaigrette over salad. Serve.

vinaigrette-style tuna salad add-ins:

- Chopped nuts, blue cheese, and Crispy Capers (page 388)
- Olives, cherry tomatoes, and orange zest
- Thawed frozen green beans and radishes
- Jalapeño (fresh or jarred), cilantro, and salsa
- Arugula, fennel, and Herbes de Provence (page 381)
- Tomatoes, cucumber, and sumac
- Kimchi and celery
- Boiled small red potatoes and olives
- Sauerkraut
- White beans, sun-dried tomatoes, and celery

crisp breaded **chicken cutlets**

SERVES 4 | TOTAL TIME: 1 HOUR

- 4 (6- to 8-ounce) boneless, skinless chicken breasts, tenderloins removed, trimmed
- ½ teaspoon table salt
- ¼ teaspoon pepper
- 4–6 slices bread, crusts removed, torn into 1½-inch pieces (1–1½ cups)
- ¾ cup all-purpose flour
- 2 large eggs
- ¾ cup vegetable or peanut oil, for frying
- Lemon wedges (optional)

why this recipe works If you think of your freezer as an extension of your pantry, it opens up a wide range of protein possibilities, and quick-cooking, versatile boneless, skinless chicken breasts top the list. For crispy cutlets that have the appeal of fried chicken with less fuss, we pound the chicken breasts ½ inch thick, bread them, and shallow-fry them. Homemade bread crumbs are easy to make from whatever bread is on hand and they add a light, crisp texture. Using a standard breading procedure (dipping in flour, beaten egg, and bread crumbs) ensures that the breading will stay in place. Finally, resting the cutlets on a paper towel–lined wire rack for about 15 seconds per side removes grease. Make sure to remove the tenderloin from each breast so the cutlets will be a uniform shape and will cook evenly; reserve the tenderloins for another use. Don't substitute store-bought bread crumbs for the fresh bread crumbs.

1   Adjust oven rack to lower-middle position and heat oven to 200 degrees. Cover chicken breasts with plastic wrap and pound to even ½-inch thickness with meat pounder. Pat cutlets dry with paper towels and sprinkle with salt and pepper.

2   Process bread in food processor to fine crumbs, 20 to 30 seconds. Transfer bread crumbs to shallow dish. Place flour in second shallow dish. Lightly beat eggs in third shallow dish.

3   Working with 1 cutlet at a time, dredge in flour, shaking off excess; dip in egg mixture, allowing excess to drip off; and coat with bread crumbs, pressing gently to adhere. Transfer to plate and let sit for 5 minutes.

4   Set wire rack in rimmed baking sheet and cover half of rack with triple layer of paper towels. Heat oil in 12-inch nonstick skillet over medium-high heat until shimmering. Place 2 cutlets in skillet and cook until deep golden brown and crisp and chicken registers 160 degrees, about 2½ minutes per side, gently pressing on cutlets with spatula for even browning.

5   Place cutlets on paper towel–lined side of prepared wire rack to dry, about 15 seconds per side. Move cutlets to unlined side of wire rack and transfer to oven to keep warm. Repeat with remaining 2 cutlets. Serve with lemon wedges, if using.

PANTRY IMPROV

use what you have Substitute 1 large pork tenderloin (about 1 pound), cut into 4 equal pieces and pounded ½ inch thick, for the chicken cutlets.

level up You can add your favorite spice blend, grated hard cheese, or fresh herbs to the bread crumbs. Make a chicken cutlet sandwich by spreading your favorite mayonnaise or mustard on bread and topping with lettuce and tomato. Top with All-Purpose Herb Sauce (page 396) or Easy Garlic Mayonnaise (page 398).

VARIATIONS

crisp breaded chicken parmesan cutlets

Mix ¼ cup grated Parmesan cheese into bread crumbs.

crisp breaded honey-mustard chicken cutlets

Whisk 2 tablespoons honey and ¼ cup Dijon mustard into eggs. Drizzle with 1 tablespoon honey before serving.

crisp breaded garlicky chicken cutlets

Mix 1 tablespoon garlic powder into bread crumbs. Heat oil and 3 smashed garlic cloves in skillet until garlic is lightly browned, about 4 minutes; discard garlic and proceed with frying cutlets as directed.

caramelized **black pepper chicken**

SERVES 4 | TOTAL TIME: 30 MINUTES

2 tablespoons vegetable oil

2 shallots, halved and sliced thin

1 teaspoon grated fresh ginger

⅓ cup packed dark brown sugar

3 tablespoons fish sauce

2 tablespoons unseasoned
rice vinegar

1 tablespoon chili-garlic sauce

1 teaspoon coarsely ground pepper

1½ pounds boneless, skinless chicken
breasts, trimmed and cut into
¾-inch pieces

¼ cup coarsely chopped fresh
cilantro leaves and stems
(optional)

why this recipe works When you're cooking from the pantry, condiments can define the dish. Case in point: this quick and full-flavored chicken inspired by Charles Phan's recipe from his cookbook *The Slanted Door: Modern Vietnamese Food*. Borrowing a technique from Phan, we streamline a Vietnamese-style fish sauce–caramel braise by using brown sugar instead of making a caramel. Potent pantry ingredients—bottled fish sauce, rice vinegar, chili-garlic sauce, and coarse-ground black pepper—let you pull off this restaurant-quality dish in a flash. The saltiness of fish sauce can vary; we recommend Red Boat 40°N Fish Sauce.

1 Heat oil in 12-inch nonstick skillet over medium-high heat until shimmering. Add shallots and ginger and cook until softened, about 2 minutes. Stir in sugar, fish sauce, vinegar, chili-garlic sauce, and pepper and bring to simmer, stirring to dissolve sugar. Cook until very thick and syrupy, about 5 minutes.

2 Stir in chicken and cook, stirring occasionally, until cooked through, 5 to 7 minutes (sauce will thin out as chicken exudes moisture). Sprinkle with cilantro, if using, and serve.

PANTRY IMPROV

use what you have Pork tenderloin can be substituted for the chicken.

level up Serve this intensely seasoned dish with plenty of steamed white rice, preferably jasmine.

lemony chicken meatballs
with quinoa and carrots

SERVES 4 | TOTAL TIME: 1¼ HOURS

why this recipe works No disrespect to ground beef, but ground chicken is just as good a candidate for freezer storage and it makes meatballs that are light and fresh-tasting. Instead of including bread crumbs in these meatballs, we cook up a big batch of quinoa and use a cup of it to lighten their texture. Hummus binds the mixture together and also makes the base for a superquick sauce. To complete the meal we reach into the crisper drawer for earthy-sweet carrots, which we brown lightly in a skillet. Be sure to use ground chicken, not ground chicken breast (also labeled 99 percent fat-free) in this recipe.

1   Cook quinoa in medium saucepan over medium-high heat, stirring frequently, until very fragrant and making continuous popping sounds, 5 to 7 minutes. Stir in 1¾ cups water and ½ teaspoon salt and bring to simmer. Reduce heat to low, cover, and simmer until quinoa is tender and water is absorbed, 18 to 22 minutes, stirring once halfway through cooking. Remove pot from heat and let sit, covered, for 5 minutes, then gently fluff with fork and set aside to cool slightly. Meanwhile, whisk ½ cup hummus, lemon juice, and 4 teaspoons oil together in bowl. Season with salt and pepper to taste; set hummus sauce aside until ready to serve.

2   Combine ground chicken, 1 cup cooled quinoa, lemon zest, ½ teaspoon salt, pepper, and remaining ¼ cup hummus in large bowl. Using your wet hands, gently knead until combined. Pinch off and roll mixture into 20 tightly packed 1½-inch-wide meatballs.

3   Heat 3 tablespoons oil in 12-inch nonstick skillet over medium-high heat until shimmering. Add meatballs and cook until well browned and cooked through, 9 to 11 minutes, turning gently as needed. Transfer meatballs to plate and tent with aluminum foil to keep warm.

4   Add carrots, remaining 3 tablespoons water, and remaining ¼ teaspoon salt to now-empty skillet. Cover and cook over medium-high heat for 2 minutes. Uncover and cook until carrots are tender and spotty brown, 3 to 4 minutes. Stir in remaining 3 cups cooled quinoa, reduce heat to medium, and cook until quinoa is warmed through, about 2 minutes. Stir in remaining 1 tablespoon oil and season with salt and pepper to taste. Drizzle quinoa with oil to taste, and serve with meatballs and hummus sauce.

1½   cups prewashed white quinoa

1¾   cup plus 3 tablespoons water, divided

1¼   teaspoons table salt, divided

¾   cup hummus, divided

1   teaspoon grated lemon zest plus 2½ tablespoons juice

4   teaspoons plus ¼ cup extra–virgin olive oil, divided, plus extra for drizzling

1   pound ground chicken

¼   teaspoon pepper

1   pound carrots, peeled and sliced thin on bias

PANTRY IMPROV

use what you have Ground turkey can be substituted for ground chicken. Any flavor hummus works here; we like plain, garlic, lemon, or roasted red pepper.

level up A dollop of yogurt or a drizzle of Rosemary Oil (page 390) are delicious on this. If your carrots come with their greens attached, chop up about ½ cup of those and sprinkle them on top, or sprinkle with parsley or cilantro.

chicken and rice with tomatoes, white wine, and parsley

SERVES 4 | TOTAL TIME: 1¼ HOURS

3 pounds bone–in chicken pieces, (split breasts, drumsticks, and/or thighs), trimmed

2 teaspoons table salt, divided

½ teaspoon pepper

2 tablespoons extra–virgin olive oil

1 onion, chopped fine

3 garlic cloves, minced

1½ cups long–grain white rice

2 cups water or broth

1 (14.5–ounce) can diced tomatoes, drained with ½ cup juice reserved

½ cup dry white wine or dry vermouth

⅓ cup chopped fresh parsley (optional)

why this recipe works This chicken casserole checks all the boxes; it's moist, flavorful, clean-tasting, and easy to make. Bonus points for relying on pantry ingredients and for adapting to different flavor profiles (see our variations). You can use white or dark meat, or both, here. Getting perfectly cooked rice in dishes like this can be tricky; we keep it light by using a modest amount of liquid. Usually stirring rice while it cooks isn't a good idea but you'll want to do it here to ensure that the top layer is moist and fully cooked.

1 Pat chicken dry with paper towels and sprinkle with 1 teaspoon salt and pepper. Heat oil in Dutch oven over medium-high heat until just smoking. Place chicken skin side down in pot and cook until well browned, 6 to 8 minutes, reducing heat if pot begins to scorch. Flip chicken skin side up and continue to cook until lightly browned on second side, about 3 minutes; transfer to plate.

2 Pour off all but 2 tablespoons fat from pot, add onion, and cook over medium heat, stirring often, until softened, about 5 minutes. Stir in garlic and cook until fragrant, about 30 seconds. Add rice and cook, stirring frequently, until coated and glistening, about 1 minute. Stir in water, tomatoes with reserved juice, wine, and remaining 1 teaspoon salt, scraping up any browned bits. Nestle chicken thighs and drumsticks into pot and bring to boil. Reduce heat to low, cover, and simmer gently for 15 minutes. Nestle chicken breasts into pot and stir ingredients gently until rice is thoroughly mixed; cover and simmer until both rice and chicken are tender, 10 to 15 minutes. Stir in parsley, if using, cover, and let dish sit for 5 minutes; serve.

PANTRY IMPROV

use what you have Substitute 2 pounds boneless thighs for the pieces of bone-in chicken. Try basmati rice instead of long-grain. Whole peeled tomatoes can be used in place of diced if you crush them by hand before adding them.

level up Serve with a sauce (see pages 396–401).

VARIATIONS

chicken and rice with saffron, peas, and paprika

Add 1 green bell pepper, cut into ¼-inch pieces, to pot along with onion. Stir 4 teaspoons paprika and ¼ teaspoon saffron into pot along with garlic. Stir 1 cup thawed frozen peas into pot along with parsley.

chicken and rice with turmeric, coriander, and cumin

Omit parsley. Add 1 cinnamon stick to pot in step 2 and cook, stirring often, until it unfurls, about 15 seconds, before adding onion and 2 green bell peppers, cut into ¼-inch pieces. Stir 1 teaspoon ground turmeric, 1 teaspoon ground coriander, and 1 teaspoon ground cumin into pot with garlic. Substitute 1 cup canned coconut milk for 1 cup of water.

chicken and rice with anchovies, olives, and lemon

Add 5 rinsed and minced anchovy fillets to pot along with onion. Stir ½ cup pitted black olives, halved, 1 tablespoon lemon juice, and 2 teaspoons grated lemon zest into pot along with parsley.

chicken sausage with braised red cabbage and potatoes

SERVES 4 | TOTAL TIME: 1 HOUR

1½ pounds small red or yellow potatoes, unpeeled, halved

¼ cup vegetable oil, divided

¾ teaspoon table salt, divided

¼ teaspoon pepper

1½ pounds cooked chicken–apple sausage

1 onion, halved and sliced thin

1 head red or green cabbage (2 pounds), halved, cored, and shredded

1½ cups apple cider

1 apple, peeled and grated

2 bay leaves

1½ teaspoons minced fresh thyme or ½ teaspoon dried

2 tablespoons cider vinegar

2 tablespoons minced fresh chives (optional)

why this recipe works This easy, rustic dinner makes the most of the affinity between juicy sausage and four pantry mainstays: potatoes, cabbage, onion, and apple. Braising the cabbage in apple cider with grated apple, bay leaves, and thyme adds complexity in short order and keeps the cabbage's texture intact. Precooked chicken sausage offers a great change of pace from pork; simmering it with the cabbage unites the dish's sweet, salty, and tart flavors, and a hit of cider vinegar rounds things out. We use small red potatoes and cook them quickly in the microwave before browning and crisping them in the skillet. If your potatoes are larger than 2 inches, cut them into 1-inch pieces. You will need a 12-inch nonstick skillet with a tight-fitting lid for this recipe. The skillet will be very full once you add the cabbage in step 3 but will become more manageable as the cabbage wilts.

1   Toss potatoes with 1 tablespoon oil, ¼ teaspoon salt, and pepper in bowl. Cover and microwave, stirring occasionally, until potatoes are tender, about 5 minutes; drain well.

2   Meanwhile, heat 1 tablespoon oil in 12-inch nonstick skillet over medium heat until shimmering. Brown sausage on all sides, about 5 minutes; transfer to plate.

3   Add onion and remaining ½ teaspoon salt to fat left in skillet and cook over medium heat until onion is softened, about 5 minutes. Stir in cabbage, cider, apple, bay leaves, and thyme. Cover and cook until cabbage is softened, about 15 minutes. Nestle sausage into vegetables, cover, and cook until cabbage is very tender, 8 to 10 minutes.

4   Uncover and simmer until liquid is almost evaporated, 2 to 3 minutes. Transfer sausage to serving platter and discard bay leaves. Stir vinegar into vegetables and season with salt and pepper to taste. Transfer vegetables to platter with sausage and tent with aluminum foil.

5   Wipe skillet clean with paper towels. Add remaining 2 tablespoons oil to now-empty skillet and heat over medium heat until shimmering. Add potatoes cut side down and cook until browned, 2 to 5 minutes. Transfer to platter with sausage and cabbage; sprinkle with chives, if using; and serve.

PANTRY IMPROV

use what you have Use any flavor of chicken sausage that you think will pair well with this dish or use pork sausage such as bratwurst. You can use fresh chicken sausage; add it along with the cabbage and cook everything for 20 to 25 minutes. Use any kind of apple; we like tart-sweet ones such as Granny Smith or Honeycrisp.

level up Stir sauerkraut into the cabbage at the end for a briny bite.

fried onion burger

SERVES 4 | TOTAL TIME: 30 MINUTES, PLUS 35 MINUTES SALTING AND RESTING

why this recipe works If you've got ground beef in the freezer, you can always make a hamburger. But this Oklahoma specialty, with its crisp crust of caramelized onions, turns burgers into something more than a default meal. Instead of layering the onions on top of the patties, we set a ball of meat on top of each mound of onions and then press the patties down onto the onions to help them stick. We place the burgers in a buttered skillet onion side down to brown the onions and seal them onto the burgers. When the onion crust is caramelized on top and slightly crisp underneath, we flip the burgers and turn up the heat to finish cooking and get a nice sear. A mandoline makes quick work of slicing the onion thin. Squeeze the salted onion slices until they're as dry as possible, or they won't adhere to the patties.

1   Toss onion with 1 teaspoon salt in colander and let sit for 30 minutes, tossing occasionally. Transfer onion to clean dish towel, gather edges, and squeeze onion dry. Sprinkle with ½ teaspoon pepper.

2   Divide onion mixture into 4 equal mounds on rimmed baking sheet. Divide ground beef into 4 equal portions, then gently shape into balls. Place beef balls on top of onion mounds and flatten beef firmly so onions adhere and patties measure ¼ inch thick.

3   Season patties with remaining ½ teaspoon salt and remaining ¼ teaspoon pepper. Melt butter and oil in 12-inch nonstick skillet over medium heat. Using spatula, transfer patties to skillet onion side down and cook until onion is deep golden brown and beginning to crisp around edges, 8 to 10 minutes. Flip patties, increase heat to high, and continue to cook until well browned on second side, about 2 minutes. Transfer burgers to platter and let rest for 5 minutes. Place 1 slice American cheese on each bun bottom. Serve burgers on buns.

1   large onion, halved and sliced ⅛ inch thick

1½   teaspoons table salt, divided

¾   teaspoon pepper, divided

1   pound 85 percent lean ground beef

1   tablespoon unsalted butter

1   teaspoon vegetable oil

4   slices American cheese (4 ounces)

4   hamburger buns, toasted if desired

PANTRY IMPROV

use what you have Ground pork or lamb works instead of beef. Sliced cheddar, Swiss, and provolone are good substitutes for the American cheese.

level up Butter and grill the buns. Top with lettuce, tomatoes, chopped onion, pickles, mustard, ketchup, and/or Pub Burger Sauce (page 398). Or for the ultimate experience, top with paté!

cuban-style **picadillo**

SERVES 6 | TOTAL TIME: 55 MINUTES

1 pound 85 percent lean ground beef

1 pound ground pork

2 tablespoons water

½ teaspoon baking soda

¾ teaspoon table salt, divided

¼ teaspoon pepper

1 green bell pepper, stemmed, seeded, and cut into 2-inch pieces

1 onion, halved and cut into 2-inch pieces

2 tablespoons vegetable oil

1 tablespoon dried oregano

1 tablespoon ground cumin

½ teaspoon ground cinnamon

6 garlic cloves, minced

1 (14.5-ounce) can whole tomatoes, drained and chopped coarse

¾ cup dry white wine

½ cup beef or chicken broth

½ cup raisins

3 bay leaves

½ cup pimento-stuffed green olives, chopped coarse

2 tablespoons capers, rinsed

1 tablespoon red wine vinegar, plus extra for seasoning

why this recipe works Traditional recipes for this Cuban dish of spiced ground meat, sweet raisins, and briny olives call for hand-chopping or grinding the beef. We turn to a pantry staple, store-bought ground beef, and supplement it with ground pork, which adds a subtle sweetness and complexity. To help the ground meat stay tender, we skip browning it and soak the meat in a mixture of baking soda and water. Pinching it off into sizable 2-inch chunks before adding it to the pot to simmer helps to keep it moist. For the spices, we use oregano, cumin, and cinnamon and bloom them to heighten their flavor. Beef broth adds a savory boost. Raisins and green olives give the picadillo a sweet-savory balance, and a couple spoonfuls of capers and a splash of red wine vinegar added at the last minute cut through the spiced meat. Serve with rice and black beans.

1 Toss ground beef and pork with water, baking soda, ½ teaspoon salt, and pepper in bowl until thoroughly combined. Set aside for 20 minutes. Meanwhile, pulse bell pepper and onion in food processor until chopped into ¼-inch pieces, about 12 pulses.

2 Heat oil in Dutch oven over medium-high heat until shimmering. Add chopped vegetables, oregano, cumin, cinnamon, and remaining ¼ teaspoon salt; cook, stirring frequently, until vegetables are softened and beginning to brown, 6 to 8 minutes. Add garlic and cook, stirring constantly, until fragrant, about 30 seconds. Add tomatoes and wine and cook, scraping up any browned bits, until pot is almost dry, 3 to 5 minutes. Stir in broth, raisins, and bay leaves and bring to simmer.

3 Reduce heat to medium-low, add meat mixture in 2-inch chunks to pot, and bring to gentle simmer. Cover and cook, stirring occasionally with 2 forks to break meat chunks into ¼- to ½-inch pieces, until meat is cooked through, about 10 minutes.

4 Discard bay leaves. Stir in olives and capers. Increase heat to medium-high and cook, stirring occasionally, until sauce is thickened and coats meat, about 5 minutes. Stir in vinegar and season with salt, pepper, and extra vinegar to taste. Serve.

PANTRY IMPROV

use what you have We like
this dish prepared with raisins,
but you can replace them with
2 tablespoons of brown sugar
added with the broth in step 2.
If you don't have ground pork,
double the quantity of ground
beef. You can substitute diced
tomatoes for the whole
tomatoes; no need to chop them.
You can substitute white wine
vinegar, sherry vinegar, or cider
vinegar for the red wine vinegar.

level up Top with chopped
parsley, toasted almonds,
and/or chopped Easy-Peel
Hard-Cooked Egg (page 274).

pan-seared shrimp with peanuts, black pepper, and lime

SERVES 4 | TOTAL TIME: 40 MINUTES

1½ pounds extra-large shrimp (21 to 25 per pound), peeled and deveined

1 teaspoon kosher salt, divided

2 teaspoons coriander seeds

1 teaspoon black peppercorns

1 teaspoon paprika

1 garlic clove, minced

1⅛ teaspoons sugar, divided

⅛ teaspoon red pepper flakes

4 teaspoons vegetable oil, divided

½ cup fresh cilantro leaves and stems, chopped (optional)

1 tablespoon lime juice, plus lime wedges for serving

3 tablespoons dry-roasted peanuts, chopped coarse

why this recipe works When it comes to stocking your freezer with proteins, shrimp just might be the ideal choice. Sold individually quick-frozen in bags, they're easy to measure out as needed, and their small size makes them relatively quick to thaw. To help these bite-size morsels brown without overcooking, we briefly salt them so that they retain their moisture and then sprinkle sugar on them just before searing them over high heat. Once the shrimp are spotty brown and pink at the edges on the first side, we remove them from the heat and quickly turn each one, letting residual heat gently cook them the rest of the way. We season them with a flavorful spice mixture pulled from the pantry and bloomed in the same pan used to cook the shrimp. A sprinkling of crunchy nuts, a squeeze of tangy citrus, and a handful of fresh herbs provide a flavorful finishing touch. This quick dish has tremendous improv potential; our variations are just the beginning.

1 Toss shrimp and ½ teaspoon salt together in bowl; set aside for 15 to 30 minutes.

2 Meanwhile, grind coriander seeds and peppercorns using spice grinder or mortar and pestle until coarsely ground. Transfer to small bowl. Add paprika, garlic, 1 teaspoon sugar, pepper flakes, and remaining ½ teaspoon salt and stir until combined.

3 Pat shrimp dry with paper towels. Add 1 tablespoon oil and remaining ⅛ teaspoon sugar to bowl with shrimp and toss to coat. Add shrimp to cold 12-inch nonstick or well-seasoned carbon-steel skillet in single layer and cook over high heat until undersides of shrimp are spotty brown and edges turn pink, 3 to 4 minutes. Remove skillet from heat. Working quickly, use tongs to flip each shrimp; let stand until second side is opaque, about 2 minutes. Transfer shrimp to platter.

4 Add remaining 1 teaspoon oil to now-empty skillet. Add spice mixture and cook over medium heat until fragrant, about 30 seconds. Off heat, return shrimp to skillet. Add cilantro, if using, and lime juice and toss to combine. Transfer to platter; sprinkle with peanuts; and serve, passing lime wedges separately.

PANTRY IMPROV

use what you have You can use any size shrimp here, but the cooking times will vary. Almonds can be used instead of peanuts.

level up Serve with rice or over greens such as baby spinach or baby kale.

VARIATIONS

pan–seared shrimp with pistachios, cumin, and parsley

Omit peppercorns and 1 teaspoon sugar from spice mixture. Substitute 1 teaspoon ground cumin for coriander and cayenne for pepper flakes. Substitute 2 tablespoons extra-virgin olive oil for vegetable oil, adding 1 tablespoon to raw shrimp and using remaining 1 tablespoon to cook spice mixture. Reduce cilantro to ¼ cup and add ¼ cup chopped fresh parsley. Substitute lemon juice for lime juice, omit lime wedges, and substitute ¼ cup coarsely chopped toasted pistachios for peanuts.

pan–seared shrimp with fermented black beans, ginger, and garlic

Omit spice mixture of coriander, peppercorns, paprika, garlic, 1 teaspoon sugar, ½ teaspoon salt, and red pepper flakes. Omit cilantro, lime, and peanuts. Combine 2 sliced scallion whites; 1 tablespoon rinsed and chopped fermented black beans; 1 tablespoon grated fresh ginger; 2 minced garlic cloves; and 1 teaspoon sugar in small bowl. In step 4, add black bean mixture to skillet and cook until ginger is just starting to brown, about 45 seconds. Add 2 sliced scallion greens, 1 tablespoon soy sauce, and 2 teaspoons toasted sesame oil with shrimp.

spanish-style **garlic shrimp**

SERVES 4 | **TOTAL TIME: 55 MINUTES**

14 garlic cloves, peeled, divided

1 pound large shrimp (26 to 30 per pound), peeled and deveined

½ cup extra-virgin olive oil, divided

½ teaspoon table salt

1 bay leaf

1 (2-inch) piece mild dried chile such as New Mexico, roughly broken, seeds included

1½ teaspoons sherry vinegar

1 tablespoon minced fresh parsley (optional)

why this recipe works Sizzling gambas al ajillo is a tempting dish served in tapas bars, but when you've got shrimp in the freezer why not make it at home? Along with the shrimp and a generous amount of garlic, all you need is oil, salt, a dried chile, vinegar, and a bay leaf—all pantry basics. We found that the shrimp don't need to swim in oil to cook evenly; we add just enough to cover them halfway and cook them over low heat, turning them halfway through. And we get layers of flavors from the garlic by using it in three ways: added raw to a marinade, browned in the oil in which the shrimp is cooked, and cooked along with the shrimp. The traditional bay leaf and chile, along with sherry vinegar (rather than sherry), brighten the richness of the oil. You can serve these garlicky shrimp with plenty of bread to soak up the juices or make them the foundation of a meal.

1 Mince 2 garlic cloves and toss with shrimp, 2 tablespoons oil, and salt in medium bowl. Let sit at room temperature for 30 minutes.

2 Meanwhile, using flat side of chef's knife, smash 4 garlic cloves. Heat smashed garlic with remaining 6 tablespoons oil in 12-inch skillet over medium-low heat, stirring occasionally, until garlic is light golden brown, 4 to 7 minutes. Remove skillet from heat and allow oil to cool to room temperature. Using slotted spoon, discard smashed garlic.

3 Slice remaining 8 garlic cloves thin. Return skillet to low heat and add sliced garlic, bay leaf, and chile. Cook, stirring occasionally, until garlic is tender but not browned, 4 to 7 minutes. (If garlic has not begun to sizzle after 3 minutes, increase heat to medium-low.) Increase heat to medium-low and add shrimp with marinade to skillet in single layer. Cook shrimp, without moving, until oil starts to gently bubble, about 2 minutes. Using tongs, flip shrimp and continue to cook until almost cooked through, about 2 minutes. Increase heat to high and add sherry vinegar and parsley, if using. Cook, stirring constantly, until shrimp are cooked through and oil is bubbling vigorously, 15 to 20 seconds. Discard bay leaf and serve immediately.

PANTRY IMPROV

use what you have You can use any size shrimp here, but the cooking times will vary. We prefer the slightly sweet flavor of dried chiles in this recipe, but ¼ teaspoon sweet paprika can be substituted. You can use 2 teaspoons dry sherry and 1 teaspoon distilled white vinegar in place of the sherry vinegar.

level up Spoon the shrimp over pasta or use them to top a mixed green salad. For tapas bar flair, transfer the shrimp to an 8-inch cast-iron skillet that's been heated for 2 minutes over medium-high heat and bring them sizzling to the table.

shrimp mozambique

SERVES 4 | TOTAL TIME: 35 MINUTES

sauce

- 2 tablespoons hot sauce
- 2 tablespoons extra-virgin olive oil
- 2 tablespoons water
- ¼ slice bread, torn into small pieces (¼ cup)
- 1 tablespoon chopped fresh parsley (optional)
- 2 garlic cloves, chopped
- 2 teaspoons paprika
- ½ teaspoon pepper

shrimp

- 2 pounds extra-large shrimp (21 to 25 per pound), peeled and deveined
- 1 teaspoon table salt, divided
- ¼ teaspoon pepper
- 1 tablespoon extra-virgin olive oil
- ½ cup finely chopped onion
- 3 garlic cloves, sliced thin
- 1 cup dry white wine or dry vermouth
- 2 tablespoons unsalted butter, cut into 2 pieces
- 2 tablespoons chopped fresh parsley (optional)

why this recipe works This bracing dish of shrimp bathed in a buttery, garlicky, peppery sauce has roots in Portugal's history in southeast Africa, where colonists cultivated the piri-piri pepper that traditionally gives this dish its heat. As a stand-in for those peppers we turn to hot sauce, blending it with olive oil, garlic, parsley, paprika, and a little bread. After cooking the shrimp with onion, garlic, and white wine, we stir in our pepper sauce and butter to bring everything together. For the hot sauce, we like Frank's RedHot Original Cayenne Pepper Sauce, which has a similar kick to piri-piris.

1 for the sauce Process all ingredients in blender until smooth, about 2 minutes, scraping down sides of blender jar as needed.

2 for the shrimp Sprinkle shrimp with ½ teaspoon salt and pepper; set aside. Heat oil in 12-inch nonstick skillet over medium heat until shimmering. Add onion and remaining ½ teaspoon salt and cook until softened, about 5 minutes. Add garlic and cook until fragrant, about 1 minute. Add wine and bring to boil. Cook until reduced by half, about 4 minutes.

3 Add shrimp and cook, stirring occasionally, until opaque and just cooked through, about 4 minutes. Stir in butter and sauce and cook until butter is melted and sauce is heated through, about 1 minute. Season with salt and pepper to taste. Sprinkle with parsley, if using, and serve.

PANTRY IMPROV

use what you have You can use any size shrimp here, but the cooking times will vary.

level up Serve with crusty bread or over white rice.

one-pan roasted salmon
with white beans and fennel

SERVES 4 | TOTAL TIME: 1 HOUR

2 (1-pound) fennel bulbs, stalks discarded, bulbs halved, cored, and sliced ¼ inch thick

2 tablespoons extra-virgin olive oil, divided

1¼ teaspoons table salt, divided

¾ teaspoon pepper, divided

2 (15-ounce) cans cannellini beans, rinsed

¼ cup dry white wine or dry vermouth

3 garlic cloves (2 sliced thin, 1 minced)

6 tablespoons unsalted butter, softened

1 teaspoon minced fresh thyme or ¼ teaspoon dried

1 teaspoon grated lemon zest plus 1 tablespoon juice

4 (6- to 8-ounce) skinless salmon fillets, 1 to 1½ inches thick

2 tablespoons chopped fresh parsley (optional)

why this recipe works What could be better than a flavorful, satisfying homemade meal with only one pan to clean? Pull some salmon fillets from your freezer, roast them with sweet-savory fennel (or onion, in a pinch) and creamy canned white beans, and that's exactly what you've got. Slathering the salmon with an herbed butter adds rich flavor, while white wine, garlic, and more herbed butter meld together to form a luscious sauce for the beans and fennel. Buy fennel with the stalks still attached. If you can find only stalkless bulbs, look for those that weigh 10 to 12 ounces each.

1 Adjust oven rack to middle position and heat oven to 450 degrees. Toss fennel, 1 tablespoon oil, ¼ teaspoon salt, and ¼ teaspoon pepper together on rimmed baking sheet. Spread fennel into even layer and roast until beginning to brown around edges, about 15 minutes.

2 Meanwhile, toss beans, wine, sliced garlic, ½ teaspoon salt, ¼ teaspoon pepper, and remaining 1 tablespoon oil together in bowl. Combine butter, thyme, lemon zest, and minced garlic in small bowl. Pat salmon dry with paper towels and sprinkle with remaining ½ teaspoon salt and remaining ¼ teaspoon pepper. Spread 1 tablespoon butter mixture on top of each fillet.

3 Remove sheet from oven. Add bean mixture to sheet with fennel, stir to combine, and spread into even layer. Arrange salmon on top of bean mixture, butter side up. Roast until centers of fillets register 125 degrees (for medium-rare), 17 to 20 minutes.

4 Transfer salmon to serving platter. Stir lemon juice and remaining 2 tablespoons butter mixture into bean mixture; transfer to serving platter with salmon; and sprinkle with parsley, if using. Serve.

easy **poached salmon**

SERVES 4 | TOTAL TIME: 30 MINUTES

why this recipe works Poaching is a near-perfect cooking method that works with a wide variety of fish, and salmon is a good place to start. A low cooking temperature prevents overcooking but you still need to create enough steam to cook the fish. The solution? White wine: The alcohol lowers the liquid's boiling point, producing more vapor even at lower temperatures. To prevent the flavor of the fish's natural juices from washing away in the liquid, we only partially submerge the fish fillets, raising them from the bottom of the skillet with lemon slices for a sort of hybrid poaching-steaming method. The lemons also protect the bottom of the fish from overcooking. Try this method with just about any fish (see Pantry Improv), pair it with any sides from pilafs to slaws to salads, and you've got yourself a meal. You will need a 12-inch skillet with a tight-fitting lid for this recipe.

1   lemon, sliced into thin rounds

4   sprigs fresh parsley (optional)

1   shallot, sliced thin

½   cup dry white wine

4   (6– to 8–ounce) skinless salmon fillets, 1 inch thick

½   teaspoon table salt

¼   teaspoon pepper

1   Arrange lemon slices in single layer across bottom of 12-inch skillet. Top with parsley sprigs, if using, and shallot, then add wine and ½ cup water. Pat salmon dry with paper towels, sprinkle with salt and pepper, and place skinned side down on top of lemon slices in skillet. Bring to simmer over medium-high heat. Cover; reduce heat to low; and cook, adjusting heat as needed to maintain gentle simmer, until centers of fillets are still translucent when checked with tip of paring knife and register 125 degrees (for medium-rare), 11 to 16 minutes.

2   Remove skillet from heat and, using spatula, carefully transfer salmon and lemon slices to paper towel–lined plate to drain. (Discard poaching liquid.) Carefully lift and tilt fillets to remove lemon slices and transfer to platter. Serve.

PANTRY IMPROV

use what you have You can substitute many varieties of fish for the salmon. If using arctic char or wild salmon, cook the fillets to 120 degrees (for medium-rare) and start checking for doneness after 8 minutes. If using black sea bass, cod, haddock, hake, or pollack, cook to 135 degrees. If using halibut, mahi-mahi, red snapper, or swordfish, cook to 130 degrees and let rest, tented with aluminum foil, for 10 minutes before serving. Any herb stems work well here.

level up Serve with Smoked Paprika Sauce; Chile-Coriander Sauce; or any other sauce on pages 396–399.

tilapia meunière

SERVES 4 | TOTAL TIME: 45 MINUTES

- 4 (6- to 8-ounce) skinless tilapia fillets, split lengthwise down natural seam
- ½ teaspoon table salt
- ¼ teaspoon pepper
- ½ cup all-purpose flour
- 2 tablespoons vegetable oil, divided
- 6 tablespoons unsalted butter, cut into 6 pieces, divided
- 1½ tablespoons lemon juice
- 2 tablespoons chopped fresh parsley (optional)

> **PANTRY IMPROV**
>
> **use what you have** You can substitute catfish, flounder, or sole for the tilapia.
>
> **level up** Sprinkle with toasted almonds, pine nuts, or walnuts. Drizzle with an herb oil (see page 390).

why this recipe works We like to stock boneless, single portion–sized tilapia fillets in our freezer for easy meals like this classic skillet dish. Lightly floured and browned, the mild fillets make a grand vehicle for soaking up a bright, lemony sauce. The perfect crust comes from simply drying the fillets, seasoning them with salt and pepper, and dredging them in flour. You'll get the most even cooking and best browning by splitting the fish down the natural seam; that way, the thick and thinner sides make full contact with the pan and can be removed as soon as they're done. Try to purchase fillets that are of similar size.

1 Adjust oven rack to middle position and heat oven to 200 degrees. Pat tilapia dry with paper towels and sprinkle with salt and pepper. Spread flour in shallow dish. Dredge fillets in flour, shaking off excess, and transfer to large plate.

2 Heat 1 tablespoon oil in 12-inch nonstick skillet over medium-high heat until shimmering. Add 1 tablespoon butter and swirl until melted. Add thick halves of fillets to skillet and cook until golden on first side, about 3 minutes. Using 2 spatulas, flip fillets and cook until second sides are golden and fish flakes apart when gently prodded with paring knife, about 2 minutes. Transfer to ovensafe platter and keep warm in oven. Wipe skillet clean with paper towels and repeat with remaining 1 tablespoon oil, 1 tablespoon butter, and thin halves of fillets.

3 Melt remaining 4 tablespoons butter in again-empty skillet over medium-high heat. Continue to cook, swirling skillet constantly, until butter is golden brown and has nutty aroma, 1 to 1½ minutes. Remove skillet from heat, add lemon juice, and season with salt to taste. Spoon sauce over tilapia and sprinkle with parsley, if using. Serve immediately.

panko-crusted tofu
with cabbage salad

SERVES 4 | **TOTAL TIME: 35 MINUTES**

why this recipe works Japanese katsu (cutlets) are all about the crunch. The technique, which dredges any thin piece of protein—often chicken or pork—in crisp panko bread crumbs and shallow-fries it to golden-brown perfection, works perfectly with tofu, which we cut into slabs and pat dry. To help the panko adhere, we dredge the tofu in a mixture of flour and egg, creating a glue-like paste that locks the panko in place. Making tonkatsu sauce, the traditional sweet-savory accompaniment, is as simple as whisking together a few pantry ingredients. Shredded cabbage (either red or green will work) makes a crunchy bed for the tofu and needs nothing more than a quick toss with some rice vinegar, toasty sesame oil, and a pinch of sugar for seasoning.

1   Whisk ketchup, Worcestershire, soy sauce, garlic powder, and ½ teaspoon sugar together in small bowl; set aside.

2   Whisk eggs and flour together in shallow dish. Place panko in large zipper-lock bag and lightly crush with rolling pin; transfer crumbs to second shallow dish. Slice tofu lengthwise into four ½-inch-thick slabs, pat dry with paper towels, and sprinkle with salt. Working with 1 slab at a time, dip tofu in egg mixture, allowing excess to drip off, then coat all sides with panko, pressing gently to adhere; transfer to large plate.

3   Place wire rack in rimmed baking sheet and line rack with triple layer of paper towels. Heat vegetable oil in 12-inch nonstick skillet over medium-high heat until shimmering. Add tofu and cook until deep golden brown, 2 to 3 minutes per side. Transfer tofu to prepared rack and let drain.

4   Combine vinegar, sesame oil, and remaining ½ teaspoon sugar in bowl. Add cabbage, toss to coat, and season with salt and pepper to taste. Drizzle tofu with reserved sauce. Serve.

¼   cup ketchup

4   teaspoons Worcestershire sauce

2   teaspoons soy sauce

1   teaspoon garlic powder

1   teaspoon sugar, divided

2   large eggs

2   tablespoons all-purpose flour

1⅓   cups panko bread crumbs

14   ounces firm or extra-firm tofu

½   teaspoon table salt

1   cup vegetable oil for frying

2½   teaspoons unseasoned rice vinegar

1½   teaspoons toasted sesame oil

3   cups shredded red or green cabbage

PANTRY IMPROV

use what you have Plant-based egg substitute can be used instead of eggs. (To make this fully vegan, use vegan Worcestershire as well.) Use shredded carrots or coleslaw mix instead of cabbage.

level up Serve on bread to make a sandwich.

seared tempeh with tomato jam

SERVES 4 | TOTAL TIME: 1 HOUR, PLUS 1 HOUR COOLING

1 (28–ounce) can diced tomatoes, drained

2 tablespoons honey or agave syrup

6 tablespoons red wine vinegar

3 garlic cloves, minced

1 tablespoon grated fresh ginger

1 teaspoon ras el hanout

1 anchovy fillet, rinsed, patted dry, and minced (optional)

¼ teaspoon ground dried Aleppo pepper (optional)

1 pound tempeh

¼ teaspoon table salt

3 tablespoons vegetable oil

2 tablespoons chopped fresh cilantro (optional)

why this recipe works As reliable pantry proteins go, tempeh deserves a shout-out. It keeps for weeks in the fridge (longer in the freezer) making it easy to have at the ready whenever you want a "meaty" base for stir-fries or even steaks like these. Searing the tempeh in oil creates a delectably crisp edge and a cohesive interior texture. Tempeh's earthy flavor pairs well with bright and bold sauces. Here we make a sweet, meaty tomato jam by cooking canned diced tomatoes with vinegar, honey, garlic and ginger. Warm spices and an optional anchovy give the jam added depth.

1   Combine tomatoes; honey; vinegar; garlic; ginger; ras el hanout; anchovy, if using; and Aleppo pepper, if using, in 12-inch nonstick skillet. Bring to boil over medium-high heat, then reduce to simmer and cook, stirring often, until tomatoes have broken down and begun to thicken, 15 to 20 minutes.

2   Mash jam with potato masher to even consistency. Continue to cook until mixture has thickened and darkened in color, 5 to 10 minutes. Let jam cool completely, about 1 hour. Season with salt and pepper to taste; set aside. (Jam can be refrigerated for up to 4 days; bring to room temperature before serving.)

3   Cut each block of tempeh into 4 even pieces, then halve each piece into approximately ¼-inch-thick slabs. Pat tempeh dry and sprinkle with salt. Heat oil in clean 12-inch nonstick skillet over medium heat until shimmering. Add 8 pieces tempeh and cook until golden brown on first side, 2 to 4 minutes. Flip tempeh, reduce heat to medium-low, and continue to cook until golden brown on second side, 2 to 4 minutes. Transfer to serving platter and tent with aluminum foil to keep warm. Repeat with remaining tempeh. Serve tempeh steaks with tomato jam, sprinkling individual portions with cilantro, if using.

PANTRY IMPROV

use what you have Any warm spice blend such as baharat or garam masala works instead of ras el hanout. You can substitute whole peeled tomatoes for the diced; crush them by hand to small pieces.

level up Serve with a verdant side such as green beans or sautéed spinach. Or chop the tempeh and add it to a grain bowl, then top with dollops of the tomato jam. Make a sandwich by layering the tempeh and jam with classic sandwich toppers such as baby greens, sliced avocado, and/or dairy or plant-based sliced cheese.

vegan **mapo tofu**

SERVES 4 TO 6 | TOTAL TIME: 1 HOUR

2 cups water

½ teaspoon table salt

½ ounce dried shiitake mushrooms, rinsed

1 tablespoon Sichuan peppercorns

12 scallions

28 ounces soft tofu, cut into ½-inch pieces

9 garlic cloves, peeled

1 (3-inch) piece ginger, peeled and cut into ¼-inch rounds

⅓ cup Asian broad bean chili paste

1 tablespoon fermented black beans

½ cup vegetable oil, divided

1 tablespoon Sichuan chili powder

4 ounces fresh shiitake mushrooms, stemmed, or oyster mushrooms, trimmed

2 tablespoons hoisin sauce

2 teaspoons toasted sesame oil

2 tablespoons soy sauce

1 tablespoon cornstarch

why this recipe works Our vegan rendition of the spicy Sichuan classic drops the minced meat and doubles down on the tofu. Poaching the soft tofu in gently salted water helps the cubes stay intact. The complex sauce uses plenty of ginger and garlic along with four Sichuan pantry powerhouses: broad bean chili paste (doubanjiang), fermented black beans, Sichuan chili powder, and Sichuan peppercorns. A small amount of finely chopped mushrooms acts as a seasoning, not a main component. In place of the chili oil often called for, we use a generous amount of vegetable oil, extra Sichuan chili powder, and toasted sesame oil. Serve with rice.

1 Microwave water, salt, and dried shiitake mushrooms in covered large bowl until steaming, about 1 minute. Let sit until softened, about 5 minutes. Drain mushrooms in fine-mesh strainer, reserving liquid; set aside soaked mushrooms and return liquid to large bowl.

2 Place peppercorns in small bowl and microwave until fragrant, 15 to 30 seconds. Let cool completely. Once cool, grind in spice grinder or mortar and pestle (you should have 1½ teaspoons).

3 Using side of chef's knife, lightly crush white parts of scallions, then cut scallions into 1-inch pieces. Place tofu and scallions in bowl with reserved mushroom liquid and microwave until steaming, 5 to 7 minutes. Let sit while preparing remaining ingredients.

4 Process garlic, ginger, chili paste, and black beans in food processor until coarse paste forms, 1 to 2 minutes, scraping down sides of bowl as needed. Add ¼ cup vegetable oil, chili powder, and 1 teaspoon peppercorns and continue to process until smooth paste forms, 1 to 2 minutes. Transfer spice paste to bowl.

5 Place reserved soaked mushrooms and fresh shiitake mushrooms in now-empty processor and pulse until finely chopped, 15 to 20 pulses (do not overprocess). Heat 2 tablespoons vegetable oil and mushroom mixture in large saucepan over medium heat, breaking up mushrooms with wooden spoon, until mushrooms begin to brown and stick to bottom of saucepan, 5 to 7 minutes. Transfer mushroom mixture to bowl.

6   Add remaining 2 tablespoons vegetable oil and spice paste to now-empty saucepan and cook, stirring frequently, until paste darkens and oil begins to separate from paste, 2 to 3 minutes. Gently pour tofu with mushroom liquid into saucepan, followed by hoisin, sesame oil, and mushroom mixture. Cook, gently stirring frequently, until dish comes to simmer, 2 to 3 minutes. Whisk soy sauce and cornstarch together in small bowl. Add cornstarch mixture to saucepan and continue to cook, stirring frequently, until thickened, 2 to 3 minutes. Transfer to serving dish, sprinkle with remaining peppercorns, and serve. (Mapo tofu can be refrigerated for up to 24 hours.)

PANTRY IMPROV

use what you have   Korean red pepper flakes (gochugaru) are a good substitute for Sichuan chili powder. Or, in a pinch, use 2½ teaspoons ancho chile powder and ½ teaspoon cayenne pepper. If you don't have fermented black beans, use an equal amount of fermented black bean paste or sauce or 2 additional teaspoons of Asian broad bean chili paste. Use other types of dried mushrooms in place of the shiitakes.

breads
& baked
goods

savory dutch baby
with prosciutto and honey

SERVES 4 | **TOTAL TIME: 45 MINUTES**

dutch baby

- ¼ cup extra-virgin olive oil, divided
- 1¼ cups (6¼ ounces) all-purpose flour
- ½ teaspoon table salt
- 4 large eggs
- 1 cup skim milk

prosciutto topping

- 1 ounce thinly sliced prosciutto or serrano ham, torn into bite-size pieces
- 1 ounce shaved Parmesan or Pecorino Romano cheese
- ½ teaspoon extra-virgin olive oil
- ½ teaspoon honey or agave syrup

PANTRY IMPROV

use what you have Any deli sliced meat, or smoked or cured fish, can be used instead of prosciutto. Or omit and simply top with cheese.

level up Sprinkle with halved cherry tomatoes, capers, olives, or fresh herbs. Top with Crispy Shallots (page 88) or quick pickled vegetables (see page 404).

---

why this recipe works A savory Dutch baby makes the perfect breakfast-for-dinner meal: Simply pour a stir-together batter of flour, egg, and milk into a skillet; bake it; and top it with whatever is handy and appealing. The edge of this skillet-size pancake puffs dramatically to form a tall, crispy rim with a texture similar to that of a popover while the base remains flat, custardy, and tender, like a thick crepe. A simple topping of prosciutto and Parmesan with a drizzle of olive oil and honey adorns our main recipe. Our variations up the ante with fresh ingredients showcasing the pancake's versatility: One combines the salty prosciutto with creamy burrata and a tangle of peppery arugula. The others top the Dutch baby with a mix of smoked salmon and creamy avocado or a salad of marinated mushrooms and crisp celery. Serve the Dutch baby directly from the skillet if you like. You can use whole or low-fat milk instead of skim, but the Dutch baby won't turn out as crisp. You can use a cast-iron or traditional skillet with this recipe.

1 **for the dutch baby** Adjust oven rack to middle position and heat oven to 450 degrees. Grease 12-inch traditional or cast-iron skillet with 2 tablespoons oil, place skillet in oven, and heat until oil is shimmering, about 10 minutes.

2 Meanwhile, whisk flour and salt together in large bowl. In separate bowl, whisk eggs until frothy, then whisk in milk and remaining 2 tablespoons oil until incorporated. Whisk one-third of milk mixture into flour mixture until no lumps remain. Slowly whisk in remaining milk mixture until smooth.

3 Quickly pour batter into skillet and bake until Dutch baby puffs and turns golden brown (edges will be dark brown), about 20 minutes, rotating skillet halfway through baking.

4 **for the prosciutto topping** Using potholders, remove skillet from oven. Being careful of hot skillet handle, transfer Dutch baby to cutting board using spatula. Top Dutch baby with prosciutto and Parmesan. Drizzle with oil and honey and sprinkle with pepper to taste. Slice into wedges and serve immediately.

VARIATIONS

savory dutch baby with smoked salmon and avocado

Omit prosciutto topping. While Dutch baby bakes, combine ½ shallot, sliced thin; 1 tablespoon extra-virgin olive oil; 1 teaspoon lemon juice; ¼ teaspoon sugar; and pinch table salt in small bowl and let stand for 10 minutes. Top Dutch baby with 4 ounces smoked salmon; 1 avocado, sliced ¼ inch thick; and shallot mixture. Drizzle with extra oil and sprinkle with minced fresh parsley or chives before slicing and serving.

savory dutch baby with celery and mushroom salad

If your celery came without its leaves, you can substitute fresh parsley leaves. Slice the mushrooms and celery as thin as possible.

Omit prosciutto topping. While Dutch baby bakes, combine 4 cremini or white mushrooms, stemmed and sliced thin; ½ shallot, sliced thin; 1 tablespoon extra-virgin olive oil; 1 teaspoon lemon juice; pinch table salt; and pinch pepper in small bowl and let stand for 10 minutes. Stir in 1 celery rib, sliced thin on bias, and ½ cup celery leaves. Top Dutch baby with mushroom-celery mixture and ¼ cup shaved Parmesan or Pecorino Romano cheese. Drizzle with extra oil before slicing and serving.

savory dutch baby with burrata, prosciutto, and arugula

Omit Parmesan. Substitute balsamic vinegar for honey. Toss ¾ cup baby arugula with oil and vinegar and season to taste with salt and pepper. Top Dutch baby with arugula mixture, prosciutto, and 4 ounces torn burrata or mozzarella cheese.

whole-wheat crepes with smoked salmon, crème fraîche, and pickled shallots

MAKES 8 CREPES | SERVES 4 | TOTAL TIME: 1½ HOURS

whole-wheat crepes

- ½ teaspoon vegetable oil
- 1 cup (5½ ounces) whole-wheat flour
- ½ teaspoon table salt
- 2½ cups milk
- 3 large eggs
- 4 tablespoons unsalted butter, melted and cooled

filling

- ⅓ cup distilled white vinegar
- 2 tablespoons sugar
- 2 shallots, sliced thin
- ¾ cup crème fraîche or sour cream
- 3 tablespoons capers, rinsed and chopped
- 3 tablespoons finely chopped chives (optional)
- 1½ teaspoons grated lemon zest plus 1½ tablespoons juice
- ¼ teaspoon table salt
- ¼ teaspoon pepper
- 8 ounces smoked salmon

why this recipe works Crepes make a delicious envelope for just about any filling you can rustle up from your pantry and fridge; here, we take inspiration from classic blini toppings and fold earthy whole-wheat crepes around a creamy smoked salmon filling. Crème fraîche may not seem like an obvious kitchen staple, but it lasts at least a month in the refrigerator and can be easily made at home (see page 398). Mixing it with lemon, chives, and chopped capers makes for a bright, briny spread to pair with the rich smoked salmon. Sliced shallots quickly pickled with vinegar and sugar offer a tangy contrasting crunch. Stacking the crepes on a wire rack allows excess steam to escape so that they won't stick together. This recipe makes enough batter for 11 crepes to allow for practicing; only eight are needed.

1 for the crepes Heat oil in 12-inch nonstick skillet over low heat for at least 5 minutes. While skillet heats, whisk flour and salt together in medium bowl. In second bowl, whisk together milk and eggs. Add half of milk mixture to flour mixture and whisk until smooth. Add melted butter and whisk until incorporated. Whisk in remaining milk mixture until smooth.

2 Using paper towel, wipe out skillet, leaving thin film of oil on bottom and sides. Increase heat to medium and let skillet heat for 1 minute. Test heat of skillet by placing 1 teaspoon batter in center and cooking for 20 seconds. If mini crepe is golden brown on bottom, skillet is properly heated; if it is too light or too dark, adjust heat accordingly and retest.

3 Lift skillet off heat and pour ⅓ cup batter into far side of skillet; swirl gently in clockwise direction until batter evenly covers bottom of skillet. Return skillet to heat and cook crepe, without moving it, until surface is dry and crepe starts to brown at edges, loosening crepe from sides of skillet with rubber spatula, about 35 seconds. Gently slide spatula underneath edge of crepe, grasp edge with your fingertips, and flip crepe. Cook until second side is lightly spotted, about 20 seconds. Transfer crepe to wire rack. Return skillet to heat for 10 seconds before repeating with remaining batter. (If at any point skillet begins to smoke, remove from burner and turn down heat.) As crepes are done, stack on rack. (Crepes can be wrapped tightly in plastic wrap and refrigerated for up to 3 days or stacked between sheets of parchment paper and frozen for up to 1 month. Allow frozen crepes to thaw completely in refrigerator before using.)

4 for the filling Combine vinegar and sugar in small bowl and microwave until sugar is dissolved and vinegar is steaming, about 30 seconds. Add shallots and stir to combine. Cover and let cool completely, about 30 minutes. Drain shallots and discard liquid.

5 Combine crème fraîche; capers; chives, if using; lemon zest and juice; salt; and pepper in medium bowl.

6 Place crepes on large plate and invert second plate over crepes. Microwave until crepes are warm, 30 to 45 seconds (45 to 60 seconds if crepes have cooled completely). Working with 1 crepe at a time, spread 2 tablespoons crème fraîche mixture across bottom half of crepe, followed by 1 ounce smoked salmon and one-eighth of shallots. Fold crepes in half and then into quarters. Transfer to plate and serve.

PANTRY IMPROV

use what you have You can substitute rye or buckwheat flour for the whole-wheat flour (do not substitute all-purpose flour); reduce the milk to 2 cups. Chopped olives can be used instead of capers. Instead of smoked salmon, fill crepes with sautéed asparagus and mushrooms, deli meats, shredded cooked chicken, Caramelized Onions (page 384), or roasted vegetables.

level up Top with baby arugula, watercress, herb leaves, or a poached or hard-cooked egg (see pages 274–275). For the ultimate experience, dollop with salmon roe or caviar before serving and top with more crème fraîche (see page 398).

socca with sautéed onions and rosemary

MAKES FOUR 10-INCH PANCAKES | SERVES 4 | TOTAL TIME: 1¼ HOURS

socca

1½ cups water

1⅓ cups (6 ounces) chickpea flour

¼   cup extra-virgin olive oil, divided,
    plus extra for drizzling

1   teaspoon table salt

¼   teaspoon ground cumin

    Flake sea salt

sautéed onions

2   tablespoons extra-virgin olive oil

2   onions, halved and sliced thin

½   teaspoon table salt

1   teaspoon chopped fresh rosemary
    or ¼ teaspoon dried

why this recipe works The beloved street food socca is a kind of pancake or flatbread made from a simple batter of chickpea flour, water, olive oil, and seasonings. Socca is excellent with just a drizzle of extra-virgin olive oil and a sprinkling of flake sea salt, but we love it even more when served with a simple topping of sautéed onions with rosemary—either way, once you taste it, you'll want to give chickpea flour a permanent place on your pantry shelf. Traditionally, the batter is poured in a thin layer into a hot oiled pan and then baked in a smoky, ripping-hot wood-fired oven until browned and crisp. Absent the large flat pans and wood oven, we use another method: cooking the batter like a crepe in a nonstick skillet on the stovetop. Letting the batter rest for 10 minutes allows the chickpea flour to hydrate and the batter to thicken. Swirling the batter in the pan makes for even socca. After a few minutes over medium-high heat, the underside turns delightfully crispy and beautifully golden brown. Chickpea flour is also sold as garbanzo flour; we don't recommend using besan or gram flour here. It's best to use a scale to weigh the flour for this recipe.

1 for the socca Adjust oven rack to middle position and heat oven to 200 degrees. Set wire rack in rimmed baking sheet and place in oven. Whisk water, flour, 4 teaspoons oil, table salt, and cumin in bowl until no lumps remain. Let batter rest while preparing onions, at least 10 minutes. (Batter will thicken as it sits.)

2 for the sautéed onions Heat oil in 10-inch nonstick skillet over medium-high heat until just smoking. Add onions and salt and cook until onions start to brown around edges but still have some texture, 7 to 10 minutes. Add rosemary and cook until fragrant, about 1 minute. Transfer onion mixture to bowl; set aside. Wipe skillet clean with paper towels.

3 Heat 2 teaspoons oil in now-empty skillet over medium-high heat until just smoking. Lift skillet off heat and pour ½ cup batter into far side of skillet; swirl gently in clockwise direction until batter evenly covers bottom of skillet.

4 Return skillet to heat and cook socca, without moving it, until well browned and crisp around bottom edge, 3 to 4 minutes (you can peek at underside of socca by loosening it from side of skillet with rubber spatula).

5 Flip socca with rubber spatula and cook until second side is just cooked, about 1 minute. Transfer socca, browned side up, to prepared wire rack in oven. Repeat 3 more times, using 2 teaspoons oil and ½ cup batter per batch.

6 Transfer socca to cutting board and cut each into 8 wedges. Serve, topped with sautéed onions, drizzled with extra oil, and sprinkled with flake sea salt.

PANTRY IMPROV

use what you have You can substitute thyme or sage for the rosemary.

level up The possibilities are endless here: Top with beans or sautéed Swiss chard or spinach; sprinkle with crispy bacon, pancetta, or Crispy Capers (page 388); top with shaved Parmesan and leafy greens; drizzle with pesto, yogurt, or Yogurt Sauce (page 396); or make them into pizzas with marinara and cheese.

sun-dried tomato, garlic, and za'atar **biscuits**

MAKES 12 BISCUITS | **TOTAL TIME: 45 MINUTES**

why this recipe works In less time than it takes your oven to heat up, you can pull together the dough for these flavor-packed cream drop biscuits: There's no cutting butter into dry ingredients and no rolling out required. Instead of adding cold liquid to the dry ingredients, we heat the cream first. The warm liquid makes the dough soft enough to be droppable, and using heavy cream provides just the right amount of both moisture and fat to create a tall, fluffy biscuit. For savory biscuits that are equally at home on the breakfast or dinner table, we dig deeper into our pantry to find additional sources of flavor, adding a few cloves of minced garlic to the cream before microwaving it and folding umami-packed sun-dried tomatoes into the dry ingredients with the cream. Brushing some of the sun-dried tomato oil on the biscuits reinforces the tomato flavor and also helps with browning. Finally, we reach into our spice rack and add a generous sprinkle of za'atar before baking. In fact, many spices or blends would work here; you could try a different seasoning every time you make these.

1 Adjust oven rack to upper-middle position and heat oven to 450 degrees. Line rimmed baking sheet with parchment paper. Whisk flour, baking powder, baking soda, sugar, salt, and pepper together in large bowl. Microwave cream and garlic in separate bowl until just warmed to body temperature (95 to 100 degrees), 60 to 90 seconds, stirring halfway through microwaving. Using rubber spatula, gently fold cream mixture and tomatoes into flour mixture until soft, uniform dough forms.

2 Spray ⅓-cup dry measuring cup with vegetable oil spray. Drop 12 level scoops of batter 2 inches apart on prepared sheet. Respray measuring cup after every 3 or 4 scoops. Brush biscuit tops with tomato oil, then sprinkle evenly with za'atar.

3 Bake until biscuits are starting to turn light golden brown, 14 to 18 minutes, rotating sheet halfway through baking. Transfer biscuits to wire rack and let cool for 5 minutes. Serve warm or at room temperature. (Biscuits can be stored in zipper-lock bag at room temperature for up to 24 hours. Reheat biscuits in 300-degree oven for 10 minutes.)

3   cups (15 ounces) all-purpose flour

1   tablespoon baking powder

¼   teaspoon baking soda

2   teaspoons sugar

1¼   teaspoons table salt

½   teaspoon pepper

2   cups heavy cream

3   garlic cloves, minced

1   cup oil-packed sun-dried tomatoes, rinsed, patted dry, and chopped fine, plus 4 teaspoons sun-dried tomato oil

1   tablespoon za'atar

PANTRY IMPROV

use what you have Vary the spices used: Try sumac, dried thyme, herbes de Provence, or Everything Bagel Seasoning (page 383). Substitute olives for the sun-dried tomatoes.

level up Make an egg sandwich: Fill each biscuit with a fried, poached, or scrambled egg; baby spinach or arugula; sliced tomato; and sliced onion.

ginger biscuits

MAKES 12 BISCUITS | TOTAL TIME: 40 MINUTES

why this recipe works A fresh, warm biscuit instantly doubles the coziness of practically anything you serve it with. These cream drop biscuits, with their tender, subtly layered crumb, can easily go in a savory direction (as with our sun-dried tomato version on page 325), or take a sweeter approach, as this version does. Two forms of ginger from the pantry—ground and crystallized—increase the flavor impact, and we add a scoop of sugar to balance the spicy heat and make the biscuits more cake-like. Just as with scones, these biscuits take well to a variety of chunky, flavorful mix-ins and spices. Brushing a couple tablespoons of melted butter on at the last second gives each biscuit a burnished sheen.

1 Adjust oven rack to upper-middle position and heat oven to 450 degrees. Line rimmed baking sheet with parchment paper. In medium bowl, whisk together flour, sugar, crystallized ginger, ground ginger, baking powder, baking soda, and salt. Microwave cream until just warmed to body temperature (95 to 100 degrees), 60 to 90 seconds, stirring halfway through microwaving. Stir cream into flour mixture until soft, uniform dough forms.

2 Spray ⅓-cup dry measuring cup with vegetable oil spray. Drop level scoops of batter 2 inches apart on prepared sheet (biscuits should measure about 2½ inches wide and 1¼ inches tall). Respray measuring cup after every 3 or 4 scoops. If portions are misshapen, use your fingertips to gently reshape dough into level cylinders. Bake until tops are light golden brown, 10 to 12 minutes, rotating sheet halfway through baking. Transfer sheet to wire rack. Brush hot biscuits with melted butter, if using, and let cool for 5 minutes. Serve warm. (Biscuits can be stored in zipper-lock bag at room temperature for up to 24 hours. Reheat biscuits in 300-degree oven for 10 minutes.)

3 cups (15 ounces) all-purpose flour

¼ cup sugar

¾ cup chopped crystallized ginger

1½ teaspoons ground ginger

1 tablespoon baking powder

¼ teaspoon baking soda

1¼ teaspoons table salt

2 cups heavy cream

2 tablespoons unsalted butter, melted (optional)

PANTRY IMPROV

use what you have You can substitute chocolate chips, any nuts, or dried fruit for the crystallized ginger. You can substitute ½ teaspoon nutmeg or cinnamon for the ground ginger.

level up Sprinkle the biscuits with granulated sugar, sanding sugar, or demerara sugar before baking.

---

butternut squash, apple, and gruyère **turnovers**

MAKES 8 TURNOVERS | SERVES 8 | TOTAL TIME: 1½ HOURS

4 tablespoons unsalted butter, divided

1 tablespoon minced fresh sage or ¾ teaspoon dried

10 ounces butternut squash, peeled, seeded, and cut into ½-inch pieces (2 cups)

1–2 Granny Smith apples, peeled, cored, and cut into ½-inch pieces (2 cups)

1 shallot, minced

3 tablespoons packed brown sugar

½ teaspoon table salt

¼ teaspoon pepper

1 teaspoon cider vinegar

5 ounces Gruyère cheese, shredded (1¼ cups), divided

2 (9½ by 9-inch) sheets puff pastry, thawed

1 large egg beaten with 1 teaspoon water

why this recipe works If you need convincing that frozen puff pastry is worth keeping on hand, these savory turnovers filled with the classic fall flavors of sweet butternut squash, tart apples, and earthy sage will do the trick. For deep, bold flavor, we bloom minced sage in butter, which we cook until browned. Adding some brown sugar to the squash, shallot, and apple promotes deeper, faster caramelization. A splash of cider vinegar ensures that the filling is well balanced and not too sweet. Cooking the filling before assembling the turnovers evaporates excess moisture from the produce, preventing the filling from leaking and turning the pastry soggy. Shredded Gruyère makes a nutty, melty binder. We sprinkle more Gruyère on top of the turnovers before baking, which adds a second level of cheesy goodness as it toasts in the oven and melts onto the pastry. To thaw frozen puff pastry, let it sit either in the refrigerator for 24 hours or on the counter for 30 minutes to 1 hour before using.

1 Adjust oven rack to middle position and heat oven to 400 degrees. Line rimmed baking sheet with parchment paper. Melt 2 tablespoons butter in 12-inch skillet over medium-high heat. Add sage and continue to cook, swirling skillet occasionally, until butter is dark golden brown and has nutty aroma, about 2 minutes. Transfer browned butter mixture to large bowl; set aside.

2 Melt remaining 2 tablespoons butter in now-empty skillet over medium heat. Add squash, apple, shallot, sugar, salt, and pepper; cover; and cook, stirring occasionally, until squash and apple are softened and lightly browned, 13 to 16 minutes. Off heat, stir in vinegar and, using potato masher, mash half of mixture until mostly smooth. Add to bowl with browned butter mixture and stir to combine. Let cool completely, about 30 minutes, then stir in ¾ cup Gruyère. (Filling can be refrigerated for up to 24 hours.)

3 Dust counter lightly with flour. Working with 1 piece puff pastry at a time, unfold pastry and roll into 10-inch square. Cut into four 5-inch squares. Space pastry squares evenly on prepared sheet. Divide squash mixture evenly among pastry squares, mounding about 3 tablespoons in center of each square, then brush edges of pastry with egg wash (reserve remaining egg wash).

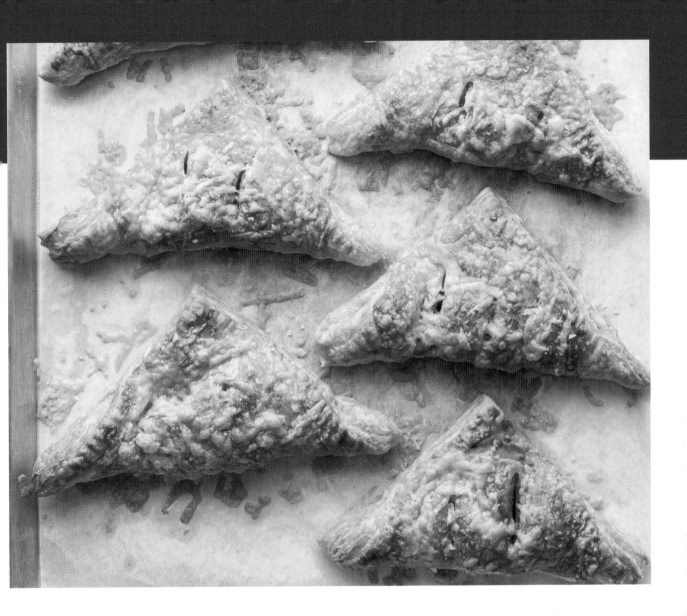

Fold pastry over filling to form triangle. Using fork, crimp edges of pastry to seal. Cut two 1-inch slits on top of each turnover (do not cut through filling). (Unbaked turnovers can be frozen in airtight container for up to 1 month.)

4 Brush tops of turnovers with remaining egg wash and sprinkle with remaining ½ cup Gruyère. Bake until well browned, 22 to 25 minutes, rotating sheet halfway through baking. Let turnovers cool on wire rack for 15 minutes. Serve warm or at room temperature.

PANTRY IMPROV

use what you have Substitute other varieties of winter squash such as buttercup, hubbard, kabocha, or sugar pumpkin for the butternut. Any variety of apple can be used here. White wine or champagne vinegar can be substituted for the cider vinegar. Cheddar, Monterey Jack, or Emmentaler cheese can be used instead of the Gruyère. You can substitute thyme, dried rosemary, or dried savory for the sage.

level up Make this a more substantial meal by serving with a salad or simply roasted vegetables.

broccoli cheese **cornbread**

SERVES 6 TO 8 | **TOTAL TIME: 1¼ HOURS, PLUS 1 HOUR COOLING**

6 tablespoons unsalted butter

1 onion, chopped fine

3 garlic cloves, minced

1 cup (5 ounces) cornmeal

1 cup (5 ounces) all-purpose flour

2 tablespoons sugar

1 tablespoon baking powder

¾ teaspoon table salt

¾ cup plain yogurt

3 large eggs

¼ cup whole milk

1 tablespoon hot sauce

12 ounces frozen broccoli florets, thawed, pressed dry with paper towels, and chopped coarse

8 ounces cheddar cheese, shredded (2 cups), divided

why this recipe works Frozen broccoli may not be first on your list of great add-ins for cornbread. But you'll change your mind after one bite of this especially moist bread, which is sort of like a cross between cornbread and spoonbread. It's substantial enough to serve as a light lunch on its own and versatile enough to pair with any soup, stew, or chili. Using convenient frozen broccoli florets, thawed and pressed dry to remove excess water, adds plenty of flavor without the extra time involved in trimming, blanching, draining, and chopping fresh broccoli. Sautéed onion and garlic underscore the bread's savory qualities, and baking the cornbread right in the same skillet gives the bread a crusty browned bottom and sides. For a little extra pizzazz, we stir in some cheddar and a tablespoon of hot sauce, and sprinkle more cheddar on top before baking for a crisp top crust. Press the thawed broccoli as dry as possible before stirring it into the batter.

1 Adjust oven rack to middle position and heat oven to 375 degrees. Melt butter in 10-inch ovensafe nonstick skillet over medium-high heat. Add onion and cook until softened, about 5 minutes. Stir in garlic and cook until fragrant, about 30 seconds. Remove from heat; set aside.

2 Whisk cornmeal, flour, sugar, baking powder, and salt together in large bowl. Whisk yogurt, eggs, milk, and hot sauce together in separate bowl. Using rubber spatula, gently fold yogurt mixture into cornmeal mixture until just combined. Stir broccoli, 1½ cups cheddar, and onion mixture into batter until thoroughly combined (batter will be thick).

3 Scrape batter into now-empty skillet and spread into even layer. Sprinkle remaining ½ cup cheddar evenly over top. Transfer skillet to oven and bake until cornbread is golden brown and toothpick inserted in center comes out clean, 40 to 45 minutes.

4 Using pot holders, transfer skillet to wire rack and let cornbread cool for 1 hour. Slide cornbread onto cutting board. Cut into wedges and serve. (Bread can be wrapped tightly in plastic wrap and stored at room temperature for up to 2 days.)

PANTRY IMPROV

use what you have Other frozen vegetables can be used instead of broccoli; try cauliflower, asparagus, spinach, or kale. Monterey Jack or other semifirm melty cheese can be subbed for the cheddar.

level up Serve with Quick Bean Chili (page 104) or Crisp Breaded Chicken Cutlets (page 284) for a hearty dinner or top with a fried egg and hot sauce for breakfast.

quick cheese bread
with bacon, onion, and gruyère

MAKES 1 LOAF | **TOTAL TIME: 1¼ HOURS, PLUS 3¼ HOURS COOLING**

- 3 ounces Parmesan or Pecorino Romano cheese, shredded (1 cup), divided
- 5 ounces bacon or pancetta, cut into ½-inch pieces
- ½ onion, chopped fine
- 2½ cups (12½ ounces) all-purpose flour
- 1 tablespoon baking powder
- 1 teaspoon table salt
- ⅛ teaspoon pepper
- ⅛ teaspoon cayenne pepper
- 4 ounces Gruyère cheese, cut into ½-inch pieces (1 cup)
- 1 cup whole milk
- ½ cup sour cream
- 1 large egg

why this recipe works One of the many joys of quick breads is that it's possible to make something special with just a mixing bowl, a little elbow grease, and ingredients you already have on hand. A case in point is this rich, hearty, cheesy bread: We use Gruyère and bacon as the main players, but it tastes fantastic with just about any semifirm cheese that has a bold flavor, and with a variety of pork products (or no meat at all). We simply mix the dry ingredients and the wet ingredients separately and then fold them together. Cutting the Gruyère into small chunks instead of shredding it makes for luscious cheesy pockets throughout the bread. For a crisp, browned crust, we coat the bottom of the pan and sprinkle the top of the loaf with shredded Parmesan. Use the large holes of a box grater to shred the Parmesan. The test kitchen's preferred loaf pan measures 8½ by 4½ inches; if you use a 9 by 5-inch loaf pan, start checking for doneness 5 minutes earlier than advised in the recipe. If, when testing the bread for doneness, the skewer comes out with what looks like uncooked batter clinging to it, try again in a different, but still central, spot. (A skewer hitting a pocket of cheese may give a false indication.) The texture of this bread improves as it cools, so resist the urge to slice the loaf when it's still warm.

1   Adjust oven rack to middle position and heat oven to 350 degrees. Grease 8½ by 4½-inch loaf pan, then sprinkle ½ cup Parmesan evenly in bottom of pan.

2   Cook bacon in 10-inch nonstick skillet over medium heat until crispy, 5 to 7 minutes. Using slotted spoon, transfer bacon to paper towel–lined plate. Pour off all but 3 tablespoons fat from skillet. Add onion to fat left in skillet and cook over medium heat until softened, about 3 minutes; set aside.

3   Whisk flour, baking powder, salt, pepper, and cayenne together in large bowl. Stir in Gruyère, bacon, and onion, breaking up clumps, until coated with flour mixture. Whisk milk, sour cream, and egg together in second bowl.

4   Gently fold milk mixture into flour mixture using rubber spatula until just combined (batter will be heavy and thick; do not overmix).

5 Transfer batter to prepared pan and smooth top. Sprinkle remaining ½ cup Parmesan evenly over surface. Bake loaf until golden brown and skewer inserted in center comes out clean, 45 to 50 minutes, rotating pan halfway through baking.

6 Let bread cool in pan on wire rack for 15 minutes. Remove bread from pan and let cool completely on wire rack, about 3 hours. Slice and serve. (Bread can be wrapped tightly in plastic wrap and stored at room temperature for up to 3 days.)

PANTRY IMPROV

use what you have Substitute any Swiss-style cheese or cheddar for the Gruyère. Instead of bacon, try prosciutto or serrano ham (it isn't necessary to cook it in step 2; just stir it into the batter along with the onions). Or simply omit the meat.

level up Stir up to ¼ cup chopped fresh herbs such as parsley or basil into the batter with the onions. Schmear slices with plain or scallion cream cheese before serving.

whole-wheat soda bread
with walnuts and cacao nibs

SERVES 6 TO 8 | TOTAL TIME: 1¼ HOURS, PLUS 1 HOUR COOLING

why this recipe works Traditional Irish soda bread, made with whole-wheat flour and without butter or eggs, is craggy, hearty, and full of whole-wheat nuttiness. The easy dough comes together in just one bowl and requires a bare minimum of shaping before it's put in a cake pan and popped into the oven. The rustic, not-too-sweet bread makes a perfect foundation for chewy or crunchy pantry ingredients such as intensely flavored cacao nibs and rich toasted walnuts. No matter what you stir into the batter—or even if you leave it plain—this bread is perfect for enjoying alongside a cup of tea or pairing with a light lunch or a wedge of cheese.

1   Adjust oven rack to middle position and heat oven to 375 degrees. Lightly grease 8-inch round cake pan. Whisk whole-wheat flour, all-purpose flour, wheat bran, wheat germ, sugar, baking powder, baking soda, and salt together in large bowl.

2   Stir in buttermilk, walnuts, and cacao nibs until all flour is moistened and dough forms soft, ragged mass. Transfer dough to counter and gently shape into 6-inch round (surface will be craggy). Using serrated knife, cut ½-inch-deep cross about 5 inches long on top of loaf. Transfer to prepared pan. Bake until loaf is lightly browned and center registers 185 degrees, 50 minutes to 1 hour, rotating pan halfway through baking.

3   Remove bread from pan and let cool on wire rack for at least 1 hour. Slice and serve. (Bread can be wrapped tightly in plastic wrap and stored at room temperature for up to 3 days.)

2   cups (11 ounces) whole-wheat flour

1   cup (5 ounces) all-purpose flour

1   cup wheat bran or oat bran

¼   cup wheat germ

2   teaspoons sugar

1½   teaspoons baking powder

1½   teaspoons baking soda

1   teaspoon table salt

2   cups buttermilk

1   cup walnuts or pecans, toasted and chopped

6   tablespoons cacao nibs

PANTRY IMPROV

use what you have You can replace the cacao nibs or some of the nuts with other stir-ins such as chopped dried fruit, crystallized ginger, or chocolate chips.

level up Spread slices with cream cheese or butter and sprinkle with cocoa powder or confectioners' sugar.

skillet **cheese pizza**

SERVES 4 | TOTAL TIME: 1 HOUR

- 1 (14.5-ounce) can whole peeled or diced tomatoes, drained with juice reserved
- 5 tablespoons extra-virgin olive oil, divided
- ½ teaspoon red wine vinegar
- ½ teaspoon dried oregano
- 1 small garlic clove, minced
- 1 pound pizza dough (see page 342), room temperature
- 8 ounces whole-milk mozzarella cheese, shredded (2 cups), divided
- 1 ounce Parmesan or Pecorino Romano cheese, grated (½ cup), divided

why this recipe works Keep a pound of pizza dough in your freezer and a fresh, crisp-crusted pizza is within reach any night of the week with this unconventional recipe. After rolling out the dough, we build the pizza in a skillet; this way, the bottom of the crust gets a jump-start toward browning on the stovetop before the skillet is transferred to the oven to bake. The simple no-cook tomato sauce is a comfy bed for sausage or other toppings, shredded mozzarella, and a little Parmesan. Let the dough sit out at room temperature while preparing the remaining ingredients and heating the oven, or it will be difficult to stretch. We like to use one of our pizza doughs (see page 342); however, you can use 1 pound of ready-made pizza dough from the local pizzeria or supermarket.

1   Adjust oven rack to upper-middle position and heat oven to 500 degrees. Process tomatoes, 1 tablespoon oil, vinegar, oregano, and garlic in food processor until smooth, about 30 seconds. Transfer mixture to 2-cup liquid measuring cup and add reserved tomato juice until sauce measures 1 cup. Season with salt and pepper to taste.

2   Grease 12-inch ovensafe skillet with 2 tablespoons oil. Transfer dough to lightly floured counter, divide in half, and gently shape each half into ball. Cover 1 dough ball with plastic wrap. Coat remaining dough ball lightly with flour and gently flatten into 8-inch disk using your fingertips. Using rolling pin, roll dough into 11-inch circle, dusting dough lightly with flour as needed. (If dough springs back during rolling, let rest for 10 minutes before rolling again.)

3   Transfer dough to prepared skillet; reshape as needed. Using back of spoon or ladle, spread ½ cup sauce in thin layer over surface of dough, leaving ½-inch border around edge. Sprinkle 1 cup mozzarella and ¼ cup Parmesan evenly over sauce.

4   Set skillet over medium-high heat and cook until outside edge of dough is set, pizza is lightly puffed, and bottom is spotty brown when gently lifted with spatula, 2 to 3 minutes. Transfer pizza to oven and bake until crust is brown and cheese is golden in spots, 7 to 10 minutes. Using pot holders, remove skillet from oven and slide pizza onto cutting board. Let pizza cool slightly before slicing and serving. Being careful of hot skillet handle, repeat with remaining 2 tablespoons oil, dough, sauce, 1 cup mozzarella, and ¼ cup Parmesan.

PANTRY IMPROV

use what you have You can use provolone or mild cheddar instead of mozzarella.

level up Feel free to add toppings before baking, such as sliced pepperoni or dime-size pieces of Italian sausage, sautéed mushrooms, and/or thinly sliced bell peppers or onions. Keep the toppings light to avoid a weighed-down, soggy crust.

VARIATIONS

skillet pizza with fontina, arugula, and prosciutto

Toss 2 cups baby arugula or spinach with 4 teaspoons extra-virgin olive oil and salt and pepper to taste in bowl. Omit Parmesan and substitute shredded fontina for mozzarella. Immediately after baking, sprinkle 4 ounces thinly sliced prosciutto, cut into ½-inch strips, and dressed arugula over top of pizza.

skillet pizza with goat cheese, olives, and infused oil

Brush one of our infused oils (see page 390) over pizza dough before adding sauce in step 3. Omit Parmesan and reduce mozzarella to 1 cup. Sprinkle 1 cup crumbled goat cheese and ½ cup pitted and halved olives over mozzarella before baking.

skillet pizza with ricotta, bacon, and scallions

Mix 1 cup ricotta, 2 thinly sliced scallions, ¼ teaspoon table salt, and ⅛ teaspoon pepper together in bowl. Omit Parmesan and reduce mozzarella to 1 cup. Dollop ricotta mixture, 1 tablespoon at a time, on top of mozzarella, then sprinkle with 4 ounces crispy cooked bacon or pancetta. Sprinkle pizza with 1 more sliced scallion before serving.

red pepper **flatbreads**

MAKES 4 FLATBREADS | SERVES 4 TO 6
TOTAL TIME: 1½ HOURS, PLUS 1¼ HOURS RESTING AND COOLING

½ cup extra–virgin olive oil, divided

2 large onions, halved and sliced thin

2 cups jarred roasted red peppers, patted dry and sliced thin

3 tablespoons sugar

3 garlic cloves, minced

1½ teaspoons table salt

¼ teaspoon red pepper flakes

2 bay leaves

3 tablespoons sherry vinegar

2 pounds pizza dough (see page 342), room temperature

¼ cup pine nuts (optional)

1 tablespoon minced fresh parsley (optional)

PANTRY IMPROV

use what you have Use red or white wine vinegar in place of the sherry vinegar. Replace jarred roasted red peppers with jarred artichokes or olives. Substitute almonds or walnuts for the pine nuts and cilantro for the parsley.

level up Serve with a green salad.

why this recipe works Thin and crunchy and sporting a myriad of toppings, the Catalan flatbreads called coques are sometimes referred to as the Spanish version of pizza. Our pantry-friendly flatbreads take inspiration from coques but start with pizza dough. To mimic the crispness of coques, we use plenty of olive oil on the baking sheets and we brush each flatbread with olive oil before baking. Parbaking the dough before topping it further promotes an evenly crisp, sturdy base. For our deeply flavorful, sweetly tangy topping, we cook onions and convenient jarred roasted red peppers with olive oil, sugar, garlic, and red pepper flakes until the vegetables turn meltingly soft and sweetly savory, and then stir in some sherry vinegar off the heat. If you can't fit two flatbreads on a single baking sheet, bake them in two batches. We like to use our pizza dough (see page 342); however, you can use 2 pounds of ready-made pizza dough from the local pizzeria or supermarket. You will need a 12-inch nonstick skillet with a tight-fitting lid for this recipe.

1 Heat 3 tablespoons oil in 12-inch nonstick skillet over medium heat until shimmering. Stir in onions, red peppers, sugar, garlic, salt, pepper flakes, and bay leaves. Cover and cook, stirring occasionally, until onions are softened and have released their juice, about 10 minutes. Remove lid and continue to cook, stirring often, until onions are golden brown, 10 to 15 minutes. Off heat, discard bay leaves. Transfer onion mixture to bowl, stir in vinegar, and let cool completely before using.

2 Divide dough into quarters and cover loosely with greased plastic wrap. Working with 1 piece of dough at a time (keep remaining pieces covered), form into rough ball by stretching dough around your thumbs and pinching edges together so that top is smooth.

3 Place ball seam side down on counter and, using your cupped hands, drag in small circles until dough feels taut and round. Space dough balls 3 inches apart, cover loosely with greased plastic, and let rest for 1 hour.

4 Adjust oven racks to upper-middle and lower-middle positions and heat oven to 500 degrees. Coat 2 rimmed baking sheets with 2 tablespoons oil each. Generously coat 1 dough ball with flour and place on well-floured counter. Press and roll into 14 by 5-inch oval. Arrange oval on prepared sheet, with long edge fitted snugly against 1 long side of sheet, and reshape as needed. (If dough resists stretching, let it relax for 10 to 20 minutes before trying to stretch it again.) Repeat with remaining dough balls, arranging 2 ovals on each sheet, spaced ½ inch apart. Using fork, poke surface of each dough oval 10 to 15 times.

5 Brush dough ovals with remaining 1 tablespoon oil and bake until puffed, 6 to 8 minutes, switching and rotating sheets halfway through baking.

6 Scatter onion mixture evenly over flatbreads from edge to edge, then sprinkle with pine nuts, if using. Bake until topping is heated through and edges of flatbreads are deep golden brown and crisp, about 15 minutes, switching and rotating sheets halfway through baking. Let flatbreads cool on sheets for 10 minutes, then transfer to cutting board using metal spatula. Sprinkle with parsley, if using; slice; and serve.

vegetable **stromboli**

SERVES 4 | TOTAL TIME: 1½ HOURS

1 teaspoon extra–virgin olive oil

2 garlic cloves, minced

¼ teaspoon red pepper flakes

6 ounces frozen broccoli florets, thawed and cut into ¼–inch pieces

2 tablespoons water

1 pound pizza dough (see page 342), room temperature

4 ounces thinly sliced aged provolone cheese

4 ounces mozzarella cheese, shredded (1 cup)

½ cup chopped jarred roasted red peppers

¼ cup chopped pitted kalamata olives

1 large egg, lightly beaten

¼ cup grated Parmesan or Pecorino Romano cheese

why this recipe works This colorful stromboli is easy to put together using ingredients from the pantry, fridge, and freezer. We layer provolone, mozzarella, sautéed broccoli, roasted red peppers, and kalamata olives (which add a bright, salty balance to the mixture) evenly over the rolled-out dough. Then we brush the borders of the dough with egg (to seal the seams) and fold the stromboli like a letter to seal in all the filling ingredients. A 375-degree oven is hot enough to promote browning but moderate enough to allow the dough in the center of the stromboli to cook through. We like to use one of our pizza doughs (see page 342); however, you can use 1 pound of ready-made pizza dough from the local pizzeria or supermarket. You will need a 12-inch nonstick skillet with a tight-fitting lid for this recipe.

1 Adjust oven rack to middle position and heat oven to 375 degrees. Line rimmed baking sheet with aluminum foil and grease foil. Heat oil in 12-inch nonstick skillet over medium heat until shimmering. Add garlic and pepper flakes and cook until fragrant, about 30 seconds. Add broccoli and water, cover, and cook until just tender, about 1 minute. Uncover and cook until liquid has evaporated, about 1 minute. Transfer broccoli to dish towel; gather corners of towel and squeeze out excess moisture.

2 Roll dough into 12 by 10-inch rectangle on lightly floured counter with long side parallel to counter edge. Shingle provolone evenly over dough, leaving ½-inch border along top and sides. Sprinkle mozzarella, red peppers, olives, and broccoli evenly over provolone.

3 Brush borders with egg (reserve remaining egg for brushing top of stromboli). Fold bottom third of stromboli in toward middle. Fold top third of stromboli down to cover first fold, creating log. Pinch seam to seal. Transfer stromboli to prepared sheet, seam side down. Pinch ends to seal and tuck underneath.

4 Brush top of stromboli with remaining egg. Using sharp knife, make 5 evenly spaced ½-inch-deep slashes, 2 inches long, on top of stromboli. Sprinkle with Parmesan. Bake until crust is golden and center registers 200 degrees, 30 to 35 minutes, rotating sheet halfway through baking. Transfer stromboli to wire rack and let cool for 10 minutes. Transfer to cutting board and cut into 2-inch-thick slices. Serve.

PANTRY IMPROV

use what you have Try pepperoncini, jarred artichokes, or peppadew instead of the roasted red peppers. Use fresh broccoli or broccoli rabe (blanched or sautéed) instead of frozen broccoli, or use frozen, thawed spinach or kale. Any deli sliced cheese works here; try fontina.

level up Serve with your favorite tomato sauce. Add any sliced deli meat or cooked, crumbled sausage to the filling.

homemade **pizza dough**

There's no denying the convenience factor of store-bought pizza dough, but making your own is quick and easy—and might just save you a shopping trip. Plus, the results are delicious. Make either of these recipes and store in the freezer: After proofing the dough, place on a baking sheet or plate lined with parchment paper, cover loosely with plastic wrap, and freeze until firm, 3 hours or up to overnight. Wrap frozen dough in plastic and store in zipper-lock bags in the freezer for up to 2 months. To thaw, unwrap ball, place in lightly oiled bowl, cover with plastic, and let sit in the refrigerator for 12 to 24 hours before making pizza.

classic pizza dough

makes 2 pounds
total time: 15 minutes, plus 1 hour rising
An equal volume of all-purpose flour can be substituted for the bread flour, but the resulting crust will be a little less chewy. Using warm water gives the yeast a head start. To make 1 pound of dough, reduce amounts of all ingredients by half; mix, knead, and let rise as directed.

- 4¼ cups (23⅓ ounces) bread flour
- 2¼ teaspoons instant or rapid-rise yeast
- 1½ teaspoons table salt
- 2 tablespoons extra-virgin olive oil
- 1½ cups warm tap water (110 degrees)

1 Pulse flour, yeast, and salt together in food processor to combine, about 5 pulses. With processor running, add oil, then water, and process until rough ball forms, 30 to 40 seconds. Let dough rest for 2 minutes, then process for 30 seconds longer. (If after 30 seconds dough is very sticky and clings to blade, add extra flour as needed.)

2 Transfer dough to lightly floured counter and knead until smooth, about 1 minute. Shape dough into tight ball, place in large lightly oiled bowl, and cover tightly with plastic wrap. (Bowl of dough can be refrigerated for up to 16 hours; let sit at room temperature for 30 minutes before using.)

3 Place in warm spot and let dough rise until doubled in size, 1 to 1½ hours.

whole-wheat pizza dough

makes 1½ pounds
total time: 15 minutes, plus 18¼ hours resting and chilling
We prefer King Arthur brand bread flour in this recipe.

- 1½ cups (8¼ ounces) whole-wheat flour
- 1 cup (5½ ounces) bread flour
- 2 teaspoons honey
- ¾ teaspoon instant or rapid-rise yeast
- 1¼ cups (10 ounces) ice water
- 2 tablespoons extra-virgin olive oil
- 1¾ teaspoons table salt

1 Process whole-wheat flour, bread flour, honey, and yeast in food processor until combined, about 2 seconds. With processor running, add ice water and process until dough is just combined and no dry flour remains, about 10 seconds. Let dough stand for 10 minutes.

2 Add oil and salt to dough and process until it forms satiny, sticky ball that clears sides of workbowl, 45 to 60 seconds. Remove from bowl and knead on oiled counter until smooth, about 1 minute. Shape dough into tight ball and place in large, lightly oiled bowl. Cover tightly with plastic wrap and refrigerate for at least 18 hours. (Dough can be refrigerated for up to 2 days.)

the many uses of **pizza dough**

Having pizza dough on hand is nothing short of a lifesaver: It freezes beautifully and works well not only for pizza but also for a hearty stromboli (see page 340), flatbread, or easy breads and rolls such as the ones on these pages. Most supermarkets (and some pizzerias) sell pizza dough in 1–pound bags—though making your own takes just 10 minutes. If buying bagged pizza dough, look for dough that is still partially frozen; the yeast is more likely to be active, which will lead to a better rise during baking. Whatever kind you use, it's important to let the dough come to room temperature before beginning the recipe.

braided dinner loaf
serves 6

Divide 1 pound pizza dough into 3 even pieces and roll each piece into 12-inch rope. Braid ropes into loaf, pinching ends to secure; transfer to parchment paper–lined baking sheet. Brush with 1 large beaten egg and sprinkle with 1 teaspoon sesame seeds, ½ teaspoon caraway seeds, ½ teaspoon fennel seeds, and ½ teaspoon kosher salt. Combine 2 tablespoons melted butter and 1 minced garlic clove in bowl. Bake in 425-degree oven until golden, about 30 minutes, brushing with garlic butter mixture halfway through baking.

garlic and herb breadsticks

makes 18 breadsticks | serves 4 to 6
total time: 45 minutes

- 1 pound pizza dough, room temperature
- 2 teaspoons minced fresh thyme or ½ teaspoon dried
- 2 teaspoons dried oregano
- 1 teaspoon garlic powder
- ½ teaspoon kosher salt
- ¼ teaspoon pepper
- 3 tablespoons unsalted butter, melted

1 Adjust oven rack to middle position and heat oven to 450 degrees. Line rimmed baking sheet with parchment paper.

2 Divide dough into 2 equal pieces. Roll and stretch 1 piece of dough into 9 by 5-inch rectangle on lightly floured counter. Transfer dough to half of prepared sheet, with short ends parallel to long sides of sheet. Repeat with remaining dough piece and place on other half of sheet.

3 Stir thyme, oregano, garlic powder, salt, and pepper together in bowl. Using pastry brush, brush doughs with half of melted butter. Sprinkle doughs with half of thyme mixture. Flip doughs, brush with remaining melted butter, and sprinkle with remaining thyme mixture.

4 Using bench scraper or chef's knife, cut doughs crosswise at 1-inch intervals to create nine 5-inch breadsticks from each piece of dough, but do not separate breadsticks. Bake until golden brown, 9 to 12 minutes. Let cool for 5 minutes. Pull breadsticks apart at seams. Serve.

VARIATION

spicy parmesan breadsticks

Combine ¾ cup grated Parmesan cheese and ½ teaspoon red pepper flakes in small bowl and sprinkle dough with mixture before baking.

easy garlic rolls

makes 10 rolls

Combine ¼ cup extra-virgin olive oil, 1 minced garlic clove, ½ teaspoon table salt, and ¼ teaspoon pepper in small bowl. Cut 1 pound pizza dough into 10 equal pieces, roll loosely into balls, and arrange on parchment paper–lined baking sheet. Brush rolls with 1 large beaten egg. Bake in 475-degree oven until golden brown, 30 to 35 minutes, brushing rolls with garlic oil halfway through baking. Serve warm.

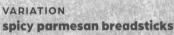

desserts

dipping hot chocolate

SERVES 4 | **TOTAL TIME: 5 MINUTES**

why this recipe works We've all experienced those nights when we're craving a bite of something sweet but it feels like there is absolutely nothing suitable in the house. Here's a solution: dipping chocolate. It's so pantry friendly that you actually don't even need chocolate. Unsweetened cocoa is fine—in fact, it's better than fine: When warmed up with cream and sugar until thick and creamy, it's delicious, reminiscent of European-style hot chocolate. In 5 minutes you'll be scouring your pantry for items to dunk: fresh or dried fruit; pretzels; potato chips; crackers; or even cookies. The possibilities are endless.

Stir cream, cocoa, and sugar in large bowl until evenly combined. Microwave at 50 percent power for 1 minute, then whisk until few lumps remain. Microwave at 50 percent power for 1 minute longer, then whisk until smooth. Serve.

1 cup heavy cream or half-and-half

½ cup (1½ ounces) unsweetened cocoa powder

½ cup (3½ ounces) sugar

PANTRY IMPROV

use what you have You can use either natural or Dutch-processed cocoa powder here.

level up Add a splash of raspberry, hazelnut, or coffee liqueur. Stir in up to ⅛ teaspoon almond, anise, orange, or vanilla extract. Dust the top with ground cinnamon, ancho, or chipotle chile powder, or coarse sea salt. Or thin it with milk for a comforting mug of drinkable hot chocolate.

pantry toppings for **ice cream**

Ice cream is the best thing to keep stashed in your freezer for an easy-to-portion dessert at a moment's notice. Plus, it welcomes a wide variety of toppings that can elevate it to a standout treat. To level up your scoops, there's no need to buy a host of toppings. Dig into your pantry for some unexpected flavor ideas. While you're at it, prepare a homemade sauce and use a Mason jar to shake up just enough whipped cream to dollop on top (see page 352 for ideas).

keep it simple

- granola and honey
- toasted nuts and espresso powder
- flaked coconut and mango
- crumbled cookies and Small-Batch Whipped Cream (page 352)
- jam and peanuts
- marshmallow crème and peanut butter
- orange zest and Classic Hot Fudge Sauce (page 352)

get creative

- matcha powder and honey
- bourbon and cinnamon
- balsamic glaze and gorgonzola
- crumbled nori and sesame seeds
- extra-virgin olive oil and flaky sea salt
- M&M'S and crumbled potato chips
- cayenne and chopped chocolate
- maple syrup and crumbled bacon
- Spiced Seeds (page 386) and maple syrup
- pomegranate seeds and white chocolate chips
- toasted cashews and curry powder
- chopped crystallized ginger and shaved chocolate

easy **dessert toppings**

When there's chocolate in the pantry and a few bags of frozen fruit in the freezer, you have a solid starting point for preparing all kinds of desserts. But one of the simplest routes is to make a sauce to pour over ice cream, Greek yogurt, fresh fruit, cookies, or anything else you like.

classic hot fudge sauce

makes 2 cups | total time: 20 minutes
This is a great sauce to keep in your fridge for whenever the mood strikes.

- 1¼ cups (8¾ ounces) sugar
- ⅔ cup whole milk
- ¼ teaspoon table salt
- ⅓ cup (1 ounce) unsweetened cocoa powder, sifted
- 3 ounces unsweetened chocolate, chopped fine
- 4 tablespoons unsalted butter, cut into 8 pieces and chilled
- 1 teaspoon vanilla extract

1 Heat sugar, milk, and salt in medium saucepan over medium-low heat, whisking gently, until sugar has dissolved and liquid starts to bubble around edges of saucepan, about 6 minutes. Reduce heat to low, add cocoa, and whisk until smooth.

2 Off heat, stir in chocolate and let sit for 3 minutes. Whisk sauce until smooth and chocolate is fully melted. Whisk in butter and vanilla until fully incorporated and sauce thickens slightly. Serve. (Sauce can be refrigerated for up to 1 month; gently warm in microwave, stirring every 10 seconds until pourable, before using.)

chocolate ice cream shell

makes about ½ cup
total time: 5 minutes, plus 20 minutes cooling

- 3 ounces bittersweet chocolate, chopped fine
- ¼ cup refined coconut oil
  Pinch table salt

Combine chocolate, oil, and salt in medium bowl. Microwave at 50 percent power, stirring occasionally until smooth, 2 to 4 minutes. Let cool completely, about 20 minutes. Spoon or pour over ice cream. (Sauce can be stored in airtight container at room temperature for up to 2 months; gently warm in microwave, stirring every 10 seconds until pourable, before using.)

small–batch whipped cream

makes ⅓ cup | total time: 5 minutes

- ¼ cup heavy cream, chilled
- ½ teaspoon sugar
- ¼ teaspoon vanilla extract

Combine all ingredients in 1- or 2-cup Mason jar. Close lid tightly, then shake jar until cream is thickened and holds shape on spoon, about 2 minutes. Serve.

strawberry–balsamic topping with pepper

makes ½ cup | total time: 10 minutes

 2 teaspoons packed brown sugar
 1 teaspoon balsamic vinegar
    Pinch pepper
 ½ cup frozen strawberries, thawed and chopped

Microwave sugar, vinegar, and pepper in small bowl until just steaming, about 30 seconds. Stir to dissolve sugar, then add strawberries and toss to coat. Serve warm or at room temperature. (Topping can be refrigerated for up to 4 days.)

blueberry compote

makes ½ cup | total time: 25 minutes

You can use fresh blueberries, though you'll need to crush one-third of them against the side of the saucepan with a wooden spoon after adding them to the butter to achieve the desired consistency.

 1 tablespoon unsalted butter
 5 ounces (1 cup) frozen blueberries
 1 tablespoon sugar, plus extra for seasoning
    Pinch table salt
 ¼ teaspoon lemon juice

Melt butter in small saucepan over medium heat. Add blueberries, sugar, and salt and bring to boil. Reduce heat to low and simmer, stirring occasionally, until sauce is thickened and about one-quarter of juice remains, 8 to 10 minutes. Remove pan from heat and stir in lemon juice. Season with extra sugar to taste. (Compote can be refrigerated for up to 4 days.)

peanut butter–chocolate
quesadillas

SERVES 4 | TOTAL TIME: 15 MINUTES

4 (10-inch) flour tortillas

½ cup creamy or chunky peanut butter

¼ cup chocolate chips

2 tablespoons unsalted butter, divided

why this recipe works A flour tortilla serves as a cross between a crepe and a pancake in this warm, satisfying pantry dessert (or anytime snack) that comes together in just a few minutes and offers far greater rewards—for no greater effort—than making a PB&J. We spread peanut butter (creamy or crunchy) over half of a tortilla, top the nut butter with a handful of chocolate chips, and fold the tortilla in half. We toast the quesadilla in a little butter until it's crispy and browned, the peanut butter is warmed through, and the chocolate chips are melty. As you might imagine, this recipe lends itself beautifully to a variety of fillings and toppings.

1 Lay tortillas on cutting board. Spread peanut butter over half of each tortilla, leaving ½-inch border around edge. Sprinkle chocolate chips over peanut butter, then fold other half of tortillas over top.

2 Melt 1 tablespoon butter in 12-inch nonstick skillet over medium-low heat. Place two filled tortillas in skillet and cook until crispy and well browned on first side, about 2 minutes. Flip quesadillas and cook until second side is crispy and well browned, 1 to 2 minutes. Transfer quesadillas to cutting board. Repeat with remaining 1 tablespoon butter and remaining filled tortillas. Let quesadillas cool slightly, then cut into wedges and serve.

PANTRY IMPROV

use what you have Use any nut butter in place of the peanut butter and any type of chocolate (chopped bar or chips) that you have on hand.

level up Add sliced pear, apple, or strawberries to the filling. Sprinkle with confectioners' sugar or cocoa powder and/or dollop with whipped cream before serving.

VARIATIONS

cannoli quesadillas

Substitute sweetened ricotta or mascarpone for peanut butter and chopped bittersweet chocolate for chocolate chips. Sprinkle 2 tablespoons toasted and chopped pistachios and/or 1 teaspoon grated lemon or orange zest over chocolate before folding tortillas.

nutella–orange quesadillas

Substitute nutella for peanut butter and chopped hazelnuts or walnuts for chocolate chips. Sprinkle 2 teaspoons grated orange zest over hazelnuts before folding tortillas.

peanut butter–banana quesadillas

Substitute 2 bananas, sliced ¼ inch thick, for chocolate chips.

skillet-roasted pears
with caramel sauce

SERVES 2 TO 4 | TOTAL TIME: 30 MINUTES

why this recipe works Sweet, juicy pears become the base for a simple yet elegant dessert. These delicate fruits are easier to keep on hand than you might think: Pears are sold unripe and storing them in the fridge slows down the ripening process. Bartlett and Bosc varieties become sweeter when cooked and retain their texture instead of becoming mushy. We pan-roast the pears in boiling sugar and water until they soften and become golden, and the sugar caramelizes. Visual cues tell us when the caramel is ready and the pears are properly cooked, so there's no need for a candy thermometer. To finish the sauce, we add heavy cream to the skillet toward the end of cooking and gently shake the pan to give the sauce a rich, glossy consistency. For the best texture, don't use pears that are either fully ripe or rock hard; choose fruit that yields slightly when pressed. You will need a 12-inch skillet with a tight-fitting lid for this recipe.

1 Add water to 12-inch skillet, then pour sugar into center of skillet (don't let it hit skillet's sides). Gently stir sugar with clean spatula to moisten it thoroughly. Bring to boil over medium heat and cook, stirring occasionally, until sugar is completely dissolved and liquid is bubbling, about 2 minutes.

2 Add pears to skillet cut side down, cover, and cook until almost tender (fork inserted into center of pears meets slight resistance), 10 to 15 minutes, reducing heat as needed to prevent caramel from getting too dark.

3 Uncover, reduce heat to medium-low, and continue to cook until sauce is golden brown and cut sides of pears are beginning to brown, about 3 minutes. Pour cream around pears and cook, shaking skillet occasionally, until sauce is smooth and deep caramel color and cut sides of pears are golden brown, 3 to 5 minutes.

4 Transfer pears cut side up to serving platter and sprinkle sauce with salt to taste. Spoon sauce over pears. Serve.

⅓ cup water

⅔ cup (4⅔ ounces) sugar

2 ripe but firm pears (8 ounces each), peeled, halved, and cored

⅔ cup heavy cream

PANTRY IMPROV

use what you have Any type of pear will work here but we prefer Bartlett or Bosc, or you can use apples.

level up Serve with ice cream, pound cake, or yogurt. Top with toasted walnuts, almonds, or pine nuts.

berry granita

SERVES 8 | **TOTAL TIME: 15 MINUTES, PLUS 3 HOURS FREEZING**

why this recipe works For a deeply fruity granita with a light, crystalline texture, we blend fresh or frozen berries with enough water to form a silky puree and enough sugar for modest sweetness and to give the puree the proper consistency when frozen. When scraped, this granita yields light, flaky ice crystals that linger briefly on the palate for a chilling pause before melting in a flood of fruity goodness. Lemon juice contributes acidity that brightens the fruit flavor. Best of all, this mostly hands-off recipe requires no special equipment—just a blender, baking dish, fork, and freezer. This recipe can be halved, if desired; use an 8-inch glass baking dish.

1   pound fresh or thawed frozen berries

¾   cup water

½   cup (3½ ounces) sugar

¼   cup lemon juice (2 lemons)

Pinch table salt

1   Process berries, water, sugar, lemon juice, and salt in blender on high speed until very smooth, 1 to 2 minutes. Strain mixture through fine-mesh strainer into 13 by 9-inch glass baking dish. Freeze, uncovered, until edges are frozen and center is slushy, about 1 hour. Using fork, scrape edges to release crystals. Stir crystals into middle of mixture and return dish to freezer. Repeat scraping and stirring, using tines of fork to mash any large chunks, every 30 minutes to 1 hour until granita crystals are uniformly light and fluffy, 2 to 3 hours.

2   Immediately before serving, scrape granita with fork to loosen. Spoon into chilled bowls or glasses and serve. (Any remaining granita can be transferred to airtight container and frozen for up to 1 week. Scrape granita again to loosen before serving.)

PANTRY IMPROV

use what you have You can use fresh or thawed frozen blueberries, raspberries, blackberries, hulled strawberries, or a combination of berries. If using fresh strawberries, weigh them after hulling. If using any type of thawed berries, do not drain them before adding them to the blender.

level up For more complexity, you can add 2 to 3 tablespoons of chopped fresh mint, 1 to 2 teaspoons of grated fresh ginger, or 1 to 2 teaspoons of grated lemon zest (do not add more than one of these) to the blender in step 1. Serve this granita on its own or garnish it with unsweetened whipped cream (layer it to make a parfait, if desired), fresh berries, or a splash of prosecco or your favorite liqueur.

any fruit **milkshakes**

SERVES 2 | TOTAL TIME: 25 MINUTES

2 cups vanilla ice cream

1 pound (3½ cups) frozen fruit, thawed

¼ cup milk

Pinch table salt

why this recipe works You can re-create thick, creamy, diner-style milkshakes at home with a couple of ingredients from your freezer: Just thaw a bag of your favorite frozen fruit, soften a pint of ice cream, and plug in the food processor. Using a processor, rather than a blender, makes quick work of turning the fruit into a smooth puree, and its larger bowl exposes more of the ice cream mixture to air and to the walls of the workbowl, resulting in a light, frothy shake that's easy to sip through a straw. The slightly higher heat generated by the processor's blade causes more of the tiny crystals to melt slightly, creating a smooth milkshake that remains cold but fluid. A pinch of salt makes the fruit flavor pop and offsets the ice cream's sweetness. Serve the milkshakes in chilled glasses to help them stay colder longer. This recipe can be easily doubled; simply blend the milkshakes in two batches.

Place 2 pint glasses in freezer and chill until ready to serve. Let ice cream sit at room temperature to soften slightly, about 15 minutes. Process fruit in food processor until smooth, about 1 minute, scraping down sides of bowl as needed. Add ice cream, milk, and salt to processor and puree until smooth, about 1 minute, scraping down sides of bowl as needed. Pour milkshakes into chilled glasses and serve.

PANTRY IMPROV

use what you have Use plant-based ice cream and milk if desired. Skip the fruit if you want: Double the amount of ice cream and milk and omit the fruit for a vanilla milkshake, or use chocolate ice cream to make a chocolate milkshake.

level up Stir caramel sauce or chocolate sauce into the milkshakes. Stir peanut butter, malted milk powder, or cocoa powder into the food processor along with the milk. Top with a dollop of whipped cream (see page 352) and crumbled cookies.

rustic **peach-ginger tart**

SERVES 4 | TOTAL TIME: 45 MINUTES

why this recipe works Making a fresh fruit pie from scratch is a delicious project—when you have the time and materials. When you don't, this recipe comes to the rescue. Chewy, spicy-sweet bits of crystallized ginger punctuate the filling of sweet and juicy frozen peaches. Forming a store-bought pie dough round into an open-faced tart is not only quick and easy, but also allows for evaporation to keep those juices in check. To prevent the tart from leaking, it is crucial to leave a ½-inch-wide border of dough around the fruit. Pie dough rounds come in packages of two; the extra round can be wrapped tightly in plastic, or in its original packaging, and frozen (or refrozen).

1   Adjust oven rack to middle position and heat oven to 500 degrees. Microwave peaches in bowl, stirring occasionally, until thawed and softened, 12 to 15 minutes.

2   Meanwhile, roll pie crust into 12-inch round on lightly floured sheet of parchment paper. Transfer dough, still on parchment, to baking sheet.

3   Drain peaches well in colander. Whisk ¼ cup sugar; peach schnapps, if using; ginger; and cornstarch together in now-empty peach bowl. Add drained peaches and toss gently to coat.

4   Mound peach mixture in center of dough round, leaving 2½-inch border of dough around edge. Being careful to leave ½ inch of space between dough edge and peach mixture, fold outermost 2 inches of dough up and over fruit, pleating it every 2 to 3 inches as needed. Brush dough with egg wash and sprinkle with remaining 1 teaspoon sugar.

5   Bake tart until crust is golden and crisp, and filling is bubbling, 12 to 15 minutes, rotating baking sheet halfway through baking. Let tart cool slightly on baking sheet. Serve warm or at room temperature. (Baked tart can be held at room temperature for up to 8 hours or refrigerated for up to 24 hours; to serve, refresh in 350 degree oven for 10 to 15 minutes before serving. Crust will be less crisp.)

1½ pounds (4½ cups) frozen peaches

1   (9-inch) store-bought
pie dough round

¼   cup (1¾ ounces) plus 1 teaspoon
sugar, divided

2   tablespoons peach schnapps
(optional)

1   tablespoon finely chopped
crystallized ginger

2   teaspoons cornstarch

1   large egg, lightly beaten with
2 tablespoons water

PANTRY IMPROV

use what you have Substitute other frozen fruit for the peaches but make sure to measure by volume, not weight. Substitute up to ¼ cup chopped dried fruit for the ginger. Use brandy or bourbon in place of the peach schnapps.

level up Add up to ¼ cup chopped and toasted nuts to the filling. Serve with whipped cream or ice cream.

no-bake **apple crisp**

SERVES 2 | TOTAL TIME: 15 MINUTES

why this recipe works You can skip your trip to the orchard: All it takes is two apples and some simple pantry ingredients to achieve a quintessential fall dessert whenever the mood strikes. We found we could "bake" an apple crisp entirely in the microwave and achieve a crispy, crunchy topping and tender, juicy fruit. The key is to cook the topping separately and stir it regularly for evenly golden, crunchy crumbles unaffected by the steam of the cooking fruit. We developed this recipe in a full-size 1200-watt microwave. If the wattage of your microwave is less than 1200 watts, you will need to increase the cooking times throughout. Be careful when handling the bowls for the filling and topping after microwaving, as they will get hot.

1 for the filling Combine apples, sugar, lemon juice, and cinnamon in bowl and microwave until apples have softened and juices have thickened, 3 to 4 minutes, stirring occasionally. Set aside to cool slightly.

2 for the topping Meanwhile, mix flour, sugar, oats, and salt together in separate bowl. Using your fingers, rub butter into flour mixture until mixture has texture of coarse crumbs. Microwave until topping is golden, about 2 minutes, stirring every 30 seconds.

3 Sprinkle topping over apples and serve.

filling

- 2 apples, peeled, cored, and cut into ¾-inch pieces
- ¼ cup (1¾ ounces) sugar
- 2 teaspoons lemon juice
- ¼ teaspoon ground cinnamon

topping

- 2 tablespoons all-purpose flour
- 3 teaspoons sugar
- 3 teaspoons old-fashioned rolled oats
- ⅛ teaspoon table salt
- 1 tablespoon unsalted butter, cut into 4 pieces

PANTRY IMPROV

use what you have We like Golden Delicious apples for this recipe, but any sweet, crisp apples you have on hand can be used.

level up Top with a dollop of whipped cream (see page 352), a drizzle of caramel, or a scoop of your favorite ice cream, gelato, or frozen yogurt. Add chopped toasted nuts (pecans, almonds, walnuts, and/or pistachios) to the topping. Add dried fruit (raisins, dried cranberries or cherries, currants, and/or chopped dried apricots) to the apples before cooking.

loaded **triple chocolate chunk cookies**

MAKES 16 COOKIES | TOTAL TIME: 1 HOUR

- 2¼ cups (11¼ ounces) all-purpose flour
- 1 teaspoon table salt
- ¾ teaspoon baking soda
- 1 cup packed (7 ounces) light brown sugar
- 12 tablespoons unsalted butter, melted
- ½ cup (3½ ounces) granulated sugar
- 2 large eggs
- 1½ teaspoons vanilla extract
- 12 ounces any combination of dark, milk, and/or white chocolate, chopped

why this recipe works The buttery brown-sugar base for these easy-to-make cookies would taste great on its own, but we jam-pack it with flavorful pantry mix-ins. Our main recipe uses any mix of dark, white, or milk chocolate. Variations incorporate crushed cookies, candy, marshmallows, and even bacon. We portion the dough in generous scoops for large, hearty cookies. Underbaking the cookies ensures that they remain chewy once cool.

1   Adjust oven rack to middle position and heat oven to 425 degrees. Line 2 rimmed baking sheets with parchment paper. Combine flour, salt, and baking soda in bowl.

2   Using stand mixer fitted with paddle, beat brown sugar, melted butter, and granulated sugar on medium speed until well combined, about 1 minute, scraping down bowl as needed. Add eggs and vanilla and beat until fully incorporated, about 30 seconds.

3   Reduce speed to low and slowly add flour mixture. Mix until mostly incorporated but some streaks of flour remain, about 30 seconds. Add chocolate and mix until evenly distributed throughout dough, about 30 seconds.

4   Divide dough into sixteen 2½-ounce portions, about ¼ cup each. Divide any remaining dough evenly among dough portions. Roll dough portions between your wet hands to make dough balls.

5   Evenly space dough balls on prepared sheets, 8 balls per sheet. Using your hand, flatten dough balls to ¾-inch thickness. (Flattened dough balls can be frozen on parchment paper–lined plate until very firm, at least 1 hour, then transferred to zipper-lock bag and stored in freezer for up to 1 month; do not thaw before baking.)

6   Bake cookies, 1 sheet at a time, until centers of cookies are puffed and still very blond, 8 to 12 minutes. (Cookies will seem underdone but will continue to bake as they cool.) Let cookies cool on sheet for 5 minutes. Using spatula, transfer cookies to wire rack and let cool for 10 minutes. Serve warm.

PANTRY IMPROV

use what you have You can use any type of chocolate (bar or chips). Incorporate other sweet stir-ins (M&M'S, Reese's Pieces, butterscotch chips) in place of the chocolate, or use chopped dried fruit, nuts, or crushed cookies. Just limit the mix-ins to 12 ounces, including the chocolate.

VARIATIONS

loaded cookies-and-cream cookies
Substitute 15 chopped Oreo cookies (1½ cups) for 8 ounces of chopped chocolate.

loaded peanut butter-bacon cookies
Substitute 1½ cups Reese's Pieces and ¾ cup cooked chopped bacon for chopped chocolate.

loaded s'mores cookies
Substitute ¾ cup mini marsh-mallows and ¾ cup lightly crushed graham crackers for 8 ounces of chopped chocolate.

chocolate mug cakes

SERVES 2 | TOTAL TIME: 20 MINUTES

why this recipe works When the craving for a decadent, fudgy cake with warm chocolate filling strikes, you need a way to satisfy it—and fast. Our solution? The microwave. For our take on a molten chocolate mug cake, we supplement bittersweet chocolate with cocoa powder; the cocoa powder provides a flavor boost, and because it has less fat it produces less steam so the batter won't overflow the mug. Microwaving the cakes gently at 50 percent power keeps the crumb light and tender, and stirring the batter halfway through ensures even cooking. We create the requisite gooey, molten center by simply dropping a couple of pieces of bittersweet chocolate into each cake. We developed this recipe in a full-size, 1200-watt microwave. If you're using a compact microwave with 800 watts or fewer, increase the cooking time to 90 seconds for each interval. For either size microwave, reset to 50 percent power at each stage of cooking. Use mugs that hold at least 12 ounces, or the batter will overflow. Be careful when handling the mugs after microwaving, as they will get hot. This recipe can be easily doubled: microwave the cakes in two batches.

4 tablespoons unsalted butter

1 ounce bittersweet or semisweet chocolate, chopped, plus 1 ounce broken into 4 equal pieces

¼ cup (1¾ ounces) sugar

2 large eggs

2 tablespoons unsweetened cocoa powder

1 teaspoon vanilla extract

¼ teaspoon table salt

¼ cup (1¼ ounces) all-purpose flour

½ teaspoon baking powder

1   Microwave butter and chopped chocolate in large bowl at 50 percent power, stirring often, until melted, about 1 minute. Whisk sugar, eggs, cocoa, vanilla, and salt into chocolate mixture until smooth. In separate bowl, combine flour and baking powder. Whisk flour mixture into chocolate mixture until combined. Divide batter evenly between two 12-ounce coffee mugs.

2   Place mugs on opposite sides of microwave turntable. Microwave at 50 percent power for 45 seconds. Stir batter and microwave at 50 percent power for 45 seconds (batter will rise to just below rim of mug).

3   Press 2 chocolate pieces into center of each cake until chocolate is flush with top of cake. Microwave at 50 percent power for 30 seconds to 1 minute (chocolate pieces should be melted and cake should be slightly wet around edges of mug and somewhat drier toward center). Let cakes sit for 2 minutes before serving.

PANTRY IMPROV

use what you have You can use chocolate chips instead of bars. If you don't have vanilla extract, substitute Grand Marnier or bourbon.

level up Add instant espresso powder, malted milk powder, cinnamon, ancho chile powder, or grated orange zest with the dry ingredients; top with your favorite ice cream or whipped cream (see page 352) or fresh berries or cherries.

tahini–banana snack cake

SERVES 8 | TOTAL TIME: 1¼ HOURS, PLUS 2¼ HOURS COOLING

1½ cups (7½ ounces) all-purpose flour

½ teaspoon table salt

½ teaspoon baking soda

4 tablespoons unsalted butter, softened

⅓ cup tahini

1¼ cups (8¾ ounces) sugar

2 large eggs

1 cup mashed ripe bananas (2 to 3 bananas)

¾ teaspoon vanilla extract

¼ cup milk

2 teaspoons sesame seeds

PANTRY IMPROV

use what you have You can substitute peanut butter or sesame paste for the tahini.

level up Serve with yogurt or whipped cream blended with a little honey.

---

why this recipe works This tender, fluffy banana snack cake demonstrates that cooking with pantry ingredients isn't just about making do; it can elevate a familiar recipe with a new flavor profile. To start, we cream tahini with softened butter and sugar, which incorporates air into the batter. Adding the tahini at this time (and using a moderate amount of butter to accommodate the tahini's fat content) ensures that it's fully incorporated so the cake isn't greasy. A cup of mashed ripe bananas is just the right amount for a moist cake with unmistakable banana flavor. Before baking the cake, we give the batter a final sprinkling of sesame seeds—a playful addition that hints at the tahini inside. This cake is simple enough to make whenever the need to snack strikes, no special occasion required. Be sure to use ripe, speckled bananas in this recipe, or your cake will be bland. (You can store ripe bananas in your freezer.) It is important to let the cake cool completely before serving.

1   Adjust oven rack to middle position and heat oven to 350 degrees. Grease 8-inch square baking pan, line with parchment paper, grease parchment, and flour pan. Whisk flour, salt, and baking soda together in bowl.

2   Using stand mixer fitted with paddle, beat butter, tahini, and sugar on medium-high speed until light and fluffy, about 3 minutes, scraping down bowl as needed. Add eggs, one at a time, and beat until combined. Add bananas and vanilla and beat until incorporated. Reduce speed to low and add flour mixture in 3 additions, alternating with milk in 2 additions, scraping down bowl as needed. Give batter final stir by hand.

3   Transfer batter to prepared pan and smooth top with rubber spatula. Sprinkle top with sesame seeds. Bake until deep golden brown and toothpick inserted in center comes out clean, 40 to 50 minutes, rotating pan halfway through baking.

4   Let cake cool in pan on wire rack for 10 minutes. Remove cake from pan, discarding parchment, and let cool completely on rack, about 2 hours. Serve. (Cake can be stored at room temperature for up to 2 days.)

emergency **chocolate cake**

SERVES 8 | TOTAL TIME: 1¼ HOURS, PLUS 1 TO 2 HOURS COOLING

2 cups (10 ounces) all-purpose flour

1¼ cups (8¾ ounces) sugar

¾ teaspoon baking soda

¾ cup (2¼ ounces) Dutch-processed cocoa powder

1¼ cups water

1 cup mayonnaise

1 tablespoon vanilla extract

why this recipe works Perhaps the original from-the-pantry dessert, this cake was invented at a time when butter and eggs could be scarce, and it replaces those two cake-recipe cornerstones with a cup of mayonnaise. It's not as odd as it sounds since mayonnaise contains both oil and eggs, plus an emulsifier called lecithin, which makes for a soft, tender texture. You don't need to wait for an emergency to make this incredibly easy, moist cake. It can be served straight from the pan as a quick after-school snack.

1 Adjust oven rack to middle position and heat oven to 350 degrees. Grease 8-inch square baking pan.

2 Whisk flour, sugar, and baking soda together in large bowl. In separate bowl, whisk cocoa and water together until smooth. Whisk in mayonnaise and vanilla. Stir mayonnaise mixture into flour mixture until combined.

3 Transfer batter to prepared pan and smooth top with rubber spatula. Bake until toothpick inserted in center comes out with few crumbs attached, about 1 hour, rotating pan halfway through baking.

4 Let cake cool in pan on wire rack, 1 to 2 hours. Serve. (Cake can be stored at room temperature for up to 3 days.)

PANTRY IMPROV

use what you have If you don't have vanilla extract, substitute Grand Marnier or bourbon.

level up Use cool brewed coffee instead of water. Serve with a dusting of confectioners' sugar.

olive oil cake

SERVES 8 | TOTAL TIME: 1¼ HOURS, PLUS 1¾ HOURS COOLING

why this recipe works Like our Emergency Chocolate Cake (page 372), this recipe shows that running out of butter doesn't mean forgoing a moist, tender cake for dessert. In fact, olive oil brings its own appealing qualities to this cake, producing a light, fine-textured plush crumb and a subtle but noticeable olive oil flavor. Whipping the sugar with whole eggs, rather than just the whites, produces a foam that is airy but sturdy enough to support the olive oil. To emphasize the defining flavor, we supplement the fruitiness of the oil with a tiny bit of lemon zest. A crackly sugar topping adds a touch of sweetness and sophistication. For the best flavor, use a fresh, high-quality extra-virgin olive oil. If your springform pan is prone to leaking, place a rimmed baking sheet on the oven floor to catch any drips.

1   Adjust oven rack to middle position and heat oven to 350 degrees. Grease 9-inch springform pan. Whisk flour, baking powder, and salt together in bowl.

2   Using stand mixer fitted with whisk attachment, whip eggs on medium speed until foamy, about 1 minute. Add 1¼ cups sugar and lemon zest, increase speed to high, and whip until mixture is fluffy and pale yellow, about 3 minutes. Reduce speed to medium and, with mixer running, slowly pour in oil. Mix until oil is fully incorporated, about 1 minute. Add half of flour mixture and mix on low speed until incorporated, about 1 minute, scraping down bowl as needed. Add milk and mix until combined, about 30 seconds. Add remaining flour mixture and mix until just incorporated, about 1 minute, scraping down bowl as needed.

3   Transfer batter to prepared pan and sprinkle remaining 2 tablespoons sugar over entire surface. Bake until cake is deep golden brown and toothpick inserted in center comes out with few crumbs attached, 40 to 45 minutes. Transfer pan to wire rack and let cool for 15 minutes. Remove side of pan and let cake cool completely, about 1½ hours. Cut into wedges and serve. (Cake can be wrapped in plastic wrap and stored at room temperature for up to 3 days.)

1¾   cups (8¾ ounces) all-purpose flour

1   teaspoon baking powder

¾   teaspoon table salt

3   large eggs

1¼   cups (8¾ ounces) plus 2 tablespoons sugar, divided

¼   teaspoon grated lemon zest

¾   cup extra-virgin olive oil

¾   cup milk

PANTRY IMPROV

use what you have Substitute lime or orange zest for the lemon zest.

level up Serve with fresh fruit and a dollop of whipped cream. Or spoon Blueberry Compote (page 353) over each serving.

---

rice pudding

SERVES 4 | TOTAL TIME: 1¼ HOURS

8 cups milk or unsweetened plant–based milk, plus extra as needed

6 tablespoons (2⅔ ounces) sugar

½ teaspoon table salt

¼ teaspoon ground cinnamon

½ cup medium–grain white rice

1 teaspoon vanilla extract

why this recipe works When it comes to simple-yet-sublime desserts, it doesn't get much better than rice pudding. Tasting of little more than sweet milk and good vanilla, this pudding relies on a short list of ingredients you're likely to have on hand. The ratio of liquid to rice is key: We combine 8 cups of milk with ½ cup of medium-grain white rice for a perfectly creamy, thick—but not stodgy—consistency. Although this pudding has a longish cook time, it is mostly hands-off and low maintenance. The basic recipe makes an excellent canvas for add-ins and spices, and using plant-based milk makes this a vegan dessert.

Combine milk, sugar, salt, and cinnamon in Dutch oven and bring to boil over medium-high heat. Stir in rice and reduce heat to low. Cook, adjusting heat to maintain gentle simmer and stirring regularly to prevent scorching, until rice is soft and pudding has thickened to consistency of yogurt, 1 hour to 1 hour 15 minutes. Stir in vanilla and adjust consistency with extra milk as needed. Serve warm or chilled. (Rice pudding can be refrigerated for up to 2 days.)

PANTRY IMPROV

use what you have We prefer the consistency of pudding made with medium-grain rice, but you can substitute long-grain rice. Any plant-based milk or dairy milk can be used here. Cardamom, nutmeg, or saffron can be used in place of the cinnamon.

level up Drizzle with maple syrup, sprinkle with fresh or dried fruit and/or toasted nuts, or dollop with whipped cream.

DIY pantry staples

spice blends

peppery coriander and dill spice rub

makes about ⅓ cup | total time: 5 minutes

We developed this blend and the variations that follow as steak rubs, but they're also good on pork chops and chicken, too. They use spices that can stand up to high heat so you can sear without fear.

- 2 tablespoons black peppercorns
- 2 tablespoons coriander seeds
- 1 tablespoon dill seed
- 1½ teaspoons red pepper flakes
- 2½ teaspoons table salt

Grind all ingredients in spice grinder until finely ground. (Rub can be stored at room temperature for up to 1 year.)

VARIATIONS

cocoa–cumin–allspice rub

makes about ⅓ cup | total time: 5 minutes

- 1 tablespoon unsweetened cocoa powder
- 4 teaspoons ground cumin
- 4 teaspoons black peppercorns
- 2 teaspoons ground allspice
- 2 teaspoons table salt

Grind all ingredients in spice grinder until finely ground. (Rub can be stored at room temperature for up to 1 year.)

star anise and coffee bean spice rub

makes about ⅓ cup | total time: 5 minutes

- 6 pods star anise
- 2 tablespoons whole coffee beans
- 1 tablespoon black peppercorns
- 2 teaspoons table salt
- 1 teaspoon sugar

Grind all ingredients in spice grinder until finely ground. (Rub can be stored at room temperature for up to 1 month.)

herbes de provence

makes about ½ cup | total time: 5 minutes

This delicate, aromatic blend of dried herbs from southern France is a good match for chicken, fish, or pork.

- 2 tablespoons dried thyme
- 2 tablespoons dried marjoram
- 2 tablespoons dried rosemary
- 2 teaspoons fennel seeds

Combine all ingredients in bowl. (Spice blend can be stored at room temperature for up to 1 year.)

adobo

makes about ¼ cup | total time: 5 minutes

Adobo seasoning is a popular Latin American and Caribbean spice blend that is used to marinate a range of proteins and pairs wonderfully with vegetables, stews, and beans. It's also delicious sprinkled on popcorn.

- 4 teaspoons onion powder
- 2 teaspoons turmeric
- 2 teaspoons ground oregano
- 2 teaspoons garlic powder
- 1 teaspoon pepper
- 1 teaspoon cumin
- ½ teaspoon table salt
- ½ teaspoon paprika

Combine all ingredients in bowl. (Spice blend can be stored at room temperature for up to 1 year.)

spice blends

ras el hanout

makes about ½ cup | total time: 15 minutes

This North African warm blend delivers complex flavor. Rub
it on meat or vegetables before roasting, use it in soups, or
make Spiced Nuts (page 52). If you can't find Aleppo pepper,
use ½ teaspoon paprika plus ½ teaspoon red pepper flakes.

- 16 cardamom pods
- 4 teaspoons coriander seeds
- 4 teaspoons cumin seeds
- 2 teaspoons anise seeds
- 2 teaspoons ground dried Aleppo pepper
- ½ teaspoon allspice berries
- ¼ teaspoon black peppercorns
- 4 teaspoons ground ginger
- 2 teaspoons ground nutmeg
- 2 teaspoons ground cinnamon

Process cardamom pods, coriander seeds, cumin seeds,
anise seeds, Aleppo pepper, allspice, and peppercorns in
spice grinder until finely ground, about 30 seconds. Stir in
ginger, nutmeg, and cinnamon. (Spice blend can be stored
at room temperature for up to 1 year.)

garam masala

makes about ½ cup | total time: 10 minutes

The warm, floral, and earthy flavor profile of garam masala
("warm spice blend" in Hindi) makes it a welcome addition
to many braises and a great seasoning for meat.

- 3 tablespoons black peppercorns
- 8 teaspoons coriander seeds
- 4 teaspoons cardamom pods
- 2½ teaspoons cumin seeds
- 1½ (3-inch) cinnamon sticks, broken into pieces

Process all ingredients in spice grinder until finely ground,
about 30 seconds. (Spice blend can be stored at room
temperature for up to 1 year.)

baharat

makes ½ cup | total time: 10 minutes

Also called seven spice blend, baharat (Arabic for "spice")
is used across North Africa and the Middle East. Its intense
flavor profile befits meats, legumes, and hearty vegetables.

- 3 (3-inch) cinnamon sticks, broken into pieces
- 4¾ teaspoons cumin seeds
- 1½ tablespoons coriander seeds
- 1 teaspoon black peppercorns
- 2 teaspoons whole cloves
- 1 teaspoon ground cardamom
- 2 teaspoons ground nutmeg

Process cinnamon sticks in spice grinder until finely ground,
about 30 seconds. Add cumin seeds, coriander seeds,
peppercorns, and cloves and process until finely ground,
about 30 seconds. Transfer to bowl and stir in cardamom
and nutmeg. (Spice blend can be stored at room temperature
for up to 1 year.)

barbecue spice blend

makes about ½ cup | total time: 5 minutes

Barbecue can mean a lot of different things, but this
spicy-sweet all-purpose rub is immediately recognizable
as "barbecue."

- 3 tablespoons chili powder
- 3 tablespoons packed brown sugar
- 2 teaspoons pepper
- ¾ teaspoon cayenne pepper

Combine all ingredients in bowl. (Spice blend can be stored
at room temperature for up to 1 year.)

jerk seasoning

makes about ½ cup | **total time: 10 minutes**

Fiery yet fruity Caribbean-style jerk rub is possible with
pantry staples and a little brown sugar.

- 5 teaspoons allspice berries
- 5 teaspoons black peppercorns
- 2 teaspoons dried thyme
- 3 tablespoons packed brown sugar
- 1 tablespoon garlic powder
- 2 teaspoons dry mustard
- 1 teaspoon cayenne pepper

Process allspice, peppercorns, and thyme in spice grinder
until coarsely ground, about 30 seconds; transfer to small
bowl. Stir in sugar, garlic powder, mustard, and cayenne.
(Seasoning can be stored at room temperature for up to
1 year.)

za'atar

makes about ⅓ cup | **total time: 10 minutes**

This eastern Mediterranean blend of herbs, spices, and
seeds is both a seasoning for cooked dishes and a raw
condiment. Sprinkle it on almost anything that could use
a bright, lemony punch.

- 2 tablespoons dried thyme
- 1 tablespoon dried oregano
- 1½ tablespoons sumac
- 1 tablespoon sesame seeds, toasted
- ¼ teaspoon table salt

Grind thyme and oregano using spice grinder until finely
ground and powdery. Transfer to bowl and stir in sumac,
sesame seeds, and salt. (Spice blend can be stored at room
temperature for up to 1 month.)

everything bagel seasoning

makes 5 teaspoons | **total time: 5 minutes**

- 1 teaspoon sesame seeds
- 1 teaspoon poppy seeds
- 1 teaspoon dried minced garlic
- 1 teaspoon dried onion flakes
- 1 teaspoon kosher salt

Combine all ingredients in bowl. (Seasoning can be stored
at room temperature for up to 3 months.)

shichimi togarashi

makes about ½ cup | **total time: 10 minutes**

This Japanese seven-spice mixture blends spices with
chile heat, toasted sesame seeds, and fragrant orange zest,
which we microwave to dry. Its complexity adds intrigue
anywhere you use it, from plain rice to noodles, soups, eggs,
tofu, and beyond.

- 1½ teaspoons grated orange zest
- 4 teaspoons sesame seeds, toasted
- 1 tablespoon paprika
- 2 teaspoons pepper
- ½ teaspoon garlic powder
- ½ teaspoon ground ginger
- ¼ teaspoon cayenne pepper

Microwave orange zest in small bowl, stirring occasionally,
until dry and no longer clumping together, about 2 minutes.
Stir in sesame seeds, paprika, pepper, garlic powder, ginger,
and cayenne. (Spice blend can be stored at room temperature
for up to 1 week.)

roasted and caramelized **alliums**

roasted garlic

makes 1–6 heads | **total time: 2 hours**

Roasting transforms sharp, pungent garlic into balanced, sweet garlic that's at once mellow and intense. We lop off the top third of up to six heads of garlic to expose the flesh, wrap the heads in foil (to allow the heads to steam), and roast them at 350 degrees for about an hour, until the cloves turn buttery soft and deep golden brown. Once the garlic is cool enough to handle, we easily squeeze the browned, nearly translucent paste out of the skins (squeezing from the root end up) and reserve it for use in anything from vinaigrettes to compound butters to garlic bread. Look for larger heads of garlic when shopping. Roasted garlic freezes beautifully.

1–6   garlic heads

Adjust oven rack to middle position and heat oven to 350 degrees. Remove any loose outer papery skin from garlic heads by rubbing with your hands. Cut off and discard top one-third (pointed tip) of heads. Wrap garlic heads in aluminum foil and roast until golden brown and very tender, 1 to 1¼ hours. Remove garlic from oven and carefully open foil. When garlic is cool enough to handle, squeeze cloves from skins; discard skins. (If making ahead, store whole heads of roasted garlic in refrigerator for up to 1 week. Let garlic come to room temperature before squeezing out of skins. To freeze, squeeze cloves from skins and freeze for up to 1 month. A scant ¼ cup of defrosted garlic is equal to 1 head.)

caramelized onions

makes about 2 cups | **total time: 40 minutes**

Steaming in a covered nonstick skillet quickly softens the onions and releases their sugars and proteins, effectively hastening the transition from raw to caramelized. A pinch of baking soda converts flavorless compounds in the onions called inulin into sucrose, which gives the onions a natural sweetness so there is no need for added sugar. We prefer yellow or Spanish onions in this recipe for their flavor but any will work. You will need a 12-inch nonstick skillet with a tight-fitting lid. Use these onions in sandwiches, grain salads, as a topping for steak, or in Pasta with Caramelized Onions, Pecorino Romano, and Black Pepper (page 112).

3   pounds onions, halved and sliced through
    root end ¼ inch thick
¾   cup plus 1 tablespoon water, divided
2   tablespoons vegetable oil
¾   teaspoon table salt
⅛   teaspoon baking soda

1   Bring onions, ¾ cup water, oil, and salt to boil in 12-inch nonstick skillet over high heat. Cover and cook until water has evaporated and onions start to sizzle, about 10 minutes.

2   Uncover, reduce heat to medium-high, and use rubber spatula to gently press onions into sides and bottom of skillet. Cook, without stirring, for 30 seconds. Stir onions, scraping fond from skillet, then gently press onions into sides and bottom of skillet again. Repeat pressing, cooking, and stirring until onions are softened, well browned, and slightly sticky, 15 to 20 minutes.

3   Combine baking soda and remaining 1 tablespoon water in bowl. Stir baking soda solution into onions and cook, stirring constantly, until solution has evaporated, about 1 minute. Transfer onions to bowl. (Onions can be refrigerated for up to 3 days or frozen for up to 1 month.)

crunchy **toppings**

dukkah

makes 2 cups | **total time: 1½ hours**

Dukkah is an Egyptian blend used in the Middle East that contains spices, nuts, and seeds. It's traditionally sprinkled on olive oil as a dip for bread, but its uses are boundless: Try it sprinkled on Hummus (page 41), roasted vegetables, salads, popcorn (see page 48), or stirred into yogurt or olive oil as a dip. For a nut-free version, substitute unsalted sunflower seeds for the pistachios.

- 1 (15-ounce) can chickpeas, rinsed
- 1 teaspoon extra-virgin olive oil
- ½ cup shelled pistachios or unsalted sunflower seeds
- ⅓ cup sesame seeds
- 2½ tablespoons coriander seeds
- 1 tablespoon cumin seeds
- 2 teaspoons fennel seeds
- 1½ teaspoons pepper
- 1¼ teaspoons table salt

1 Adjust oven rack to middle position and heat oven to 400 degrees. Pat chickpeas dry with paper towels and transfer to rimmed baking sheet. Drizzle oil over chickpeas, toss to coat, and spread in even layer. Roast until browned and crisp, 40 to 45 minutes, stirring every 5 to 10 minutes. Transfer to wire rack and let cool completely.

2 Meanwhile, toast pistachios in 8-inch skillet over medium heat, stirring frequently, until lightly browned and fragrant, 3 to 5 minutes; transfer to small bowl and let cool completely. Add sesame seeds to now-empty skillet and toast, stirring frequently, until fragrant, about 1 minute; transfer to separate small bowl and let cool. Add coriander seeds, cumin seeds, fennel seeds, and pepper to now-empty skillet and toast, stirring frequently, until fragrant, about 30 seconds; transfer to food processor.

3 Process spices in food processor until finely ground, 2 to 3 minutes; transfer to medium bowl. Process chickpeas in now-empty processor until coarsely ground, about 10 seconds; add to bowl with spices. Pulse pistachios in now-empty processor until coarsely ground, about 15 pulses; add to bowl with spices. Pulse sesame seeds and salt in food processor until coarsely ground, about 5 pulses; add to bowl with spices.

4 Toss dukkah until well combined. (Spice blend can be stored at room temperature for up to 3 months.)

spiced seeds

makes ½ cup | **total time: 10 minutes**

Salty, crunchy, spicy seeds are an easy topping that elevates a salad, soup, or grain bowl in a snap.

- 2 teaspoons extra-virgin olive oil or vegetable oil
- ½ cup pepitas or sunflower seeds
- ½ teaspoon paprika
- ½ teaspoon coriander
- ¼ teaspoon table salt

Heat oil in 12-inch skillet over medium heat until shimmering. Add pepitas, paprika, coriander, and salt. Cook, stirring constantly, until pepitas are toasted, about 2 minutes; transfer to bowl and let cool. (Seeds can be stored at room temperature for up to 5 days.)

crunchy **toppings**

crispy capers

makes ¼ cup | total time: 10 minutes

These are a home-run topping; they impart pops of crispy vegetal brininess that make anything taste better. Sprinkle them on dips and pureed soups, use them as a garnish for seared fish fillets or chicken breasts, or stir them into pasta dishes such as Spaghetti al Tonno (page 122).

- ¼ cup capers, rinsed
- ½ cup extra–virgin olive oil for frying

Microwave capers and oil in medium bowl (capers should be mostly submerged) until capers are darkened in color and have shrunk, about 5 minutes, stirring halfway through. Using slotted spoon, transfer capers to paper towel–lined plate (they will continue to crisp as they cool). Use immediately.

crispy shallots

makes ½ cup | total time: 20 minutes

The microwave makes frying shallots (and garlic) a breeze; use them to top fried rice, fill sandwiches, and garnish soups.

- 3 shallots, sliced thin
- ½ cup vegetable oil for frying

1   Combine shallots and oil in medium bowl. Microwave for 5 minutes. Stir and continue to microwave for 2 minutes. Repeat stirring and microwaving in 2-minute increments until beginning to brown (4 to 6 minutes).

2   Repeat stirring and microwaving in 30-second increments until deep golden brown (30 seconds to 2 minutes). Using slotted spoon, transfer shallots to paper towel–lined plate; season with salt to taste. Let drain and crisp for about 5 minutes. (Shallots can be stored at room temperature for up to 1 month; shallot oil can be stored in refrigerator for up to 1 month.)

VARIATION
crispy garlic

Substitute ½ cup sliced or minced garlic cloves for shallots. After frying, sprinkle garlic with 1 teaspoon confectioners' sugar (to offset any bitterness) before seasoning with salt. Use immediately. (Garlic oil can be stored in refrigerator for up to 3 days.)

pita chips

serves 8 | total time: 50 minutes

Both white and whole-wheat pita breads will work well here. We prefer the larger crystal size of sea salt or kosher salt here; if using table salt, reduce the amount of salt by half.

- 4 (8–inch) pita breads
- ½ cup extra–virgin olive oil
- 1 teaspoon sea salt or kosher salt

1   Adjust oven racks to upper-middle and lower-middle positions and heat oven to 350 degrees. Using kitchen shears, cut around perimeter of each pita and separate into 2 thin rounds.

2   Working with 1 round at a time, brush rough side generously with oil and sprinkle with salt. Stack rounds on top of one another, rough sides up, as you go. Using chef's knife, cut pita stack into 8 wedges. Spread wedges, rough sides up and in single layer, on 2 rimmed baking sheets.

3   Bake until wedges are golden brown and crisp, about 15 minutes, switching and rotating sheets halfway through baking. Let cool before serving. (Pita chips can be stored at room temperature for up to 3 days.)

classic croutons

makes about 3 cups | **total time: 50 minutes**

Either fresh or stale bread can be used in this recipe, although stale bread is easier to cut and crisps more quickly in the oven.

- 6 slices bread, crusts removed, cut into ½-inch pieces (about 3 cups)
- 3 tablespoons unsalted butter, melted, or extra-virgin olive oil

Adjust oven rack to middle position and heat oven to 350 degrees. Toss bread with melted butter in bowl, season with salt and pepper to taste, and spread onto rimmed baking sheet. Bake until golden brown and crisp, 20 to 25 minutes, stirring halfway through baking. Let cool before serving. (Croutons can be stored at room temperature for up to 3 days.)

VARIATIONS

garlic croutons

Whisk 1 minced garlic clove into melted butter before tossing with bread.

herbed croutons

Whisk 1 teaspoon minced fresh parsley and ½ teaspoon minced fresh thyme into melted butter before tossing with bread.

umami croutons

Opt for extra-virgin olive oil instead of butter, and increase amount to ¼ cup. Whisk oil with 3 tablespoons nutritional yeast, 1 teaspoon white or brown miso, 1 teaspoon Dijon mustard, ¼ teaspoon distilled white vinegar, and ⅛ teaspoon table salt before tossing with bread. Reduce baking time to 13 to 15 minutes.

tortilla strips

makes 2 cups | **total time: 30 minutes**

For crunchy strips that add texture to salads and soups (including Tortilla Soup, page 70) we turn to oven frying.

- 8 (6-inch) corn tortillas, cut into ½-inch-wide strips
- 1 tablespoon vegetable oil

Adjust oven rack to middle position and heat oven to 425 degrees. Toss tortilla strips with oil; spread on rimmed baking sheet; and bake, stirring frequently, until deep golden brown and crispy, 8 to 12 minutes. Transfer to paper towel–lined plate and season with salt to taste. (Tortilla strips can be stored at room temperature for up to 1 week.)

parmesan crisps

makes 3 crisps | **total time: 15 minutes**

Cheese usually lends a soft or creamy element to a dish, but when you turn it into frico, it brings the crunch. Try other aged hard cheeses here as well, such as Asiago or Manchego.

- ½ ounce Parmesan or Pecorino Romano cheese, shredded (3 tablespoons)

Mound Parmesan in 3 piles on large plate (1 tablespoon per mound), then spread each pile into 2½-inch-wide circle. Microwave until golden brown, about 2 minutes. Using thin metal spatula, carefully transfer wafers to wire rack and let cool, about 10 minutes. Once cool to touch, crumble into bite-size pieces. (If wafers aren't crisp after 2 minutes of cooling, blot dry with paper towels, then return wafers to microwave in 15-second bursts until crisp.) Use immediately.

flavored **oils**

rosemary oil

makes 1 cup
total time: 5 minutes, plus 4 hours resting
You can strain the finished oil through a fine-mesh strainer just before serving, if desired.

- 1 cup extra-virgin olive oil
- 2 tablespoons dried rosemary

Heat oil and rosemary in small saucepan over medium-low heat until fragrant and starting to bubble, 2 to 3 minutes. Off heat, let sit until flavors meld, about 4 hours. (Oil can be refrigerated for up to 1 month.)

VARIATIONS

chipotle-coriander oil

Substitute vegetable oil for olive oil. Substitute 3 tablespoons cracked coriander seeds and 1 teaspoon chipotle chile powder for rosemary.

fennel-orange oil

Substitute 3 tablespoons cracked fennel seeds and 2 (2-inch) strips orange zest for rosemary.

sichuan chili oil

makes about 1½ cups
total time: 40 minutes, plus 12 hours resting
Sichuan chili powder is milder and more finely ground than red pepper flakes, but ground dried Aleppo pepper or gochugaru (Korean red pepper flakes) are good alternatives. Drizzle on noodles, soups, steamed vegetables, eggs, or rice.

- ½ cup Sichuan chili powder
- 2 tablespoons sesame seeds
- 2 tablespoons Sichuan peppercorns, crushed, divided
- ½ teaspoon table salt
- 1 cup vegetable oil
- 1 (1-inch) piece ginger, sliced into ¼-inch-thick rounds and smashed
- 2 bay leaves
- 3 star anise pods
- 5 green cardamom pods, crushed

Place chili powder, sesame seeds, half of peppercorns, and salt in heatproof bowl. Heat oil, ginger, bay leaves, star anise, cardamom, and remaining peppercorns in small saucepan over low heat. Cook, stirring occasionally, until spices have darkened and mixture is very fragrant, 25 to 30 minutes. Strain oil mixture through fine-mesh strainer into bowl with chili powder mixture (mixture may bubble slightly); discard solids in strainer. Stir well to combine. Let cool completely, transfer mixture to airtight container, and let sit for at least 12 hours before using. (Oil can be stored at room temperature for up to 1 week or refrigerated for up to 3 months.)

chili pastes

chili crisp

makes about 1½ cups
total time: 1 hour, plus 12 hours resting

Chili crisp, aka Lao Gan Ma, or "Godmother Sauce," is a spicy Chinese condiment that is used as a dipping sauce for dumplings or as a sauce for noodles, rice, or stir-fried greens. For even cooking, slice the shallots to a consistent thickness. Sichuan chili powder is milder and more finely ground than red pepper flakes, but ground dried Aleppo pepper or gochugaru (Korean red pepper flakes) are good alternatives. You'll find monosodium glutamate in the spice aisle under the brand name Accent.

- ½ cup Sichuan chili powder
- ½ cup salted dry-roasted peanuts, chopped
- 2 tablespoons Sichuan peppercorns, crushed
- 1½ teaspoons kosher salt
- ¼ teaspoon monosodium glutamate (optional)
- 1 cup vegetable oil
- 2 large shallots, sliced thin
- 4 large garlic cloves, sliced thin
- 1 (1-inch) piece ginger, unpeeled, sliced into ¼-inch-thick rounds and smashed
- 3 star anise pods
- 10 green cardamom pods, crushed
- 2 cinnamon sticks
- 2 tablespoons toasted sesame oil

1 Combine chili powder; peanuts; peppercorns; salt; and monosodium glutamate, if using, in heatproof bowl and set fine-mesh strainer over bowl. Cook vegetable oil and shallots in medium saucepan over medium-high heat, stirring frequently, until shallots are deep golden brown, 10 to 14 minutes. Using slotted spoon, transfer shallots to second bowl. Add garlic to vegetable oil and cook, stirring constantly, until golden brown, 2 to 3 minutes. Using slotted spoon, transfer garlic to bowl with shallots.

2 Add ginger, star anise, cardamom, and cinnamon sticks to vegetable oil; reduce heat to medium; and cook, stirring occasionally, until ginger is dried out and mixture is very fragrant, 15 to 20 minutes. Strain ginger mixture through fine-mesh strainer into bowl with chili powder mixture (mixture may bubble slightly); discard solids in strainer. Stir well to combine. Once cool, stir shallots, garlic, and sesame oil into ginger–chili powder mixture. Transfer to airtight container and let stand for at least 12 hours before using. (Chili crisp can be refrigerated for up to 3 months.)

harissa

makes about 1 cup | **total time: 15 minutes**

Harissa is a Tunisian condiment that is great for flavoring soups, sauces, and dressings or dolloping on lamb, hummus, eggs, and sandwiches. If you can't find Aleppo pepper, you can substitute 1½ teaspoons paprika and 1½ teaspoons finely chopped red pepper flakes.

- ¾ cup extra-virgin olive oil
- 12 garlic cloves, minced
- ¼ cup paprika
- 2 tablespoons ground coriander
- 2 tablespoons ground dried Aleppo pepper
- 2 teaspoons ground cumin
- 1½ teaspoons caraway seeds
- 1 teaspoon table salt

Combine all ingredients in bowl and microwave until bubbling and very fragrant, about 1 minute, stirring halfway through microwaving. Let cool completely before serving. (Harissa can be refrigerated for up to 4 days. Bring to room temperature before serving.)

dressings

make-ahead vinaigrette

makes about 1 cup | total time: 15 minutes

This vinaigrette can be stored in your fridge without separating thanks to two emulsifiers, mustard and mayonnaise, as well as some molasses, which acts as a stabilizer. After a few days, a very thin layer of vinegar will settle to the bottom of the jar but is easily reincorporated with a quick shake before serving.

- 1 tablespoon regular or light mayonnaise
- 1 tablespoon molasses
- 1 tablespoon Dijon mustard
- ½ teaspoon table salt
- ¼ cup white wine vinegar
- ½ cup extra-virgin olive oil, divided
- ¼ cup vegetable oil

1 Combine mayonnaise, molasses, mustard, and salt in 2-cup jar with tight-fitting lid. Stir with fork until mixture is milky in appearance and no lumps of mayonnaise or molasses remain. Add vinegar; seal jar; and shake until smooth, about 10 seconds.

2 Add ¼ cup olive oil; seal jar; and shake vigorously until combined, about 10 seconds. Repeat with remaining ¼ cup olive oil and vegetable oil in separate additions, shaking vigorously until combined after each addition. Vinaigrette should be glossy and lightly thickened after all oil has been added, with no pools of oil on surface. Season with salt and pepper to taste. (Vinaigrette can be refrigerated for up to 1 week; shake to recombine before using.)

VARIATIONS

make-ahead sherry-shallot vinaigrette

Add 2 teaspoons minced shallot and 2 teaspoons minced fresh thyme to jar with mayonnaise. Substitute sherry vinegar for white wine vinegar.

make-ahead balsamic-fennel vinaigrette

Toast the fennel seeds in a skillet and crack them in a mortar and pestle or on the counter using the bottom of a heavy skillet. Press firmly to crack them.

Add 2 teaspoons toasted and cracked fennel seeds to jar with mayonnaise. Substitute balsamic vinegar for white wine vinegar.

make-ahead cider-caraway vinaigrette

Toast the caraway seeds in a skillet and crack them in a mortar and pestle or on the counter using the bottom of a heavy skillet. Press firmly to crack them.

Add 2 teaspoons toasted and cracked caraway seeds to jar with mayonnaise. Substitute cider vinegar for white wine vinegar.

tahini-lemon dressing

makes ½ cup | total time: 10 minutes

We balance the rich sesame flavor of tahini with lemon juice and garlic in a dressing that's great with greens, grains, chicken, or fish.

- 2½ tablespoons lemon juice
- 2 tablespoons tahini
- 1 tablespoon water
- 1 garlic clove, minced
- ½ teaspoon table salt
- ⅛ teaspoon pepper
- ¼ cup extra-virgin olive oil

Whisk lemon juice, tahini, water, garlic, salt, and pepper together in bowl. Whisking constantly, slowly drizzle in oil until emulsified. (Dressing can be refrigerated for up to 4 days; whisk to recombine before using.)

sauces

all-purpose herb sauce

makes about ¾ cup
total time: 10 minutes, plus 1 hour resting
Don't let fresh herbs go to waste! Use them up here.

- 2 cups fresh parsley, basil, cilantro, tarragon, chives, and/or dill leaves
- 1 slice bread, lightly toasted and cut into ½-inch pieces (about ¾ cup)
- 1 small garlic clove, minced
- ⅛ teaspoon table salt
- 2 tablespoons lemon juice
- ½ cup extra-virgin olive oil

1 Pulse parsley, bread, garlic, and salt in food processor until finely chopped, about 5 pulses. Add lemon juice and pulse briefly to combine.

2 Transfer mixture to medium bowl and slowly whisk in oil until incorporated. Cover and let sit at room temperature for at least 1 hour to allow flavors to meld. Season with salt and pepper to taste. (Sauce can be refrigerated for up to 2 days. Bring to room temperature and whisk to recombine before serving.)

VARIATIONS

smoked paprika sauce

Choose combination of parsley and basil. Add ½ teaspoon smoked paprika to processor with remaining ingredients.

chile-coriander sauce

Choose combination of parsley and cilantro. Add 2 stemmed and seeded jalapeños or 4 stemmed and seeded Thai chiles. Add ½ teaspoon each coriander and cumin to processor with remaining ingredients.

mint, anchovy, and caper sauce

Choose combination of parsley and mint. Add 2 tablespoons capers and 2 anchovy fillets to processor with remaining ingredients.

yogurt sauce

makes about 1 cup
total time: 5 minutes, plus 30 minutes resting
Refreshing and light, yogurt-based sauces can bring a dish to life with just a few simple pantry ingredients. Do not substitute low-fat or nonfat yogurt here.

- 1 cup plain whole-milk yogurt
- 1 teaspoon grated lemon zest plus 2 tablespoons juice
- 1 garlic clove, minced

Whisk all ingredients together in bowl and season with salt and pepper to taste. Cover and refrigerate for at least 30 minutes to allow flavors to meld. (Sauce can be refrigerated for up to 4 days.)

VARIATIONS

cucumber-herb yogurt sauce

Omit lemon juice and zest. Toss 1 (12-ounce) cucumber, peeled, halved lengthwise, seeded, and shredded with ½ teaspoon table salt in colander and let drain for 15 minutes. Stir into yogurt along with 2 tablespoons minced fresh mint and/or dill.

curry-cilantro yogurt sauce

Heat 1 tablespoon vegetable oil in 8- or 10-inch skillet over medium-high heat until shimmering. Add 1 minced shallot and cook until softened, about 2 minutes. Stir in 2 teaspoons curry powder and ¼ teaspoon red pepper flakes; cook until fragrant, about 1 minute. Substitute lime zest and juice for lemon, and curry mixture for garlic. Stir in 2 tablespoons minced fresh cilantro.

sauces

avocado–lime yogurt sauce

makes about 1/2 cup | **total time: 10 minutes**

Drizzle into tacos or on grain bowls, or use as a spread for sandwiches.

- 1/2 avocado, pitted and chopped
- 1/4 cup chopped fresh cilantro
- 3 tablespoons water
- 1 tablespoon lime juice
- 1 tablespoon plain yogurt

Process all ingredients in food processor until completely smooth, about 1 minute, scraping down sides of bowl as needed. Season with salt and pepper to taste. (Sauce can be refrigerated with plastic wrap pressed flush to surface for up to 2 days.)

crème fraîche

makes 1 cup

total time: 5 minutes, plus 12 hours resting

Tangy and rich, crème fraîche makes a perfect addition to your refrigerator staples, and if you have extra heavy cream on hand and a bit of buttermilk (which can be frozen), this is a great way to use them up. Don't use ultrapasteurized or UHT cream for this recipe—organic pasteurized cream works best. The ideal temperature for the crème fraîche to culture is 75 degrees. It will work at lower temperatures but may take up to 36 hours.

- 1 cup pasteurized heavy cream, room temperature
- 2 tablespoons buttermilk, room temperature

Combine cream and buttermilk in 1-pint jar. Cover jar with triple layer of cheesecloth and secure with a rubber band. Let sit in warm place (about 75 degrees) until thickened but still pourable, 12 to 24 hours. Stir to recombine before serving. (Crème fraîche can be refrigerated for up to 1 month.)

easy garlic mayonnaise

makes about 1¼ cups | **total time: 15 minutes**

Homemade mayonnaise is amazingly easy to make and tastes worlds better than store-bought.

- 2 large egg yolks
- 2 teaspoons Dijon mustard
- 2 teaspoons lemon juice
- 1 garlic clove, minced
- 3/4 cup vegetable oil
- 1 tablespoon water
- 1/4 cup extra–virgin olive oil
- 1/2 teaspoon table salt
- 1/4 teaspoon pepper

Process yolks, mustard, lemon juice, and garlic in food processor until combined, about 10 seconds. With machine running, slowly drizzle in vegetable oil, about 1 minute. Transfer to bowl and whisk in water. Whisking constantly, slowly drizzle in olive oil, about 30 seconds. Whisk in salt and pepper. (Mayo can be refrigerated in for up to 4 days.)

pub burger sauce

makes about 1 cup | **total time: 10 minutes**

Simple pantry staples create a fantastic burger sauce.

- 3/4 cup mayonnaise
- 2 tablespoons soy sauce
- 1 tablespoon packed dark brown sugar
- 1 tablespoon Worcestershire sauce
- 1 tablespoon minced fresh chives (optional)
- 1 garlic clove, minced
- 3/4 teaspoon pepper

Whisk all ingredients together in bowl. (Sauce can be refrigerated for up to 4 days; bring to room temperature before serving.)

tartar sauce

makes about 1 cup | total time: 20 minutes

- ¾ cup mayonnaise
- 3 tablespoons minced cornichons plus 1 tablespoon brine
- 1 scallion, minced
- 1 small shallot, minced
- 1 tablespoon capers, rinsed and minced
- ½ teaspoon pepper

Combine all ingredients in small bowl. Cover with plastic wrap and refrigerate for about 15 minutes. (Sauce can be refrigerated for up to 4 days.)

infinite sauce

makes ½ cup sauce | total time: 15 minutes

The name speaks to the number of ways you'll want to use this combo of soy sauce, browned butter, and lemon: On grilled steak, roasted vegetables, pasta, and more . . .

- 8 tablespoons unsalted butter
- 1 tablespoon soy sauce
- 1 teaspoon lemon juice

Melt butter in 10-inch skillet over medium-high heat. Reduce heat to low and continue to cook, swirling skillet constantly, until butter is dark golden brown and has nutty aroma, 6 to 8 minutes longer. Off heat, stir in soy sauce. Transfer sauce to heatproof bowl, making sure to scrape out butter solids with rubber spatula. Stir in lemon juice. (Sauce can be stored at room temperature for up to 5 days or refrigerated for up to 2 weeks.)

peanut–sesame sauce

makes ⅔ cup | total time: 10 minutes

This versatile sauce is great on meat, tofu, grains, or greens.

- 3 tablespoons chunky peanut butter
- 3 tablespoons toasted sesame seeds
- 2 tablespoons soy sauce
- 1½ tablespoons rice vinegar
- 1½ tablespoons packed light brown sugar
- 1½ teaspoons grated fresh ginger
- 1 garlic clove, minced
- ¾ teaspoon hot sauce

Process all ingredients in blender until smooth and mixture has consistency of heavy cream, about 1 minute (adjust consistency with warm water, 1 tablespoon at a time, as needed). Season with salt and pepper to taste. (Sauce can be refrigerated for up to 3 days; add warm water as needed to loosen before using.)

brown sugar–balsamic glaze

makes about ½ cup | total time: 35 minutes

This sophisticated glaze works well on scallops, salmon, pork, and carrots, but also tastes great drizzled on fresh strawberries or ice cream.

- ⅔ cup packed dark brown sugar
- ½ cup balsamic vinegar
- ¼ teaspoon table salt

Bring all ingredients to simmer in small saucepan over medium heat and cook until thickened and reduced to about ½ cup, 3 to 5 minutes. Let cool to room temperature. (Glaze can be refrigerated for up to 1 week; gently warm in microwave before using.)

bottom-of-the-jar
sauces and dressings

When you reach the bottom of the jar of one of your beloved condiments, don't throw it away! Often the dregs of the container can be mixed with other items in your pantry to make a new and interesting sauce, vinaigrette, or glaze to drizzle on food.

AN ALMOST-EMPTY JAR OF

honey	+ soy sauce	= *soy honey*
	+ Sichuan Chili Oil (page 390)	= *spicy honey*
	+ melted butter	= *honey butter*
	+ hoisin	= *honey-hoisin glaze*
	+ Thai chili paste	= *honey-chili paste*
jam *(microwave jam to melt first)*	+ whole-grain/Dijon mustard, vinegar, and oil	= *fruit vinaigrette*
	+ fresh fruit	= *glazed fruit topping*
	+ melted butter	= *fruity butter spread*
	+ water, minced garlic, minced ginger, and soy sauce	= *fruity soy-ginger glaze*
	+ chopped fresh herbs and water	= *sweet and herby glaze*
mayonnaise	+ Thai curry paste	= *thai curry mayonnaise*
	+ lime/lemon juice and zest	= *citrus mayonnaise*
	+ horseradish and Worcestershire	= *steakhouse mayonnaise*
	+ chipotle chile in adobo	= *chipotle mayonnaise*
	+ curry powder or Ras el Hanout (page 382)	= *spiced mayonnaise*
sun-dried tomatoes	+ vinegar, mustard, and minced shallot	= *sun-dried tomato vinaigrette*
	+ mayonnaise	= *sun-dried tomato mayonnaise*
miso	+ mirin, oil, and minced ginger	= *miso dressing*
	+ mayo, maple syrup, toasted sesame oil, and vinegar	= *miso-maple vinaigrette*
	+ melted or softened butter	= *miso butter*
hoisin	+ unseasoned rice vinegar, minced ginger, and chopped scallions	= *hoisin vinaigrette*
peanut butter	+ oats and water (1:1 ratio); let sit overnight	= *overnight peanut butter oats*
	+ unseasoned rice vinegar, hot water, and curry paste	= *peanut sauce*
	+ chocolate syrup and hot milk	= *peanutty hot chocolate*
red curry paste	+ coconut milk and lime juice	= *red curry sauce*
mustard	+ vinegar, honey, oil, and herbs	= *classic vinaigrette*
tahini	+ water, lemon, minced garlic, and Za'atar (page 383)/Aleppo pepper/chili flakes	= *tahini sauce*
	+ soy sauce and vinegar	= *tahini-soy dressing*
gochujang	+ soy sauce, rice vinegar, minced ginger, minced garlic, and toasted sesame oil	= *gochujang sauce*

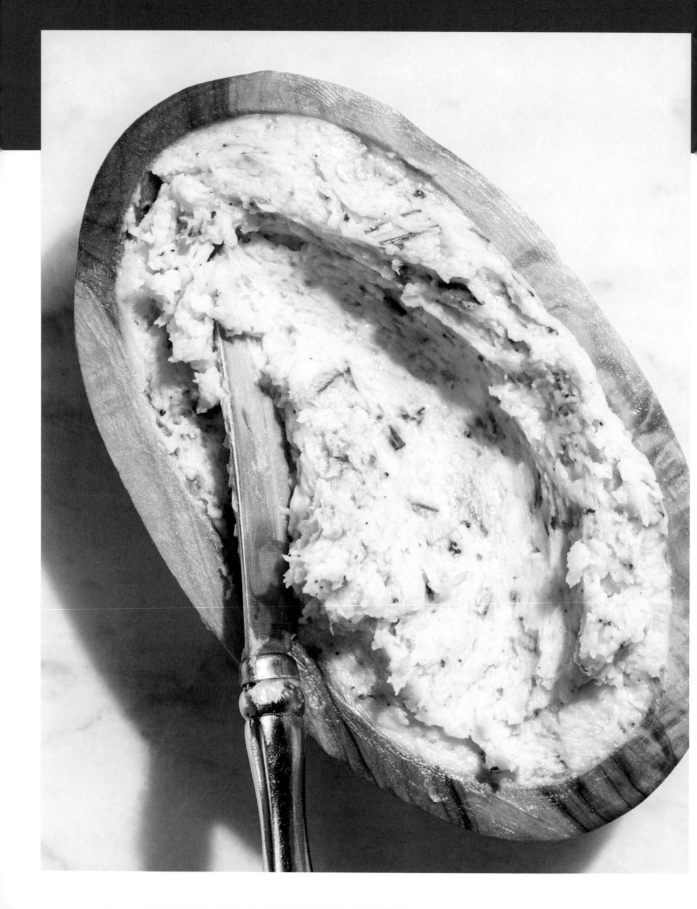

butter

compound butter

makes about ½ cup | **total time: 20 minutes**

Whip 8 tablespoons softened unsalted butter in bowl with fork until light and fluffy. Mix in any of the following ingredient combinations and season with salt and pepper to taste. Cover with plastic wrap and let rest so flavors meld, about 10 minutes, or roll into log and refrigerate. (Butter can be refrigerated for up to 4 days or frozen, wrapped tightly in plastic wrap, for up to 2 months.)

FLAVOR COMBINATIONS

chipotle–cilantro compound butter

- 2 teaspoons minced canned chipotle chile in adobo sauce, plus 2 teaspoons adobo sauce
- 4 teaspoons minced fresh cilantro
- 2 garlic cloves, minced
- 2 teaspoons honey
- 2 teaspoons grated lime zest

chive–lemon miso compound butter

- ¼ cup white miso
- 2 teaspoons grated lemon zest plus 4 teaspoons juice
- ¼ teaspoon pepper
- ¼ cup minced fresh chives

parsley–caper compound butter

- ¼ cup minced fresh parsley
- 4 teaspoons capers, rinsed and minced

parsley–lemon compound butter

- ¼ cup minced fresh parsley
- 4 teaspoons grated lemon zest

tarragon–lime compound butter

- ¼ cup minced scallion
- 2 tablespoons minced fresh tarragon
- 4 teaspoons lime juice

roasted garlic–rosemary compound butter

- 1 head Roasted Garlic (page 384), squeezed to extrude garlic
- 1 tablespoon chopped fresh rosemary
- ¼ teaspoon table salt
- ¼ teaspoon pepper

ghee

makes about 1½ cups | **total time: 3½ hours**

Indispensable in Indian cooking, ghee is made by slowly simmering butter until all of its moisture has evaporated and its milk solids begin to brown. These solids are then strained out, and the remaining pure butter fat has a nutty flavor and aroma and an ultrahigh smoke point that make it suitable for high-heat applications such as frying and making popcorn. This recipe can easily be doubled.

- 1 pound unsalted butter

1 Adjust oven rack to middle position and heat oven to 250 degrees. Place butter in Dutch oven and bake uncovered until all water evaporates and solids are golden brown, 2½ to 3½ hours.

2 Line fine-mesh strainer with triple layer of cheesecloth that overhangs edges; set over large bowl. Let ghee cool slightly, then transfer to prepared strainer and let sit until all ghee is extracted; discard solids. (Cooled ghee can be stored at room temperature for up to 3 months or refrigerated for up to 1 year.)

quick **pickles**

quick bread and butter pickles

makes 1 quart

total time: 35 minutes, plus 3 hours chilling

Pickles are a pantry cook's secret weapon for perking up the flavor of all kinds of dishes. These quick pickles are so easy to make that once you try making them, it's hard to stop. The basic method is to warm up a mixture of vinegar, water, salt, sugar, and seasonings and pour the hot liquid over sliced vegetables. Once cooled, cover the jars and refrigerate until the pickles are chilled. Quick pickles don't keep nearly as long as traditional pickles (they last for about a week) but are ready to eat as soon as they've cooled. Be sure to use seasoned rice vinegar.

- 1 pound pickling cucumbers, sliced crosswise ¼ inch thick
- 5 sprigs fresh dill
- 1¼ cups seasoned rice vinegar
- ¼ cup water
- 2 garlic cloves, peeled and halved
- ½ teaspoon turmeric
- ¼ teaspoon black peppercorns
- ¼ teaspoon yellow mustard seeds

Place cucumbers and dill in 1-quart glass jar with tight-fitting lid. Combine vinegar, water, garlic, turmeric, peppercorns, and mustard seeds in small saucepan and bring to boil. Pour brine into jar, making sure all vegetables are submerged. Let cool completely. Affix jar lid and refrigerate for at least 3 hours before serving. (Pickles can be refrigerated for up to 1 week.)

VARIATIONS

quick carrot pickles

Substitute 1 pound carrots, peeled and cut into 4 by ½-inch sticks, for cucumbers and 5 sprigs fresh tarragon for dill. Omit turmeric.

quick fennel pickles

Substitute 1 fennel bulb, stalks discarded, bulb halved, cored, and cut crosswise into ¼-inch-thick slices, for cucumbers. Omit dill and turmeric. Add two 1-inch strips orange zest and ½ teaspoon fennel seeds to saucepan with vinegar.

quick giardiniera

Substitute 6 ounces cauliflower, cut into 1-inch florets; 1 celery rib, sliced ¼ inch thick; and 1 carrot, sliced ¼ inch thick, for cucumbers. Omit dill and turmeric. Add ½ teaspoon red pepper flakes to saucepan with vinegar.

quick sweet and spicy pickled red onions

Substitute 1 halved and thinly sliced red onion and 2 jalapeños, sliced crosswise into ¼-inch-thick rings, for cucumbers. Omit dill and turmeric. Add two 1-inch strips lime zest and 5 allspice berries to saucepan with vinegar.

HOMEMADE SEASONED RICE VINEGAR

makes ½ cup | total time: 10 minutes

Commercial seasoned rice vinegar contains added salt and sugar. You can also make your own. Table salt dissolves most readily here, but if all you have is kosher salt, increase the amount to 2 tablespoons. This recipe can be doubled or tripled.

- ½ cup unseasoned rice vinegar
- ¼ cup sugar
- 1 tablespoon table salt

Combine ingredients in bowl and let sit for 5 minutes. Whisk constantly until sugar and salt dissolve, about 3 minutes. (Vinegar can be stored at room temperature for up to 1 week.)

pantry **stocks and broth**

chicken stock

makes 8 cups | total time: 5½ hours

4	pounds chicken backs, wings, or parts
3½	quarts water
1	onion, chopped
2	bay leaves
2	teaspoons table salt

1 Bring chicken and water to boil in large stockpot or Dutch oven over medium-high heat, skimming off any scum that rises to surface. Reduce heat to low and simmer gently for 3 hours.

2 Add onion, bay leaves, and salt and continue to simmer for 2 hours. Strain broth through fine-mesh strainer into large pot or container, pressing on solids to extract as much liquid as possible. Let broth settle for about 5 minutes, then skim off fat. (Cooled stock can be refrigerated for up to 4 days or frozen for up to 1 month.)

quick shrimp stock

makes about 1½ cups | total time: 25 minutes
Freeze your shrimp shells to make a quick stock to flavor risotto, gumbo, rice, grits, or soups. Adjust the quantity of water to accommodate fewer or more shrimp shells. The water should cover the majority of the shells in the skillet.

1	tablespoon vegetable oil
1½	cups shrimp shells
1	tablespoon tomato paste
2	cups water

Heat oil in 12-inch skillet over medium-high heat until shimmering. Add shrimp shells and cook until spotty brown, 5 to 7 minutes. Stir in tomato paste and cook for 30 seconds. Add water and bring to boil. Cover, reduce heat to low, and simmer for 5 minutes. Strain stock, pressing on solids to extract as much liquid as possible; discard shells. (Cooled stock can be refrigerated for up to 1 week or frozen for up to 2 months.)

vegetable broth base

makes about 1¾ cups base; enough for 7 quarts broth
total time: 20 minutes
Remove a tablespoon at a time to reconstitute. The coarseness of the kosher salt aids in grinding the vegetables.

2	leeks, white and light green parts only, chopped and washed thoroughly (2½ cups or 5 ounces)
½	small celery root, peeled and cut into ½-inch pieces (¾ cup or 3 ounces)
2	carrots, peeled and cut into ½-inch pieces (⅔ cup or 3 ounces)
½	cup (½ ounce) fresh parsley leaves and thin stems
3	tablespoons dried minced onion
2	tablespoons kosher salt
1½	tablespoons tomato paste
3	tablespoons soy sauce

1 Process leeks, celery root, carrots, parsley, dried onion, and salt in food processor, scraping down sides of bowl frequently, until paste is as fine as possible, 3 to 4 minutes. Add tomato paste and process for 1 minute, scraping down sides of bowl every 20 seconds. Add soy sauce and continue to process for 1 minute.

2 Transfer mixture to airtight container and tap firmly on counter to remove air bubbles. Press small piece of parchment paper flush against surface of mixture and cover. Freeze for up to 6 months.

3 To make 1 cup broth: Stir 1 tablespoon fresh or frozen broth base into 1 cup boiling water. If particle-free broth is desired, let broth steep for 5 minutes, then strain through fine-mesh strainer.

nutritional information for our recipes

To calculate the nutritional values of our recipes per serving, we used The Food Processor SQL by ESHA research. When using this program, we entered all the ingredients, using weights wherever possible. We also used our preferred brands in these analyses. Any ingredient listed as "optional" was excluded from the analyses. If there is a range in the serving size, we used the highest number of servings to calculate nutritional values. We did not include additional salt or pepper for food that's seasoned to taste.

	CALORIES	TOTAL FAT (G)	SAT FAT (G)	CHOL (MG)	SODIUM (MG)	TOTAL CARB (G)	DIETARY FIBER (G)	TOTAL SUGARS (G)	PROTEIN (G)
anytime snacks									
one-minute tomato salsa	15	0	0	0	300	4	0	2	1
one-minute smoky tomato and green pepper salsa	20	0	0	0	310	5	0	2	1
one-minute tomato, pinto bean, and red pepper salsa	25	0	0	0	320	6	1	2	1
one-minute tomato and avocado salsa	45	2.5	0	0	300	6	1	2	1
spicy carrot dip	80	4.5	0.5	0	190	9	3	4	1
garlic and rosemary white bean dip	170	11	1.5	0	220	14	4	1	5
provençal-style anchovy dip	170	14	1.5	10	420	5	1	2	6
hummus	150	11	1.5	0	300	10	3	0	5
spicy whipped feta	230	21	10	50	520	3	0	2	8
spinach and artichoke dip	300	27	10	50	560	5	1	2	10
vegan nacho dip	90	5	0	0	310	9	1	1	2
parmesan-pepper popcorn	70	5	1.5	5	80	5	1	0	2
buttermilk ranch popcorn	70	4.5	1	5	45	5	1	0	1
chocolate popcorn	70	4.5	1.5	5	40	5	1	1	1
sriracha-lime popcorn	70	4.5	1	5	50	5	1	0	1
maple-pecan skillet granola	320	18	1.5	0	150	37	5	14	5
bbq party mix	230	9	4	15	330	32	0	5	3
spiced roasted chickpeas	190	10	1.5	0	440	20	7	0	7
spiced nuts	230	20	2	0	150	12	3	9	3
devils on horseback	190	13	5	25	280	12	1	11	5
deviled eggs	50	4	1	95	75	0	0	0	3
blue cheese deviled eggs	60	5	1.5	95	110	0	0	0	4
dill pickle deviled eggs	50	4	1	95	80	0	0	0	3
herbed deviled eggs	50	4	1	95	80	0	0	0	3
spanish-style deviled eggs	70	5	1.5	95	130	1	0	0	4
anything in a blanket	240	16	7	20	660	15	1	4	8

	CALORIES	TOTAL FAT (G)	SAT FAT (G)	CHOL (MG)	SODIUM (MG)	TOTAL CARB (G)	DIETARY FIBER (G)	TOTAL SUGARS (G)	PROTEIN (G)
anytime snacks *(cont.)*									
quesadillas	230	12	6	25	560	20	0	1	10
gochujang and cheddar pinwheels	160	10	5	5	160	13	0	1	5
kimchi jeon	340	21	1.5	0	1330	30	1	14	7
soups, stews & chilis									
empty-your-pantry vegetable soup	330	7	1	0	1400	60	8	7	6
spring vegetable soup with pesto	350	14	2	0	1540	50	9	8	7
vegetable soup with eggplant and harissa	360	8	1	0	1510	63	15	13	7
vegetable soup with mushrooms, paprika, and dill	400	8	1	0	1310	73	14	6	9
hearty cabbage soup	100	4	2.5	10	660	14	2	3	2
winter squash and white bean soup	180	6	3.5	15	910	29	7	5	6
tortilla soup	250	9	1.5	45	620	16	2	3	23
quick beef and vegetable soup	370	18	7	75	1760	25	5	6	27
miso soup with wakame and tofu	60	2.5	0	5	770	7	2	1	9
miso soup with white fish and carrots	110	2	0	30	810	9	3	3	17
miso soup with squash and spinach	60	1	0	5	770	10	3	2	7
miso soup with udon and mushrooms	200	2	0	5	870	35	2	2	14
chickpea noodle soup	240	9	1	0	100	31	7	4	10
almost-instant miso ramen	370	13	1.5	0	1860	50	4	4	12
almost-instant miso ramen with soft-cooked egg	400	16	2.5	95	1890	50	4	4	16
almost-instant miso ramen with pork and kimchi	740	41	11	0	1800	58	4	5	33
rich and creamy miso ramen with shiitake mushrooms and bok choy	470	21	3	95	1960	52	5	6	17
creamy leek (or onion) and potato soup	210	9	5	25	780	27	2	6	4
creamless creamy tomato soup	150	7	1	0	600	18	2	9	3
butternut squash soup	160	5	0.5	0	490	29	5	6	3
butternut squash soup with fennel, blue cheese, and pine nuts	150	5	0.5	0	510	25	5	7	3
butternut squash soup with sausage and apple	230	8	2	10	700	34	6	10	9
southwestern butternut squash and lentil soup	230	6	0.5	10	500	39	8	6	9
shrimp bisque	440	28	18	225	310	17	1	6	19
easy canned black bean soup	210	3.5	1	5	1150	39	0	3	12
easy canned chickpea and garlic soup	230	7	1.5	5	950	31	10	1	12
easy canned white bean and sun-dried tomato soup	260	6	2.5	10	1070	36	10	4	17
easy canned lentil and chorizo soup	510	23	8	50	1480	44	17	4	33

	CALORIES	TOTAL FAT (G)	SAT FAT (G)	CHOL (MG)	SODIUM (MG)	TOTAL CARB (G)	DIETARY FIBER (G)	TOTAL SUGARS (G)	PROTEIN (G)
soups, stews & chilis *(cont.)*									
red lentil soup with warm spices	230	6	0.5	0	800	34	8	3	12
italian pasta and bean soup	210	7	1.5	5	950	28	5	5	9
spicy pinto bean soup	260	8	0.5	0	1260	34	7	5	11
lablabi	340	18	2	0	630	55	2	3	15
tomato, bulgur, and red pepper soup	180	7	1	0	1070	21	3	10	4
wild rice soup with coconut and lime	490	34	25	0	840	41	3	6	10
quick bean chili	230	4	0	0	1600	44	3	7	13
quick bean chili with tequila and lime	250	4	0	0	1600	47	3	10	13
smoky bean chili with sweet potatoes	270	4	0	0	1630	54	5	10	13
quick bean chili with ground meat	470	21	7	75	1680	43	3	7	34
butternut squash and peanut chili with quinoa	640	46	21	0	1410	50	9	10	13
pasta & noodles									
pasta with garlic and oil	430	15	2	0	0	63	3	2	11
pasta with shrimp, lemon, and parsley	510	16	2	145	170	65	3	2	26
pasta with capers and raisins	460	15	2	0	230	69	3	7	12
pasta with olives and almonds	540	25	2.5	0	480	68	5	2	13
pasta with caramelized onions, pecorino romano, and black pepper	370	7	3.5	0	440	63	4	2	14
bottom-of-the-box pasta with butter and cheese	550	23	13	60	800	62	3	2	23
pasta alla gricia	590	25	9	55	1270	62	3	2	27
pasta e ceci	540	23	4.5	15	1510	65	9	5	20
spaghetti al tonno	550	17	2.5	30	1180	68	4	4	29
pasta with pesto, potatoes, and green beans	610	27	7	25	300	78	6	7	17
bucatini with peas, kale, and pancetta	460	8	2.5	15	710	71	6	5	21
fideos with chickpeas, fennel, and kale	550	17	2	0	1290	78	15	11	19
skillet tortellini supper	620	40	20	130	1190	44	3	7	23
gnocchi, cauliflower, and gorgonzola gratin	650	45	28	125	1200	50	7	10	18
cheese ravioli with pumpkin cream sauce	600	46	26	130	950	35	1	11	13
pantry pesto (per ⅓ cup)	210	23	3	0	45	2	0	0	2
sun-dried tomato pesto (per ⅓ cup)	220	23	3.5	0	65	3	1	0	2
kale and sunflower seed pesto (per ⅓ cup)	120	12	2	0	50	2	1	0	2
green olive and orange pesto (per ⅓ cup)	120	12	1.5	0	125	2	1	0	2
classic marinara sauce (per ⅓ cup)	90	5	0.5	0	570	10	2	5	2
vodka cream marinara sauce (per ⅓ cup)	170	11	4	15	570	10	2	6	2

pasta & noodles *(cont.)*

	CALORIES	TOTAL FAT (G)	SAT FAT (G)	CHOL (MG)	SODIUM (MG)	TOTAL CARB (G)	DIETARY FIBER (G)	TOTAL SUGARS (G)	PROTEIN (G)
simple (any) meat sauce (per ⅓ cup)	130	7	2.5	25	260	8	2	4	9
chickpea-mushroom bolognese (per ⅓ cup)	120	10	1	0	510	12	3	5	3
puttanesca sauce (per ⅓ cup)	190	11	4	20	1310	17	1	8	5
white clam sauce (per ⅓ cup)	170	13	4.5	35	750	6	0	1	7
garlic cream sauce (per ⅓ cup)	340	29	18	85	320	8	0	5	7
one-pot penne with quick tomato sauce	560	13	1.5	0	810	98	8	11	17
one-pot penne with sausage ragu	710	18	3.5	15	1160	104	9	13	27
one-pot shrimp fra diavolo	720	25	3.5	105	1370	100	8	11	29
one-pot penne with olives, capers, and eggplant	600	14	1.5	0	920	105	11	15	19
fresh pasta without a machine	280	11	3	245	130	35	0	0	10
fresh spinach pasta without a machine	290	11	3	245	160	36	0	0	10
fresh tomato pasta without a machine	300	14	4	370	55	30	0	1	11
fresh lemon–black pepper pasta without a machine	290	11	3	245	130	35	0	0	10
buttered spaetzle	310	9	4.5	155	630	43	0	0	11
sautéed buttery egg noodles with cabbage and fried eggs	420	19	8	265	460	47	2	5	16
pasta salad with salami and sun-dried tomato vinaigrette	810	52	19	100	1760	49	4	1	35
farfalle salad with broccoli and avocado	610	40	5	0	180	56	12	3	13
tortellini salad with grilled eggplant, zucchini, and peppers	540	31	5	5	590	55	7	9	14
orecchiette salad with asparagus and tomatoes	430	22	3	0	240	48	5	5	11
browned butter–soy noodles with pan-seared tofu	500	31	12	80	1060	37	1	28	17
chilled soba noodles with miso dressing	330	9	1	0	380	52	1	8	8
soba noodles with pork, scallions, and shichimi togarashi	530	13	2	110	2200	48	1	8	49
spicy peanut rice noodles	690	32	4.5	0	980	85	2	11	18
gochujang-tahini noodles	470	11	2.5	0	1030	77	1	7	16
singapore noodles	350	15	2	195	820	40	1	2	14
pad thai	480	20	3	185	1110	64	2	13	14
vegetable lo mein	320	17	4	20	1680	35	2	23	6
vegetable lo mein with hot-and-sour sauce	320	17	4	20	1760	36	2	24	6
vegetable lo mein with garlic-basil sauce	320	17	4	20	1680	36	2	23	6
vegetable lo mein with sesame sauce	340	20	4	20	1710	35	2	24	6
biang biang mian	580	35	3	0	1040	54	2	2	10

	CALORIES	TOTAL FAT (G)	SAT FAT (G)	CHOL (MG)	SODIUM (MG)	TOTAL CARB (G)	DIETARY FIBER (G)	TOTAL SUGARS (G)	PROTEIN (G)
grains & beans									
grain salad with dried fruit, cheese, and nuts	660	24	4	5	400	96	17	6	19
barley salad with celery and miso dressing	150	4	0.5	0	350	28	4	4	2
simple fried rice	490	12	2.5	150	840	76	1	2	19
broccoli, bean sprout, and ham fried rice	480	12	2.5	150	840	74	0	1	19
mushroom, chicken, and napa cabbage fried rice	490	12	2.5	170	620	74	0	1	22
three pea fried rice	500	11	2	140	480	85	1	2	17
kimchi bokkeumbap	470	15	1.5	15	1030	69	2	4	14
nasi goreng	570	18	2.5	185	1500	85	2	6	18
congee	120	0	0	0	580	27	0	0	3
stir-fried ground pork	170	13	4.5	40	290	2	0	1	10
no-fuss parmesan polenta	310	15	8	35	1400	31	3	0	16
savory oatmeal with corn, jalapeños, and cotija	320	11	4.5	20	760	43	6	3	12
almost hands-free risotto with parmesan	600	18	9	40	1410	84	4	7	19
almost hands-free risotto with fennel and saffron	610	18	9	40	1440	88	6	9	19
almost hands-free risotto with chicken	730	21	10	125	1460	84	4	7	44
almost hands-free red wine risotto with beans	840	32	14	85	2350	100	8	8	33
mushroom farrotto	380	14	9	40	1100	50	6	1	16
black beans and rice	400	8	1	0	940	71	5	1	12
red beans and rice with andouille	520	15	3.5	35	1470	75	1	4	22
lentils and rice with spiced beef	570	17	4.5	40	860	79	9	3	27
butter beans and rice with tomato salad	480	15	2	0	930	77	8	5	12
lentil salad with oranges, celery, and pecans	360	20	2.5	0	460	38	9	9	11
white bean and tuna salad	290	14	2	15	660	23	7	3	17
palak dal	400	13	7	30	910	49	13	2	23
stovetop white bean casserole	410	19	2.5	0	1260	50	9	10	13
stovetop white bean casserole with zucchini, smoked paprika, and parmesan croutons	450	21	3.5	5	1390	52	9	11	17
stovetop white bean casserole with bacon, spinach, and rosemary	410	16	4.5	20	1470	51	9	10	17
stovetop white bean casserole with chicken thighs and butternut squash	690	39	8	120	1460	52	8	8	33
chana masala	320	15	1	0	1110	36	11	3	12

	CALORIES	TOTAL FAT (G)	SAT FAT (G)	CHOL (MG)	SODIUM (MG)	TOTAL CARB (G)	DIETARY FIBER (G)	TOTAL SUGARS (G)	PROTEIN (G)
grains & beans (cont.)									
sweet potato and bean tacos	550	19	4.5	0	1660	79	7	7	16
sweet potato, bean, and poblano tacos	580	21	5	0	1660	83	9	9	17
sweet potato and bean tacos with mango and cabbage slaw	580	19	4.5	0	1830	87	9	13	17
smoky sweet potato and mushroom tacos	560	19	4.5	0	1660	81	7	9	17
spiced chickpea gyros with tahini yogurt	500	20	7	10	1570	62	8	4	23
chickpea salad sandwiches	550	26	3.5	10	1180	65	7	7	13
black bean burgers	320	12	2	0	700	46	0	4	10
beans and greens	190	9	2	5	700	18	7	3	9
white bean gratin with rosemary and parmesan	260	11	3	10	850	26	7	4	14
vegetables									
carrot and white bean salad with raisins and almonds	420	26	2.5	0	1140	45	8	21	9
caesar vegetables	350	22	4.5	15	660	26	5	6	10
shaved celery salad with pomegranate-honey vinaigrette	270	19	4	10	430	20	3	9	7
succotash salad	350	15	2	0	320	48	9	10	10
succotash salad with bell pepper, avocado, and cilantro	380	23	3	0	520	42	10	9	8
succotash salad with bacon, cherry tomatoes, and arugula	430	30	9	25	870	33	6	11	13
succotash salad with zucchini, dill, and feta	450	22	6	25	590	48	8	11	14
esquites	240	13	4	20	590	26	1	3	7
charred cabbage salad with torn tofu and plantain chips	430	31	4.5	0	1210	30	4	16	13
stir-fried cabbage with shallot and fish sauce	100	4.5	0.5	0	390	13	4	8	2
skillet-charred green beans with crispy sesame topping	180	14	1.5	0	450	10	4	3	4
bubble and squeak	410	23	14	60	370	46	10	7	9
anytime hash	280	11	1.5	0	490	44	6	9	5
sweet potato and ham hash with kale salad	400	20	3.5	25	1280	39	5	7	16
potato, kimchi, and radish hash with fried eggs	320	19	3.5	185	710	27	2	3	10
beet and potato hash with smoked salmon	330	12	2	5	960	42	5	9	10
skillet-roasted carrots with spicy maple bread crumbs	170	10	0.5	0	480	20	4	9	0
vegetable tagine with chickpeas and olives	460	21	2	0	1820	62	13	16	11

	CALORIES	TOTAL FAT (G)	SAT FAT (G)	CHOL (MG)	SODIUM (MG)	TOTAL CARB (G)	DIETARY FIBER (G)	TOTAL SUGARS (G)	PROTEIN (G)
vegetables (cont.)									
vindaloo-style sweet potatoes	300	8	0.5	0	950	50	6	9	6
bagna cauda potatoes	480	29	4	10	680	43	0	0	10
hasselback potato casserole	410	18	8	40	740	45	4	3	18
twice-baked potatoes with cheddar and scallions	390	19	12	60	580	44	3	3	13
twice-baked stuffed potatoes with ham, peas, and gruyère	450	21	12	75	890	46	4	4	21
twice-baked potatoes with chorizo and chipotle	510	30	15	80	910	43	3	3	19
twice-baked potatoes with smoked salmon and chives	310	12	6	35	580	42	3	2	11
potato and parmesan tart	390	25	13	80	500	31	1	1	9
potato tart with blue cheese and sun-dried tomatoes	410	27	14	85	600	32	1	1	11
potato tart with brie and crispy bacon	440	29	16	95	650	31	1	1	13
potato tart with caramelized onions and goat cheese	410	26	14	85	530	32	1	1	11
savory onion-apple tarte tatin	370	22	8	0	500	49	2	16	5
rustic butternut squash and spinach tart	400	25	9	0	500	48	5	6	6
pantry proteins									
scrambled eggs with pinto beans and cotija cheese	390	23	6	380	740	24	6	1	22
scrambled eggs with asparagus, smoked salmon, and chives	270	21	4.5	375	380	3	1	1	17
scrambled eggs with shiitake mushrooms and feta cheese	280	22	6	380	360	6	2	3	15
scrambled eggs with arugula, sun-dried tomatoes, and goat cheese	290	23	6	375	340	5	1	2	16
spicy chilaquiles with fried eggs	780	47	12	400	1200	67	4	13	26
fried eggs with parmesan and potato roesti	580	30	15	420	1010	52	0	0	22
shakshuka with chickpeas, red peppers, and tomatoes	390	19	4.5	370	1710	36	10	12	22
tofu shakshuka with white beans and zucchini	360	14	3	10	1800	40	10	15	21
garam masala–spiced shakshuka with spinach and yogurt	430	20	4.5	375	1700	38	11	12	25
shakshuka with black beans, chiles, and avocado	500	25	5	370	1710	51	9	13	25
smoked salmon and potato frittata	450	30	11	500	750	16	2	3	24
empty-your-breadbox skillet strata	560	32	13	330	1010	36	1	10	27
easy-peel hard-cooked eggs (per egg)	70	5	1.5	185	70	0	0	0	6
soft-cooked eggs (per egg)	70	5	1.5	185	70	0	0	0	6

	CALORIES	TOTAL FAT (G)	SAT FAT (G)	CHOL (MG)	SODIUM (MG)	TOTAL CARB (G)	DIETARY FIBER (G)	TOTAL SUGARS (G)	PROTEIN (G)
pantry proteins (cont.)									
perfect fried eggs (per egg)	110	9	2	185	70	0	0	0	6
perfect poached eggs (per egg)	70	5	1.5	185	70	0	0	0	6
matzo brei	370	21	11	315	400	30	1	3	13
cheese enchiladas	730	48	21	100	1440	53	3	8	32
tartiflette	650	42	21	105	1510	41	1	3	23
creamy tuna salad	410	31	5	65	660	1	0	1	30
vinaigrette-style tuna salad	420	29	4.5	40	1040	2	1	0	34
crisp breaded chicken cutlets	470	19	3	215	520	26	1	2	46
crisp breaded chicken parmesan cutlets	500	21	4	220	640	26	1	2	49
crisp breaded honey-mustard chicken cutlets	540	19	3	215	880	39	1	14	46
crisp breaded garlicky chicken cutlets	480	19	3	215	520	28	1	2	46
caramelized black pepper chicken	370	11	1.5	125	670	24	1	20	40
lemony chicken meatballs with quinoa and carrots	720	40	6	100	1070	59	9	9	31
chicken and rice with tomatoes, white wine, and parsley	760	16	3	250	1590	62	1	4	83
chicken and rice with saffron, peas, and paprika	800	16	3	250	1590	69	3	6	85
chicken and rice with turmeric, coriander, and cumin	890	28	14	250	1590	67	2	5	84
chicken and rice with anchovies, olives, and lemon	790	18	3.5	255	1890	64	1	4	84
chicken sausage with braised red cabbage and potatoes	780	37	9	110	1790	71	7	26	40
fried onion burger	510	29	13	105	1540	27	1	6	32
cuban-style picadillo	470	29	8	105	690	18	3	12	29
pan-seared shrimp with peanuts, black pepper, and lime	220	10	1.5	215	530	6	1	2	25
pan-seared shrimp with pistachios, cumin, and parsley	140	8	1	105	320	3	1	1	13
pan-seared shrimp with fermented black beans, ginger, and garlic	210	9	1	215	680	5	0	2	25
spanish-style garlic shrimp	360	29	4	145	460	7	0	0	17
shrimp mozambique	340	18	5	230	1130	8	1	2	24
one-pan roasted salmon with white beans and fennel	670	39	15	105	1290	43	15	13	36
easy poached salmon	390	23	5	95	390	2	0	1	35
tilapia meunière	430	26	12	130	380	11	0	0	36
panko-crusted tofu with cabbage salad	410	23	2.5	95	800	37	1	9	16
seared tempeh with tomato jam	300	12	2	5	710	31	2	6	17
vegan mapo tofu	370	28	2	0	1510	17	2	4	13

	CALORIES	TOTAL FAT (G)	SAT FAT (G)	CHOL (MG)	SODIUM (MG)	TOTAL CARB (G)	DIETARY FIBER (G)	TOTAL SUGARS (G)	PROTEIN (G)
breads & baked goods									
savory dutch baby with prosciutto and honey	420	22	5	200	700	36	0	4	18
savory dutch baby with burrata, prosciutto, and arugula	460	27	8	215	660	36	0	3	20
savory dutch baby with smoked salmon and avocado	510	30	5	195	580	40	3	4	19
savory dutch baby with celery and mushroom salad	440	24	5	195	500	38	1	4	16
whole-wheat crepes with smoked salmon, crème fraîche, and pickled shallots	580	36	20	220	1020	41	5	16	24
socca with sautéed onions and rosemary	380	24	3.5	0	900	30	6	7	10
sun-dried tomato, garlic, and za'atar biscuits	300	17	10	45	410	30	1	2	5
ginger biscuits	330	16	10	50	390	40	0	14	5
butternut squash, apple, and gruyère turnovers	420	27	15	60	490	37	1	10	11
broccoli cheese cornbread	390	21	13	125	630	36	3	6	15
quick cheese bread with bacon, onion, and gruyère	430	20	9	70	890	42	0	3	19
whole-wheat soda bread with walnuts and cacao nibs	400	15	3.5	5	670	56	11	5	13
skillet cheese pizza	650	35	12	45	1410	60	0	11	25
skillet pizza with fontina, arugula, and prosciutto	720	41	13	65	2050	62	0	11	30
skillet pizza with goat cheese, olives, and infused oil	670	38	14	45	1290	60	0	10	24
skillet pizza with ricotta, bacon, and scallions	740	40	14	65	1860	60	0	10	36
red pepper flatbreads	600	23	4	0	1700	86	1	20	12
vegetable stromboli	520	21	11	45	1370	59	1	9	27
classic pizza dough (per 4 ounces dough)	340	3.5	0.5	0	440	61	2	0	11
whole-wheat pizza dough (per 4 ounces dough)	280	6	1	0	680	49	5	2	9
braided dinner loaf	240	7	3	40	550	37	0	5	7
easy garlic rolls	170	7	1.5	20	390	22	0	3	4
garlic and herb breadsticks	70	2	1	5	130	10	0	0	2
spicy parmesan breadsticks	90	3.5	2	10	210	10	0	0	4
desserts									
dipping hot chocolate	330	23	15	70	20	33	4	27	4
classic hot fudge sauce (per 2 tablespoons)	130	6	3.5	10	40	19	1	16	1
chocolate ice cream shell (per 2 tablespoons)	230	23	18	0	35	11	1	0	1

	CALORIES	TOTAL FAT (G)	SAT FAT (G)	CHOL (MG)	SODIUM (MG)	TOTAL CARB (G)	DIETARY FIBER (G)	TOTAL SUGARS (G)	PROTEIN (G)
desserts (cont.)									
small-batch whipped cream (per 2 tablespoons)	90	9	6	25	5	2	0	2	1
strawberry-balsamic topping with pepper (per 2 tablespoons)	15	0	0	0	0	4	0	3	0
blueberry compote (per 2 tablespoons)	50	3	2	10	35	7	1	6	0
peanut butter–chocolate quesadillas	530	32	10	20	460	48	2	10	14
cannoli quesadillas	430	24	11	30	340	44	1	1	11
nutella-orange quesadillas	530	29	9	15	330	57	1	21	9
peanut butter–banana quesadillas	530	29	8	15	450	57	3	12	14
skillet-roasted pears with caramel sauce	320	15	9	45	15	48	3	43	1
berry granita	70	0	0	0	20	19	2	17	0
any fruit milkshakes	360	16	10	60	190	54	5	39	7
rustic peach-ginger tart	380	14	6	55	300	64	2	31	5
no-bake apple crisp	300	6	3.5	15	150	62	4	49	2
loaded triple chocolate chunk cookies (per cookie)	340	17	10	45	220	44	1	18	4
loaded cookies-and-cream cookies (per cookie)	310	14	8	45	260	44	0	23	4
loaded peanut butter–bacon cookies (per cookie)	330	14	9	50	350	43	0	28	7
loaded s'mores cookies (per cookie)	290	12	7	45	250	42	1	20	4
chocolate mug cakes	530	33	19	245	470	49	1	25	10
tahini-banana snack cake	390	13	5	60	250	64	2	37	7
emergency chocolate cake	460	21	3	10	220	62	0	31	5
olive oil cake	470	24	4	70	310	58	0	35	6
rice pudding	440	16	9	50	500	58	0	40	17
DIY pantry staples									
peppery coriander and dill spice rub (per 1 tablespoon)	20	0.5	0	0	970	3	2	0	1
cocoa-cumin-allspice rub (per 1 tablespoon)	15	0	0	0	780	2	1	0	1
star anise and coffee bean spice rub (per 1 tablespoon)	20	0.5	0	0	780	4	1	1	1
herbes de provence (per 1 tablespoon)	10	0	0	0	0	2	1	0	0
adobo (per 1 tablespoon)	25	0	0	0	300	5	1	0	1
ras el hanout (per 1 tablespoon)	20	0.5	0	0	220	4	2	2	1
baharat (per 1 tablespoon)	15	1	0	0	0	3	2	0	1
garam masala (per 1 tablespoon)	20	0.5	0	0	0	5	3	0	1
barbecue spice blend (per 1 tablespoon)	30	0.5	0	0	135	7	1	5	1
jerk seasoning (per 1 tablespoon)	40	0.5	0	0	0	8	1	5	1

	CALORIES	TOTAL FAT (G)	SAT FAT (G)	CHOL (MG)	SODIUM (MG)	TOTAL CARB (G)	DIETARY FIBER (G)	TOTAL SUGARS (G)	PROTEIN (G)
DIY pantry staples (cont.)									
za'atar (per 1 tablespoon)	15	1	0	0	100	2	1	0	1
everything bagel seasoning (per 1 tablespoon)	40	3	0	0	560	4	2	0	2
shichimi togarashi (per 1 tablespoon)	15	1	0	0	0	2	1	0	1
roasted garlic (per clove)	5	0	0	0	0	1	0	0	0
caramelized onions (per ¼ cup)	50	2	0	0	120	8	1	4	1
dukkah (per 1 tablespoon)	60	4	0	0	240	5	2	0	3
spiced seeds (per 1 tablespoon)	60	5	1	0	75	1	1	0	2
crispy capers (per 1 tablespoon)	130	14	2	0	200	0	0	0	0
crispy shallots (per 1 tablespoon)	50	5	0	0	0	2	0	1	0
crispy garlic (per 1 tablespoon)	60	5	0	0	0	3	0	0	1
pita chips (per ¼ cup)	80	0	0	0	450	17	0	0	3
classic croutons (per ¼ cup)	60	4	0.5	0	60	5	0	1	1
garlic croutons (per ¼ cup)	60	4	0.5	0	60	5	0	1	1
herbed croutons (per ¼ cup)	70	2	1	5	75	11	0	2	2
umami croutons (per ¼ cup)	50	3	0	0	80	5	0	2	2
tortilla strips (per ¼ cup)	80	3	0	0	10	14	0	2	2
parmesan crisps (each)	20	1.5	0.5	5	85	0	0	0	2
rosemary oil (per 1 tablespoon)	120	14	2	0	0	0	0	0	0
chipotle-coriander oil (per 1 tablespoon)	123	14	4	0	0	0	0	0	0
fennel-orange oil (per 1 tablespoon)	124	14	4	0	0	1	0	0	0
sichuan chili oil (per 1 tablespoon)	100	10	1	0	125	1	1	0	1
chili crisp (per 1 tablespoon)	110	11	1.5	0	150	2	1	0	1
harissa (per 1 tablespoon)	110	11	1.5	0	150	2	1	0	1
make-ahead vinaigrette (per 1 tablespoon)	100	11	1.5	0	100	1	0	1	0
make-ahead sherry-shallot vinaigrette (per 1 tablespoon)	110	11	1.5	0	100	1	0	1	0
make-ahead balsamic-fennel vinaigrette (per 1 tablespoon)	110	11	1.5	0	100	2	0	2	0
make-ahead cider-caraway vinaigrette (per 1 tablespoon)	110	11	1.5	0	100	1	0	1	0
tahini-lemon dressing (per 1 tablespoon)	90	9	1.5	0	150	1	0	0	1
all-purpose herb sauce (per 1 tablespoon)	100	10	1.5	0	40	3	0	0	1
smoked paprika sauce (per 1 tablespoon)	100	10	1.5	0	40	3	0	0	1
chile-coriander sauce (per 1 tablespoon)	100	10	1.5	0	60	3	0	0	0
mint, anchovy, and caper sauce (per 1 tablespoon)	100	10	1.5	0	115	3	0	0	1

	CALORIES	TOTAL FAT (G)	SAT FAT (G)	CHOL (MG)	SODIUM (MG)	TOTAL CARB (G)	DIETARY FIBER (G)	TOTAL SUGARS (G)	PROTEIN (G)
DIY pantry staples (cont.)									
yogurt sauce (per 1 tablespoon)	20	1	0.5	5	15	2	0	2	1
cucumber-herb yogurt sauce (per 1 tablespoon)	25	1	0.5	5	160	2	0	2	1
curry-cilantro yogurt sauce (per 1 tablespoon)	40	3	1	5	20	2	0	2	1
avocado-lime yogurt sauce (per 1 tablespoon)	45	4	0.5	0	0	3	2	0	1
crème fraîche (per 1 tablespoon)	50	5	3.5	15	5	1	0	1	0
easy garlic mayonnaise (per 1 tablespoon)	110	12	1	20	70	0	0	0	0
pub burger sauce (per 1 tablespoon)	80	8	1	5	220	1	9	1	9
tartar sauce (per 1 tablespoon)	70	8	1	5	85	1	0	1	0
infinite sauce (per 1 tablespoon)	100	11	7	30	150	0	0	0	0
peanut-sesame sauce (per 1 tablespoon)	110	7	1.5	0	400	8	1	5	4
brown sugar–balsamic glaze (per 1 tablespoon)	70	0	0	0	75	19	0	18	0
compound butter (per 1 tablespoon)	130	15	9	40	0	0	0	0	0
chipotle-cilantro compound butter (per 1 tablespoon)	130	15	9	40	0	0	0	0	0
chive-lemon miso compound butter (per 1 tablespoon)	130	15	9	40	0	0	0	0	0
parsley-caper compound butter (per 1 tablespoon)	130	15	9	40	0	0	0	0	0
parsley-lemon compound butter (per 1 tablespoon)	130	15	9	40	0	0	0	0	0
tarragon-lime compound butter (per 1 tablespoon)	130	15	9	40	0	0	0	0	0
roasted garlic-rosemary compound butter (per 1 tablespoon)	130	15	9	40	0	0	0	0	0
ghee (per 1 tablespoon)	130	15	9	40	0	0	0	0	0
quick bread and butter pickles (per ¼ cup)	35	0	0	0	530	8	0	7	0
quick carrot pickles (per ¼ cup)	45	0	0	0	540	10	1	8	0
quick fennel pickles (per ¼ cup)	40	0	0	0	540	10	1	7	0
quick giardiniera (per ¼ cup)	35	0	0	0	530	8	0	7	0
quick sweet and spicy pickled red onions (per ¼ cup)	35	0	0	0	540	8	0	7	0
chicken stock (per ¼ cup)	60	4	1	35	170	0	0	0	5
quick shrimp stock (per ¼ cup)	10	0.5	0	10	15	0	0	0	1
vegetable broth base (per ¼ cup broth)	5	0	0	0	90	1	0	0	0

conversions & equivalents

Some say cooking is a science and an art. We would say that geography has a hand in it, too. Flours and sugars manufactured in the United Kingdom and elsewhere will feel and taste different from those manufactured in the United States. So we cannot promise that the loaf of bread you bake in Canada or England will taste the same as a loaf baked in the States, but we can offer guidelines for converting weights and measures. We also recommend that you rely on your instincts when making our recipes. Refer to the visual cues provided. If the dough hasn't "come together in a ball" as described, you may need to add more flour—even if the recipe doesn't tell you to. You be the judge.

The recipes in this book were developed using standard U.S. measures following U.S. government guidelines. The charts below offer equivalents for U.S. and metric measures. All conversions are approximate and have been rounded up or down to the nearest whole number.

example:

1 teaspoon = 4.9292 milliliters, rounded up to 5 milliliters
1 ounce = 28.3495 grams, rounded down to 28 grams

VOLUME CONVERSIONS:

U.S.	metric
1 teaspoon	5 milliliters
2 teaspoons	10 milliliters
1 tablespoon	15 milliliters
2 tablespoons	30 milliliters
¼ cup	59 milliliters
⅓ cup	79 milliliters
½ cup	118 milliliters
¾ cup	177 milliliters
1 cup	237 milliliters
1¼ cups	296 milliliters
1½ cups	355 milliliters
2 cups (1 pint)	473 milliliters
2½ cups	591 milliliters
3 cups	710 milliliters
4 cups (1 quart)	0.946 liter
1.06 quarts	1 liter
4 quarts (1 gallon)	3.8 liters

WEIGHT CONVERSIONS:

ounces	grams
½	14
¾	21
1	28
1½	43
2	57
2½	71
3	85
3½	99
4	113
4½	128
5	142
6	170
7	198
8	227
9	255
10	283
12	340
16 (1 pound)	454

CONVERSIONS FOR COMMON BAKING INGREDIENTS:

Baking is an exacting science. Because measuring by weight is far more accurate than measuring by volume, and thus more likely to produce reliable results, in our recipes we provide ounce measures in addition to cup measures for many ingredients. Refer to the chart below to convert these measures into grams.

ingredient	ounces	grams
flour		
1 cup all-purpose flour*	5	142
1 cup cake flour	4	113
1 cup whole-wheat flour	5½	156
sugar		
1 cup granulated (white) sugar	7	198
1 cup packed brown sugar (light or dark)	7	198
1 cup confectioners' sugar	4	113
cocoa powder		
1 cup cocoa powder	3	85
butter†		
4 tablespoons (½ stick or ¼ cup)	2	57
8 tablespoons (1 stick or ½ cup)	4	113
16 tablespoons (2 sticks or 1 cup)	8	227

* U.S. all-purpose flour, the most frequently used flour in this book, does not contain leaveners, as some European flours do. These leavened flours are called self-rising or self-raising. If you are using self-rising flour, take this into consideration before adding leaveners to a recipe.

† In the United States, butter is sold both salted and unsalted. We generally recommend unsalted butter. If you are using salted butter, take this into consideration before adding salt to a recipe.

OVEN TEMPERATURES:

fahrenheit	celsius	gas mark
225	105	¼
250	120	½
275	135	1
300	150	2
325	165	3
350	180	4
375	190	5
400	200	6
425	220	7
450	230	8
475	245	9

CONVERTING TEMPERATURES FROM AN INSTANT-READ THERMOMETER:

We include doneness temperatures in many of the recipes in this book. We recommend an instant-read thermometer for the job. Refer to the table above to convert Fahrenheit degrees to Celsius. Or, for temperatures not represented in the chart, use this simple formula:

Subtract 32 degrees from the Fahrenheit reading, then divide the result by 1.8 to find the Celsius reading.

example:
"Roast chicken until thighs register 175 degrees."

to convert:
175°F – 32 = 143°
143° ÷ 1.8 = 79.44°C, rounded down to 79°C

index

Note: Page references in *italics* indicate photographs.

C

G

Garam Masala, 382
Garlic
    Bagna Cauda Potatoes, *248,* 249
    -Basil Sauce, Vegetable Lo Mein
        with, 167
    and Chickpea Soup, Easy Canned,
        91, *91*
    Cream Sauce, 141
    Crisp Breaded Garlicky Chicken
        Cutlets, 285
    Crispy, 388
    Croutons, 389
    freezing, 31
    frying in the microwave, 10
    granulated, subbing for fresh, 6
    Harissa, 392, *393*
    and Herb Breadsticks, 345, *345*
    Mayonnaise, Easy, 398
    and Oil, Pasta with, 110–11
    Pasta with Capers and Raisins,
        111, *111*
    Pasta with Olives and Almonds,
        111, *111*
    Pasta with Shrimp, Lemon, and
        Parsley, 111, *111*
    powder, hydrating, 24
    Roasted, 384, *385*
    Roasted, –Rosemary Compound
        Butter, 403
    Rolls, Easy, 345, *345*
    and Rosemary White Bean Dip, 38, *38*
    Shrimp, Spanish-Style, 300–301, *301*
    storing, 29
    substitute for, 26
    Sun-Dried Tomato, and Za'atar
        Biscuits, *324,* 325
Ghee, 403
Giardiniera, Quick, 404, *405*
Ginger
    Biscuits, *326,* 327
    Chili Crisp, 392, *393*
    Fermented Black Beans, and Garlic,
        Pan-Seared Shrimp with, 299, *299*
    fresh, freezing, 6, 31
    fresh, storing, 29
    fresh, substitute for, 26
    -Peach Tart, Rustic, *362,* 363
    Ras el Hanout, *380,* 382
    Sichuan Chili Oil, 390, *391*
Glaze, Brown Sugar–Balsamic, 399

Gnocchi, Cauliflower, and Gorgonzola
    Gratin, *132,* 133
Gochugaru
    gochujang made from, 15
    substitutes for, 26
Gochujang
    about, 15
    bottom-of-the jar, ideas for, 401
    and Cheddar Pinwheels, 59, *59*
    -Tahini Noodles, *160,* 161
    Kimchi Bokkeumbap, 180
Grain(s)
    bowl combinations, 172–73
    cooked, freezing, 30
    cooking directions, 173
    Salad with Dried Fruit, Cheese,
        and Nuts, 174, *175*
    types of, 4–5
    see also specific grains
Granita, Berry, *358,* 359
Granola, Maple-Pecan Skillet, 49, *49*
Green Beans
    Caesar Vegetables, *222,* 223
    Pesto, and Potatoes, Pasta with,
        124, *125*
    Quick Beef and Vegetable Soup,
        72, 73
    Skillet-Charred, with Crispy Sesame
        Topping, 234–35, *235*
    Succotash Salad, 226–27
    Succotash Salad with Bacon, Cherry
        Tomatoes, and Arugula, 227, *227*
Greens
    Beans and, 214, *215*
    see also specific greens
Grits, about, 5
Gyros, Spiced Chickpea, with Tahini
    Yogurt, *208,* 209

H

Half-and-half, substitutes for, 27
Ham
    Broccoli, and Bean Sprout Fried
        Rice, 179
    Peas, and Gruyère, Twice-Baked
        Stuffed Potatoes with, 253, *253*
    and Sweet Potato Hash with Kale
        Salad, 239, *239*

Harissa
    about, 15
    and Eggplant, Vegetable Soup with, 65
    homemade, 392, *393*
    ideas for, 22
    Lablabi, 98, *99*
Hash
    Anytime, 238–39
    Beet and Potato, with Smoked
        Salmon, 239
    Potato, Kimchi, and Radish, with
        Fried Eggs, 239
    Sweet Potato and Ham, with Kale
        Salad, 239, *239*
Hazelnuts
    Cheese Ravioli with Pumpkin Cream
        Sauce, 134, *135*
    Nutella-Orange Quesadillas, 355, *355*
Herb(s)
    dried, cooking with, 15
    fresh, freezing, 31
    fresh, storing, 29
    fresh, substitute for, 26
    and Garlic Breadsticks, 345, *345*
    garnish alternatives, 18
    Herbed Croutons, 389
    Herbed Deviled Eggs, 54
    Herbes de Provence, *380,* 381
    Pantry Pesto, *136,* 137
    Sauce, All-Purpose, 396, *397*
    stems, freezing, 30
    sturdy, drying, 32
    substituting, 18
    see also specific herbs
Hoisin sauce
    about, 13
    bottom-of-the jar, ideas for, 401
    ideas for, 23
Honey
    bottom-of-the jar, ideas for, 401
    -Mustard Chicken Cutlets, Crisp
        Breaded, 285
    storing, 28
    substitutes for, 26
    uses for, 19
Hot Chocolate, Dipping, *348,* 349
Hot Fudge Sauce, Classic, 352, *353*
Hot sauces
    buying, 15
    cholula, uses for, 23
Hummus, *40,* 41
    ideas for, 23
    topping suggestions, 42–43

I

Ice cream
Any Fruit Milkshakes, 360, *361*
pantry toppings for, 350–51
Infinite Sauce, *397*, 399

J

Jam, bottom-of-the jar, ideas for, 401
Jerk Seasoning, 383

K

Kale
Chickpeas, and Fennel, Fideos with, 128–29, *129*
Peas, and Pancetta, Bucatini with, *126*, 127
Salad, Sweet Potato and Ham Hash with, 239, *239*
and Sunflower Seed Pesto, 137
Kecap manis, about, 19
Ketchup, uses for, 19
Kimchi
about, 16
Bokkeumbap, 180–81, *181*
Jeon, 60, *61*
and Pork, Almost-Instant Miso Ramen with, 79, *79*
Potato, and Radish Hash with Fried Eggs, 239
Kombu
about, 13
Dashi, 74

L

Lablabi, 98, *99*
Leaveners, 21
Leek(s), 6
(or Onion) and Potato Soup, Creamy, *80*, 81
storing, 29
substitute for, 26
Lemon(s)
–Black Pepper Pasta, Fresh, without a Machine, 144, *145*
-Chive Miso Compound Butter, 403
flavoring dishes with, 16
-Parsley Compound Butter, 403
substitute for, 26
-Tahini Dressing, 395
Tilapia Meunière, 308, *309*
Lentil(s), 5
and Butternut Squash Soup, Southwestern, 85
and Chorizo Soup, Easy Canned, 91, *91*
Palak Dal, 200–201, *201*
Red, Soup with Warm Spices, *92*, 93
and Rice with Spiced Beef, 195, *195*
Salad with Oranges, Celery, and Pecans, 196–97, *197*
Lime(s)
-Avocado Yogurt Sauce, 398
flavoring dishes with, 16
-Sriracha Popcorn, 48
substitute for, 26
-Tarragon Compound Butter, 403

M

Mango and Cabbage Slaw, Sweet Potato and Bean Tacos with, 207, *207*
Maple (syrup)
Bread Crumbs, Spicy, Skillet-Roasted Carrots with, *242*, 243
-Pecan Skillet Granola, 49, *49*
storing, 28
uses for, 19
Mapo Tofu, Vegan, 314–15, *315*

Marinara Sauce
Classic, 138, *138*
Vodka Cream, 138
Marjoram
Herbes de Provence, *380*, 381
Marshmallows
Loaded S'mores Cookies, 367, *367*
Matzo Brei, *276*, 277
Mayonnaise
bottom-of-the jar, ideas for, 401
Garlic, Easy, 398
ideas for, 18
Pub Burger Sauce, 398
Tartar Sauce, *397*, 399
Meat
(Any), Sauce, Simple, 139, *139*
cured, types of, 8
freezing, 30
frozen, stocking up on, 8
Ground, Quick Bean Chili with, 105, *105*
trimmings, freezing, 30
see also Beef; Pork; Veal
Meatballs, Lemony Chicken, with Quinoa and Carrots, *288*, 289
Milk
Any Fruit Milkshakes, 360, *361*
cow's, substitutes for, 27
whole, substitutes for, 27
Mint
Anchovy, and Caper Sauce, 396
Cucumber-Herb Yogurt Sauce, 396
Mirin
about, 19
substitute for, 26
Miso
about, 13
bottom-of-the jar, ideas for, 401
Chive-Lemon Compound Butter, 403
Dressing, Chilled Soba Noodles with, 154, *155*
Dressing and Celery, Barley Salad with, *176*, 177
Ramen, Almost-Instant, 78–79
Ramen, Almost-Instant, with Pork and Kimchi, 79, *79*
Ramen, Almost-Instant, with Soft-Cooked Egg, 79, *79*
Ramen, Rich and Creamy, with Shiitake Mushrooms and Bok Choy, 79, *79*
Soup with Squash and Spinach, 75, *75*

P

Pad Thai, 164–65, *165*
Palak Dal, 200–201, *201*
Pancakes
    Kimchi Jeon, 60, *61*
    see also Dutch Baby
Pancetta
    Pasta alla Gricia, *118,* 119
    Peas, and Kale, Bucatini with, *126,* 127
Panko, toasting, 24
Pantry cooking
    acidic & pickled foods, 16
    baking items, 20–21
    cooking liquids, 20
    creamy & rich ingredients, 18
    crispy, crunchy, & chewy toppings, 10
    fats, 20
    favorite flavor boosters, 22–23
    flavor-boosting tips, 24–25
    flavorful broths and stocks, 33
    fresh produce, 29
    kitchen substitutions, 26–27
    long-storage vegetable & aromatics, 6
    proteins, 8–9
    savory condiments, seasonings, & sprinkles, 13
    spices, chiles, & hot sauces, 15
    starchy foods, 4–5
    stocking your freezer, 30–31
    storage smarts, 28
    sweet & sweet-tart ingredients, 19
    using food scraps and leftovers, 32
Paprika
    Harissa, 392, *393*
    Shichimi Togarashi, *380,* 383
    Smoked, Sauce, 396
    Spiced Roasted Chickpeas, 51, *51*
    Spiced Seeds, 386, *387*
Parsley
    All-Purpose Herb Sauce, 396, *397*
    -Caper Compound Butter, 403
    Chile-Coriander Sauce, 396
    Green Olive and Orange Pesto, 137
    -Lemon Compound Butter, 403
    Mint, Anchovy, and Caper Sauce, 396
    Smoked Paprika Sauce, 396
Parsnips
    Anytime Hash, 238–39
    Beet and Potato Hash with Smoked Salmon, 239
Party Mix, BBQ, 50, *50*

Pasta
    alla Gricia, *118,* 119
    and Bean Soup, Italian, *94,* 95
    Bottom-of-the-Box, with Butter and Cheese, 114, *115*
    Bucatini with Peas, Kale, and Pancetta, *126,* 127
    Buttered Spaetzle, *146,* 147
    with Capers and Raisins, 111, *111*
    with Caramelized Onions, Pecorino Romano, and Black Pepper, 112, *113*
    Cheese Ravioli with Pumpkin Cream Sauce, 134, *135*
    Chickpea Noodle Soup, 76, *77*
    e Ceci, 120–21, *121*
    Farfalle Salad with Broccoli and Avocado, 151, *151*
    Fresh, without a Machine, 144
    Fresh Lemon–Black Pepper, without a Machine, 144, *145*
    Fresh Spinach, without a Machine, 144, *145*
    Fresh Tomato, without a Machine, 144, *145*
    with Garlic and Oil, 110–11
    Gnocchi, Cauliflower, and Gorgonzola Gratin, *132,* 133
    with Olives and Almonds, 111, *111*
    One-Pot Penne with Olives, Capers, and Eggplant, 143
    One-Pot Penne with Quick Tomato Sauce, 142–43, *143*
    One-Pot Penne with Sausage Ragu, 143
    One-Pot Shrimp Fra Diavolo, 143
    Orecchiette Salad with Asparagus and Tomatoes, 151, *151*
    with Pesto, Potatoes, and Green Beans, 124, *125*
    Salad with Salami and Sun-Dried Tomato Vinaigrette, 150–51, *151*
    sauces for, 137–41
    with Shrimp, Lemon, and Parsley, 111, *111*
    Skillet Tortellini Supper, 130, *131*
    Spaghetti al Tonno, 122–23, *123*
    substituting shapes, 27
    3-ingredient combinations, 116–17
    Tortellini Salad with Grilled Eggplant, Zucchini, and Peppers, 151, *151*
    types of, 4
    see also Noodles
Peach-Ginger Tart, Rustic, *362,* 363

Peanut Butter
    –Bacon Cookies, Loaded, 367, *367*
    –Banana Quesadillas, 355, *355*
    bottom-of-the jar, ideas for, 401
    –Chocolate Quesadillas, 354–55
    Peanut-Sesame Sauce, *397,* 399
    Spicy Peanut Rice Noodles, *158,* 159
    substitutes for, 27
    uses for, 18
Peanut(s)
    Black Pepper, and Lime, Pan-Seared Shrimp with, 298–99, *299*
    and Butternut Squash Chili with Quinoa, 106–7, *107*
    Chili Crisp, 392, *393*
    Pad Thai, 164–65, *165*
Pears
    Skillet-Roasted, with Caramel Sauce, *356,* 357
    storing, 29
Pea(s)
    Almost Hands-Free Risotto with Chicken, 191
    Almost Hands-Free Risotto with Parmesan, 190–91, *191*
    Ham, and Gruyère, Twice-Baked Stuffed Potatoes with, 253, *253*
    Kale, and Pancetta, Bucatini with, *126,* 127
    Saffron, and Paprika, Chicken and Rice with, 291
    Simple Fried Rice, 178–79, *179*
    Skillet Tortellini Supper, 130, *131*
    Three, Fried Rice, 179
Pecan(s)
    Grain Salad with Dried Fruit, Cheese, and Nuts, 174, *175*
    -Maple Skillet Granola, 49, *49*
    Oranges, and Celery, Lentil Salad with, 196–97, *197*
Pepitas
    Spiced Seeds, 386, *387*
Pepper(s)
    Bell, Avocado, and Cilantro, Succotash Salad with, 227, *227*
    Eggplant, and Zucchini, Grilled, Tortellini Salad with, 151, *151*
    fresh red bell, substitute for, 26
    Green, and Tomato Salsa, One-Minute Smoky, 36
    Red, Chickpeas, and Tomatoes, Shakshuka with, 268–69, *269*
    Red, Flatbreads, 338–39, *339*
    Red, Tomato, and Bulgur Soup, *100,* 101

R

Radish(es)
 Pad Thai, 164–65, *165*
 Potato, and Kimchi Hash with
  Fried Eggs, 239
Raisins
 and Almonds, Carrot and White Bean
  Salad with, *220,* 221
 and Capers, Pasta with, 111, *111*
 Cuban-Style Picadillo, 296–97, *297*
 Provençal-Style Anchovy Dip, 39, *39*
 Vegetable Tagine with Chickpeas
  and Olives, *244,* 245
Ras el Hanout, *380,* 382
Rice
 Almost Hands-Free Red Wine Risotto
  with Beans, 191
 Almost Hands-Free Risotto with
  Chicken, 191
 Almost Hands-Free Risotto with
  Fennel and Saffron, 191
 Almost Hands-Free Risotto with
  Parmesan, 190–91, *191*
 Black Beans and, 194–95, *195*
 brown, cooking directions, 173
 and Butter Beans with Tomato Salad,
  195, *195*
 Chicken and, with Anchovies, Olives,
  and Lemon, 291
 Chicken and, with Saffron, Peas, and
  Paprika, 291
 Chicken and, with Tomatoes, White
  Wine, and Parsley, 290–91, *291*
 Chicken and, with Turmeric,
  Coriander, and Cumin, 291
 Congee, *184,* 185
 cooked, freezing, 30
 Fried, Broccoli, Bean Sprout, and
  Ham, 179
 Fried, Mushroom, Chicken, and
  Napa Cabbage, 179
 Fried, Simple, 178–79, *179*
 Fried, Three Pea, 179
 Kimchi Bokkeumbap, 180–81, *181*
 and Lentils with Spiced Beef,
  195, *195*
 Nasi Goreng, 182–83, *183*
 Pudding, 376, *377*
 Red Beans and, with Andouille,
  195, *195*

Rice *(cont.)*
 types of, 4
 wild, cooking directions, 173
 Wild, Soup with Coconut and Lime,
  102, *103*
Risotto, Almost Hands-Free
 with Chicken, 191
 with Fennel and Saffron, 191
 with Parmesan, 190–91, *191*
 Red Wine, with Beans, 191
Rolls, Easy Garlic, 345, *345*
Rosemary
 and Garlic White Bean Dip, 38, *38*
 Herbes de Provence, *380,* 381
 Oil, 390, *391*
 and Parmesan, White Bean Gratin
  with, *216,* 217
 –Roasted Garlic Compound
  Butter, 403
 and Sautéed Onions, Socca with,
  322–23, *323*
Rye berries, cooking directions, 173

S

Saffron
 and Fennel, Almost Hands-Free
  Risotto with, 191
 Peas, and Paprika, Chicken and Rice
  with, 291
Salads
 Barley, with Celery and Miso
  Dressing, *176,* 177
 Carrot and White Bean, with Raisins
  and Almonds, *220,* 221
 Charred Cabbage, with Torn Tofu and
  Plantain Chips, 230–31, *231*
 Esquites, *228,* 229
 Farfalle, with Broccoli and Avocado,
  151, *151*
 Grain, with Dried Fruit, Cheese, and
  Nuts, 174, *175*
 Lentil, with Oranges, Celery, and
  Pecans, 196–97, *197*
 Orecchiette, with Asparagus and
  Tomatoes, 151, *151*
 Pasta, with Salami and Sun-Dried
  Tomato Vinaigrette, 150–51, *151*

Salads *(cont.)*
 Shaved Celery, with Pomegranate-
  Honey Vinaigrette, *224,* 225
 Succotash, 226–27
 Succotash, with Bacon, Cherry
  Tomatoes, and Arugula, 227, *227*
 Succotash, with Bell Pepper,
  Avocado, and Cilantro, 227, *227*
 Succotash, with Zucchini, Dill, and
  Feta, 227, *227*
 Tortellini, with Grilled Eggplant,
  Zucchini, and Peppers, 151, *151*
 Tuna, Creamy, 282, *282*
 Tuna, Vinaigrette-Style, 283, *283*
 White Bean and Tuna, *198,* 199
Salami
 Almost Hands-Free Red Wine Risotto
  with Beans, 191
 and Sun-Dried Tomato Vinaigrette,
  Pasta Salad with, 150–51, *151*
Salmon
 One-Pan Roasted, with White Beans
  and Fennel, 304–5, *305*
 Poached, Easy, *306,* 307
 Smoked, and Avocado, Savory
  Dutch Baby with, 319
 Smoked, and Chives, Twice-Baked
  Potatoes with, 253, *253*
 Smoked, and Potato Frittata, 270, *271*
 Smoked, Asparagus, and Chives,
  Scrambled Eggs with, 263
 Smoked, Beet and Potato Hash
  with, 239
 Smoked, Crème Fraîche, and Pickled
  Shallots, Whole-Wheat Crepes
  with, 320–21, *321*
Salsa, One-Minute
 Smoky Tomato and Green Pepper, 36
 Tomato, 36, *36*
 Tomato, Pinto Bean, and Red
  Pepper, 36
 Tomato and Avocado, 36
Salt
 flake sea, 10
 flavored, ideas for, 25
 seasoning with, 25
 table, substitutes for, 27
Sambal oelek, about, 15
Sandwiches
 Chickpea Salad, *210,* 211
 Spiced Chickpea Gyros with Tahini
  Yogurt, *208,* 209

T

Tacos
Sweet Potato, Bean, and Poblano, 207
Sweet Potato and Bean, 206–7, *207*
Sweet Potato and Bean, with Mango and Cabbage Slaw, 207, *207*
Sweet Potato and Mushroom, Smoky, 207, *207*

Tagine, Vegetable, with Chickpeas and Olives, *244, 245*

Tahini
about, 18
-Banana Snack Cake, 370, *371*
bottom-of-the jar, ideas for, 401
-Gochujang Noodles, *160,* 161
Hummus, *40, 41*
ideas for, 22
-Lemon Dressing, 395
substitutes for, 27
Yogurt, Spiced Chickpea Gyros with, *208,* 209

Tajín, ideas for, 22

Tamarind juice concentrate, substitute for, 26

Tarragon
All-Purpose Herb Sauce, 396, *397*
-Lime Compound Butter, 403

Tartar Sauce, *397,* 399

Tartiflette, 280–81, *281*

Tarts
Butternut Squash and Spinach, Rustic, 258–59, *259*
Peach-Ginger, Rustic, *362,* 363
Potato, with Blue Cheese and Sun-Dried Tomatoes, 255
Potato, with Brie and Crispy Bacon, 255
Potato, with Caramelized Onions and Goat Cheese, 255
Potato and Parmesan, 254–55, *255*
Savory Onion-Apple Tarte Tatin, 256, *257*

Tempeh
about, 8
Seared, with Tomato Jam, 312–13, *313*

Tequila and Lime, Quick Bean Chili with, 105

Thai curry paste
bottom-of-the jar, ideas for, 401
red, ideas for, 22
uses for, 15

Thyme
Herbes de Provence, *380,* 381
Za'atar, *380,* 383

Tilapia Meunière, 308, *309*

Toasts, toppings for, 240–41

Tofu
Panko-Crusted, with Cabbage Salad, *310,* 311
Pan-Seared, Browned Butter–Soy Noodles with, *152,* 153
Shakshuka with White Beans and Zucchini, 269
Torn, and Plantain Chips, Charred Cabbage Salad with, 230–31, *231*
types of, 8
Vegan Mapo, 314–15, *315*
and Wakame, Miso Soup with, 74–75

Tomato(es)
and Asparagus, Orecchiette Salad with, 151, *151*
and Avocado Salsa, One-Minute, 36
Bulgur, and Red Pepper Soup, *100,* 101
canned, versatility of, 6
canned crushed, substitute for, 26
Chana Masala, 204–5, *205*
Cherry, Bacon, and Arugula, Succotash Salad with, 227, *227*
Chickpea-Mushroom Bolognese, 140, *140*
Chickpeas, and Red Peppers, Shakshuka with, 268–69, *269*
Classic Marinara Sauce, 138, *138*
fresh, substitutes for, 26
Garam Masala–Spiced Shakshuka with Spinach and Yogurt, 269
and Green Pepper Salsa, One-Minute Smoky, 36
Jam, Seared Tempeh with, 312–13, *313*
One-Pot Penne with Olives, Capers, and Eggplant, 143
One-Pot Penne with Sausage Ragu, 143
One-Pot Shrimp Fra Diavolo, 143
Pasta, Fresh, without a Machine, 144, *145*
Pinto Bean, and Red Pepper Salsa, One-Minute, 36
Puttanesca Sauce, 141
Salad, Butter Beans and Rice with, 195, *195*
Salsa, One-Minute, 36, *36*

Tomato(es) *(cont.)*
Sauce, Quick, One-Pot Penne with, 142–43, *143*
Shakshuka with Black Beans, Chiles, and Avocado, 269
Simple (Any) Meat Sauce, 139, *139*
Skillet Cheese Pizza, 336–37, *337*
Skillet Pizza with Fontina, Arugula, and Prosciutto, 337
Skillet Pizza with Goat Cheese, Olives, and Infused Oil, 337
Skillet Pizza with Ricotta, Bacon, and Scallions, 337
Soup, Creamless Creamy, 82, *83*
Spaghetti al Tonno, 122–23, *123*
Spicy Pinto Bean Soup, 96–97, *97*
Sun-Dried, and Blue Cheese, Potato Tart with, 255
Sun-Dried, and White Bean Soup, Easy Canned, 91, *91*
Sun-Dried, Arugula, and Goat Cheese, Scrambled Eggs with, 263
sun-dried, bottom-of-the jar, ideas for, 401
sun-dried, flavor in, 13
Sun-Dried, Garlic, and Za'atar Biscuits, *324,* 325
Sun-Dried, Pesto, 137
Sun-Dried, Vinaigrette and Salami, Pasta Salad with, 150–51, *151*
Tofu Shakshuka with White Beans and Zucchini, 269
Tortilla Soup, 70–71, *71*
Vindaloo-Style Sweet Potatoes, 246–47, *247*
Vodka Cream Marinara Sauce, 138
White Wine, and Parsley, Chicken and Rice with, 290–91, *291*

Tomato paste
about, 13
cooking with aromatics, 24
freezing, 31

Toppings
crispy, crunchy, & chewy, 10
easy dessert, 352–53
pantry, for ice cream, 350–51
savory crunchy, 386–89

Tortilla(s)
Cheese Enchiladas, 278, *279*
Quesadillas, 58, *58*
Soup, 70–71, *71*
Spicy Chilaquiles with Fried Eggs, 264–65, *265*